Successful Schools and Educational Accountability

Concepts and Skills to Meet Leadership Challenges

KENNETH K. WONG

Brown University

ANNA NICOTERA

Peabody College at Vanderbilt University

JAMES W. GUTHRIE
Series Editor

Peabody College at Vanderbilt University

PEARSON

Boston New York San Francisco
Mexico City Montreal Toronto London Madrid Munich Paris
Hong Kong Singapore Tokyo Cape Town Sydney

Senior Editor: Arnis Burvikovs
Development Editor: Christien Shangraw
Editorial Assistant: Erin Reilly
Marketing Manager: Tara Kelly
Production Editor: Gregory Erb
Editorial Production Service: Nesbitt Graphics, Inc.
Composition Buyer: Linda Cox
Manufacturing Buyer: Linda Morris
Electronic Composition: Nesbitt Graphics, Inc.
Interior Design: Nesbitt Graphics, Inc.
Cover Designer: Joel Gendron

For related titles and support materials, visit our online catalog at www.ablongman.com.

Between the time website information is gathered and then published, it is not unusual for some sites to have closed. Also, the transcription or URLs can result in typographical errors. The publisher would appreciate notification where these errors occur so that they may be corrected in subsequent editions.

Library of Congress Cataloging-in-Publication Data

Wong, Kenneth K.
    Successful schools and educational accountability: concepts and skills to meet leadership challenges/
    Kenneth K. Wong, Anna Nicotera; James W. Guthrie, series editor.
        p. cm.
    Includes bibliographical references and index.
    ISBN 0-205-47478-0
    1. Educational accountability—United States. 2. School improvement programs—United States.
    I. Nicotera, Anne Maydan   II. Guthrie, James W.   III. Title
    LB2806.22.W66 2007
    379.1'58—dc22

                                                                                        2006049822

Printed in the United States of America

10 9 8 7 6 5 4 3 2 1 RRD-VA 10 09 08 07 06

To Jonathan Kusumi
and
Tony, Vicki, and Santo Nicotera
and
Michelle and Ellen Wong
for all of their support.

Brief Contents

Contents   vi
Series Preface   xi
Preface   xiv
About the Authors   xvi

PART I **Accountability Challenges   1**

CHAPTER ONE
Current Dilemmas in Accountability   1

PART II **The Context of Accountability   24**

CHAPTER TWO
Evolving Public Policy and the Educational Accountability Context   24

CHAPTER THREE
Changing Expectations for Leadership in Educational Accountability   39

CHAPTER FOUR
Intergovernmental Considerations in Educational Accountability   58

PART III **Accountability's Operational Components   75**

CHAPTER FIVE
Standards and Expectations   75

CHAPTER SIX
Assessment and Measurement of Progress   108

CHAPTER SEVEN
Reporting, Monitoring, and Consequences in Systems
of Educational Accountability   130

PART IV **Leadership Accountability Tools   160**

CHAPTER EIGHT
Using Student- and School-Performance Indicators   160

CHAPTER NINE
Professional Development and Educational Accountability   174

Appendices (A–G)   192
Glossary   237
Bibliography   249
Index   263

Contents

Series Preface   xi

Preface   xiv

About the Authors   xvi

PART I Accountability Challenges 1

CHAPTER ONE

Current Dilemmas in Accountability   1

■ LEARNING OBJECTIVES 1

■ INTRODUCTION 1

■ THE EMERGENCE OF EDUCATIONAL ACCOUNTABILITY: SHIFT
   IN EDUCATIONAL GOALS AND EXPECTATIONS 3

   A Nation at Risk 3

   The Standards-Based Reform Movement 5

   Changes in Federal Legislation: The Emergence of Educational
     Accountability 6

■ LOGIC OF PERFORMANCE-BASED ACCOUNTABILITY 8

■ NEW LEADERS FACE NEW CHALLENGES 10

   Focus on Student Learning 11

   Instructional Organization and Practices 11

   School Leaders 12

   System-Wide Capacity 13

■ OBJECTIVES AND ORGANIZATION OF THE CHAPTERS 13

Summary 15

Case Studies and Discussion Questions 15

▭ Tackling an Impossible Job 15

▭ Theory of Action 20

PART II The Context of Accountability 24

CHAPTER TWO

Evolving Public Policy and the
Educational-Accountability Context   24

   ■ LEARNING OBJECTIVES 24

   ■ INTRODUCTION 24

■ EDUCATIONAL ACCOUNTABILITY: THE THEORY OF CHANGE 25
   Reciprocal Accountability 27
   High-Quality Standards 27
   Valid and Reliable Assessments 28
   System of Accountability 28
■ EDUCATIONAL ACCOUNTABILITY DEFINED: MEDIATING COMPONENTS 29
   Educational Roles Change: Lead by Results 30
   Standards Guide Curriculum, Instruction, and Assessments 31
   Assessment Results Inform School Improvement 31
   Reporting, Monitoring, and Sanctions and Support 31
   Educational Accountability Tools 32
■ EDUCATIONAL ACCOUNTABILITY CHALLENGES 33
   Weak Implementation 33
   Lack of Organizational Capacity to Reform 34
   Unintended Consequences of Accountability Sanctions 34
Summary 35
Commentary and Discussion Questions 35
▱ Juggling Accountabilities: The Leaders' Turn 36

CHAPTER THREE
Changing Expectations for Leadership in Educational Accountability

39
   ■ LEARNING OBJECTIVES 39
   ■ INTRODUCTION 39
   ■ LEADING BY RESULTS VERSUS MANAGING BY RULES 40
      Managing by Rules 41
      Leading by Results 41
      Knowledge and Skills 42
      Building Capacity 46
      Collaborative Inquiry and Reflection 46
      Share Leadership 47
   ■ LEADERSHIP THEORIES FOR EDUCATIONAL ACCOUNTABILITY 48
      Instructional Leadership 48
      Distributed Leadership 49
      Transformational Leadership 51
      Results-Driven Leadership 52
   ■ RESPONSE TO NEW LEADERSHIP EXPECTATIONS 53
   Summary 54
   Article and Discussion Questions 55
   ▱ A Challenging Offer for Potential Principals 55

CHAPTER FOUR
Intergovernmental Considerations in Educational Accountability

58
   ■ LEARNING OBJECTIVES 58
   ■ INTRODUCTION 58

■ INTERGOVERNMENTAL NATURE OF EDUCATION SYSTEM: FEDERAL,
STATE, AND LOCAL LEVELS 59
    Federal Level 60
    State Level 63
    Local Level 65
    Changes in Intergovernmental Roles and Responsibilities with
    Educational Accountability 66
■ IMPLEMENTATION OF EDUCATIONAL ACCOUNTABILITY
IN INTERGOVERNMENTAL CONTEXT 67
    Variability in Implementation of Educational Accountability 67
    Capacity to Implement Educational Accountability 69
■ EDUCATIONAL ACCOUNTABILITY CHALLENGES WITH THE
INTERGOVERNMENTAL SYSTEM 70
Summary 71
Commentary and Discussion Questions 72
▭ Accountability Is a Shared Responsibility 72

PART III Accountability's Operational Components 75

CHAPTER FIVE
Standards and Expectations   75
    ■ LEARNING OBJECTIVES 75
    ■ INTRODUCTION 75
    ■ EDUCATIONAL ACCOUNTABILITY: HOW STANDARDS FUNCTION 77
        Academic Standards 78
        Performance Standards 89
    ■ ALIGNING STANDARDS WITH CURRICULUM, INSTRUCTION,
    AND ASSESSMENT 91
        Aligning Standards with Curriculum 91
        Aligning Standards with Instruction 94
        Aligning Standards with Assessment 101
    Summary 102
    Article and Discussion Questions 105
    ▭ States Confront Definition of "Proficient" as They Set the Bar for Lots
    of New Tests 105

CHAPTER SIX
Assessment and Measurement of Progress   108
    ■ LEARNING OBJECTIVES 108
    ■ INTRODUCTION 108
    ■ TYPES OF STUDENT ASSESSMENTS 109
        Norm-Referenced Tests 111
        Criterion-Referenced Tests 113
        Formative Assessments 119
    ■ TESTING ISSUES: RELIABILITY AND VALIDITY 123
        Reliability 123
        Validity 124

■ MEASURING CHANGE IN STUDENT PERFORMANCE   124
   Measuring Change in Average Achievement   125
   Measuring Gains in Achievement   126
Summary   128
Editorial and Discussion Questions   128
🗀 Stay on Reform Track   128

CHAPTER SEVEN
Reporting, Monitoring, and Consequences in Systems of Educational Accountability   130
   ■ LEARNING OBJECTIVES   130
   ■ INTRODUCTION   130
   ■ ACCOUNTABILITY SYSTEMS: REPORTING   132
      Academic Standards, Performance Standards, and Assessments   133
      Aggregated and Disaggregated Data   134
      Adequate Yearly Progress   136
      School Report Cards   137
   ■ ACCOUNTABILITY SYSTEMS: MONITORING   141
      Starting Points   142
      Intermediate Goals   143
      Safe Harbor Provision   148
   ■ ACCOUNTABILITY SYSTEMS: CONSEQUENCES   149
      School Improvement   150
      Corrective Action   154
      Restructuring   155
Summary   156
Commentary and Discussion Questions   157
🗀 Subgroup Reporting and School Segregation: An Unhappy Pairing
   in the No Child Left Behind Equation   157

Part IV Leadership Accountability Tools   160

CHAPTER EIGHT
Using Student- and School-Performance Indicators   160
   ■ LEARNING OBJECTIVES   160
   ■ INTRODUCTION   160
   ■ CONDITIONS NECESSARY FOR MAKING EFFECTIVE
     SCHOOL-IMPROVEMENT DECISIONS   162
      Environment Conducive to Inquiry and Reflection   162
      Types of Data-Driven Decisions   165
   ■ DECISION-MAKING PROCESS FOR SCHOOL IMPROVEMENT   166
      Collect Data from Multiple Sources   167
      Conduct Needs Assessment   168
      Set Goals for Improvement   168
      Adapt Instructional Practices   169
      Evaluate Impact of Decisions   169

Summary   170
Article and Discussion Questions   170
📁 Benchmark Assessments Offer Regular Checkups on Student Achievement   170

CHAPTER NINE
Professional Development and Educational Accountability   174
■ LEARNING OBJECTIVES   174
■ INTRODUCTION   174
■ EFFECTIVE PROFESSIONAL-DEVELOPMENT STRATEGIES   176
   Problems with Traditional Professional Development   176
   Research on Effective Professional-Development Strategies   177
   System-Wide Professional Development   180
■ PROFESSIONAL DEVELOPMENT AND EDUCATIONAL ACCOUNTABILITY:
   CREATE OPPORTUNITIES FOR TEACHER COLLABORATION   183
   Professional Learning Communities   183
   Peer Coaching   186
Summary   189
Commentary and Discussion Questions   189
📁 To Improve Schools, Focus on Teachers   190

APPENDIX A
No Child Left Behind Act of 2001   192

APPENDIX B
A Nation at Risk   209

APPENDIX C
Colorado Legislation to Provide Exemptions for No Child Left
Behind Assessments   216

APPENDIX D
School Leaders Licensure Assessment (1010)   219

APPENDIX E
Interstate Leaders Licensure Consortium (ISLLC) Indicators   222

APPENDIX F
NEA Lawsuit against Unfunded Mandates of No Child Left Behind   229

APPENDIX G
Tennessee Language Arts Curriculum Standards for Reading, Eighth Grade   231

Glossary   237
Bibliography   249
Index   263

Series Preface

■ THE PEABODY EDUCATION LEADERSHIP SERIES

Vanderbilt University's Peabody College is one of the world's foremost schools of education and human development. The Peabody faculty is in the vanguard of research and knowledge creation, while a long tradition of collaboration "on the ground" with learners, educators, policy-makers and organizations ensures that, at Peabody, theory and practice inform each other. In addition to conferring a full range of graduate, professional, and undergraduate degrees, the College is committed to strengthening current educators and organizational leaders in their efforts to propel greater achievement and enhance human development.

This book and others in the Allyn & Bacon Peabody Education Leadership Series are published to facilitate wider understanding of the means by which human learning takes place and how greater learning can be fostered. Much of the nation's most forward thinking regarding learning and instruction emanates from Peabody. For example, the National Research Council's famous research synthesis, *How People Learn*, was undertaken with the leadership of Peabody faculty. Current faculty members are generating research and constructing the paradigms that will influence the teaching of reading, mathematics, and science well into the future.

Consistent with its mission and its own research, Peabody strives to model good instruction. In that spirit, each book in the Educational Leadership Series has a number of instructional aids. These include full outlines of the volume's substantive material, complete tables of contents, indexes filled with significant concepts and citations, technical glossaries, chapter previews with summaries of what has been and is to be covered, extensive use of topical case studies, clearly understandable graphics, and discussion questions. These aids will enable readers to grasp the complexities associated with what 21st-century leaders need to know about such topics as leadership, finance, accountability, community relations, organizational dynamics, or education law.

■ TEXT SUPPLEMENTS

Each text in this series is accompanied by a **Companion Website**. Students and instructors should visit www.ablongman.com/Peabody for test cases, simulation exercises, sample data for end-of-chapter exercises, URLs for further research and interest, added bibliographies, and other up-to-date information.

Students can find help with research projects using **Research Navigator**, which provides access to three exclusive databases of credible and reliable source material, including EBSCO's ContentSelect Academic Journal Database, the *New York Times* Search by Subject Archive, and the "Best of the Web" Link Library. Research Navigator is available through

Allyn & Bacon's **MyLabSchool**, located at www.mylabschool.com. MyLabSchool needs to be requested by the instructor with a separate ISBN that is free with new books.

An **Instructor's Manual** with teaching resources and test items is also available to adopting instructors through their local Allyn & Bacon representative.

■ THE PEABODY EDUCATION LEADERSHIP SERIES AND EDUCATION'S EVOLVING CONTEXT

Education today must respond as never before to a set of global economic and cultural conditions. These rapidly changing conditions, and the competition they are creating, serve as a subtext for virtually every concept covered by books in this textbook series.

For most of the nation's history, it was possible for an individual to forego formal schooling and still own land, acquire relatively well-paying employment, participate in civic life as an informed citizen, and achieve a substantial degree of personal fulfillment. For many, probably most, individuals, these comfortable circumstances have changed. Modern economies render formal education crucial for individual success, social mobility, and engagement with the demands of the workforce, the environment, and government. The eventual outcome of these relatively new challenges now matters as much for a child being raised on a family farm in South Dakota as to one from a farm family in South Africa.

What has become true for individuals also applies to nations. A people once flourished or floundered based on what they could extract from the ground. Today, a nation is more likely to survive and prosper based on what it can extract from the minds of its citizens.

Readers of this series also will have to grapple with the challenges posed by global changes. Many of the divisive questions facing society as a whole have powerful implications for the conduct of education, as well.

- How can immigrants be fully integrated into American society?
- How many languages can schools reasonably be expected to offer or to use for instruction?
- How much testing is too much?
- How much should be spent on schools to ensure that all students have an opportunity to achieve the learning standards that governments set?
- How should teachers be trained and licensed?
- Should private providers be permitted to offer public schooling?
- Should the public pay for preschool and interschool programs?
- Should high school exit examinations determine graduation?
- What should class sizes be to maximize the positive effects of instruction?

These questions illustrate the complicated and interconnected policy and practical dilemmas upon which books in this series will attempt to shed light. The goal is not so much to provide direct answers to such questions as it is to arm readers with the tools that will enable them to keep pace with and contribute solutions to these and future problems. Specifically, this series will:

- Harness useful concepts and evidenced-based practical understandings applicable to understanding and solving emerging policy challenges and to managing and reforming modern organizations

- Provide readers with technical understanding of important components of education resource deployment, policy development, organizational development, and institutional governance and operation
- Suggest research-based means by which education institutions and practices can be undertaken to greater effect and with greater efficiency
- Enable educators to participate better in policy-related and professional debates regarding best practice

We welcome your comments and suggestions as a reader, researcher, or other user of this book, or other books in the series.

James W. Guthrie
Series Editor
Professor of Public Policy and Education

Camilla P. Benbow
Patricia and Rodes Hart
Dean of Education and Human Development

Peabody College
Vanderbilt University
Nashville, Tennessee

Preface

Successful Schools and Educational Accountability offers an analytical foundation for school leaders to meet new expectations in educational accountability. It was only a generation ago that a national commission raised public attention to the challenge of academic performance for all students. The commission's report, *A Nation at Risk*, claimed, "The educational foundations of our society are presently being eroded by a rising tide of mediocrity that threatens our very future as a Nation and a people" (NCEE, 1983, p. 5). While the extent of our schools' "mediocrity" is subject to debate, the report's ripple effect on policy has been extensive. In the last 25 years, the educational community has rapidly adopted standards-based reform, restructured services for disadvantaged students, and improved transparency in reporting school and student performance. While states have been active in setting curriculum standards, the Congress and the president came to an agreement on educational accountability in the passage of the No Child Left Behind Act of 2001. Consequently, today's school leaders operate in a policy environment that demands a completely new set of skills and knowledge.

In this new context, *Successful Schools and Educational Accountability* integrates current theory and evidence-based practices on leadership and school change. **We provide a road map to position our school leaders so that they can succeed in meeting educational accountability**. Instead of managing their organization by rules and regulations, the new breed of leaders need to lead by results, build organizational capacity, encourage collaborative inquiry, and institute shared decision making. We believe that it is equally important for school leaders to develop the knowledge and skills in managing the accountability system. **This book clarifies the importance of aligning standards with curriculum, instruction, and assessment, and provides extensive discussion on different types of student assessments**. From a policy perspective, the book examines the reporting, monitoring, and consequences of accountability as stipulated in the No Child Left Behind Act. Finally, we introduce various leadership tools that are instrumental in school-improvement decisions and in developing more effective professional development strategies. These tools, when grounded in the relevant knowledge base, are necessary to sustain school success.

Students in school leadership and educational policy courses at both graduate and advanced undergraduate levels will benefit from the many unique features of this book. Each chapter opens with a set of learning objectives to guide readers through the materials. Throughout the text, theories and concepts are clearly defined in the proper organizational and historical context. Data trends, schematic illustrations, glossaries, and policy documents are integrated into the text to deepen the understanding of key themes. Evidence-based practices and reflective questions are included for discussion so that students can think about how to apply concepts and theories in their own setting. In short,

Successful Schools and Educational Accountability offers a research-based, practice-informed, comprehensive approach to the complex issue of accountability.

Supplements are available with this text and are described in the Series Preface.

In completing this book, we have received a great deal of support and advice from many colleagues. In particular, we would like to thank Arnis Burvikovs, Christien Shangraw, and Greg Erb at Allyn and Bacon for their professional support. At Vanderbilt University, we benefited from our numerous conversations with James W. Guthrie, the editor for the Peabody Leadership Series, Matthew Springer, Eric Houck, Robert Crowson, Dale Ballou, Kristie Rowley, Lauren Pachucki, Bettie Teasley, Patrick Schuermann, and Warren Langevin. At Brown University, we received helpful suggestions from colleagues in the Department of Education and the Annenberg Institute for School Reform and from Edward Socha in the Urban Education Policy Program. Finally, we greatly appreciate the thoughtful suggestions of the outside reviewers: Saul Grossmann, Temple University; Virginia Johnson, Saint Joseph's University; Michael Kirst, Stanford University; Scott McLeod, University of Minnesota; and Anthony Normore, Florida International University.

Kenneth K. Wong

Anna Nicotera

About the Authors

Kenneth K. Wong is the Walter and Leonore Annenberg Chair for Education Policy, director of the Urban Education Policy Program, and a professor of education, political science, and public policy at Brown University. Professor Wong, who holds a BA, MA, and PhD from the University of Chicago, is nationally known for his research in the politics of education, policy innovation, outcome-based accountability and governance redesign, including city and state takeover, management reform, and Title I schoolwide reform. He has advised the U.S. Congress, state legislatures, governor and mayoral offices, and the leadership in several large urban school systems on how to redesign the accountability framework. Professor Wong was the founding director of the federally funded National Center on School Choice, Competition and Student Achievement. Currently, he is co-editor of a major educational policy journal, *Education Evaluation and Policy Analysis*.

Anna Nicotera is a pre-doctoral fellow in the Experimental Education Research Training (ExpERT) program funded by the U.S. Department of Education's Institute of Education Sciences (IES). Ms. Nicotera received her BA in political science from the University of Chicago, and is working toward a PhD in education policy and research methods at Vanderbilt University. Her experience includes conducting program evaluations of nationwide whole-school reform models and professional development initiatives in urban school districts. Her research interests include the theories, policies, and practices of educational accountability, as well as the interaction between student mobility and peer effects on student achievement.

CHAPTER ONE

Current Dilemmas in Accountability

LEARNING OBJECTIVES

- Understand the process by which educational accountability gains prominence in school reform.
- Describe how educational goals and expectations shifted in the early 1980s away from rules and regulations to a focus on standards and student results.
- Examine the rationale and the logic of accountability.
- Recognize the new challenge that new school leaders face in an era of accountability.

■ INTRODUCTION

A new era of educational accountability has transformed the agenda in public school reform. *A Nation at Risk*, a 1983 report issued by a presidential commission to propose recommendations on school improvement, marked the beginning of a national movement toward standards-based reform. Recognizing that education is a national challenge, the commission's report signaled the need for national leadership in reforming the entire system of education. For the first time in American history, the president used his bully pulpit to define the problems in the nation's public education. During the first 12 months following the release of the report, the media quoted President Ronald Reagan over 100 times as referring to its findings and recommendations. Further, the commission and its activities mobilized a wide range of societal interests, resources, and expertise to address educational problems. Building on the work of the Commission, two subsequent national educational summits involved the president, the governors, businesses, civic, and educational leaders. The passage of the No Child Left Behind Act of 2001 signaled broad, bipartisan support for standards-based reform with measurable results for all students.

Not surprisingly, the policy reform agenda poses new challenges for educational leaders. For decades, educational leadership programs have been designed to train leaders to lead a more or less hierarchical organization where formal authority comes from the top. The classical depiction of the Weberian bureaucracy is reinforced by a commonly accepted notion that organizational procedures are institutionalized and that the technical core only evolves incrementally. Insiders' knowledge is closely tied to years of experience within the same district. Administrative career is seen as a process of organizational socialization and job promotion from the instructional ranks toward assuming the principalship. Effective principals are then recruited by the district leadership to take on administrative responsibilities in the central office. Similarly, vacancies in the district leadership often result in promotion from within the administrative cadres in the same district. Particularly important is the strong professional identity that focuses on collegiality and trust among members within the organization. This governing culture of self regulation has thrived for many years and in many districts where the "external" environment is stable. Nonpartisan election of school board members and a strong culture of professional training further insulate the school organization from other social and political institutions.

To be sure, organizational inertia remains a key in the operation of public school system. However, the culture of professional self governance now faces a formidable challenge from an increasingly dynamic and changing policy environment. The emergence of educational accountability has redefined the organizational purpose of public school institution. Whereas organizational trust and collegiality dominated the educational sector a generation ago, measurable results for all students now becomes the driving force in today's schools. The most visible sign of the new era is the No Child Left Behind (NCLB). Building on the 1994 Improving America's Schools Act, NCLB has its primary focus on the academic achievement of all students, particularly low-performing students in disadvantaged schools. NCLB mandates that states must establish and implement an accountability plan with well-defined standards for academic proficiency. It also requires states to hire highly qualified teachers who are trained in their instructional areas. Students are required to take annual tests in grades three through eight with results disaggregated by several subgroups, including racial and ethnic groups, students with disabilities, low-income students, and English language learners. Additionally, NCLB allows for supplemental services and school transfers for students in school identified as low-performing. Clearly, achievement for all students must now be a primary objective of educational reform. To see the specific assessment provisions that NCLB applies to all states, Appendix A provides the legislative details for Part A, Subpart 1, Section 1111 of the law.

In this context of new accountability, this book addresses the challenges that the next generation of school leaders face. "Accountability refers to the systematic collection, analysis, and use of information to hold schools, educators and other responsible for student performance" (Armstrong, 2002, p. 1). Among these include a strong focus on student learning, implementation of effective instructional practices, sustainability in leadership skills and qualities, and sound policy analysis. Equally important, we contextualize these challenges within the broader institutional landscape of public school reform at the federal, state, and local level. Public expectation on academic performance has steadily grown over the last decade. An increasing number of governors, mayors, and state lawmakers are asking for evidence on student outcomes to aid in their appropriations decisions. Parents are demanding more information in their children's school report card and a growing number of them are selecting educational alternatives outside of their neighborhood schools.

From our perspective, public schools are at a crossroad. The new accountability dynamics merit a more comprehensive, multidisciplinary approach to provide the knowledge and training for our next generation of school leaders. We believe that our new school leaders need to use data to make decisions on an ongoing basis, ask policy questions on program effectiveness, and recognize the necessity to balance incentives, competition, and sanctions in the multi-layered school policy system. In many cases, school leaders are expected to "alter the incentives facing school personnel in such a way as to increase student performance" (Ladd & Zelli, 2002, p. 496). The school leadership of the 21st century, in short, will be open-minded to a wide range of strategies to deliver a highly performing organization for all students.

■ THE EMERGENCE OF EDUCATIONAL ACCOUNTABILITY: SHIFT IN EDUCATIONAL GOALS AND EXPECTATIONS

While educational accountability may be synonymous for many educators with the policies and mandates of the recent No Child Left Behind Act of 2001, the demand for high academic standards and the focus on student results emerged in the early 1980s with the seminal report, *A Nation at Risk*. The report emerged in response to the poor performance of students from the United States on the Second International Mathematics Study (SIMS) in the early 1980s. Results from SIMS alarmed policymakers, educators, and business people about the prospects for international competition. Specifically, there was concern that the U.S. education system was not adequately preparing students to compete against their peers in other nations in mathematics and science. The report condemned the public education system and presented a set of recommendations for improvement covering accountability, curriculum standards, instructional practices, and assessment of student performance. The push for national educational excellence originated with the federal government, but was soon embedded in education policy and practice at the state, district, and school levels. This section will follow the development of educational accountability from *A Nation at Risk* to the resultant standards-based reform movement and finally to changes in federal and state legislation that now define accountability for public school educators.

A Nation at Risk

In 1983, the National Commission on Excellence in Education (NCEE) released the report, *A Nation at Risk: The Imperative for Education Reform*. The report was commissioned under President Ronald Reagan by U.S. Secretary of Education Terrell H. Bell in response to lagging U.S. student performance on mathematics and science tests in comparison to international students. The report asserted that widespread low student performance had placed the U.S. education system in ruins and compromised the nation's preeminence economically, technologically, and militarily (Guthrie & Springer, 2004). The report claimed, "The educational foundations of our society are presently being eroded by a rising tide of mediocrity that threatens our very future as a Nation and a people" (NCEE, 1983, p. 5). It is now widely accepted that the report made erroneous claims about the demise of student academic achievement compared to previous generations. Nonetheless, it brought about the type of national attention toward public schools that had not been seen in the United States since the Soviet Union launched the satellite, Sputnik, in 1957 and questions were raised about the quality of high school curriculum (Angus & Mirel, 1999).

The authors of *A Nation at Risk* were particularly concerned with the quality of core content areas and the trend toward differentiated curriculum tracks, in which students were placed in separate curricular tracks with vocational or college preparatory focuses. Not surprisingly, differentiated curricular tracks were creating unequal learning opportunities for students based on content coverage and expectations for student performance. Oakes (1985) found that curricular tracking was responsible for sorting and labeling students based on intellectual capabilities and accomplishments, categorizing students in the minds of teachers as a certain ability level, defining students as part of a particular group, and creating different learning opportunities and experiences for students. Based on these concerns, the report recommended strengthening the core content areas by developing rigorous and common academic content standards with high expectations for all students, improving the use of instructional time and time on task, requiring quality teachers and instructional practices, and making comparisons of students nationally and internationally based on standardized tests of achievement.

A Nation at Risk's recommendations, which are included in Appendix B, required that significant changes be made to the U.S. education system. However, the report neglected to propose a design for a system of accountability to ensure that recommendations were put in place. The report merely suggested that citizens should make educators accountable for student performance. In their analysis of *A Nation at Risk* after twenty years, the Koret Task Force on K–12 Education find, "[The Commission] seemed not to realize that the system lacked meaningful accountability and tangible incentives to improve, that it exhibited the characteristic flaws of a command-and-control enterprise" (Koret Task Force on K–12 Education, 2003, p. 11). Despite the fact that the report did not include an accountability mechanism for making certain the recommendations were followed through by educators across the nation, the report had a significant impact on the education system.

A Nation at Risk laid the foundation for educational accountability in its recommendations for standards, high-quality instruction, and standardized tests. However, it was the results-driven nature of the report that dramatically shifted the goals of the education system. Prior to the report, the education system was held accountable through the inputs of rules, regulations, and procedural compliance rather than educational outcomes such as student performance indicators (Murphy, 1971; Peterson, Rabe & Wong, 1988). Adams and Kirst (1999) state that these type of management and fiscal procedures for accountability were representative of public administration strategies in the 1960s and 1970s, such as "planning, programming, budgeting systems (PPBS), management by objectives (MBO), management information systems (MIS), uniform accounting systems, program evaluation, and zero-based budgeting (ZBB)" (p. 465). The focus on procedural and regulatory compliance had unintended consequences that are particularly evident in the federal Title I compensatory education program. To ensure that Title I funds were targeted to low-income students, policymakers mandated that Title I be used for pull-out instructional programs. While good intentions are evident in the policy, the pull-out Title I programs were typically taught by noncertified paraprofessionals. Timar (1994) observes, "In order to comply with federal regulations, compensatory students were segregated from others. The resulting separation between students identified as disadvantaged and low-achieving from the rest simply exacerbated the isolation of Title I students and services" (p. 68). Researchers subsequently found that Title I resources and services are more effective for improving student performance when resources are implemented schoolwide (U.S. Department of Education, 1993). In effect, the focus on procedural compliance in government hindered the ability of educational programs to assist low-performing students.

The shift to performance-based accountability recommended by *A Nation at Risk* significantly altered the goals and functioning of the public education system. The report had a foremost impact on the switch in focus of the education system from rules and regulations to results-driven accountability. In particular, the report's recommendations for academic standards and changes in instructional practices turn out to be key components when considering educational accountability as a reform for improving schools.

The Standards-Based Reform Movement

A Nation at Risk set the tone for changes in the public education system based on high-quality instruction and high expectations. The report provided the impetus for the standards-based reform movement. However, the report was a federal policy document without legislative authority. In 1989, President George Bush met with the National Governors' Association (which was led by Arkansas Governor Bill Clinton) for an Education Summit in Charlottesville to address public education and set broad national performance goals to be achieved by 2000. The goals included preparing students to attend school, reducing the achievement gap between minority and white students, increasing the high school graduation rate, improving academic performance in mathematics, science, and foreign languages, raising college participation rates, and recruiting high quality teachers (Ravitch, 1995; U.S. Department of Education, 1991). Following the summit, the National Education Goals Panel and the National Council on Educational Standards and Testing (NCEST) were established by the U.S. Congress to address the academic subject areas that should be covered in the goals, student assessments that should be used, and standards of performance to be set (Kendall & Marzano, 1996). Subsequently, the National Council of Teachers of Mathematics (NCTM) released *Curriculum and Evaluation Standards for School Mathematics* in 1989 and *Professional Standards for Teaching Mathematics* in 1991, which set in motion the use of standards-based educational practices for math in schools across the country (NCTM, 2000). The National Research Council put together the National Committee on Science Education Standards and Assessment in 1992 and released the *National Science Education Standards* in 1996 (NRC, 1996). In 1996, the National Council of Teachers of English released the *Standards for the English Language Arts* (NCTE, 1996).

Standards-based reform challenged the central practices of the education system that had been differentiating content and instruction based on perceptions of student ability (Linn, 2000). In fact, the theory behind standards-based reform claimed that all students can perform well irrespective of background characteristics. Weiss, Knapp, Hollweg, and Burrill (2001) note that the separate academic content standards share similar characteristics, including "affirmation of the importance of increased expectations, opportunities, and achievement of all students, including groups largely bypassed historically, such as girls and ethnic and language minorities" (p. 25). In turn, educators must recognize diversity in the classroom and create learning opportunities for every student. Spillane (1999) comments, "The standards movement's central doctrine calls for more intellectually demanding content and pedagogy for everyone. The movement challenges deeply rooted beliefs about who can do intellectually demanding work in school and questions popular conceptions of teaching, learning, and subject matter" (p. 547). Specifically, standards-based reform maintained that students learn as a consequence of what is taught; the implication being that educators must take a different approach with teaching, one defined by skill and understanding (Elmore, 2000; Fink & Thompson, 2001). The necessary changes to teaching practices include aligning curriculum design, instructional practices, and student assessment with academic content standards. In this way, standards-based reform has a similar purpose as the current system of educational accountability. Educational accountability encompasses standards-based goals and strategies while also developing and implementing mechanisms that hold schools accountable for student performance.

Changes in Federal Legislation: The Emergence of Educational Accountability

Legislative mandates in education may be faulted for a variety of reasons, such as lack of specificity, inadequate funding, and unintended consequences. While legislation may not be perfect, it is often used to push for and facilitate significant reform initiatives. Elmore (2000) states that in terms of education:

> Policy can set the initial expectations and conditions with which large scale improvements will occur, it can set targets for practice and performance, it can open and stimulate public discussion about content and performance in schools, and it can alter the incentives under which schools and school systems work. (p. 26)

The political environment following *A Nation at Risk* supported results-driven education with a general consensus that the education system should have high expectations, be challenging, and establish specific demands for student outcomes (Adams & Kirst, 1999). Accordingly, these components of standards-based reform were embraced by policymakers and thrust into federal and state legislation. Over the course of time, legislative mandates for accountability mechanisms were increasingly developed and defined, which resulted in the emergence of educational accountability that is reflected in the current education system.

It should be noted, however, that policy mandates for standards-based reform may have had ulterior motives. Legislation based on results-driven reform is politically attractive given its nature of visible, rapid, and quantifiable results (Thompson, 2001). Linn (2000) lists the political appeal of focusing on student performance:

- Tests and assessments are relatively inexpensive;
- Testing and assessment can be externally mandated;
- Testing and assessment changes can be rapidly implemented; and
- Results are visible. (p. 4)

Standards-based reform entails considerable effort from educators to make changes in curriculum, instruction, and assessment that are necessary to improve student learning. Given the politics that surround policymaking in education, the resulting policy may not reflect the intricacies and complexity of large-scale school-improvement reform. As we describe the progression of federal legislation that leads to the current state of educational accountability, it is important to be aware that policy may not capture the intended theory of reform. In fact, standards-based reform and educational accountability will not have their proposed impact on student achievement by merely implementing high-stakes tests. Legislation that focuses too heavily on testing will be limited in its ability to facilitate significant change.

The 1983 report, *A Nation at Risk*, recommended that the federal government take a more active role in setting educational standards and demands for student outcomes. At the same time, President Ronald Reagan proposed dismantling the U.S. Department of Education, reducing federal funds to schools, and shifting all the educational functions to the states to improve federal governmental efficiency (Barfield, 1981). However, by 1987 the Reagan administration had discontinued its effort to reduce federal spending in education. With the federal role in education intact, federal legislation brought about by the reauthorizations of the Elementary and Secondary Education Act (ESEA) began to reflect the goals of standards-based education, specifically for the principal federal education compensatory program, Title I.

The first federal reauthorization of ESEA after the release of *A Nation at Risk* was the Hawkins-Stafford Elementary and Secondary School Improvement Amendments of 1988. Prior to 1988, ESEA legislation had directed attention to administrative compliance, fiscal audits, supplemental resources, separate curriculum for Title I students, pull-out programs, and little academic comparison between Title I and non-Title I students (P.L. No. 100-297). Similar to the recommendations of *A Nation at Risk*, the Hawkins-Stafford Amendments proposed changes in the areas of accountability, curricular standards, instructional practices, and assessment of performance (Wong & Nicotera, 2004a). In terms of accountability, the federal legislation proposed local and state evaluations of Title I program effectiveness and school performance. In accordance with recommendations for common standards and quality instruction, the Hawkins-Stafford Amendments suggested coordination between Title I and regular school curriculum and schoolwide instructional programs. Compared to the report's recommendations, federal legislation in 1988 did not mandate student performance comparisons. However, the legislation did require that the national test of student achievement, the National Assessment of Educational Progress (NAEP), include specific data on student performance in the academic content areas of reading, writing, and math. Merely five years after the release of *A Nation at Risk*, standards-based reform was taking root in national educational policy.

If the education legislation in Hawkins-Stafford Amendments of 1988 began to reflect the purposes of standards-based reform, the Improving America's Act (IASA) of 1994 continued the momentum for high standards and quality education. Explicit in the 1994 reauthorization is the purpose to "establish a Title I program for helping disadvantaged students meet high standards" (P.L. No. 103-382). IASA changed the nature of accountability in federal legislation by shifting away from procedural compliance and instead establishing the notion that the federal government would approve flexibility in Title I program requirements in exchange for greater accountability for student performance. This accountability arrangement is referred to as tight-loose coupling and it is a centerpiece of educational accountability. IASA encouraged states to develop a system of challenging academic content and student performance standards, as well as define annual levels of adequate yearly progress for all students. Included in the state systems should be state assessments administered to all students. In terms of instruction, IASA promoted the use of effective teaching practices and extended learning time in schoolwide programs rather than traditional pull-out Title I programs for low-performing students. Additionally, IASA shifted accountability mechanisms to the school-level such that schools instead of districts were responsible for the performance of students.

The national push for accountability facilitated activity at the state-level where states increased the stakes and consequences for educational accountability (Adams & Kirst, 1999). Chatterji (2002) states:

> As the federal government became increasingly involved in setting the education reform agenda on a national level, the term standards-based reform was used to refer to the ways in which individual states responded to push for high standards and school accountability. (p. 346)

IASA provided states with the flexibility to make instructional, structural, and fiscal changes to achieve academic and student performance standards. It appeared that the states were making progress developing systems for standards and assessments. However, the federal government grew impatient with states' responses to IASA (Linn, 2003; Valencia & Wixson, 2001). The political reality was that holding schools and districts accountable to high-stakes mandates was not desirable.

The most recent reauthorization of federal education legislation, the No Child Left Behind Act of 2001, intensifies federal mandates for results-driven and high-stakes education. The legislative intent of NCLB is to improve the academic achievement of all students by enhancing state systems of accountability, requiring clearly defined statewide standards for academic proficiency, mandating teacher and paraprofessional quality standards, enacting annual testing in third through eighth grades with results disaggregated by subgroups, and calling for the use of instructional practices based on scientifically based research. Additionally, NCLB allows for choice mechanisms such as supplemental educational services and school transfers for students in schools identified as low performing (P.L. No. 107-110).

To a large extent, NCLB illuminates the changing state role in educational reform throughout the 1990s. State government has taken an increasingly activist agenda in public school improvement. By the time Congress enacted NCLB, many states had established accountability standards, and a few of them were ready to take more direct intervention, such as taking over a failing districts or a cluster of low-performing schools. In 2000, state mandates on testing and academic standards varied in a number of aspects, such as number of tests given in grades one through eight in English and mathematics, number of tests given in grades nine through twelve in English and mathematics, statewide practice in assigning ratings to all schools, state efforts to identify low-performing schools, and state listing of low-performing schools. Based on these measures, states differed in their degree of state-led academic policies (Wong, 2003). Strong accountability states included Alabama, California, Florida, West Virginia, North Carolina, Louisiana, New Mexico, Maryland, Tennessee, Virginia, and Kentucky. Among the states that played a limited accountability role were Nebraska, Wyoming, New Jersey, New Hampshire, Montana, Minnesota, Maine, and Iowa.

As of December 2003, all state educational accountability plans had been approved by the U.S. Department of Education. The reform rhetoric, purposes, and goals of *A Nation at Risk* and standards-based reform culminate in the state accountability plans mandated by NCLB. Nonetheless, variations in the difficulty and specificity of state standards and accountability plans have been identified (Kingsbury, Olson, Cronin, Hauser, & Houser, 2003). We go into further detail on the specifics of the NCLB legislation in subsequent chapters.

■ LOGIC OF PERFORMANCE-BASED ACCOUNTABILITY

The theory of educational accountability requires that considerable changes be made to strategies and practices in leading schools and districts. These changes in educational practices pose major challenges to policymakers and school professionals. Our system of educational governance is designed in such a way as to encompass various theories of change when considering issues of accountability (Adams & Kirst 1999). The theories are grounded in perspectives that are oriented toward bureaucratic, legal, professional, political, moral, and market accountability. Bureaucratic accountability functions through the roles of hierarchy and control in the education system and the provision of rules and regulations for fiscal and compliance audits (p. 467). Legal accountability operates through contractual obligations where a legal overseer, such as state legislatures or courts, hold schools accountable with legal mandates and the threat of sanctions (pp. 467–469). With professional accountability, educators take responsibility and ensure professional standards of practice for teaching and learning (pp. 469–470). Political accountability functions through elected representatives taking into account constituents' value preferences to improve schools (p. 470). In moral accountability, educators improve schools based on their personal obligation or sense of duty for the school system (pp. 470–471). And lastly, market accountability works through customer choice based on school performance where the ultimate consequence for schools is that they can lose their students (pp. 471–472).

In reality, analytic perspectives are not necessarily mutually exclusive and that are likely to overlap and conflict with each other. Previous practices are seldom entirely phased out as new expectations permeate through different layers of the policy organization (Wong, 1999). In special education, for example, procedural guidance remains extensively detailed since the enactment of the program in the mid 1970s. At the same time, the notion of bureaucratic accountability was the leading theory in U.S. education when the goal was to increase the efficiency and management of the inputs of schooling. In recent years, the goals of schooling success have shifted to a results-driven system. The theory of educational accountability that was specifically designed for particular states or districts has been replaced by standards-based broad scale efforts. NCLB clearly signals the increasing reliance on the theory of legal accountability for school improvement.

While the scope and content of accountability policy systems may vary across states and districts, the logic of the new system of accountability is straightforward: "Schools and school systems should be held accountable for their contribution to student learning" (Elmore & Fuhrman, 2001, p. 4). From a policy system perspective, Baker and Linn (2002) identify seven conditions for accountability:

- The reported results are accurate
- The results are widely interpreted
- Individuals are willing to act and can motivate action by team members
- Alternative actions to improve the situation are known and available
- Individual and team members possess the knowledge to apply alternative methods
- The selected action is adequately implemented
- The actions selected will improve results (p. 1)

These general conditions are applicable to different levels of the educational policy system. The superintendents, for example, need to focus on evidence on "what works." At the same time, superintendents and school boards must now rely on reliable data to make decisions to raise school performance. In some districts, data-driven decisions may involve such unconventional strategies as converting failing neighborhood schools into a charter school or outsourcing them with outsider vendors. In Philadelphia, CEO Paul Vallas has contracted the lowest-performing forty schools with universities, nonprofit and for-profit organizations to raise student performance. Likewise, community-based organizations and parental groups now use data frequently to push for policy preferences.

The logic of new accountability can be further articulated at the level of the principal-ship in the school building level. The principles of effective school-level accountability may include (Reeves, 2002a, pp. 19–24):

- Congruence: Accountability must bring together, strategy, rewards, recognition, and personnel evaluations under a unifying theme (i.e., prioritizing standards).
- Specificity: What specific strategies are associated with improved student achievement? Principals need to focus on behaviors of adults, not just test scores.
- Relevance: Direct relationship between strategies employed and improvement in student learning.
- Respect for Diversity: Make diversity a moral and intellectual part of curriculum. This focus requires different approaches, techniques, and teaching strategies in different schools.
- Continuous Improvement: Annual reporting on student performance is far from sufficient for the purpose of improving teaching and learning during the course of an academic year.
- Focus on Proficient Achievement: School-level educators must sharpen their primary focus on whether all students meet high expectations.

Although some skeptics may claim that standards and accountability can be stifling for teachers and students, others have provided evidence that teachers and principals in some of the higher performing districts and schools are embracing them and thriving (DeRoche, 2004, p. 37). Clearly, accountability calls for a systematic rethinking about strategic choices. These critical decisions may involve trade-offs, but they can lead to a proper balance of rewards, support, and sanctions at both the district and school building levels.

■ NEW LEADERS FACE NEW CHALLENGES

In Easton Elementary School on the eastern shore of the Chesapeake Bay in Maryland, Kelly Griffith redefines the responsibilities of a school principal in this school that enrolls 610 students in grades 2 through 5 (see Case 1: Tackling An Impossible Job). Unlike many of her peers throughout the nation, Principal Kelly does not have to spend her time to deal with noninstructional administrative tasks, such as ordering supplies and supervising the custodial staff. With the assistance of a county-funded "school manager" in her building, Griffith is able to focus on the core challenge. "I'm in the classrooms every day," Griffith points out. When teachers need to observe their peers in another class, Griffith take over the instructional task for them. She frequently spends time observing classroom teaching so that she can develop strategies to support professional development. School leadership, in other words, is prioritized to support teaching and learning.

Even though they are geographically far apart, California's Gilroy Unified Schools and Tennessee's Clarksville–Montgomery County are leading the way in building district-wide capacity to meet accountability standards (see Case 2: Theory of Action). With external support from the Stupski Foundation, these two districts are able to implement district-wide content standards and instructional approaches, including teacher training in using student achievement data to gauge their classroom practices. In observing these districts as well as reflecting on his own experience as a former superintendent in Seattle, Joseph Olchefiske comments, "You've got to set standards, you've got to create and implement assessments that are for all kids, regardless of the school, and have very clear accountability, which means consequences." At issue is finding the appropriate balance between district-led initiatives and school-level sense of ownership.

These two cases, one situates at the school building level and the other at the district level, speak to the reality of how school leadership is undergoing transformation in the context of accountability. The two cases, in essence, suggest several new challenges. These include focusing on student learning, thinking instructional organization and practices, redefining the tasks of leading a school, and reforming the functions and responsibilities of the district leadership.

Focus on Student Learning

School leaders face a complex challenge in meeting the public expectation on student performance. At issue is what knowledge students acquire from their schooling. The near term reaction tends to focus on raising the test scores in standardized tests as a way to meet the NCLB requirements. The longer term challenge, however, has to enhance the life of the students' mind. "The bottom line for school improvement initiatives is student learning" (Spillane & Seashore Louis, 2002, p. 83). This new paradigm of student-centered learning has far reaching implications for school policy and school organization (Darling-Hammond, 1997). In response to differential academic needs among our increasingly diverse student populations, schools need:

- To teach for understanding: That is, to teach all students not just a few, to understand ideas deeply and perform proficiently.
- To teach for diversity: That is, to teach in ways that help different kinds of learners find productive paths to knowledge as they also learn to live constructively together. (p. 5)

In substantive terms, these goals can be realized when students develop various skill sets, including thinking and learning, motivation and engagement, and self-regulation and autonomy (Hill, 2002).

Instructional Organization and Practices

The accountability reality also challenges instructional practices. Given data transparency and disaggregation of test results by subgroups in each school, teachers and principals must confront the formidable task of academic proficiency for all students. Many urban schools face a wide range of environmental constraints that are counter to their efforts. Economic disenfranchisement and lack of social support in many urban communities have led to alienation and low expectation among teachers, students, and parents. Highly qualified teachers, for example, often select schools that enroll a higher proportion of stable families where children are better prepared for academic work. Inner-city schools are doubly disadvantaged with social problems outside of school and an absence of qualified teachers inside the school building.

To improve instructional effectiveness across all learning circumstances, school leaders need to consult evidence-based instructional practices on an ongoing basis. Local adaptation of what works may pose additional challenges. Nonetheless, the new accountability requires schools and districts to rethink new ways to engage students in academic tasks. Research shows that there are teacher practices that are associated with effective student learning (Hill, 2002, p. 55). These include:

- Time on task
- Closeness of content to assessment instrument
- A structured approach: specific objectives, frequent assessment, corrective feedback

- Types of adaptive instruction that can be managed by teachers
- High expectations of student achievement
- Engaged learning time
- Focused teaching

Further, the emergence of data-driven instruction and technology-enhanced practices encourages teachers, principals, and students to access and use resources that are well beyond the boundary of the school and the district. Science experiments, for example, can be substantially informed by NASA resources and images from the latest space explorations on Mars and Saturn. Internet-based research projects can be widely promoted in various subject areas, including history and literature. In other words, while accountability seems to put new pressure on school leaders to evaluate student success, teachers are now enabled by technology and data tools to enhance their instructional practices to improve student learning.

School Leaders

While the logic of accountability provides the "why" to new reform initiatives, school building leaders need to develop the skills and knowledge to be able to know "when" and "how" to take the necessary steps to raise student performance. In their study of the principalship in San Diego, Schnur and Gerson (2005) observed five core beliefs underlying the vision for the new principalship (pp. 97–99):

- The first belief is that actions taken by adults—especially teachers, principals, and instructional leaders—in the San Diego public schools are a primary determinant of student achievement.
- The quality of classroom instruction provided by teachers is the single greatest determinant of student achievement.
- There is a specific instructional and pedagogical agenda that should be carried out in every San Diego public school classroom.
- The best way to drive any change is through leadership and transfer of knowledge. School leaders must set tone and agenda, provide teachers necessary skills and knowledge through professional development and coaching, and hold teachers accountable to using new strategies to change practice.
- These instructional leadership and management practices can only be carried out effectively if principal and other instructional leaders have the knowledge and skills to play this role—especially knowledge about "what good instruction looks like" and "how to organize adult learning" at the school site around improvement in instruction.

In reality, the varying context of schools contributes to mixed leadership outcomes. For example, principals in focus groups know and believe that on the job they should be instructional leaders, but principals in advantaged communities can only spend 40% of their time on instructional matters, while their peers in urban, low-performing schools are constantly addressing emergencies (Tucker & Codding, 2002, p. 5). Further, principals feel competing pressure on a daily basis. Due to accountability policy, principals in some districts are granted a different mix of authority. Most dramatically, Houston, Chicago, and several urban districts have eliminated tenure for principals in exchange of better compensation package and more discretion in budgeting and personnel recruitment. The changing nature of the school-level leadership in the context of accountability is a central theme of this book.

System-Wide Capacity

As NCLB-like accountability institutionalizes across states, there is growing concern over the gap between policy talk and classroom practice. Historians Tyack and Cuban (1995) observed, "To bring about improvement at the heart of education—classroom instruction . . . has proven to be the most difficult kind of reform, and it will result in the future more from internal changes created by the knowledge and expertise of teachers than from the decisions of external policymakers" (pp. 134–135). Hess (1999), in his study of 57 urban districts in the mid-1990s, found that rapid churning of reform activities at the district level tend to have the unintended effect of maintaining the status quo at the school and classroom levels. The gap between policy talk and instructional improvement is structurally reinforced by the incentive practices and organizational loose coupling within our decentralized educational system (Elmore, Abelmann, & Fuhrmann, 1996; Ogawa, Sandholtz, Martinez-Fiores, & Scribner, 2003; Wong & Anagnostopoulos, 1998). Teacher discretion in using "structured curriculum" is seen even when Chicago's central office mandated the lesson plans during the six-week summer bridge program (Wong, Anagnostopoulos, Rutledge, Lynn, & Dreeben, 1999).

Given the concerns on the policy-practice gap, we believe that the critical connecting link lies with the district. What can the district do to provide sufficient support for schools and teachers to do their job well? How can the district use data to implement evidence-based practices? Does the district have the capacity to address growing public demands on student performance? When should the district use sanctions and incentives to change school practices? Answers to these questions will begin to form the basis for a new way of thinking about district capacity to raise student performance.

■ OBJECTIVES AND ORGANIZATION OF THE CHAPTERS

The chapters in this book are structured to present educational leaders with the context of educational accountability, the theory of education accountability reform and its operational components, and leadership tools for making significant school improvement with educational accountability. Educational-accountability reform is a large-scale improvement initiative that is focused on improving instructional practices and student improvement. Each of the chapters addresses the purpose of educational accountability.

Chapter 2 provides the context on the theory and assumptions behind educational accountability. The logic behind accountability is to set high academic expectations and to focus our reform efforts and resources on improving instructional practices to raise student performance. Particularly important are the operational components that translate the power of the theoretical logic into a series of reform actions and desirable student outcomes. Chapter 2 examines four of the key bridging components.

Having laid out the logic model of accountability, Chapter 3 explores how the changing expectations redefine educational leadership. Clearly, accountability has shifted the educational system from regulatory compliance (or the traditional model of accountability) to the current outcome-based accountability. Educational leaders at all levels of the school policy organization must lead by results rather than managing by top-down directives and rules. Chapter 3 examines the types of knowledge and skills that school and district leaders need to acquire to fully address accountability issues. Chapter 3 also provides an overview on different configurations of leadership, ranging from focused to dispersed arrangements.

With the No Child Left Behind Act, the federal government and states have expanded their programmatic involvement in school reform. From a broader institutional perspective, instructional efforts and schoolwide improvement are "nested" in a multilayered policy organization. Chapter 4 considers school leadership within our complex intergovernmental system, where multiple centers of power exist in shaping decisions on school funding and accountability policy. School leadership at different levels also engages in a division of functions and roles. At the state and local level, we will examine variability in policy implementation. Politics, policies, and funding are among the factors may constrain or foster effective school leadership.

Policymakers and the public often assume that raising educational and performance standards would be sufficient for improving schools and student performance. Chapter 5 begins with a discussion on the importance and the process of developing state standards. Further, Chapter 5 argues that academic standards by themselves are not sufficient. Drawing on experience in several states, this chapter shows how standards need to be closely connected to policies and strategies that support, assess, and reward teaching and learning. A challenge for school leadership is to rethink practices that enable students who are currently low-performing to attain academic proficiency within the time frame established in the state accountability standards.

The No Child Left Behind Act marks an era of high stakes accountability. A challenge for school leadership is to design and implement a system of student assessment that meets the standards of reliability and validity. Chapter 6 focuses on the design and technical dimensions of student testing. Beginning with a comparison of major types of student assessments (such as norm- versus criterion-referenced tests), this chapter discusses the promises and limits of measuring student performance that is grounded in only one state-approved standardized test in the spring of each academic year. In this regard, the chapter examines the current NCLB standards, or the "status" approach, that compare the average achievement of a specified grade/cohort of students (such as 3rd grade reading) with that of the same grade/cohort of different students in the following year. This approach is different from alternative models that measure gains in achievement of the same students who move from one grade to another.

Chapter 7 further examines how reliable data on student performance can be, institutionalized as a key policy system to improve teaching and learning on an ongoing basis. A critical issue is to make sure that data reporting and monitoring are designed to detect in a timely manner when schools and students are not improving. Data disaggregation and benchmarking targets, for example, are analytic tools that school leaders are expected to employ frequently to adjust their school wide and instructional practices. The level of professional skills, data analytic practices, and content knowledge, among others, may form the basis for supporting "a culture of evidence" at both the school and district level.

Chapter 8 presents the first of two tools educational leaders should employ on an ongoing basis in order to bring about the changes required in educational-accountability reform. The chapter describes how educators throughout the school should be engaging in data-driven school-improvement decisions to change instructional practices and improve student learning. Conditions necessary for effectively using data-driven decisions are explored, such as creating a school environment conducive for collaborative inquiry and reflection. The chapter also illustrates the process by which educators make school-improvement decisions as an iterative cycle.

The quality of schooling services often depends on the quality of professional development activities. Chapter 9 focuses on professional development strategies that show evidence of effectiveness in improving teaching and learning for all students. Further, the chapter addresses issues of central concerns from the perspective of a community of teaching professionals. Specifically, teacher collaboration is essential in the forging a closer alignment of assessment, curriculum, and instruction. Professional learning communities and peer coaching are among the collaborative models that this chapter examines.

Summary

- Accountability calls for a systematic rethinking about strategic choices on school-reform policy and practice.
- Decisions at the system-wide and school levels are likely to involve trade-offs in terms of rewards, support, sanctions, as well as the purpose of schooling.
- Leaders at the system and school levels must be prepared to face the reality of accountability.
- New leaders are expected to focus on student learning, implement instructional organization and practices, redefine the task of leading, and enhance the analytic capacity of themselves and their organizations.

Case Studies and Discussion Questions

Tackling an Impossible Job
By Jeff Archer
Education Week, September 15, 2005

Kelly Griffith's job description is most notable for what it doesn't include.

The principal at Easton Elementary School in Easton, Md., doesn't handle maintenance. She doesn't help arrange field trips. She doesn't oversee her building's cafeteria workers. Nor does she supervise the buses before and after school.

Instead, she spends her time in classrooms, observing educators and showing them new methods of instruction. She analyzes test scores. She plans professional-development activities for her teachers aimed at boosting student achievement.

Griffith can focus on teaching and learning because school leaders in her district made a conscious effort to let principals do so. Two years ago, the 4,500-student Talbot County system put "school managers" in its buildings to free principals of administrative duties and let them concentrate on raising student performance.

"It really has given me more of a hands-on approach to being an instructional leader," says Griffith, who's been a principal for 13 years. Before her building got a school manager, she says, "you were putting your fingers in the holes in the dike."

After years of hearing that a principal's main job should be to raise the quality of instruction, districts and states are experimenting with ways to make that ideal a reality. New policies are emerging to give principals more of the time, training, and tools to become leaders of school improvement, rather than managers of operations.

Like Talbot County, some school systems are lightening the load for principals, particularly when it comes to noninstructional matters. Others are grounding the preparation of new administrators more in the real work of improving school performance, as in Massachusetts, where state policymakers have empowered districts to run their own licensing programs for principals.

There's also renewed talk of giving building leaders more decisionmaking authority. An agreement with the teachers' union in Memphis, Tenn., for example, will give principals in low-performing schools more flexibility on personnel issues. And across the country, evaluation systems and professional-development efforts for administrators are placing a greater premium on raising student achievement.

"There really is a growing consensus about what the center of education administration is supposed to be about," says Joseph F. Murphy, an expert on educational leadership at Vanderbut University. "Ten years ago, even seven years ago, I wouldn't have said that."

To be sure, such changes are hardly the norm. Surveys suggest that many of the nation's 84,000 public school principals remain largely caught up in the "administrivia" of the job, lacking the authority and wherewithal to carry out significant changes in their schools. But the press to re-engineer the work of principals has never been stronger. Under the federal No Child Left Behind Act, school leaders are judged on their ability to raise test scores for all groups of students. Some of the law's stiffest sanctions for low-performing schools kick in this year.

Marc S. Tucker, the president of the National Center on Education and the Economy, a Washington-based policy group that runs a training program for principals, says the federal law underscores a sea change in the expectations for administrators. No longer is it enough for school leaders to keep things running smoothly.

"For the first time in the history of American education, with the advent of the accountability movement, bad things happen to school leaders who don't improve student performance, and good things happen to those who do," he says.

Principals don't teach students, but they do affect student achievement. Kenneth Leithwood, a professor of educational leadership and policy at the University of Toronto who co-wrote a new review of research on leadership effectiveness, says leadership characteristics are the second-strongest predictor of a school's effeet on student results. Only classroom factors, such as teacher quality, are stronger.

"It's not that those in leadership roles are having a dramatic direct influence," says Leithwood. "But those things that do have a direct influence are quite substantially affected by what people in leadership do."

Another recent research summary by MidContinent Research for Education and Learning shows how good principals leave their mark. Based in Aurora, Colo., McREL analyzed 70 studies and identified the most critical parts of a principal's job. Among them: fostering shared beliefs, monitoring the effectiveness of school practices, and involving teachers in implementing policy.

The bad news is that many principals have little opportunity to perform those functions. Their days are consumed with student discipline, parent complaints, maintenance problems, and paperwork. A 1998 poll by the National Association of Elementary School Principals showed that 72 percent of building leaders nation-wide agreed that "fragmentation of my time" was a major concern.

Such frustrations are why the Talbot County system, located on the eastern shore of the Chesapeake Bay in Maryland, created its "school manager" position in 2002. Eight of its nine schools now have such managers, who handle virtually all of their buildings' noninstructional administrative tasks. They order supplies and re-pairs, supervise the food service and custodial workers, and track staff attendance.

Griffith, the principal at Easton Elementary, says the change has been a god-send. Her school serves 610 pupils in grades 2–5 on a campus that includes a sepa-rate school for prekindergarten through 1st grade. The benefits of the managerial position were clear last year, when a new roof at the school kept leaking—a prob-lem that, in the old days, Griffith would have had to resolve herself.

Not only is Griffith able to spend more time modeling instruction for her teach-ers, but she also can cover their classes herself so the teachers can observe col-leagues elsewhere in the building. Districtwide, the number of teacher observations by principals has tripled since the schools got their managers, district officials say.

"I'm in the classrooms every day," says Griffith.

Other districts have tried similar steps to make principals' jobs more doable. For the past four years, the 4,900-student Mansfield, Mass., public schools have had two principals at each elementary school. In California, the 97,000-student Long Beach Unified uses pairs of "co-principals" at its six regular high schools.

The tactic isn't without challenges. Talbot County lost two of its school man-agers the first year of the system, when leaders discovered that the intense multi-tasking demanded of the position requires a special temperament. Also, district leaders say, some principals were so used to acting as managers that they found it hard to shed their administrative roles.

"There are some principals that would not benefit from having a school man-ager," says Griffith. "They are very comfortable being a school manager themselves."

Indeed, many of today's principals feel ill-prepared for the role of instructional leader. They do know instruction: More than 99 percent of them are former teach-ers. But a common complaint is that traditional administrator preparation programs don't focus on how to carry out the kind of organizational change that's needed to significantly improve a school's performance.

Frederick M. Hess, an education expert at the American Enterprise Institute in Washington, has surveyed the course content of university-based preparation pro-grams, and he's been struck, he says, by their emphasis on "what principals are al-lowed." They stress the mechanics of school law, finance, and teacher evaluation, but not how to restructure academic programs, he says.

"They're being trained to nibble around the edges," he contends.

Hess' answer is to infuse the profession with new blood. He argues that states should pare back licensure rules to allow leaders from fields other than teaching to serve as principals, as Florida and Michigan have done. Other experts counter that some exposure to teaching, while not sufficient, is nonetheless critical for anyone charged with improving instruction.

Regardless, there's little disagreement in the field that administrator preparation in the United States needs an overhaul. Says Tucker of the National Center on Education and the Economy: "The quality of leadership and management training in our schools of education is, on the whole, terrible."

Some districts are taking matters into their own hands. Last year, the 60,000-student Boston public schools launched an initiative that trains principal-candidates in one-year "residencies," during which participants work as administrators under the tutelage of practicing school leaders in the city. The program graduated its first class of 10 "Boston principal fellows" this summer.

One of them is Oscar Santos, who spent his residency at Irving Middle School, which serves a diverse student enrollment in the southwest part of the city. While there, he helped disaggregate student test scores for staff members working on the school's improvement plan. He also organized a Saturday mathematics camp to offer extra help for struggling students.

"I was fully involved in the change process," says Santos, 32, who has since become the headmaster—as principals in Boston are called—at a district high school.

A key objective of the fellowship program is to produce principals who understand Boston's own brand of school improvement. Fellows take part in seminars that teach such skills as how to use the district's datamanagement system. With funding from the Los Angeles-based Broad Foundation and a federal grant, Boston pays full salaries to the trainees during the year.

Other district-led principal-training programs have sprung up recently in Los Angeles and Springfield, Mass. New Leaders for New Schools, a 3-year-old non-profit group that trains aspiring principals through a one-year residency, has contracts with the school districts in Chicago, the District of Columbia, Memphis, and its headquarters of New York City.

Meanwhile, some states are prodding universities to change how they train school leaders. Louisiana's administrator-preparation programs have until next July to redesign themselves or face closure. State officials there have required that the programs strengthen candidates' field experience by forming closer ties with districts. A similar push is under way in Iowa.

Elsewhere, there's been less progress. The Southern Regional Education Board, an Atlanta-based policy group, recently surveyed 126 higher education institutions that prepare administrators, and it found them lacking in offering practical experience. Fewer than one-quarter have participants lead activities aimed at improving instruction. Shadowing experienced principals is more often the norm.

"What colleges tell us is that when the state requires something different, they will do differently," says Betty Fry, who directs an SREB project that advises universities on the redesign of their educational leadership programs. "But as long as they're able to get principals licensed and get them jobs, there's not much real compelling reason for them to do differently."

Funding for the project comes from the New York City–based Wallace Foundation.

Preservice training programs can't take all the blame for the way many principals go about their work. For most of the past century, building administrators have been hired, rewarded, and promoted based on considerations other than their ability to raise the level of instruction in their schools.

"A lot of what a principal is, is what their school board wants them to be," says Carole Kennedy, a principal-in-residence at the National Board for Professional Teaching Standards, a private group based in Arlington, Va., that offers a process for recognizing highly skilled teachers. "If they're satisfied with management, that's what they'll get."

Gradually, though, principals are being held more accountable for students' learning. In a national survey last year by Public Agenda, a New York City–based polling group, 29 percent of principals said they were much more likely than in the past to be reassigned because of student performance. And almost twice as many, 57 percent, said they were evaluated based on "their ability to judge and improve teacher quality."

As one example of what states are doing to alter principals' behavior, Delaware is now pilot-testing what state policymakers say will become a mandatory, statewide evaluation system for school administrators. While requiring principals to show that they've mastered the state's standards for educational leadership, the plan also demands evidence of improved student performance.

Kennedy cites the 140,000-student San Diego school system as a district that has largely transformed its expectations for school-level administrators. There, specialists in instruction from the central office regularly take principals on "walk-throughs" in their own buildings to show them how to identify effective teaching.

"If you don't know how to analyze instruction in pretty sophisticated ways, then I don't believe you can plan for change in a school," says Ann Van Sickle, who directs the district's Leadership Academy, which provides training to aspiring and current principals.

Of course, principals can't change their schools if they're not allowed to, and many building leaders say they're not. A 2001 Public Agenda poll showed that only 30 percent of the nation's principals agreed that "the system helps you get things done." In contrast, 48 percent said they had to "work around" the system to accomplish their goals.

That climate represents a major barrier to school improvement, contends William G. Ouchi, the author of *Making Schools Work: A Revolutionary Plan to Get Your Children the Education They Need*. He favors strategies used in Seattle, Houston, and Edmonton, Alberta, all of which have shifted much decisionmaking authority over budget and personnel issues to the school level.

"Every school has a different mixture of children with different kinds of educational needs," says Ouchi, who is a professor of management at the University of California, Los Angeles. "If you impose on every school the same formula for the number of 8th grade science teachers or 3rd grade reading teachers, then you're necessarily giving them something different from what they need."

Memphis offers another model for giving school leaders more authority. In hiring New Leaders for New Schools to train 60 new principals over the next three years, the district struck a deal with the local teachers' union that will give graduates of the program greater latitude in their staffing decisions if they agree to lead one of the district's lowest-performing schools.

"If you have a strong instructional leader at the school-site level, you want to give them as much flexibility as possible, as long as they get results," says Carol R. Johnson, the superintendent of the 118,000-student district.

Johnson says she learned the importance of doing so in her former job as the chief of the 50,000-student Minneapolis school district. While there, she let Patrick Henry High School use money designated for two assistant-principal positions to release five teachers from the classroom so they could work with other educators at the school to improve their instruction.

The school was, and continues to be, one of the best-performing in the city. The lesson underscores another point many experts make about instructional leadership: Fostering improvements in teaching and learning often requires that principals elevate others in their buildings to leadership positions.

"It's about principals," says Johnson, "but it's also about empowering the school site so that teachers and others own the results and the decisions around the changes."

Theory of Action

By Jeff Archer
Education Week, September 14, 2005

Not long ago, a popular theory about school improvement went something like this: Put in strong principals and dedicated staff members, and then get out of their way. When it came to improving teaching and learning, the thinking went, the central office had little to add.

The upshot was an era of policies that limited the role of district-level leadership in matters of instruction. Site-based management and "whole-school reform" models flourished in the 1990s on the premise that individual schools alone could raise achievement.

And the idea worked. Or rather, it worked for some schools, while others languished. As a result, a new consensus is emerging in the field that strong district leadership is needed to bring about large-scale improvement-now a mandate under the federal No Child Left Behind Act.

"Either you believe in district reform, or you're going to have to be extremely patient in waiting for a school-by-school turnaround," says Jane Hammond of the Stupski Foundation, a Mill Valley, Calif.–based group that helps districts with strategic planning.

Education Week is focusing on leadership at the district level for its second annual "Leading for Learning" special report. The key question is: What strategies should district leaders pursue to influence the quality of teaching and learning?

To answer that, we tell the stories of two school systems that re-established the role of the central office in guiding instructional improvement: the 10,000-student Gilroy Unified schools in California and the 26,000-student Clarksville-Montgomery County system in Tennessee.

The two districts—both of which work with the Stupski Foundation—have sought greater consistency across schools in content and teaching methods. They've created new ways for teachers to learn together and use student data. And, they've each seen more students succeed academically.

To get a sense of how widespread such approaches are, the Education Week Research Center also commissioned a poll of superintendents that asked what practices they use to improve instruction. The results show district leaders across the country embracing many of the strategies employed in Gilroy and Clarksville-Montgomery County.

True, districts still reflect a range of approaches. Some are more explicit in telling schools what instruction should look like-a method that some are now calling "managed instruction." Others prefer to set broader boundaries and then step in where they see problems.

Many experts see the growing assertiveness of district leaders as a natural consequence of the movement for higher academic standards that has dominated education policymaking for more than a decade. It's too much, they say, to presume that every school has within it the capacity to bring its students to the levels of achievement now demanded of them.

"When you have a policy environment now that expects change to occur at scale, that means that districts have to improve all schools, essentially simultaneously," says Warren Simmons, the executive director of the Annenberg Institute for School Reform, located in Providence, R.I.

Tellingly, the Bill & Melinda Gates Foundation—one of the strongest promoters of designs for small schools—has drafted a new white paper arguing that schools are most likely to succeed if they're part of a supportive district, or, in the case of charter schools, part of a larger network of schools.

"We've spent over a billion dollars on almost 2,000 schools, and what we found is that most people don't know what to do, and how to do it," says Tom Vander Ark, the executive director for education at the Seattle-based foundation.

Mounting evidence suggests that effective schools are most often found in districts with strong systemwide guidance. In 2002, the Council of the Great City Schools identified some parallels among improving districts in an influential report, "Foundations for Success."

The council described strategies employed in Charlotte-Mecklenburg, N.C.; Houston; Sacramento, Calif.; and the subset of schools in New York City then known as the Chancellor's District.

Each district had a common curriculum, and had set up training and monitoring systems to ensure consistent approaches toward instruction across schools. The districts also made frequent use of student-performance data to inform educators' decisions.

"You have to take responsibility for the overall instructional program," says Michael D. Casserly, the executive director of the Washington-based council, "rather than just abandon that to the individual schools without providing direction, technical assistance, or professional development, and just hoping for the best."

Chrys Dougherty, the director of research at the National Center for Educational Accountability, says much the same is true in most of the districts named as finalists and winners for the annual Broad Prize for Urban Education, which recognizes improved student performance.

"When you go to effective schools that are in a district that has certain things in place, they will say their job was made infinitely easier by the fact that the district did these things," says Dougherty, whose Austin, Texas-based center collects the data used to make the Broad Prize selections.

On the surface, this larger role for the central office might seem at odds with the concurrent push to give families more options. Some of the biggest urban districts, for example, are creating large numbers of new schools with different designs—what's come to be called a "portfolio" model.

Likewise, decentralized decisionmaking still has plenty of proponents, as seen in the number of districts giving school sites more power to hire whom they want and to spend their budgets as they see fit.

But strong district leadership is needed for empowerment of school sites to succeed, says Joseph Olchefske, a former superintendent of the Seattle public schools. As a district chief, he gave schools considerable leeway to design their own programs, but that didn't mean anything goes.

"You've got to set standards, you've got to create and implement assessments that are for all kids, regardless of the school, and have very clear accountability, which means consequences," says Olchefske, who is now the managing director of a new consulting group at the American Institutes for Research, located in Washington.

Michael Fullan, an expert on school system management at the University of Toronto, says one of a superintendent's biggest challenges is finding the right balance between central authority and site-based autonomy. Ideally, he argues, schools should feel ownership of a commopi vision of instruction.

'"If you're too loose, you don't get the focus, but if you're too focused, you get prescription, and narrowness, and rebellion," he says. "The holy grail of school reform on a large scale is large-scale ownership."

Whether most districts in the United States can achieve that balance remains to be seen. But as the survey results and the stories of the two districts in this report suggest, few district leaders are leaving things to chance.

1. Review Cases 1 and 2 and pick one or two themes at the district and the school level that may be applicable to your school and district. For each of these issues, develop three open-ended questions on accountability. Conduct a brief interview with a school-site and district staff, such as superintendent, assistant superintendent, resource coordinator, principal, and teachers. Provide a summary on similarities and differences in their views on accountability. Can you explain why such differences exist? Do you see any imbalance in the way accountability is distributed between the district and the school levels?

2. Suppose you are asked to develop a three-year school-improvement plan for your school or your district. Considering the logic of accountability in this chapter, what

are the supportive and impeding conditions in your school and your district? What do you propose to address these conditions?

3. Do you aspire to be the same type of principal as in Easton Elementary School in Maryland (Case 1)? If so, how would you develop a road map that will enable you to advance toward that goal in your school? If not, what are your key reservations about the Easton leadership model?

4. More generally, what kind of leadership is needed to face the challenge of accountability at the school and district/state level? What skill set do new leaders need to meet the new accountability expectations?

CHAPTER TWO

Evolving Public Policy and the Educational-Accountability Context

LEARNING OBJECTIVES

- Understand the underlying assumptions of educational accountability, its defining characteristics, and fundamental challenges with the reform.
- Explore the assumptions of the educational accountability theory of change.
- Define the general components of a comprehensive accountability system.
- Understand the challenges that may arise when implementing educational accountability.

■ INTRODUCTION

Although testing has been used to determine student academic progress throughout the history of U.S. education, educators must now contend with an education system dominated by student assessments and high expectations for results. The goals of education in the United States have been redefined. The ways we measure success have shifted. And the ways we think about improving schools have changed. Traditional educational practices have not met the needs of many students and educators. We cannot continue to do more of the same if we want to drastically improve the education system. The problems of the educational system are multifaceted; these problems cannot be solved with reform strategies that focus on single dimensions, such as teacher hiring practices, autonomy over budgeting, or school governance. Indeed, there is a growing dissatisfaction in "content-free improvement and reform initiatives" (Hill, 2002, p. 49). In order to make significant and necessary changes in our schools, we need a comprehensive, process-oriented, school-improvement framework. Educational accountability, with its focus on challenging academic standards, curriculum, instructional practices, student outcomes, assessment, consequences, and customer satisfaction, provides such a framework for defining how schools must function to improve student academic achievement.

    In order to effectively implement accountability mechanisms for large-scale improvement of schools, it is important to understand the underlying assumptions of educational accountability, its defining characteristics, and fundamental challenges with the reform. This chapter addresses each of these components while providing conceptual and contextual understanding about educational change dynamics.

■ EDUCATIONAL ACCOUNTABILITY: THE THEORY OF CHANGE

Comprehensive and systematic reform is necessary to make significant improvements in the U.S. education system. The multilevel and multifaceted nature of the U.S. education system makes it intrinsically resistant to large-scale change. However, the education system has not created equal educational opportunities for all students and change is needed to ensure that every student is in a school that creates an educational environment conducive to learning. Education reform with this level of desired change entails a broad and clear vision. Elmore (2000) notes:

> *Improvement, then, is change with direction, sustained over time, that moves entire systems, raising the average level of quality and performance while at the same time decreasing the variation among units, and engaging people in analysis and understanding of why some actions seem to work and others don't. (p. 13)*

Educational-accountability reform provides the necessary vision and framework for such large-scale improvement.

To reasonably make the argument that accountability strategies and mechanisms will bring about improvements in student academic achievement, we must thoroughly describe the assumptions underlying the theory of change of educational-accountability reform. Weiss (1998) describes theories of change as "Explanation[s] of the causal links that tie program inputs to expected program outputs" (p. 55). In addition, Shadish, Cook, and Campbell (2002) state that theories of change can be used "to explicate the theory of a treatment by detailing the expected relationships among inputs, mediating processes, and short- and long-term outcomes" (p. 501). It should be noted that the educational accountability theory of change we convey in this book may not correspond directly with NCLB legislative accountability mandates. This is because the federal and state legislation may not reflect the theory supporting educational accountability in its entirety. Additionally, changes may be made to federal or state accountability legislation with a new Congress or presidential administration. What we describe in this book is the theory of how educational accountability is supposed to function to improve student performance irrespective of political decisions. Gaps between theory and policy present critical areas for concern and should be addressed if educational accountability is to be used for large-scale changes in the U.S. education system.

Weiss, Knapp, Hollweg, and Burrill (2001) suggest that there are three channels by which reform can influence the education system: curriculum, teacher development, and assessment and accountability. Each of these channels is interactive and directly impacts teachers and their practices, which in turn influences student learning. Seeing as Weiss et al. identify accountability as one of their core channels of influence, it may seem that educational accountability is one of the core channels. However, Weiss et al. conceptualize the core channel of accountability as a set of assessment-based consequences. This conceptualization differs from the theory of educational accountability that we present as a large scale reform initiative. Specifically, the theory of educational accountability is not simply defined by test-based compliance (Elmore & Fuhrman, 2001). Rather, educational accountability is

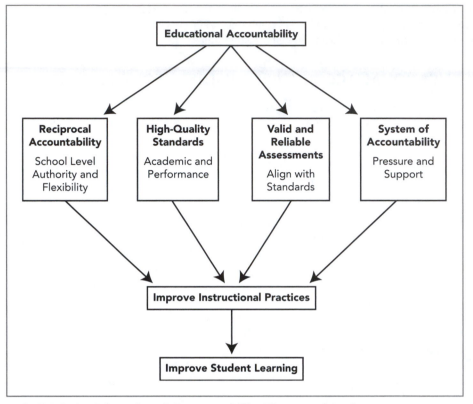

FIGURE 2.1   Educational Accountability Theory of Action

a reform initiative with components that work through each of the three core channels to bring about improvements in instructional practices and student learning.

The theory of change for educational accountability is presented in Figure 2.1. Similar to the channels of influence developed by Weiss et al. (2001), the figure illustrates that in order for improvements to be made in student learning, improvements must be made in instructional practices. Accordingly, educational accountability requires that all attention and support within the education system be directed at improving instructional practices by influencing roles and responsibilities, academic standards, assessments, and accountability mechanisms. As seen in Figure 2.1, the four major assumptions of results-driven accountability for improving instructional practices are:

1. Allocate commensurate authority and flexibility to the school level to make educational changes.
2. Establish clear goals for academic and performance standards.
3. Provide valid and reliable information to make educational decisions.
4. Facilitate the motivation for change through a combination of pressures and support.

These assumptions that we identify as critical for the theory of educational accountability are consistent with research and literature on educational-accountability reform. For example, Newmann, King, and Rigdon (1997) claim:

The assumption is that teachers will try harder and become more effective in meeting goals for student performance when goals are clear, when information on the degree of success is available, and when there are real incentives to meet the goals. (p. 43)

The four assumptions for educational accountability are interconnected and each essential to bringing about improvements in student performance. We will explore each of the assumptions to provide a better understanding of how educational accountability is designed to impact the education system to improve instruction and student learning.

Reciprocal Accountability

The first assumption of educational accountability maintains that educators at the school level will receive commensurate authority and flexibility appropriate for their given role to make necessary improvements in instructional practices. Accountability is reciprocal in the sense that because educators receive authority and flexibility in exchange for producing results, they must also receive sufficient support and resources from the district and state levels to make change. Educational accountability will not function properly if principals, teachers, and students are the only individuals being held accountable for results. Educators at the district and state levels are also accountable to schools.

The key aspect to reciprocal accountability is being able to identify clear causality between the practices implemented and outcomes desired. In particular, educators must believe that they have direct control over the factors they are asked to change. Schlechty (2002) comments, "In an effective results-oriented management system, those who are held accountable for results believe that these results are important and that they themselves can do something about them" (p. 193). The theory of educational accountability demands that educators believe they can make changes to improve student performance after acquiring new flexibility and authority. Of course, educators will need to be aware of the types of knowledge and skills to use with the flexibility and authority allotted to them by educational accountability if they want to make significant improvements in academic achievement for students who have not traditionally done well in our education system.

The assumption of commensurate authority and flexibility is directly related to the theory of tight-loose coupling (Fennell, 1994; Firestone, 1985; Weick, 1976). With tight-loose coupling, schools are given the flexibility and authority to make educational changes as long as they meet the established performance standards. Education reform based on tight-loose coupling recognizes that educators would not be able to meet the demands of educational accountability without the power to experiment with new strategies.

High-Quality Standards

The establishment of clear goals for academic and performance standards is the second assumption of the theory of educational accountability. Specifically, the goals must be entirely centered on aligning curriculum, instruction, and student assessment to high-quality academic content standards to improve student learning and performance. Adams and Kirst (1999) state that accountability promotes academic achievement by focusing "educational policy, administration, and practice directly on teaching and learning" (p. 464). In this sense, the goals must be the same and clear for all actors in the education system from policymakers to administrators to teachers. In addition, all actors must believe in the goals of academic and performance standards to secure the will and capacity to reform (Spillane, 1999). The theory suggests that when goals throughout the education system are focused on academic and performance standards, teachers will have the capacity to make changes to their instructional practices and increase academic press. Academic press consists of a combination of high-quality homework, course content, and teacher expectations (Chatterji, 2002).

Valid and Reliable Assessments

The theory of educational accountability assumes that when educators are provided with valid and reliable information regarding student performance, they will be able to make effective instructional decisions for improving student learning. There is an additional underlying notion that using the provided information to make comparisons between schools and districts will stimulate school improvement. Information should be in the form of multiple assessments of student performance aligned to the standards. Chatterji (2002) calls attention to the necessary conditions for the use of information: "validity of data from standards-based assessment; consistency of decisions on individual students, teachers, and schools; and a search for appropriate indicators of school quality" (p. 368). The assumption about the provision of information relies on the education system's ability to both measure appropriate indicators of school quality and report results accurately (Baker & Linn, 2002). Critical here is that the information collected and reported be relevant to the practice of teaching and learning (O'Day, 2002). The assumptions regarding information also depend on individuals within the education system having the requisite knowledge and skills, or capacity, to use the information to make effective changes (Baker & Linn, 2002). Interpretations of the provided information must be made and turned into decisions. If the information is to be used to change educational practices, educators must then be able to identify and apply alternative methods. The use of information to make important education decisions may seem intuitive, but in reality it relies on intricate psychometric, methodological, and cognitive theories of action and learning (Baker & Linn, 2002; Spillane, 1999).

System of Accountability

Many people believe that the single driving force behind educational accountability is that the added pressure on individuals and schools in the education system motivates them to make changes that result in improvements in student performance. Even though this is the most widely recognized and discussed assumption of the theory of educational accountability, we have placed the assumption about pressure at the end of the list to emphasize the interconnected nature and importance of all the identified assumptions. Additionally, putting pressure on schools in the form of mandates, high-stakes decisions, sanctions, and consequences alone is not educational accountability and will not bring about large-scale improvement in schools. First, focusing on pressure neglects the importance of providing support to educators and schools, such as adequate resources for technical assistance, extra time to attend to reform, materials, and high-quality professional development. And second, using pressure to motivate assumes that individuals and schools are willing to participate. Ladd and Zelli (2002) claim that only when the conditions of an incentive contract are satisfied will educators be willing to participate in accountability. Specifically, "The agent must find the job sufficiently attractive to be willing to participate and, given that the participation constraint is met, the incentives provided to the agent must be compatible with the desired outcomes" (Ladd & Zelli, 2002, p. 501). The combination of pressure and support is necessary to motivate educators to make the large-scale changes required by the theory of educational accountability.

Our description of the theory and assumptions supporting educational accountability should highlight its complexity and comprehensiveness as a school-reform strategy. The theoretical assumptions should also emphasize the logic of educational accountability for school improvement. The current system of education has not served all of our students equally. If we want to instill high expectations and quality education for all students, then the theory of educational accountability shows how it can be done. Specifically, we need to focus all of our efforts and resources on the core channels of influence in the education system to change instructional practices that will improve student performance. We must ensure that educators have the appropriate flexibility and authority to make necessary changes in instructional practices for improvements in student performance. We must set clear goals for academic standards and performance. We must make certain that educators receive accurate information that can be used to change instructional practices. And we must use a combination of pressure and support to motivate educators. The next section will provide the specific components that make up educational accountability strategies for school improvement.

■ EDUCATIONAL ACCOUNTABILITY DEFINED: MEDIATING COMPONENTS

The assumptions described in the previous section illustrate how the theory of change for educational accountability is supposed to function to facilitate changes in instructional practices that improve student performance. With the theory in place, we will now describe the components that make up educational accountability. Figure 2.2 illustrates the theory of educational accountability with its components. The components can be viewed as mediating factors that "identify the essential processes that must occur in order to transfer an effect" (Shadish, Cook, & Campbell, 2002, pp. 89–90). They are the specific strategies and elements of the intervention that stand between the theoretical assumptions of the reform and desired improvements in instructional practices that lead to student outcomes. We have identified the following four components of educational accountability:

1. Change expectations for educational leaders and determine who is accountable to whom in the education system.
2. Develop and implement academic and performance standards.
3. Design assessment tools that accurately measure school quality and inform school-improvement decisions.
4. Construct a system to evaluate how effectively schools have met the academic and performance standards and put into action a set of pressure and support mechanisms for low-performing schools.

These four components are consistent with research on systems of educational accountability. For example, O'Day (2002) explains that the components of educational-accountability reform for student improvement are manifested in an emphasis on student outcomes, the school as the unit of analysis and responsibility, public reporting of student achievement data, and the attachment of rewards and sanctions to student performance levels. As we describe the components of educational accountability in this section, we will also note the chapters in this book that go into further detail.

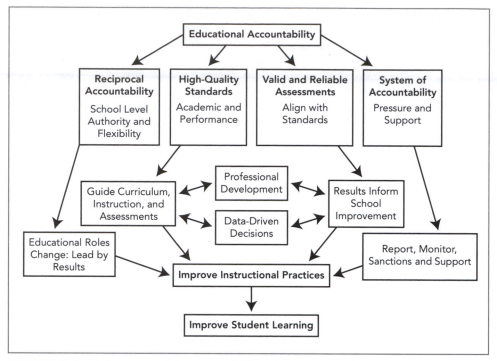

FIGURE 2.2   Educational Accountability Theory of Action with Operational Components

Educational Roles Change: Lead by Results

The first component of educational accountability is that educational roles within the system change. In turn, determining who is accountable to whom in the education system is important. First of all, in a change from traditional school governance structures, educational accountability places the school, rather than the district, as the unit of accountability (Elmore & Fuhrman, 2001). The change in focus from the district to the school infers new roles and interactions between the state and school levels of education. The district level of education still maintains a central role in providing technical assistance and resources to schools to support changes in instructional practices, but in actuality the schools are accountable to the state, which could be state legislatures and educational politicians or bureaucrats in the state department of education. Second, declaring that the school is now the unit of accountability ignores the important levels within schools that influence student performance and must also be held accountable (Waters, Marzano, & McNulty, 2003). Individual and schools should only be held accountable for factors and actions over which they have control and responsibility. This does not grant permission to educators to shirk responsibility for student performance. It merely indicates that the component of who is accountable to whom holds reciprocal responsibility across levels of the education system. School leaders must convey a clear vision of challenging standards-based goals while creating a professional environment conducive for instructional changes. Teachers must make changes to their curriculum design and instructional practices. And students must be engaged and motivated to make progress toward mastering the curriculum. Chapter 3 addresses the changing expectations and roles for educational leaders in educational accountability. Further discussion concerning the varying roles in the education system can be found in Chapter 4.

Standards Guide Curriculum, Instruction, and Assessments

The second assumption of the theory of educational accountability states that clear goals regarding academic and performance standards have to be established. Correspondingly, the first component of educational accountability is to develop and adopt challenging academic content and performance standards for all students. These academic and performance standards should in turn guide the instructional practices of selecting curriculum, instruction, and assessment. As part of the federal push for standards-based and results-driven reform, NCLB has required that all states design systems for academic and performance standards. Currently this is the way in which the standards component of educational accountability is being characterized and implemented. In turn, state departments of education and state legislatures have assumed responsibility for devising statewide academic-content standards that specify what students are expected to know, contain coherent and rigorous content, and promote the use of advanced academic skills. States have also defined performance standards that are aligned with the state academic-content standards. In general, the performance standards are arranged into three levels of achievement including two levels of high achievement—such as advanced and proficient—that determine how well students are mastering the standards, and a basic level of achievement for low-achieving students to gauge their progress toward mastering the proficient and advanced levels of achievement. The design and use of academic and performance standards are carefully examined in Chapter 5.

Assessment Results Inform School Improvement

The third component of educational accountability is designing assessment tools that accurately measure school quality, such as student mastery of the curriculum. Additionally, results from assessments should be used by educators to improve instructional practices. Adams and Kirst (1999) comment:

> *Indicators should be selected that measure the central features of schooling, measure what is actually taught or considered important for schools to know, provide information that is policy-relevant, focus on schools, allow for fair comparisons, and balance information's usefulness against burden for collecting it. Indicators also should be valid, measuring what they purport to measure, and reliable, operating free from errors of measurement and data collection. (p. 477)*

Although these are arguably the elements of schooling that we would like to know about when using educational accountability mechanisms, it is debatable whether indicators have been developed that can meet all of the assessment demands identified (Linn, 2000). Chapter 6 addresses the different types of assessments available for determining student performance.

Reporting, Monitoring, and Sanctions and Support

The fourth component of educational accountability entails constructing a system to monitor and evaluate how effective schools are in meeting academic and performance standards. The system must be effectively designed to judge "the quality of success of organizational performance" (Newmann, King, & Rigdon, 1997, p. 43). In developing such a system, decisions must be made regarding the levels at which data will be collected, data reported, and comparisons made (Adams & Kirst, 1999). The legislative mandates of NCLB currently delegate the responsibility to the states of designing systems for evaluating school quality under educational accountability. The states have created measures of adequate yearly progress that determine the percentage of students within a school meeting academic proficiency based on the levels of achievement of the performance standards. Data is collected at the school-level, but disaggregated for subgroups including economically disadvantaged students, students from major racial and ethnic groups, students with disabilities, and English Language Learner (ELL) students. The NCLB system provides one interpretation of how to evaluate schools. Unfortunately, the NCLB system does not currently have the capacity to monitor the provision of equal learning opportunities for all schools as it is based on a single indicator of student success: a test score (Sirotnik & Kimball, 1999). Educators should not let the NCLB system for evaluating schools preempt the use of more authentic monitoring procedures. The issues of reporting and monitoring school quality under educational accountability are discussed in Chapter 7.

Once the performance of schools has been evaluated, educational accountability requires that a process for applying pressure and support mechanisms in low-performing schools be put into place. Significant improvements in instructional practices to improve student performance necessitate considerable support and a little push from other levels of the education system. Many educators are quite familiar with educational accountability sanctions given current NCLB provisions, such as student performance reporting, probation, school-improvement plans, reconstitution, and the threat of choice to name a few. When we described the assumptions behind the theory of educational accountability in the previous section, we emphasized the dual nature of pressure and support. Sanctions and consequences may be easier to implement than support to schools attempting to make large scale improvements, but support strategies cannot be thrown to the wayside in educational accountability. Adequate financial, technical, and political resources need to be made available to aid schools in facilitating the use of effective school-improvement strategies. As educational accountability is a process-oriented reform strategy for improving student learning, resources cannot be prescribed with a one-size-fits-all mentality. Rather, districts and states need to supply resources to schools that match the context of the problem. Chapter 7 covers the process of applying pressure and support through educational accountability.

Educational Accountability Tools

In Figure 2.2 there are two components within the theory of educational accountability that differ slightly in character from the four mediating components we have just described. While professional development and data-driven decision-making strategies also have the purpose of improving instructional practices, they are tools that should be used by schools to facilitate the alignment of academic and performance standards and results from multiple assessments with changes in instructional practices. The tools should be used through an iterative process where standards and results from assessments inform professional development activities and data-driven decisions at the same time that professional development and data-driven decisions work to improve alignment of the standards and the use of assessment results. This is indicated by the double-ended arrows between the tools and the mediating components of standards and assessments. Using student and school performance indicators to make educational decisions are discussed in Chapter 8, while professional development strategies are described in Chapter 9.

▪ EDUCATIONAL ACCOUNTABILITY CHALLENGES

Although the theory of change supporting educational accountability suggests that the reform will make significant improvements in student performance by focusing on changes to instructional practices, there is the potential for challenges and difficulties to arise. One of the primary reasons schools may find it difficult to make substantial improvements in student performance with educational accountability or any other school-reform initiative is that low-performing schools often find themselves in a "policy churn" situation where they are constantly being asked to implement new programs and practices in response to changing legislation and policies (Hess, 1999). In addition to the notion of education reform "policy churn," we identify the following three challenges that surface when employing educational accountability:

1. Weak implementation
2. Lack of organizational capacity to reform
3. Unintended consequences of accountability sanctions

If any of these three challenges are permitted to persist and not systematically addressed, educational accountability will not impact instructional practices and student performance in its intended manner. This section describes the ways these challenges have manifested in attempts to use the strategies of educational accountability.

Weak Implementation

Research on implementation of education reforms suggests that when a theoretically sound initiative is implemented to its full extent, the probability of attaining the intended educational impact is higher (Rossi, Freeman, & Lipsey, 1999). However, in reality it is unlikely that any education reform initiative, educational accountability included, will be fully implemented. In turn, it is imperative that we deal with the potential challenges that may arise when implementing educational accountability to improve student learning. There are various reasons why a reform initiative does not get fully or correctly implemented (Pressman & Wildavsky, 1984). Institutional fragmentation, multiple and confusing goals, numerous decision points, inadequate funding, and varying perspectives are just a few of the impediments to full program implementation. In the case of educational accountability, weak implementation is by and large a result of educators throughout the system failing to accept changes required by the reform. For example, educational accountability hinges on teachers making improvements in their instructional practices. In reality, they may only make minimal changes. Butzin (2004) finds, "In response to high-stakes testing and higher standards for even the most challenging students, schools have responded by talking louder. They haven't changed the way they teach. Instead, they push more papers in front of the kids" (p. 307). If educational accountability is to be used to improve student performance, then educators cannot merely spend more time on traditional activities that have not proven to be effective for low-performing students.

Educational accountability asks educators to expand their expectations and practices regarding academic content and curriculum, rather than narrowing them to any particular assessment. Nonetheless, many educators believe that the purpose of results-driven accountability is to force educators to teach to the test. Teaching to the test is an unintended consequence of accountability and an example of incorrect implementation of the reform (Thompson, 2001). Of course, it is not only teachers in the education system who may fail to implement the reform in its entirety. For example, the state legislature of Colorado has introduced a bill that allows parents to opt-out of having their children tested according to NCLB requirements (see Appendix C for the proposed legislation). The NCLB legislation is the current manifestation of the theory of educational accountability and Colorado's proposed legislation functions to make changes to the federal accountability legislation. While educators may not agree with NCLB, the theory of educational accountability rests on the assumption that schools will be tested in order to receive support, as well as to be held accountable for performance. In turn, Colorado's proposed legislation may make it difficult for educational-accountability reform to make significant improvements in the education system if parents opt-out of testing.

Weak implementation of educational accountability may arise because of resistance to change or due to the belief that certain aspects of the reform effort are not necessary. The federal NCLB legislation is only one interpretation of educational accountability. The theoretical assumptions of educational accountability identified in this chapter should be used to determine whether the federal program, if fully implemented, will bring about large-scale improvements in the education system. The variety of responses to implementing educational accountability will certainly change the way in which educational accountability is intended to function to improve student performance.

Lack of Organizational Capacity to Reform

We cannot be surprised by weak implementation of educational accountability when schools lack the necessary organizational capacity to make the required changes in teaching and learning. Newmann, King, and Rigdon (1997) observe, "Schools with strong external accountability tended to be low in organizational capacity" (p. 54). The implication is that schools with the least ability to make required educational accountability changes due to their organizational capacity find themselves with the most severe external accountability demands. The lack of organizational capacity is evident in rudimentary technology, inadequate support and resources, and the problematic distribution of authority (Adams & Kirst, 1999). This again raises the issue that applying pressure alone will not bring about substantial school improvement. If we want low-performing schools to make significant improvements in student performance and we expect them to do it with accountability mechanisms, then we have to ensure that these schools receive sufficient support.

Unintended Consequences of Accountability Sanctions

The third challenge to educational accountability is how sanctions can result in unintended outcomes. The application of sanctions depends on the way in which success is defined in systems of accountability. When educational success is determined by a single indicator, such as a test score, ensuing consequences for failure may not be commensurate with the problem. In turn, educators and students in schools identified as low performing and impacted by negative sanctions may feel demoralized, devastated, or destabilized, which may hinder their will to reform (Acker-Hocevar & Touchton, 2002). Education researchers have questioned the rationale behind negative sanctions. O'Day (2002) states, "Reliance on negative incentives undermines innovation and risk-taking in threatened schools and diverts attention to organizational survival rather than student learning" (p. 20). Furthermore, Spillane (1999) finds that mandates "can also undermine the educative potential of the ideas promoted through state standards" (p. 567). Nonetheless, pressure is a necessary theoretical assumption and component of education accountability when appropriately combined with adequate support. If the accountability sanctions of NCLB that educators have become familiar with are not implemented with proportional support, then the accountability mechanisms of NCLB do not reflect the intent of educational accountability for improvements in student performance.

These potential challenges to realizing educational accountability are important and should not be forgotten when progressing through the rest of the book. When educational leaders think about their role in educational accountability, they should remember that these challenges may need to be addressed.

Summary

- Extensive and comprehensive reform is needed to make significant improvements in the education system. Furthermore, educational-accountability reform may provide the necessary framework for large-scale improvement.
- Education reform with this level of desired change entails a broad and clear vision. In addition, educational accountability requires a great deal of attention and support within the education system directed at improving instructional practices, as well as providing the proper balance between pressures and support.
- Challenges that surface when employing educational accountability include weak implementation, lack of organizational capacity, and unintended consequences of accountability sanctions.
- Educational leaders need to develop accountability-based strategies in anticipation of these challenges.

Commentary and Discussion Questions

The following commentary discusses the challenging nature of school administrators' roles today. Now that the notion of accountability has been brought directly into the classroom and placed on teachers and students, education reformers are looking to ensure this trend is applied to school and district leaders also. Dorothy Shipps and William Firestone argue that such reform is almost always advocated by individuals external from schools. While students and teachers have had to manage with one form of accountability, school leaders have to perform to five unique types: "political, bureaucratic, professional, market and moral." Each one requires the administrator to assume different norms and behave differently. Recent research may provide a more coherent solution to accountability issues—internal accountability. Such a system would put administrators', teachers', and parents' expectations of high performance at the center of accountability.

Juggling Accountabilities: The Leaders' Turn

By Dorothy Shipps and William A. Firestone
Education Week, June 18, 2003

Accountability for public school leaders is all the rage. First we devised standards to make teachers answerable for student outcomes. Then we expanded testing so that students would take responsibility for their accomplishments and failures. Now the big goal on the accountability agenda is to require principals and superintendents to answer for the performance of the schools under their guidance. But will another round of defining responsibilities and setting standards improve schools? Is it wise (or fair) to ratchet up the mandates that leaders face from state and federal governments while ignoring their obligations to others?

The idea that public school leaders owe a justification for why schools succeed or fail comes from reform advocates, often education outsiders, promoting a particular vision of change. Each such reform vision would realign school and district leaders' responsibilities in particular ways, usually deputizing them as representatives, salesmen, or instruments of the advocate's goals. The reformer typically describes the newly imagined accountability as if all other responsibilities on leaders' shoulders could be ignored.

Missing from the debate is a view that takes the perspective of the leader. Looking at accountability from the inside, as it is experienced in a school or district, reveals that public school leaders already face multiple, simultaneous obligations that often conflict.

School and district leaders respond to at least five distinct types of external accountability. Each requires that they behave differently:

- Political accountability
- Bureaucratic accountability
- Professional accountability
- Market accountability
- Moral accountability

Leaders experience these multiple accountability claims simultaneously, making their task of creating coherence out of mixed signals vastly more complex than it appears to most reform advocates. To make matters worse, these obligations often conflict. A few examples should clarify:

Political accountability conflicts with bureaucratic accountability when local constituents insist on greater involvement in decisionmaking while education agencies require that schools implement standardized programs. For instance, New York City parents, accustomed to choosing their children's schools with care and having a voice on systemwide policies, have been in an uproar over a mandated reading and mathematics curriculum that about 1,000 of its nearly 1,200 schools must adopt. These conflicting pressures push school and district leaders in opposite directions. The compromises that will result when Schools Chancellor Joel I. Klein permits school-by-school exceptions to mollify vocal parents undermine the credibility of the curricula and leave parents even more suspicious of school leaders.

Professional accountability clashes with bureaucratic accountability when agency functionaries ignore or mistrust professional standards of good practice. For instance, at least 27 state education departments threaten to quickly impose sanctions on low-performing schools (or students) if they do not raise their test scores in short order. Until sanctions are administered, most schools leave local educators to figure out how to raise scores with existing resources. Yet current professional standards encourage leaders to build the instructional capacity of teachers and the self-confidence of low-achieving students, both of which take new resources and much time. The too-frequent compromise includes both teaching to the test and educational triage in which school and district leaders show quick improvements by focusing limited resources on students whose test scores are very near the mark, a strategy that meets neither goal.

Market accountability competes with moral accountability when experiments in mission-driven and market-based schooling—like charter schools—confront the ethical obligation to educate all students, including those with disabilities. Legal or bureaucratic attempts to resolve these tensions are less successful than it first appears, and the results vary widely. States like Arizona, where charters function highly independently, put a premium on competition and charter school survival, creating disincentives for enrolling special education children. Others, like Connecticut, mandate links between charter schools and districts for the provision of special education services, encouraging families to apply to charter schools, but leaving district administrators and school heads with open-ended responsibilities. In both cases, school leaders must create coherence from the incentives and ambiguities that result often only after the first special education student is actually enrolled.

These examples, and many others like them, make it obvious that *increasing* leaders' accountability is a nostrum unlikely to improve public education. Leaders already face many competing obligations. Making any one of them stronger simply adds to the confusion and courts unforeseen and unintended consequences. Moreover, the use of rigid rules and strong external sanctions implies weakness, not the inherent strength of the important goals sought. Powerful accountability is more clearly demonstrated when influence is understated and models are voluntarily copied.

While reformers demand more external accountability—more testing, more choices, more community control, more training—a small but growing body of evidence suggests that schools where children really learn feature a strong sense of *internal* accountability. The principal, teachers, and families share an expectation of strong performance, definitions of the practices that meet ambitious goals, and mutual obligations to monitor their performance. Such schools are always exceptional, but they suggest that reformers might have gotten the problem backwards.

The challenge for improving public schooling is less about strengthening any one of the many external accountabilities that educators face, and more about building an internal consensus at each school over a common direction and the obligations that principals, parents, teachers, and students have to one another.

1. When considering the commentary by Dorothy Shipps and William Firestone, discuss what possible issues could arise in your school/district if a notion of *internal accountability* was implemented. What would be your solution(s) to such matters?
2. How would you develop a school-improvement plan that reflects the principles and practices of internal accountability? Discuss the key assumptions behind the theory of educational accountability.
3. How would you describe the implementation process in meeting your state's accountability standards? Do you see strong or week implementation? Discuss whether your school and district have strong educational capacity.
4. How do you assess the unintended consequences of accountability sanctions in your state and district?

CHAPTER THREE

Changing Expectations for Leadership in Educational Accountability

LEARNING OBJECTIVES

- Understand why the traditional leadership role of managing by rules is not likely to improve student outcomes.
- Recognize the necessity of shifting to a new leadership frame of mind that can be characterized by a process of leading by results.
- Describe the strategies educational leaders will need to adopt in order to lead by results, including acquiring appropriate knowledge and skills, building school capacity centered on student performance, ensuring collaborative inquiry and reflection, and sharing leadership to attain student performance results.
- Connect the results-driven strategies to four educational leadership theories that are frequently cited in research on educational accountability initiatives. These theories include instructional leadership, distributed or shared leadership, transformational leadership, and results-driven leadership.

■ INTRODUCTION

The era of results-driven goals and high expectations for all students calls for reform that will bring about drastic improvements in student performance. The key to making substantial change is using the theory and strategies of educational accountability to focus attention on instructional practices. Educators must have the appropriate knowledge and skills to align high academic content standards with curriculum design, instruction, and student assessments. As such, educational leaders are critical to the process of improving student performance with educational accountability by preparing themselves to provide teachers with the necessary knowledge and skills to make significant improvements. Grogan and Andrews (2002) note:

> There is a direct link between what good teachers are able to do and the quality of the school where they teach. Furthermore, the school principal is a key lynchpin between teacher development and school improvement. The superintendent is the key lynchpin between principal development and good schools. (p. 249)

School leaders and superintendents will have to be prepared to provide leadership and support that properly match the school-improvement needs of individual schools, teachers, and students.

If we want to ensure the success of large-scale educational accountability initiatives to improve student outcomes, educational leaders at the district and school levels must understand and accept that leadership expectations have appreciably changed. With the focus on instructional practices, educational leaders at the district level are obliged to provide a clear vision and sufficient technical resources to support the capacity of schools and school leaders. At the school level, principals can no longer view their role as simply a building manager who handles spending restrictions, personnel proscriptions, instructional material provision, and process specifications. Rather, principals must balance and align these duties with knowledge and skills about educational practices to guide teachers toward best practices for teaching and student outcomes. Many states, such as New Jersey and Pennsylvania, have introduced standardized tests as part of school leader certification (see Appendix D for an example from the "School Leaders Licensure Assessment" designed and administered by the Educational Testing Service [ETS]).

Educational accountability shifts the education system away from procedural compliance and input efficiency to the monitoring of student performance by measuring outcomes. Given the emergence of educational accountability described in the previous chapter, it should not be surprising that expectations about the roles of educational leaders have changed. Explicitly, educational leaders must lead schools by results rather than managing by rules. In this chapter we explain how school leadership expectations have evolved for principals and superintendents. Additionally, we consider theories of leadership that correspond with the changing demands required by educational accountability. At the end of the chapter we provide examples of the strategies and leadership styles school leaders have adopted in response to the new expectations.

∎ LEADING BY RESULTS VERSUS MANAGING BY RULES

For decades the role of the school leader has been defined by the bureaucratic nature of the education system. Hierarchical arrangements, supervision and discipline, and strict divisions of labor were believed best practices in order to garner organizational efficiency. However, organizational efficiency does not necessarily produce rigorous expectations or powerful outcomes for all students. In reality, under mechanisms of procedural compliance, the education system failed many students and created sizable achievement gaps. Fortunately, the shift to results-driven educational goals presents the opportunity to make significant changes for students who have not traditionally found educational success. The roles educational leaders assume and the strategies they adopt are critical to the transformation of the education system. Educational leaders must balance managerial duties with leadership for teaching and learning to improve student performance. Marsh (2002) states, "Successful principals will evolve the roll to include setting the strategic direction for the school—a direction that requires considerable insight about education and the new interface between management support and educational reform" (p. 129). Superintendents must also embrace a shifting role that focuses on improving instructional practices throughout their districts.

This section will first explain why the traditional leadership role of managing by rules will not produce desired student outcomes. We then describe the shift in expectations for educational leaders to a process of leading by results. Finally, we describe the strategies educational leaders will need to adopt in order to lead by results, including acquiring appropriate knowledge and skills, building school capacity centered on student performance, ensuring collaborative inquiry and reflection, and sharing leadership to attain student performance results.

Managing by Rules

In an education system dominated by hierarchical and bureaucratic processes, school administrators have typically assumed supervisory and managerial roles to lead schools. Murphy (2002) states, "The educational roots of the profession of school administration atrophied over the course of the 20th century as the field gravitated toward conceptions of leadership based on scientific images of business management and social science research" (p. 76). While educational-accountability reform also calls for practices grounded in scientifically based research, Murphy refers to the focus on management practices to increase input efficiency. Educational accountability, on the other hand, involves scientifically based research practices that indicate the types of teaching and learning approaches that will improve student performance outcomes.

In general, the focus for school administrators at the district and school levels has been on procedural and programmatic managerial compliance rather than inquiry-based and results-driven leadership. The bureaucratic structure of the education system along with demands for procedural compliance created starkly clear divisions in the roles of educators, manifested for many schools in teacher isolation and a lack of schoolwide discussions about effective teaching and learning practices. It is not to say that educators cared less about students or did not want schools to succeed under the bureaucratic form of education. Instead, the education system and the way that roles were defined reflected trends in public administration of social programs during the 1960s and 1970s. Specifically, organizations were arranged hierarchically with attention to principles of scientific management for the purpose of achieving efficiency of inputs. The principles of scientific management suggest that data about the workplace can be collected to aid in hiring practices, facilitate cooperation between management and workers, and inform the division of labor and job specialization (Taylor, 2001). Lunenburg and Ornstein (1991) note, "Historically, scientific management focused on the management of work and workers" (p. 5). In terms of the function of hierarchy, Max Weber's classic theory of management claims, "The principles of office hierarchy and of levels of graded authority mean a firmly ordered system of super- and sub-ordination in which there is a supervision of the lower offices by the higher ones" (Weber, 2001, p. 73). Accordingly, in the bureaucratic system of schooling, the principal was viewed as the lone leader of the school who made executive decisions and supervised teachers to efficiently ensure that programmatic procedures were followed. In this system, leaders work to ensure efficiency rather than to encourage and support innovative instructional practices that improve student achievement. We classify this style of school leadership as managing by rules.

Leading by Results

The belief that school administrators should manage by rules and procedural compliance is in direct conflict with the new goals of the educational system that insist on high expectations for all students and demand student-performance results. To meet the new goals and make significant improvements in student performance, all attention throughout the education system must be focused on the processes of teaching and learning. Schlechty (2002) notes:

> *If schools are to become the dynamic organizations they must be to satisfy the conditions of the twenty-first century, then the school's management and leadership style must shift from management-by-programs (making sure people do things right) to leadership-by-results (insisting that people do the right things and giving them latitude to judge what those things are). (p. 192)*

The shift away from managing by rules will require considerable modifications in leadership practices at the district and school levels. We borrow Schlechty's terminology of *leading by results* to refer to the leadership style that will be necessary to respond to results-driven educational goals. Leading by results consists of the following leadership strategies:

1. Obtain and adopt knowledge and skills about effective teaching and learning practices.
2. Build school capacity centered on improving student performance.
3. Establish norms of collaborative inquiry and reflection about teaching and learning.
4. Share leadership to attain teacher support and sustain results.

We will address the changing expectations for educational leaders encompassed in each of these strategies of leading by results.

It should be noted that the managerial duties that have been the primary responsibility for educational leaders will not disappear in the era of results-driven educational accountability. It is more likely the case that school leaders will be asked to take on more managerial duties while also attempting to make changes in instructional practices. It should not be surprising that school leaders may feel too overwhelmed or overburdened to focus on teaching and learning. Neuman and Pelchat (2001) quote a principal:

> *That's the balance I was talking about earlier between management and instructional issues. This year I told my secretary that I would take no phone calls from anyone between 9 a.m. and 1 p.m. "Tell them I'm in the classrooms with the children." Now this created some real irate parents! "What do you mean, you can't find her? Go get her and put her on the phone!" When I call parents back now at 5 or 6 p.m. and they say, "I couldn't reach you," I tell them, "Well, that's because I was with the children, and I think that's where I'm supposed to be." And then I hear silence on the other end of the phone. And I say, "But I did get back to you. And in the same day." (p. 735)*

Observing the dilemma inherent in shifting to results-driven leadership, Goldring and Greenfield (2002) claim that educational leaders will need to take notice of "the necessity to manage and develop *internal* operations while concurrently monitoring the environment and anticipating and responding to *external* exigencies" (p. 13). As we describe the strategies of leading by results, it is important to be mindful of the delicate balance educational leaders will have to maintain between managerial duties and instructional leadership.

Knowledge and Skills

To lead by results, district and school leaders will need to have substantial knowledge and skills regarding how to bring about the use of effective instructional practices. In the system of managing by rules, district and school leaders are typically chosen through rigid channels of seniority and for personality qualities, such as charisma and loyalty. Elmore (2000) refers to the traditional recruitment process as "trait theories of competence" where leaders are chosen for having desirable personal attributes for leading schools, but may lack necessary knowledge and skills. Furthermore, leaders are not generally selected or promoted "because they have mastered some body of professional knowledge or because they work in an organizational environment in which they are expected to be competent at what they do as a condition of employment" (Elmore, 2000, p. 8). In general, the system of managing by rules overlooked and undervalued the knowledge and skills educational leaders must possess to improve student performance. To meet the demands of educational accountability, educational leaders will have to be cognizant of the knowledge and skills that are relevant to the leadership demands of changing instructional practices to improve student performance.

Reviewing research on effective leadership practices related to making significant changes in student performance, Waters, Marzano, and McNulty (2003) find:

> *Effective leadership means more than simply knowing what to do—it's knowing when, how, and why to do it. Effective leaders understand how to balance pushing for change while at the same time, protecting aspects of culture, values, and norms worth preserving. They know which policies, practices, resources, and incentives to align and how to align them with organizational priorities. They know how to gauge the magnitude of change they are calling for and how to tailor their leadership strategies accordingly. Finally, they understand and value the people in the organization (p. 2).*

The central feature of these findings is that when faced with challenging reform initiatives, effective educational leaders recognize that the nature of the reform, along with the context of the school, should determine how they respond. The use of appropriate methods necessitates a "repertoire of strategies for engaging students and staff members in meaningful learning and action oriented toward effective school change" (Grogan & Andrews, 2002, p. 243). Understanding the magnitude of change required by educational accountability is fundamental to determining suitable strategies. Changes in schools can be characterized as either first-order or second-order depending on the degree of disruption the reform brings to the school (Green, 2001; Waters, Marzano, & McNulty, 2003). First-order changes involve minimal disruption as they coincide with norms and values present in the school. The changes can be realized with existing knowledge and skills. And individuals within the school agree that the reform is the right type of change for the school. Second-order changes, on the other hand, are considered rather disruptive as there may not be consensus regarding the reform as the right initiative for the school and the changes require that individuals in the school learn new strategies and practices. For many schools, large-scale reform, such as educational accountability, will be second-order change. In turn, it will be imperative for educational leaders to emphasize the strength of the theory for making improvements in student performance and to use effective strategies for guiding the reform.

The field of educational administration has established a set of standards for the knowledge, skills, and strategies that leaders of effective schools with low-performing and disadvantaged students typically employ (Murphy, 2003). Table 3.1 presents six standards for school leaders developed in 1996 by the Council of Chief State School Officers (CCSSO) and its designated Interstate Leaders Licensure Consortium (ISLLC). The purpose of the ISLLC standards is to provide focus for teaching and learning practices, as well as the tools to create powerful learning environments (Buchanan & Roberts, 2001). The ISLLC standards and their corresponding indicators for knowledge, disposition, and performance

TABLE 3.1   Interstate Leaders Licensure Consortium (ISLLC) Standards

Standard 1	A school administrator is an educational leader who promotes the success of all students by facilitating the development, articulation, implementation, and stewardship of a vision of learning that is shared and supported by the school community
Standard 2	A school administrator is an educational leader who promotes the success of all students by advocating, nurturing, and sustaining a school culture and instructional program conducive to student learning and staff professional growth
Standard 3	A school administrator is an educational leader who promotes the success of all students by ensuring management of the organization, operations, and resources for a safe, efficient, and effective learning environment
Standard 4	A school administrator is an educational leader who promotes the success of all students by collaborating with families and community members, responding to diverse community interests and needs, and mobilizing community resources
Standard 5	A school administrator is an educational leader who promotes the success of all students by acting with integrity, fairness, and in an ethical manner
Standard 6	A school administrator is an educational leader who promotes the success of all students by understanding, responding to, and influencing the larger political, social, economic, legal, and cultural context

Source: Council of Chief State School Officers. (1996). *Interstate school leaders licensure consortium (ISLLC): Standards for school leaders.* Washington, DC: Author. Retrieved February 1, 2005, from http://www.ccsso.org/content/pdfs/isllcstd.pdf.

(see Appendix E) reflect a broad range of important and practical knowledge and skills useful for thinking about the process of leading by results. The standards cover the development of learning goals, the facilitation of instructional improvements, efficient management, parent and community involvement, ethical behavior, and social justice in educational practices. The merit of the ISLLC standards for educational leaders in times of change is evident in the principles that guided the development of the standards (CCSSO, 1996, p. 7):

- Standards should reflect the centrality of student learning
- Standards should acknowledge the changing role of the school leader
- Standards should recognize the collaborative nature of school leadership
- Standards should be high, upgrading the quality of the profession
- Standards should inform performance-based systems of assessment and evaluation for school leaders
- Standards should be integrated and coherent
- Standards should be predicated on the concepts of access, opportunity, and empowerment for all members of the school community

In effect, the ISLLC standards reflect the process-oriented nature of how educational accountability functions. Educational leaders will have to determine the appropriate knowledge and skills for the context of their needs. The ISLLC standards provide a valuable resource to educational leaders at the district- and school-levels as a set of guidelines for thinking about the knowledge and skills necessary for leading by results to make significant improvements in student performance.

In schools where all students achieve high standards, educational leaders possess the expertise to articulate and align the standards with practices, policies, resources, and incentives (Goldring & Greenfield, 2002). Educational leaders in these successful schools recognize that the demands of educational accountability entail different types of strategies for different school-improvement needs. Hill (2002) observes:

> *Particularly in schools serving poor and minority students, these pressures have tended to cause principals to focus more on the bottom line and to seek to learn why some schools are successful in ensuring that most students attain high standards while all too many do not. (p. 49)*

Process-oriented reform, such as educational accountability, require in struggling schools that educational leaders think about the school-improvement issues pertinent to the context of their schools. In addition, educational leaders will have to understand and promote the interrelationship between effective use of standards and assessments and improvements in instructional practices (Tucker & Codding, 2002).

The knowledge and skills necessary to improve the processes of teaching and learning may be unfamiliar to many educational leaders. Elmore (2000) finds, "direct involvement in instruction is among the least frequent activities performed by administrators of any kind at any level" (p. 7). When leading by results, educational leaders cannot remain disconnected from the technical core of schooling. Lugg, Bulkley, Firestone, and Garner (2002) identify the following questions that educational leaders should raise when making changes to instructional practices:

- How do I mobilize the time, funds, knowledge, and staff leadership resources needed to help improve instruction?
- How do I ensure that responses to state testing improve instruction for all children rather than become a motivation for ignoring some students (e.g., especially high or low achievers) and pushing unsuccessful children out of the school?
- What do I do to ensure that "untested" content areas are not ignored?
- How do I work with my staff to maintain a humane environment where children learn to enjoy learning and do more than just prepare for tests? (pp. 31–32)

Each of these questions is important to consider as it is the responsibility of educational leaders to bring proper knowledge and skills to their schools to progress the development of excellent instructional practices (Neuman & Pelchat, 2001). Educational leaders who lead by results with educational accountability engage in the practice of modeling behavior and practices to emphasize the importance of reform. The activities of the school leaders should include, but are not limited to, introducing the reform idea, participating in and monitoring the process of curriculum design, developing a productive and reasonable timetable for success, and obtaining technical assistance from the district in the form of subject-area specialists (Rettig, McCullough, Santos, & Watson, 2004).

Our discussion of leading by results with knowledge and skills would be remiss if we did not mention the importance for educational leaders of taking advantage of continuing education and training programs to master necessary strategies for large-scale educational improvements. Teachers are not the only educators who should be receiving continuous and sustained professional development regarding improvements in instructional practices. Novice and expert educational leaders alike will benefit from the provision of new information and dialogue on strategies for results-driven initiatives.

Building Capacity

While obtaining appropriate knowledge and skills is important for leading by results, it is also necessary that educational leaders build capacity to support the improvement of instructional practices that lead to increases in student performance. Newmann, King, and Rigdon (1997) state, "The critical defining feature of organizational capacity is the degree to which the human, technical, and social resources of an organization are organized into an effective collective enterprise" (p. 47). In other words, educational leaders must build capacity in their schools that collectively focuses on the demands of results-driven reform and brings about change from within the school.

First, educational leaders who lead by results will build capacity by setting clear goals. Adams and Kirst (1999) comment, "[The] administrators' primary responsibilities involve gaining agreement on performance goals, communicating goals constantly, and fostering commitment to goals through school communities, as well as aligning resources with goals, analyzing performance and fixing problems" (p. 482). Goals that foster capacity building will concentrate on improvements in instructional practices that meet the school-improvement needs of the school. Second, leading by results requires that school leaders use effective communication strategies to underscore the importance of reform initiatives to educators throughout the school, as well as provide examples of the instructional practices that should be put in place. Third, leading by results to build capacity includes valuing each individual within the school (Waters, Marzano, & McNulty, 2003). Fourth, in order to demand results for student performance, educational leaders must create opportunities for collaboration with and between teachers. Finally, organizational capacity depends largely on ensuring organizational stability. Goldring and Greenfield (2002) note, "The concurrent expectation is to lead the school toward the improvement of instruction and to manage the school so that there is enough stability and certainty for the organization to function efficiently" (p. 12). This last component of building school capacity for educational-accountability reform highlights the balance between managerial duties and leading by results that we mentioned earlier in this chapter. Effective managerial strategies work to bring individuals into the organization who believe in the mission and purpose of that organization, as well as to keep committed individuals in the organization for institutional stability.

Collaborative Inquiry and Reflection

Educational leaders who lead by results establish norms of collaborative inquiry and reflection about the practices of teaching and learning. The processes of collaborative inquiry and reflection differ from supervisory roles of leadership in that they encourage school leaders and teachers to think about the instructional practices that will bring about desired improvements in student performance (Reitzug, 1997). Collaborative inquiry "entails not merely teachers engaged in inquiry, but teachers and others collaboratively and collegially seeking better to understand and thus improve aspects of the schooling experience" (Brubacher, Case, & Reagan, 1994). Educational leaders play an essential role in the school in establishing the conditions necessary to promote collaborative inquiry. Educational leaders must create a school environment that values curiosity, develops mutual respect, and allows educators to try new teaching practices. Collaborative inquiry and reflection about school practices go hand in hand.

Sergiovanni (1987) distinguishes between traditional supervision and the process of reflection:

> *Reflective practice requires the establishment of a* differentiated system of supervision *that provides teachers with an array of options and formats from which they may choose; and it also provides for different supervisory techniques in recognition of the need for a variety of teaching and learning repertoires. Further, supervisory options are a reflective response to differences in personality, needs, professional development levels, and learning styles. (p. 169)*

As educational accountability is a process-oriented reform, reflective practices support the reform by encouraging dialogue and action toward improvements in instructional practices to meet school needs. Additionally, Rallis and Goldring (2000) find that reflective leaders "question and process and learn from their experiences" as well as "examine their situations, make choices, and work with others to enable goals to be reached" (p. 132). The approaches of collaborative inquiry and reflection represent a break with traditional school arrangements of teacher isolation. One way to set about employing these strategies is through the process of reflective dialogue.

Reflective dialogue is part of a continuous inquiry approach that builds on naturalistic elements of changing teaching practices through the constructivist theory of learning and teacher expertise (Richardson, 2003). As reflective dialogue requires that teachers and administrators conduct conversations around tough questions, challenged assumptions, and disagreements over practices in an environment of trust and mutual support, the capacity to develop productive reflective dialogue may only occur gradually. Little, Gearhart, Curry, and Kafka (2003) identify a set of challenges to implementing reflective dialogue, including the necessary time, effort, and resources to introduce the approach, concern for personal comfort and collegial relationships, productive use of time, and the ability to identify the critical issues to be brought up through the practice. As the collaborative inquiry and reflection may be unfamiliar to many educational leaders, they may want to enlist the assistance of trained facilitators and conversation protocols.

Share Leadership

The final component of leading by results is sharing leadership throughout the school to attain teacher support for reform initiatives, as well as to sustain results. Rather than hinder the ability of educational leaders to make improvements in student performance, sharing leadership should support reform initiatives. Grogan and Andrews (2002) state, "Behind this conceptualization of the role is the idea that the executive power of the educational leader is expanded, rather than reduced, through the sharing of power" (p. 243). The theory behind sharing leadership is that leadership should be viewed as a way to facilitate a collective agenda for the organization, such as results-driven educational accountability. Smylie, Conley, and Marks (2002) comment, "as a social influence process, leadership permeates organizations rather than residing in particular people or formal positions of authority. As a result, leadership can come from and be exercised by a wide range of organizational participants" (p. 167). Educational leaders who make educational accountability a reality recognize that it will take the talent and skills of every educator in the school to bring about significant improvements in instructional practices. In turn, sharing leadership should not be viewed as threatening to the position of school leaders. Rather, educational leaders should think about sharing leadership as a way to make certain that their school meets the educational needs of every student. We will further explore the theory of shared leadership in the next section when we address leadership theories that may be appropriate for meeting changing expectations and achieving educational-accountability reform.

■ LEADERSHIP THEORIES FOR EDUCATIONAL ACCOUNTABILITY

The emergence of educational-accountability reform in the education system and ensuing changes in expectations for educational leaders may leave educational leaders at a loss for how to ground the results-driven strategies we have suggested in a theory of leadership. We will present four educational leadership theories that are frequently cited in research on educational accountability initiatives. These theories include instructional leadership, distributed or shared leadership, transformational leadership, and results-driven leadership. Instructional leadership is the theory most commonly referred to when considering applicability to the demands of educational accountability. For instance, Winter and Morgenthal (2002) claim that educational leadership "is now more challenging because school reform mandates place greater emphasis on principals being instructional leaders directing the effort to improve student achievement" (p. 333). However, current calls for instructional leadership differ from the initial conceptualizations of the theory that identified the school principal as the sole instructional leader in the school. Researchers and educators now commonly refer to a version of instructional leadership that encompasses aspects of distributive, transformational, and results-driven leadership theories. While educational leaders may lean toward one type of leadership theory over another, using the theories independently may limit a leader's ability to respond to the demands of educational-accountability reform. Instead, we suggest that educational leaders take into account aspects from each of the theories to provide a more integrated and comprehensive view of leadership. In addition, employing an integrated theory of leadership will better prepare educational leaders to take into consideration the particular educational context of the school.

Instructional Leadership

The initial conceptualizations of the theory of instructional leadership emerged in the 1980s from research in instructionally effective schools. The early theory of instructional leadership maintained that the school leaders in these effective schools directly managed instructional practices. For example, Hallinger and Murphy (1985b) find that in effective high-poverty schools:

> [Principals] have a clear vision of how the school should be organized and tend to exercise relatively tight control over classroom instruction. They are forceful in establishing high expectations and standards for staff and students and in holding themselves and staff accountable for student achievement. (p. 194)

These findings suggest that the initial conceptualization of instructional leadership was influenced by the trend toward standards-based reform initiatives. Additionally, the findings indicate that the principal should be the primary instructional leader in the school and be directly involved in matters of curriculum and instruction. From the research on instructionally effective schools, Hallinger and Murphy (1985a) suggest an early classification of the role of the instructional leader, which includes "defining the school mission, managing the instructional program, and promoting a positive learning climate" (p. 220). Murphy

(1990) further developed the characterization of the instructional leader, which include the following strategies:

- Promoting quality instruction
- Supervising and evaluating instruction
- Allocating and protecting instructional time
- Coordinating the curriculum
- Promoting content coverage
- Monitoring student progress

In effect, the role of instructional leadership encompasses prioritizing curriculum design and instructional practices, aligning resources to accomplish learning goals, and creating an environment of high academic expectations (Grogan & Andrews, 2002).

As the theory of instructional leadership was developing and being implemented, concerns arose regarding the nature of the school principal as the only instructional leader in the school. Lunenburg and Ornstein (1991) highlight troubling aspects of early instructional leadership theory:

> Data suggest that teachers do not view curriculum-instructional leadership as a major responsibility of principals, do not see much evidence of such leadership on the part of principals, are reluctant to accept principals in this capacity, often feel that principal are not capable of providing such leadership, and don't always want principal's assistance in these technical areas that teachers consider to be more appropriate for peer coaching and collegial staff development. (p. 340)

Despite the fact that teachers express reservations about having the school principal involved in the processes of teaching and learning, schools that make significant improvements in student performance possess school leaders who focus their efforts on instructional practices. In turn, the teachers' response to principals being the only instructional leader suggests that there needs to be more balance. In results-driven reform, such as educational accountability, school leaders have to be directly involved in instructional practices. On the other hand, the concerns of teachers reveals the weakness of the instructional leadership theory that identifies the principal as the only instructional leader in the school. Principals must make instructional practices a priority, but they must do so in collaboration with educators throughout the school.

Given the theoretical weaknesses in singling out the school principal as the solitary instructional leader in the school, as well as role ambiguity and role overload, researchers no longer consider instructional leadership alone to be the proper approach for bringing about results-driven reform (Marsh, 2002). Instead, educational researchers suggest that schools will make significant improvements in student performance if they practice distributed or shared leadership that spreads instructional leadership throughout the school.

Distributed Leadership

If educational-accountability reform demands that schools focus their attention on changes in instructional practices to improve student performance, it is difficult to imagine how one individual could take on all of the responsibility to bring about the necessary instructional change as suggested by early notions of instructional leadership theory. Furthermore, teachers have expertise and distinct capabilities that should be employed in instructional reform. Elmore and Fuhrman (2001) find, "individual teachers' conceptions of their own responsibility have the greatest influence over how schools address accountability issues" (p. 68). In turn, educational leaders must capitalize on the talents and skills of educators throughout their schools. Given the demands of educational accountability, as well as the value of actively engaging and empowering teachers in reform, the theory of distributed leadership responds by proposing collaboration between principals and teachers to examine and enhance the processes of teaching and learning. With distributed or shared leadership, the principal appreciates teacher ideas, insights, and expertise by seeking them out and incorporating them into school functioning. In addition, educational leaders share leadership responsibility with teachers and provide resources and support for changing curriculum and instructional practices (Marks & Printy, 2003; Spillane, Halverson, & Diamond, 2004).

The theory of distributed leadership corresponds with the components of leading by results that we discussed earlier in this chapter. In terms of the new knowledge and skills, educational leaders have to acquire and employ to meet the demands of educational accountability, distributed leadership will help schools build capacity to make use of strategies that have been identified as effective for improving student learning. Spillane and Seashore Louis (2002) state:

> *A distributed perspective on leadership will help considerably in determining how school principals might manage the daunting task of school improvement and supporting organizational learning—particularly when the core improvement processes involve detailed knowledge of cutting-edge pedagogy and content in multiple disciplines. (pp. 97–98)*

The theory of educational accountability proposes that improvements in student performance will occur through significant changes to instructional practices. As educational accountability does not prescribe any particular educational programs or practices, schools in need of improvement must use the knowledge and skills of educators throughout the school to make instructional changes that meet the needs of individual students. The instructional practices that work for upper elementary mathematics will not be the same as those that positively impact struggling readers in early grade levels. Through process-oriented reform and shared leadership, school leaders can make use of the full range of educational talents within their schools.

The successful implementation of process of reflection and collaborative inquiry requires that school leaders simultaneously embrace the tenets of distributed leadership for collective school reform and collective decision-making practices that focus on student learning and performance (Copland, 2003). Collaborative inquiry and reflection are processes that can facilitate the ability of schools to tailor improvement responses of educational accountability to the contexts of the school. Crow, Hausman, and Scribner (2002) comment, "to achieve this type of school environment, principals will also have to be open to leadership that emanates from anywhere in the organization and thus create learning opportunities for teachers" (p. 197). The processes that bring about instructional improvement cannot be viewed as practices that occur on an occasional basis. Rather, reflection and collaborative inquiry toward improving the practices of teaching and learning must be continuous processes throughout the school. Distributed leadership establishes an educational environment that promotes and sustains constant discussions about school improvement.

The theory of distributed leadership is an improvement over the theory of instructional leadership with its focus on the school principal as the sole instructional leader.

With distributed leadership, principals become the leader of instructional leaders (Mark & Printy, 2003). Distributed leadership builds on the value of people in the organization by drawing on individual expertise and competency to tackle difficult instructional reform. Additionally, distributed leadership does not require that principals relinquish all of their authority. In fact, Goldring and Greenfield (2002) state that principals will "need to balance participatory leadership with the simultaneous imperative to assume the responsibility to make and implement difficult decisions that may not be endorsed by the collective" (p. 14). Tough decisions about school-improvement need to be made by a strong educational leader to move educational-accountability reform forward. As distributed leadership does not specifically speak to the processes of leading schools through tumultuous school improvement, we also present the theories of transformational leadership and results-driven leadership to fill this theoretical gap.

Transformational Leadership

The theory of transformation leadership presents strategies to address the reality that it is often difficult to make significant and wide-spread changes in the education system. Individuals throughout the education system are reluctant to make changes for a variety of reasons. It is not hard to imagine a low-performing school that has been asked to take part in every school-reform initiative that has cycled through the education system. Educators in this low-performing school may be disinclined to participate in educational accountability because they believe that it will eventually be replaced by another school-reform initiative. While this mentality is not to be blamed given the way in which education reform initiatives are allowed such little time to make improvements, educational-accountability reform is a theory for school improvement that is grounded in sound educational practices. Basically, the theory of educational accountability asks that schools use high-quality academic content and performance standards to guide decisions around the selection of curriculum, instruction, and assessments. Additionally, educational accountability changes the roles of educators throughout the education system by encouraging flexibility in exchange for results. Pressure and support mechanisms are included in educational accountability to make certain that low-performing schools do not lose their focus on changing instructional strategies to improve student performance. In turn, for educational accountability to work properly, educational leaders must use concepts from transformational leadership to promote the values of the reform initiative and the actions necessary to make improvement a reality.

Transformational leadership provides an approach that focuses primarily on the process of influencing school outcomes based on a particular school vision (Bush, 2003; Leithwood & Poplin, 1992). Northouse (2004) comments, "Transformational leadership involves an exceptional form of influence that moves followers to accomplish more than what is usually expected of them" (p. 169). Educational leaders may use transformational leadership to promote the acceptance and adoption of promising school-reform initiatives, such as educational accountability. More specifically, Norton (2005) states:

> *Transformational leaders are able to build worker commitment by (a) raising followers' levels of consciousness about the importance and value of designated outcomes and ways of reaching these goals, (b) getting followers to set aside their own self-interests for the sake of the team, the organization, or the bigger picture, and (c) raising followers' need levels to a higher-order, such as from self-esteem needs to self-actualization, or by expanding their portfolio of needs. (p. 50)*

With transformational leadership there is the potential for the leader's actions to appear manipulative. However, the potential for manipulation can be overcome if transformational leadership is integrated with instructional and shared leadership to develop capacity and ownership within the school toward the strategies designed to bring about school improvement.

In the transformational leadership model, educational leaders tackle resistance to school-improvement initiatives and work to produce commitment to the reform. In many schools, leaders will need to increase confidence in the vision and strategies of educational accountability. Educational accountability does ask educators to make drastic changes in their instructional practices, which may be a difficult sell. However, the theory of educational accountability suggests that standards-based and results-driven changes to the practices of teaching and learning will improve student performance. In turn, educational leaders will have to know how to build buy-in among their staff to support educational accountability.

Results-Driven Leadership

The theory of results-driven leadership may not be explicitly defined in many discussions or texts about educational leadership. However, it is an interesting framework in light of the emergence of new educational goals that focus on high expectations and demands for student-performance outcomes. Marsh (2002) describes the essential leadership components of the theory:

> a) Leadership focused on results-indicators/accountability within the tightly-coupled educational and social system, and b) substantive leadership for reshaping the school as an organization to help all students meet the high performance standards while also achieving quality/market goals. (p. 132)

Results-driven leadership differs from instructional, distributed, and transformational leadership in the sense that it goes beyond the general call to focus on instructional practices by sharing leadership or bringing about school reform through transformational leadership. Instead, the theory suggests that school leaders develop strategic thinking to focus on the best practices for student performance results. Marsh (2002) claims that educational leaders who use the results-driven leadership theory make use of performance indicators as "anchors for decisions, program priorities, and support services" (p. 138). Practices include planning school-improvement strategies using backward-mapping, linking teaching and learning to results, and employing high-quality professional development to address educational problems. These strategies are directly related to the process-oriented practices educational leaders should be engaging in to bring about improvements in student performance through educational accountability.

Instructional leadership and distributed leadership theories suggest ways to engage the school community in educational-accountability reform. Transformational leadership theory provides strategies for contending with low support and commitment for the reform initiative. Results-driven leadership theory puts the impetus on leadership to facilitate process-oriented school improvement, including the use of data to make decisions and the development of professional development that targets school needs. Each of the theories provides valuable elements for leadership practices. The theories should be thought about in an integrated manner to contend with the changing expectations for educational leaders in educational accountability.

■ RESPONSE TO NEW LEADERSHIP EXPECTATIONS

The process of matching leadership practices to school-improvement needs is a critical component of educational-accountability reform to bring about improvements in instructional practices and student learning. In this section we will describe findings from research on the practices of educational leaders who have met the new leadership expectations.

Sebring and Bryk (2000) examine principals in Chicago who received increased autonomy in exchange for accountability for results. Principals of productive schools shared common leadership styles, strategies, and focus on key issues. In terms of leadership styles, principals of productive schools favored an inclusive and facilitative orientation toward the schools' reform visions, maintained a schoolwide focus on student learning, ensured efficient management, and combined pressure and support. The strategies these principals used included first identifying and quickly addressing highly visible problems, establishing a long-term focus on the instructional core, developing a school-improvement plan based on data, and creating programmatic coherence throughout the school. Finally, principals of productive schools focused on several key issues. These were strengthening the school's connection with parents and the community, building capacity by developing teachers' knowledge and skills, and promoting a schoolwide professional community that facilitates reflective dialogue and collaboration on instructional practices.

The National Science Foundation provides financial support to the Distributed Leadership Study at Northwestern University to apply the distributed leadership lens to the examination of educational leadership issues in urban schools. Archer (2004) reports findings from a school using distributed leadership practices:

> *Take the Kelly School, a nearly all-black, high-poverty school on Chicago's West Side. (The name is a pseudonym for research purposes.) The school, whose percentile scores on the Iowa Tests of Basic Skills jumped from the 20s to the 70s over the past decade, has an official "leadership team" of four teachers. But another important way in which staff members there influence one another is through regular meetings focused on instruction.*
>
> *By arranging its schedule so that students are dismissed at 12:30 p.m. on Fridays, Kelly is able to hold schoolwide gatherings each week to let teachers share ideas about improving their work. Recently, staff members there also took it upon themselves to launch what they're calling a "focus group," a series of smaller, regular meetings of teachers who voluntarily come together to study and discuss specific instructional issues.*
>
> *As a result, teachers at Kelly aren't left to sink or swim, remarks one staff member there. "When you're a teacher, you learn all this theory, and then you go in to teach and the theory goes out the door," she said recently. "So you're either a natural-born teacher, or you quit at the end of the day, if you don't have anyone to help you."*
>
> *Barbara Eason-Watkins, the chief education officer for the Chicago public schools, who is familiar with James Spillane's work, agrees that good principals foster an atmosphere in which such exchanges can happen. "It's not just about governance," she says of distributed leadership. "It's truly about making the appropriate instructional decisions about teaching and learning within that school."*
>
> *It's also not necessarily democratic, as the researchers saw. Even where teachers were encouraged to offer ideas, school administrators played a central role. As the principal at Kelly said recently: "I see my job as setting the tone." She tells teachers how she wants their classrooms to look—bright, clean, and colorful—and she makes clear that student discipline is a collective responsibility of the whole staff. (p. 50)*

The findings indicate that the school made significant improvements by creating opportunities for teachers to meet and discuss instructional practices. The focus of the school is instructional improvement to increase student learning, but the example also shows that the principal must balance the overall focus of the school with other pertinent issues, such as school discipline and maintenance of the school facility.

Rettig et al. (2004) suggest that principals who guide their schools through the process of aligning academic standards with instruction and assessment employ several keys to success. The principals balance pressure and support, embed the alignment process into the school's culture, establish clear goals and a prescribed time line for completion, encourage the use of collaborative work, facilitate communication, use time wisely, and maintain momentum.

DeMoss (2002) examines leadership styles in eight elementary schools that were initially identified as low performing. The principals of two schools showed leadership qualities that supported systemic school improvement. DeMoss (2002) states:

> *Both schools demonstrated strong gains based on solid principles of school improvement. The principals were committed to teachers' meaningful participation in instructional decisions. They led their schools using a philosophy based on professionalism and empowerment. Curriculum improvements rather than test scores were seen as the primary target for teachers' efforts, with the tests serving as a source of information by which teachers could gauge their instructional efforts. (p. 127)*

In this study, schools that were not identified as having leaders who exhibited practices to support systemic school improvement focused on basic academic skills, lacked a strong instructional focus, and attempted to deceitfully avoid accountability consequences.

Results from educational leaders' responses to new leadership expectations suggest that school leaders who lead by results create schools conducive for instructional and student learning improvements. Specifically, effective school leaders focus on knowledge and skills about effective teaching and learning practices, build school capacity focused on instruction, establish norms for collaborative inquiry and reflection, and share leadership throughout the school.

Summary

- Understand the challenge of large-scale educational accountability and the need to raise leadership expectations.
- Develop knowledge and skills to balance and align leadership roles and accountability at the district, school, and classroom levels.
- Recognize that the instructional leadership and distributed leadership theories suggest ways to engage the school community in educational reform.
- Understand that the transformational leadership theory provides strategies for contending with low levels of commitment and support for school-reform initiative.
- Understand that the results-driven leadership theory focuses on the use of data to make decisions and the development of professional development that targets school needs.
- Recognize that each of the theories provides distinct, key leadership elements for addressing accountability issues.

Article and Discussion Questions

The following article discusses the issue of principal supply shortages within the United States. The shortage stems from the increasing number of accountability standards principals are expected to meet. As the age of the average principal gets older each year, we must make it more attractive for younger teachers to look to such a profession as a possible career-advancement. Those teachers who demonstrate the qualities of a good school administrator must be recognized and given every opportunity to explore the nature of being a principal. Incentives such as on-the-job training and tuition reimbursement for administration-related classes may begin to reinvigorate interest in such a profession.

A Challenging Offer for Potential Principals

By Nancy Trejos
The Washington Post, June 28, 2001

It means long days. Lots of paperwork. The pressure to improve standardized test scores. Bus duty and cafeteria duty. Having to discipline misbehaving, sometimes even dangerous, youngsters. Those are all part of what it takes to be a school principal.

"The principal is accountable for everything, but he or she can't do everything," La Plata High School Principal Donald Cooke told an audience of Charles County teachers and vice principals thinking about taking on those responsibilities.

Bracing for a potential shortage of principals within the next five years, Charles County school officials last week for the first time held a five-day workshop for many of those they hope to groom for jobs as administrators. Speakers from the Maryland Department of Education, area universities and other school districts described what it takes to become principals.

"It's a way to home-grow some leadership, we hope," Ronald Cunningham, associate superintendent, said of the workshop. "The idea is to try to expose them to it."

The U.S. Department of Labor estimates that 40 percent of the nation's 93,000 principals are at or close to retirement age. Most will leave in the next five years. In that time, the Maryland Department of Education expects the state's schools will lose about half their principals, said Mary Bea Preston, chief of staff development for the agency.

And there are not enough teachers clamoring to move into the principal's office. "People look at the job, they look at the time, and they decide not to do it," said John Cox, assistant superintendent of instruction in Charles County. "In my view, there are a lot of good candidates who decide not to do it."

The reason? Principals these days have a hefty agenda. They must deal with standardized tests, school violence, the teacher shortage, changes brought by increasing diversity. They are their schools' property managers, business managers, customer service representatives.

"It's a critical shortage, so we've got to be training these folks to get them ready to move up," Preston said during one of the workshop's sessions.

School systems, already dealing with a dearth of teachers, are starting to do just that. Many in Maryland and Virginia are creating programs to train teachers to become administrators. Some, including Charles, are letting those in the classes earn credit toward a master's degree.

After 16 years of teaching, Don King, a social studies instructor at Piccowaxen Middle School, was intrigued by the idea of running a school some day. He wants to become a principal for a simple reason: "It'll give me a chance to reach out to a larger group of students," he said.

King has already taken on some responsibilities at his school. When the top administrators are out of the building, King, 39, is often the one who handles disciplinary problems.

The hours don't scare him. He has had his fair share of early mornings and late nights. When he coached basketball at La Plata High School, he often opened the school at 6 a.m. to let the students in for pre-class practice.

"We see administrators every day. I don't think we appreciate the responsibilities they carry with them," he said.

One day last week, he sat at a table inside Middleton Hall in Waldorf, a binder and handouts in front of him, as the group talked about the changing role of the principal.

"Fourth grade doesn't look anything like it did even five, 10 years ago," said Carol Geck, vice principal of Dr. James Craik Elementary School.

Some of those changes have come into focus as states have adopted standardized tests to determine whether schools are teaching students what they should be learning.

"I don't ever remember the word 'accountability' being used," Cooke told the audience. "Recently I've seen tremendous change."

Standing in front of the aspiring administrators one day last week, John Cox, assistant superintendent for instruction, asked them to turn their attention to the overhead projector.

"The data will drive the effort," it said.

He turned to the aspiring administrators. Ask yourself one question before changing instruction in any way, he said. "What does the data say?"

It said a lot during a role-playing session that followed his talk. Cox pretended to be a principal charged with the duty of firing a teacher whose students' standardized test scores have lagged behind other teachers' pupils.

The woman who played the teacher protested. She said she didn't think it was fair. Cox kept repeating his mantra: "To be honest, the data tells it all."

Jeremy Campbell has already had a taste of being an administrator. He was a special education teacher at Mary H. Matula Elementary School before his principal asked him this year to become an administrative assistant. He has taken on the duties of a vice principal without actually being a vice principal.

Before this year, he was not sure if he wanted to become a principal. Now, after a year of "learning on the fly," he said, he's sure he does. "I can really influence kids' lives more this way than as a teacher."

1. In reference to Nancy Trejos's article, what do you see as the largest demotivating factor for teachers considering advancement to principal positions in your school system? What policy change would you suggest to address this issue?
2. Can you identify leaders who are "leading by results" in your school system?
3. Do you agree with the ISLLC standards in defining the knowledge and skills necessary for "leading by results"? If you agree, discuss how this might look in practice. If you disagree, how could the ISLLC standards be revised to define appropriate knowledge and skill development?
4. Do you find the notion of an integrated theory of leadership useful in thinking about ways to make significant school improvement? Explain your reasoning.

CHAPTER FOUR

Intergovernmental Considerations in Educational Accountability

LEARNING OBJECTIVES

- Explore the intergovernmental nature of the U.S. education system, including the ways in which educational accountability requires changes in roles and responsibilities at each level.
- Recognize the institutional and organizational complexity in implementing a large scale improvement initiative, such as the No Child Left Behind reform.
- Understand what conditions are needed for sustainable implementation of education reform, including support, coordination, and reciprocal accountability between each level of the education system.
- Suggest strategies for educational leaders to use that may direct the resources and support more effective toward instructional changes and student learning.

■ INTRODUCTION

The governance structure of the U.S. education system, parallel to the overall U.S. system of government, is a federalist, multilevel system divided into federal, state, and local levels. While each level of the education system has designated roles and responsibilities, a significant degree of interaction between the levels of government is needed to secure efficient operation. Of course, the education system rarely functions efficiently. To begin with, unresolved tensions persist in determining what each level of government values for the education system (Stout, Tallerico, & Scribner, 1995). Concurrently, allocation of funding largely depends on the politics of defining values and preferences throughout the system. And furthermore, intergovernmental policies, which can be both complex and ambiguous, may not be interpreted or implemented properly. If the education system is to successfully achieve the new educational goals of high expectations and demands for improvement in student performance, the issues that impact intergovernmental interaction must be understood and addressed. Specifically, the issues of politics, policies, and funding create a multidimensional lens for intergovernmental considerations in the education system. We will use this perspective to address the ways in which the education system responds to educational accountability.

To meet the rigorous demands and challenges of educational-accountability reform and make significant improvements in student performance, educators and policymakers throughout the system must shift their focus and support to ensure appropriate changes and improvements in instructional practices. In actuality, the present manifestation of educational accountability in the form of NCLB legislation has not fulfilled this critical component of the theory of educational-accountability reform. Across the levels of the education system, common goals of standards-based reform and the excellence movement have been embraced (Goertz, 2001). At the same time, however, the education system has failed to reallocate adequate resources to the core technology of schooling and has put in place sanctions that may undermine the ability of school leaders to bring meaningfully change to the processes of teaching and learning. This chapter we use a multidimensional perspective to explore the intergovernmental nature of the U.S. education system, including the ways educational accountability requires changes in roles and responsibilities at each level. Next, we address how educational accountability is implemented in the intergovernmental education system. Finally, in response to the intergovernmental challenges of educational accountability, we suggest strategies for educational leaders that may direct the resources and support of the education system on instructional changes.

■ INTERGOVERNMENTAL NATURE OF EDUCATION SYSTEM: FEDERAL, STATE, AND LOCAL LEVELS

The education system is a three-level system where issues of politics, policies, and funding interact within, as well as between, levels. The intergovernmental nature of the education system brings great complexity when considering the implementation of a large-scale improvement initiative, such as educational accountability. Effective and sustainable implementation of education reform requires support and coordination between each level of the education system (Datnow & Stringfield, 2000). However, efforts to increase coordination between the politics, policies, and funding of the three levels of the education system will undoubtedly contend with institutional fragmentation (Fuhrman, 1993; Spillane, 1999). Institutional fragmentation in the education system is evident in the widespread existence of categorical and disjointed policies, programs, and funding mechanisms. Often institutional fragmentation leads to incoherent policy interpretation and implementation. Wong and Sunderman (2000) state, "multiple centers of power exist both inside and outside the school system. Incoherence in implementing educational policy can result when these institutional actors compete for authority over important policy issues" (p. 359). If educational accountability is to function well in the education system, institutional fragmentation will have to be considered and addressed.

As educational accountability theory suggests that the entire education system targets resources and support to improving instructional practices, we use our multidimensional politics, policies, and funding perspective to describe the respective roles and responsibilities of federal, state, and local jurisdictions in matters of large-scale reform. Additionally, this section examines how roles and responsibilities have changed due to educational accountability, paying particular attention to which levels generate accountability policy and oversee accountability practices and results.

Federal Level

In recent years, the federal government has become more involved in defining and promoting goals for the education system. The most visible demonstration of the rising federal role in education is the No Child Left Behind (NCLB) Act of 2001. As we describe in Chapter 2, NCLB differs from previous federal legislation by providing specific guidelines for the substance of standards-based and results-driven reform initiatives to increase academic achievement for all students (Goertz, 2001). Although federal legislation is now familiar to most educators due to NCLB, federal involvement in the education system occurs in various forms, including presidential agendas, congressional legislation, judicial rulings, and U.S. Department of Education regulations (Marshall & Gerstl-Pepin, 2005). With a three-level system, any initiative sponsored at the federal level will need to be interpreted and implemented by the state and local levels to impact the education system. Additionally, the federal level will have to determine whether funding for federal initiatives will be appropriated at the federal level or necessitate state and local contributions. While the federal role in the education system has always comprised elements of national agenda setting, this role has increased with the enactment of NCLB. As the federal government has not matched its entire national agenda with adequate funding, federal policy has imposed larger financial demands and responsibilities on state and local levels to meet the national objectives for education. With this, the National Education Association (NEA) has filed a lawsuit along with plaintiffs from the states of Michigan, Connecticut, Delaware, Illinois, Maine, Oklahoma, Wisconsin, and the District of Columbia against the U.S. Secretary of Education, Margaret Spellings, for mandating a federal requirement while not funding its entirety (see Appendix F for an excerpt from the complaint).

The federal government has historically been engaged in issues of educational equality. These equality issues include the 1954 Supreme Court racial desegregation ruling in *Brown v. Board of Education*, the federal compensatory education legislation Elementary and Secondary Education Act (ESEA) of 1965, educational rights for students with disabilities in the 1975 Education for All Handicapped Children Act (now Individuals with Disabilities Education Act [IDEA]), and federal legislation to meet the needs of English language learners (ELL). Wong (1992) comments, "the national government has both the fiscal capacity and the political resources (often facilitated by interest groups) to respond to social needs" (p. 11). Prior to the standards-based reform movement, federal initiatives had not typically focused on, or provided suggestions for, the technical core of education, such as processes of teaching and learning. The federal government left these decisions for the state and local levels. While the federal government has focused on educational equality, it should be noted that the way in which the federal level defines educational equality has changed significantly over the years, resulting in our current notion of educational accountability for equal educational opportunities. Changes in the meaning of educational equality reflect the politics, policies, and funding decisions at the federal level of the education system.

The politics of the education system at the federal level revolve around tensions and compromises in values and preferences between many political actors (Sroufe, 1995). In our pluralistic political system "differences must be negotiated, plans must be delayed, and policies must be modified" (Peterson, 1981, p. 89). The political focus of the federal level on equality in education was initiated by President Lyndon Johnson in the 1960s when he set an administrative agenda to target the poor and needy with his Great Society programs. In a 1965 speech, Johnson stated:

> *We seek not just freedom but opportunity. We seek not just legal equity but human ability, not just equality as a right and a theory but equality as a fact and equality as a result . . . To this end equal opportunity is essential, but not enough, not enough. (Johnson, 1965)*

Johnson's ambitious views of equality in society were apparent in the purposes of the 1965 federal legislation of ESEA. In particular, ESEA intended to provide additional resources to school districts to enable the provision of programs and services that would meet the needs of high-poverty and low-achieving students (Martin & McClure, 1969). Murphy (1971) comments, "The main thrust for aid to poverty schools came from reformers in the Executive Branch who had a double objective: the establishment of the principle of federal aid to schools and a redirection of local priorities" (p. 38). In other words, ESEA firmly established the federal role in education as one of social redistribution. While there were subsequent political debates about the federal role in education, including President Ronald Reagan's proposal to dismantle the U.S. Department of Education in the 1980s in favor of schools of choice and increases in state-level authority, federal involvement in the education system prior to NCLB can be characterized as functioning through social redistribution for equality.

The federal level's ability to perform redistribution of resources is a function of the federal funding structure. Wong (1999) states, "The federal government enjoys a broader revenue base in which taxes are raised primarily on the ability-to-pay principle and represents a constituency with heterogeneous demands" (p. 18). The federal government may only contribute to roughly 7% of the distribution of revenue in public schools (see Table 4.1), but it has the leverage to use the funding to target disadvantaged students and address funding inequities as well as direct national attention to particular educational agendas.

Before the enactment of NCLB, the federal level had been reluctant to get involved in regular education programs, focusing rather on redistribution by targeting compensatory

TABLE 4.1   Source of Revenue for Elementary and Secondary Schools, 1951–1952 to 2000–2001

Year	Federal (%)	State (%)	Local (%)
1951–1952	3.5	38.6	57.9
1961–1962	4.3	38.7	56.9
1965–1966	7.9	39.1	53.0
1970–1971	8.4	39.1	52.5
1974–1975	9.0	42.0	49.0
1980–1981	9.2	47.4	43.4
1984–1985	6.6	48.9	44.4
1990–1991	6.2	47.2	46.7
1994–1995	6.8	46.8	46.4
2000–2001	7.3	49.7	43.1

Source: Compiled by authors from National Center for Education Statistics. (2003). *Digest of education statistics and figures.* U.S. Department of Education. Retrieved on June 1, 2005, from http://nces.ed. gov//programs/digest/d03/tables/dt156.asp.

resources to disadvantaged students across the nation to improve their chances of equality (Peterson, Rabe, & Wong, 1986). However, changes in federal policy regarding the funding formula for Title I compensatory resources have increased the federal role in regular education programs (Wong & Nicotera, 2004b). Federal Title I funding was initially used to administer categorical or pull-out programs for targeted students. The operation of categorical programs was not a function of beliefs about effective educational practices. Instead, local levels employed categorical programs to fulfill procedural compliance and demonstrate to the federal level that Title I funds were indeed being targeted to disadvantaged students. While categorical programs became the norm, research emerged suggesting that student poverty affects all students in a school and pull-out programs hinder the educational opportunities of Title I students. In turn, demands were placed on the federal level to change legislation to allow Title I funds to be used for schoolwide initiatives. The 1994 ESEA federal legislation permitted limited changes, which were then increased further with NCLB. Now most schools receiving Title I funds use them for schoolwide programs. Wong and Meyer (2001) state, "instead of serving only students who qualify, Title I programs now can implement schoolwide strategies that use Title I resources for all students, holding them all to the same high academic standards" (p. 197). In this way, the federal level has increased its role in the entire education system, not just compensatory education.

The increasing federal role in the education system has been accompanied by increases in federal funding. For example, Table 4.2 describes the increases in federal Title I funding between 1994 and 2004. However, it is debatable whether the increases in funding match the mandates the federal government has placed on states, districts, and schools. Besides marginal increases in federal funds, the challenge for federal policy has

TABLE 4.2   Title I Funding Appropriations (1994–2004)

Appropriations Year	Title I Grants to Local Educational Agencies	Increase in Title I Grants	Percent Increase in Title I Grants
1994	6,336,000	—	—
1995	6,698,356	362,356	5.7%
1996	6,730,348	31,992	0.5%
1997	7,295,232	564,884	8.4%
1998	7,375,232	80,000	1.1%
1999	7,732,397	357,165	4.8%
2000	7,941,397	209,000	2.7%
2001	8,762,721	821,324	10.3%
2002	10,350,000	1,587,279	18.1%
2003	11,684,311	1,334,331	12.9%
2004	12,350,000*	665,689†	5.7%‡

*President Bush's budget request for 2004.

†Estimated increase in Title I Grants for 2004.

‡Estimated percent increase in Title I Grants for 2004.

Source: Compiled by authors from U.S. Department of Education. (2003). *Education Department Budget History Table.*

been garnering political capital to target funds to schools with high concentrations of poverty. For example, Title I schools with poverty below 35 percent receive larger allocations on average per low-income student than schools serving high-poverty populations of 50 percent poverty or more (U.S. Department of Education, 2000, p. 37). While spreading limited federal resources broadly across constituents may be politically appealing, the practice puts into question the ability of federal policy to adequately achieve equality, whether equality means meeting the needs of disadvantaged students through social redistribution or raising expectations for standards and performance.

The federal role in education has certainly increased since the enactment of ESEA in 1965 in terms of national agenda setting as well as initiating substantial reform with the NCLB manifestation of educational accountability. A larger federal role in education subsequently entails greater demands on the state and local levels to meet national objectives for education, all while balancing their own values and preferences.

State Level

Although the federal level of the education system may presently hold the most visible role in setting policy and legislative agendas to meet results-driven education goals, according to the federal Constitution, education is not the function of the federal government. Rather, education is the function of the states. It is through education or equal protection clauses in state constitutions that the state level of government maintains the power and responsibility to govern education. If it appears that the federal government imposes too hefty a role in guiding education reform given its constitutional standing, the states follow national directives because federal mandates are tied to funding streams that the states are unwilling to forfeit.

The state level has the ability as the chief operative of education to make substantial changes in the education system as well as in the technical core of education, such as focusing resources and support to the improvement of instructional practices per the theory of educational-accountability reform. The actors in the state level include the governor, state legislators, state courts, state boards of education, and state departments of education. The primary responsibilities of the state government in education include enacting legislation to collect taxes and finance local schools; establishing personnel training, certification, and salary standards, administering student tests; providing guidance for curriculum design; and developing criterion for school buildings and facilities (Lunenburg & Ornstein, 1991; Marshall & Gerstl-Pepin, 2005). This section discusses the general politics, policies, and funding issues that determine the state-level roles and responsibilities.

While the state level of government has not assumed social redistribution in the form of compensatory education programs like the federal government, there are examples of state activism to improve equality between students. The primary example is school-finance reform where state supreme courts have ruled on the constitutionality of state systems of school finance based on inequities in expenditures between localities. Local resources are typically tied to property values of the tax base, which can vary widely between districts in a state. The structure of the state finance systems raises the constitutional question of whether local disparities in funding lead to unequal access to educational resources. McUsic (1999) comments on the political nature of state education funding:

> *Litigation must play a central role in any hope for transforming the educational delivery system, as school finance reform favoring poor students does not occur in the usual course of*

legislative action. The political arena does not prefer the poor school district, and at least in the pasty twenty years or so has seldom preferred increased educational funding over reduced taxes. (p. 89)

As of 1999, state supreme courts in 17 states had ruled to overturn state finance systems. Another 13 states have appeals pending (Hurst, Tan, Meek, & Sellers, 2003). State supreme court rulings and subsequent state legislative action have facilitated fiscal and structural changes as well as given the state-level governments greater control over financing schools to encourage fiscal neutrality between districts (Dayton, 1996). Murray, Evans, and Schwab (1998) find "evidence that court-mandated finance reforms generate results consistent with its goals—within-state inequality is substantially reduced and expenditures in the poorest districts are increased" (p. 807). The central issue of school-finance reform is the likely continued boost to state authority in funding public education. Reform of state finance systems will undoubtedly remain a critical political issue for the state level of the education system.

Besides school-finance reform, the states have taken responsibility for results-driven reform. Although the 1983 report *A Nation at Risk* set the national agenda for standards-based and results-driven reform, several states had been discussing and making progress toward accountability models for education based on theories of efficiency and productivity (Mazzoni, 1995). Due to particular state-level forces, the excellence movement identified in *A Nation at Risk* was able to gain momentum and grow. Mazzoni (1995) tracks the materialization of results-driven reform at the state level and finds five major enabling forces. First, state-level networking organizations, such as the National Governors Association (NGA) and the Council for Chief State School Officers (CCSSO) embraced standards-based reform and created opportunities for diffusion of policy between states. Second, the existence of institutional capacity at the state level enabled legislators and policymakers to take action on demands for school reform. Third, by the mid-1980s the recession had diminished and states experienced a recovery of revenue that could be used for school-reform efforts. Fourth, states could attract economic resources by having the reputation of good schools. And finally, state court interventions in systems of school finance established school-reform agendas and energized state responses. Given these enabling forces, the state level of the education system was able to make noticeable but varying degrees of headway on results-driven reform. However, as we noted in Chapter 2, the federal government became impatient with state progress and responded with the legislative mandates of NCLB. The accountability mandates of NCLB differed from most state reform in the areas of annual high-stakes testing, proficiency levels for performance, reporting and monitoring subgroup performance, demands for high-quality teachers, and school choice options.

The state-level education system holds primary responsibility for providing education. With this responsibility, the state level can generate considerable impact on educational practices. In terms of educational accountability, states are in the process of meeting the demands of federal legislative mandates in NCLB. Regrettably, the notion of educational accountability reflected in NCLB does not directly correspond with the theory and components of educational accountability to make significant improvements in student performance. Severe sanctions for poor student performance on single indicators of success focus attention in NCLB on preparing students for standardized tests as opposed to making substantial changes in the processes of teaching and learning. Seeing as the states have the ability to make changes in the technical core of education, this is the level where authentic changes in instructional practices can be proposed and supported to bring about the improvements suggested by educational-accountability reform.

Local Level

The third level of the education system is the local level, which encompasses both districts and schools. The roles and responsibilities of the school in the local level of governance have not traditionally been considered because the district has been viewed as the vehicle for translating politics, policies, and funding into educational practices. However, standards-based and results-driven reform has restructured the governance structure such that schools are directly accountability to the state, as opposed to the district, for student performance. Subsequently, considerations of the local level in the education system must take into account both the district and school levels.

The local level of the education system has functioned as the primary unit for governing schools throughout most of the history of U.S. education. Iannaccone and Lutz (1995) comment, "the myth of local control is embedded in the culture and values of the people, who tend to believe that control of 'their' public schools is and should be a matter of local control" (p. 43). The local level is considered the locus of authentic democracy, where individuals can more easily participate in public decisions and enjoy direct representation. It is still the case that individuals are able to get more involved in making decisions through the local school district than the state or federal levels of the system. Most local school boards are elected as they are intended to directly represent their constituents. The duties of local school boards include managing fiscal resources for the district, appointing a superintendent, delegating the hiring of employees to the superintendent's district office, following state guidelines for curriculum design, engaging in community relations, and translating state and federal policy mandates into practice (Lunenburg & Ornstein, 1991). As for the superintendent and the central district office, conventional understanding of district level roles and responsibilities are characterized by managerial procedures. Barr, Dreeben, and Wiratchai (1983) state:

> *Activities occurring at this managerial level have* nothing directly *to do with running schools or teaching students but rather are concerned with the acquisition of resources, with general supervision, and with the maintenance of relations with the surrounding community including suppliers of labor. (p. 5)*

Nonetheless, the combination of district consolidations, low voter participation in school board elections, higher levels of the education system assuming former local responsibilities, and educational accountability placing the school rather than the district as the unit of analysis, suggests that our conceptions of the local level need to be redefined. More specifically, schools take on greater responsibility for student performance results with educational accountability in exchange for flexibility and commensurate authority. In a sense, the schools adopt from the district the locus of participation and representation in the education system.

As low-performing schools are no longer allowed to elude the attention and consequences of the state level of education, the school district must refocus its efforts to function as a capacity-builder (Foley, 2001; Ladd & Zelli, 2002). In a role of capacity-building, the district level would reallocate resources to provide adequate technical assistance and support to schools to aid in the difficult process of changing instructional practices. The capacity-building role relies on the ability of the district level to interpret state and federal policies into tangible practices that are consistent with the local context of schools (Cohen & Hill, 2000; Elmore, 1993; Spillane, 1999). Regardless of differences in resource and funding capacity, schools will be held responsible for achieving student performance results. In turn, the district level has the responsibility to rethink district strategies to ensure that attention is directed to the processes of teaching and learning. For example, school districts spend between about 2 and 5% of their budgets on professional development for teachers (Killeen, Monk, & Plecki, 2002). This degree of spending should be closely examined to determine whether it is adequate in both amount and quality to support improvements in instructional practices.

The local level of the education governance structure now incorporates roles and responsibilities of both districts and schools. Given recent changes in school authority and flexibility to make school improvements, the school district will have to restructure from managing schools through programmatic compliance to developing capacity-building strategies to support the processes of teaching and learning.

Changes in Intergovernmental Roles and Responsibilities with Educational Accountability

The beginning of this section discussed the need for coordination and support between the three levels of the education system. This is especially the case with large-scale school-improvement initiatives, such as educational accountability. In our descriptions of the three governance levels of the education system, we addressed the general changes in intergovernmental roles and responsibilities due to educational accountability. The federal level sets policy mandates to direct results-driven reform, while the state level establishes content and performance standards aligned with student assessments, and the local level is given flexibility and commensurate authority to make changes in instructional practices to improve student performance. While fulfilling the respective roles and responsibilities defined by the levels of the education system is important in intergovernmental considerations of educational accountability, it will not be enough to make significant changes. Educational accountability must be designed to include reciprocal or symmetric accountability between the levels of the education system (Elmore, 2000; Porter & Chester, 2002). Elmore (2000) comments on the logic of reciprocal accountability, "if the formal authority of my role requires that I hold you accountable for some action or outcome, then I have an equal and complementary responsibility to assure that you have capacity to do what I am asking you to do" (p. 21). The notion of reciprocal accountability extends from the federal level to the state level to the local level of the education system.

With reciprocal accountability, the federal government can use legislative mandates to require that states develop and implement detailed statewide accountability systems, but the federal level must provide appropriate resources and support to ensure that the states have the ability to successfully meet federal goals. O'Day (2005) defines reciprocal accountability for states and district levels that hold schools accountable:

> If the district (or state) is to hold schools accountable for producing specified outcomes for their students, the district (or state) has the responsibility to provide those schools with the resources (human, material, and intellectual) and the conditions necessary to produce those outcomes. (p. 119)

The resources and support necessary to bring about changes in instructional practices and improvements in student performance are not easy to define. While it may seem like a simple answer, in reality the resources and support needed by states, districts, and schools will vary by their respective conditions. Take for example the technical assistance districts and states need to provide schools that are in need of improvement. Reid (2004) reports:

> State departments of education and local districts often face similar obstacles in following the federal law: they don't have enough people to provide hands-on intervention in their struggling schools. They lack the expertise on their staffs to tackle the schools' myriad challenges. They don't have the money to expand school improvement efforts they're already pursuing. (p. 16)

Reid (2004) further reports that several districts are providing districtwide initiative, rather than develop resources for the individual needs of schools. As educational accountability depends on high quality support and resources from the district and state levels, these responses to the provision of technical assistance need to be examined carefully to determine if they hinder school improvement.

While the resources and support necessary at each level of the education system may differ, we do know what educational leaders need in order to make significant improvements in student performance given the theory and components of educational accountability. Specifically, each of the levels of the education system need to work together to make certain that educational leaders have, and put to use, the proper knowledge and skills to make changes in the processes of teaching and learning possible (Schnur & Gerson, 2005).

▪ IMPLEMENTATION OF EDUCATIONAL ACCOUNTABILITY IN INTERGOVERNMENTAL CONTEXT

Implementation of large-scale improvement initiatives in the education system is by no means an easy endeavor. Tyack and Cuban (1995) describe the complicated components of translating policy into institutional actions, "the *time lag* between advocacy and implementation; the *uneven penetration of reform* in the different sectors of public education; and the *different impact* of reform on various social groups" (p. 55). The intergovernmental nature of the education system means that consistent implementation of an initiative such as educational accountability will rarely occur. If it is unlikely that uniform and full implementation of reform efforts will be realized in the education system, then the critical issue becomes the determination of an acceptable level of variation where the reform will still bring about significant improvements in student performance in different types of schools. Once the acceptable level of variation has been resolved, strategies must be identified to reduce differences in implementation to the specified level. In this section we discuss the variability that is evident in present educational accountability systems. We also address the capacity to implement educational accountability, which is highly influenced by local interpretations of policy.

Variability in Implementation of Educational Accountability

The theory of educational accountability suggests that giving schools greater flexibility and authority to make improvements in exchange for student performance results will create the necessary incentive for significant changes in the education system. The institutional bargain implied by educational-accountability reform creates a tradeoff between flexibility for results and uniform schooling practices (Goertz, 2001). The points of interest in this tradeoff are determining how much variability is acceptable to achieve results and in which levels of the education system should variability be allowed to exist. These issues are not mutually exclusive as it may be the case that variability between respective levels of the education is not as great of a concern as variability within the levels.

Elmore (2000) suggests that effective school improvement led with clear direction and purpose should improve quality and reduce variability in educational practices. The claim that educational accountability will reduce variability in the processes of teaching and learning may seem to run counter to the theoretical grounding of accountability where flexibility is transferred to schools in return for results. It would seem that educational accountability grants schools the ability to use any type of schooling practice as long as they can prove that the practice led to demonstrable improvements in student performance. While this is indeed the theory of educational accountability, the assertion for a reduction in variability anticipates that once the other components of educational accountability are put in place, like processes of collaborative inquiry and reflection for school leaders and teachers, educators will determine best practices for improving student performance. The best practices for one school with a particular set of needs may be quite different than the practices another school finds effective for its students. For this reason, the claim about reducing variability in educational practices may entail a caveat about the level of the education system. Variability between schools will likely be greater than within school variability. Likewise, variability between districts may be greater than within district variability if the district works to transfer effective practices between schools with similar characteristics and needs.

In the case of the state level, variations in curriculum, assessments, and educational programs are inclined to exist between states given the governance structure of the U.S. education system described earlier in this chapter. While NCLB established rigid federal mandates in vision and purpose for educational accountability, the legislation allows for variation in state responses. For example, states have the flexibility to develop academic standards, establish performance levels for proficiency, determine starting points and methods to achieve proficiency, and employ sanctions for low-performing schools. In turn, it should not be surprising that researchers have found variations in the specifics and strategies between state accountability systems (Linn, 2000; Kingsbury, Olson, Cronin, Hauser, & Houser, 2003). However, researchers have also determined that variability persists within states when examining subject areas across grade levels and between subject areas within grade levels (Kingsbury et al., 2003). First, Kingsbury et al. (2003) consider the extent to which states calibrate their performance proficiency levels across grade levels within subject areas, such as math or reading from 3rd to 8th grade. Kingsbury et al. (2003) explain the potential problem with this type of within state variability:

> Standards that are not calibrated give students, parents, and educators an inaccurate perception about the child's standing relative to the expected level of performance. Students are reported as proficient in one grade who may not remain proficient in later grades even if they show normal growth. (p. 15)

The researchers find that most of the states in their study overestimate the number of proficient students in 3rd grade who would actually be on track to proficiency by 8th grade standards.

Second, Kingsbury et al. (2003) examine whether variation exists within states between subject areas in a given grade level and find that proficiency standards for math are typically more challenging than proficiency standards for reading. The researchers recommend that states work to calibrate their proficiency levels and address differences in proficiency levels between subject areas.

Variations between schools and districts in the types of educational practices they use exist due to new permissions for experimentation. This type of variability in educational accountability systems is appropriate as it allows schools to determine the educational practices that will improve student performance given their contextual factors. Educational accountability should extract ineffective educational practices by sanctioning low-performing schools while also providing additional support to build the capacity of schools to determine effective instructional practices. On the other hand, inconsistent and incomparable proficiency levels that may be present within states do not represent an acceptable level of variability in educational accountability. More specifically, this type of within-state variability undermines the ability of the education system to measure student progress on academic proficiency standards.

Capacity to Implement Educational Accountability

While variability may exist in implementing educational accountability initiatives at the school and district levels as a result of collaborative and reflective practices to determine appropriate educational practices for improving student performance, variability may be caused by the complex nature of reform efforts and school or district capacity to translate federal and state policy into practice. The instructional practices that will be necessary to bring about substantial improvements in student performance may not be familiar to educators at the district or school levels. Educators must align educational practices including curriculum design, instruction, and assessment to academic and performance standards. Certainly, there will be instructional practices that will be more challenging and complex to implement than others given that educators cannot merely respond to accountability by doing more of the same. This will require educators to change their conceptions of the processes of teaching and learning. In other words, "they would have to learn a great deal" (Spillane, 1999, p. 563).

A corollary to the complexity of reform efforts, and a central issue in school and district capacity to implement educational accountability, is the way policies are interpreted at the local level and adapted into practice. Several researchers focus on the important role of teachers and educational leaders in the process of translating policy into practice. Sandholtz, Ogawa, and Scribner (2004) claim, "decisions and actions of local school districts and schools are the critical link between standards and the instructional practice of teachers" (p. 1197). Identifying teachers as key mediators between policy and practice, Cohen and Hill (2000) state, "students' achievement is the ultimate dependent measure of instructional policy, and teachers' practice is both an intermediate dependent measure of policy enactment and a direct influence on students' performance" (p. 295). Furthermore, Spillane (1999) suggests a cognitive approach to understand how meanings constructed from policies influence implementation at the local level:

> Policy messages are not carried solely by policy signals to be extracted by implementers; rather, the meaning or message of a policy signal is constructed by local enactors in the interaction of policy signals with their knowledge, experiences, and situation. In this view, although policy signals a problem with practice and offers cues about the nature of that problem and the solution to it, implementers are active agents who construct ideas about reforming practice from those signals. (p. 549)

The research on the ways local interpretations of policy impact implementation indicate that while educators at the local level will likely respond in some way to reform initiatives, the responses may not reflect the intentions of federal or state policy. For example, educators may respond by increasing the amount of time in the day spent on educational practices that were not effective for low-achieving students in the first place. In turn, a good measure of success for educational accountability has to be the degree to which the initiative substantially changes instructional practices to improve student performance (Goertz, 2001).

As described earlier in this chapter, educational accountability demands that the district assume the roles and responsibilities of capacity building to support schools' ability to make necessary changes to instructional practices. While the capacity-building role for districts is central to implementing educational accountability, districts have more frequently responded to reform with the purpose of evading state intervention rather than to aid schools in improving instructional practices (Malen, Croninger, Muncey, & Redmond-Jones, 2002; Sandholtz, Ogawa, & Scribner, 2004). District-level educational leaders should avoid the inclination to resist large-scale improvements on account of reservations about state encroachment into district practices. Instead, the district level must focus all attention to supporting the capacity of schools to implement instructional changes. Goertz and Duffy (2003) find that districts who take on the role of capacity builders engage in similar practices. "District strategies included enhancing teacher professionalism, curriculum reform aligned to state standards, data-driven decision making, and assistance targeted on low performing schools" (p. 10). Implementation of educational accountability initiatives is dependent on district leaders developing facilitative environments that create opportunities for school leaders and teachers to learn and adopt innovative instructional practices.

▪ EDUCATIONAL ACCOUNTABILITY CHALLENGES WITH THE INTERGOVERNMENTAL SYSTEM

The education system with its intergovernmental structure proves to be a difficult environment for implementing any type of large-scale education reform initiative. The governance structure presents particular challenges for educational-accountability reform where supportive interactions between the three levels are essential to making significant improvements in student performance. Specifically, ambiguity may persist regarding the designated roles and responsibilities of educational accountability at each level of the education system. Adam and Kirst (1999) state, "the political and intergovernmental character of education, and the dispersion of responsibility for learning, make it difficult to know certainly who is accountable to whom" (pp. 481–482). Not only should responsibility be shared throughout the education system, but each level needs to remain attentive to targeting resources and support to schools to assist in focusing on student performance and the processes of teaching and learning. In this section we will discuss challenges at each level of the education system that may persist and obstruct the processes of educational accountability.

The increasing involvement of the federal level in educational agenda setting generates challenges regarding commensurate support in the design and funding of effective reform initiatives. The federal level's penchant for measuring the success of educational accountability with single indicators reflects the desire for politically appealing, relatively inexpensive, and easy-to-interpret results rather than an authentic understanding of how difficult it is to make substantial changes in student performance (Adams & Kirst, 1999; Linn, 2000). If the federal government mandates the use of educational accountability, then it must also demand accountability designs that provide schools with sufficient resources to make difficult improvements in educational practices. Addressing this challenge may entail greater levels of federal funding. Mintrop and Trujillo (2005) state, "the gap between what is federally required for successful corrective action and redesign and what states are able or willing to offer at this point is large in many instances" (p. 28). Educational-accountability reform is not an easy endeavor; a challenge that must be reflected in federal policy and funding.

As states have the responsibility of designing systems of academic and performance standards, they must be cognizant of the challenges in developing well-defined and clear sets of standards and sanctions. Underdeveloped standards or mandates that focus on particular measurement indicators over others may result in districts and schools misinterpreting the intentions of educational accountability (Spillane, 1999). Additionally, states should further their efforts to make certain that proficiency levels for standards are calibrated such that they can accurately assess student progress across grade levels as well as between content areas (Kingsbury et al., 2003).

At the district level, the educational accountability challenge will be to make the shift from dealing with schools through supervisory compliance to becoming centers of support and resources that help schools build capacity for changes in instructional practices. Converting into capacity-building entities will require that districts determine the multiple types of technical assistance and support that will facilitate changes in instructional practices. The resources and support necessary to bring about substantial change will likely vary between districts given differences in school contextual factors. Additionally, districts will need to avoid responses to educational accountability that reflect concerns about state involvement in educational practices. Fink and Thompson (2001) state, "the bureaucratic log jams that stall so many reform efforts arise from the habitual preoccupation with turf and territory" (p. 239). Educational accountability will only be successful when the different levels of the education system cooperate to improve student performance.

Finally, the present manifestation of intergovernmental educational accountability is designed in such a way that fails to appreciate mechanisms for schools' internal accountability. Educators at the school level do need pressure and support from the higher levels of the education system to acquire and adopt knowledge and skills, build school capacity, develop processes for collaborative inquiry and reflection, and share leadership. However, the accountability system should not overlook the reality that "a school's commitment to monitor its progress and offer its own set of rewards and sanctions can lead to higher consensus and skill development among staff" (Newmann, King, & Rigdon, 1997, p. 48). In turn, the challenge for external accountability systems in the intergovernmental context is that they should not be so severe that they limit the ability of schools to hold themselves accountable for student performance.

Summary

- Large-scale reforms, such as the No Child Left Behind Act, requires that the federal, state, and local government share their responsibilities and coordinate their resources and efforts.

- Each level of the complex intergovernmental policy system needs to remain attentive to targeting resources and support to schools to assist in focusing on student performance and the processes of teaching and learning.
- Understand the challenges at each level of the education system, including conditions that may persist and obstruct the processes of educational accountability.

Commentary and Discussion Questions

The following commentary is about a fourth-grade teacher turned state teachers union president. It focuses on recognizing who is driving educational-accountability reform within Washington state. The author argues that "politicians and non-educators" are those who are in control of the debate and choose legislation that punishes schools instead of promoting effective change and providing the necessary resources for such change. Those involved with the direct provision of education should be the central voices consulted when education reform is on the legislative table. Finally, the author argues that there is now "accountability" at all levels of public education except on those legislators who initiate the reform.

Accountability Is a Shared Responsibility
By Charles Hasse
The Seattle Post-Intelligencer, August 2, 2001

Before he assumed the presidency of the Washington Education Association July 7, Charles Hasse was a fourth-grade teacher in the Highline School District.

Since education reform began in 1993, the Washington Education Association and its members have helped lead the quest for higher academic achievement. Test scores, graduation rates, SAT scores and other measures of academic achievement show that public schools have made great progress over the past eight years.

As the state's largest professional organization for public school employees, WEA is dedicated to making public schools the best they can be for students, staff and communities. We're proud of our role in improving public education and we believe our state's new learning standards can benefit all students.

That's why it's frustrating when the *Post-Intelligencer* editorial page misrepresents WEA's position on so-called "school accountability" legislation ("Lawmakers duck educational accountability," July 24).

Throughout this year's legislative sessions, we supported several versions of the accountability bill, including the final one approved by Republicans and Democrats in the Senate. That bill died in the House of Representatives, despite our support.

Unfortunately, many of the politicians and non-educators involved in the accountability debate focused on punishing schools rather than helping them improve. Instead of emphasizing assistance for struggling schools, much of the discussion centered around blaming school employees.

The *Post-Intelligencer* and others have claimed WEA wanted "veto" power over school changes. That's not true, but common sense says teachers and other school employees should be involved in key decisions about improving student achievement.

Many of the school accountability proposals excluded school staff members from having a voice in those changes. In fact, some of the proposed bills would allow state officials to force major changes on a school, waiving existing school laws and employee contracts even without agreement from all of the parties involved, including staff and parents.

That means outsiders could unilaterally dictate major changes in a school's operation without regard for the staff's experience, expertise or morale.

"I don't think we need hammers for kids to be successful," said Dan Wilson, a high school teacher who testified before the Legislature. Rather than passing a flawed accountability bill that punishes schools and doesn't adequately support students, the Legislature should take the time to do it right.

For example, we believe in using more than one method to measure whether students have met the higher standards. Contrary to what the *Post-Intelligencer* argues, it's unfair and misleading to use a single test—such as the Washington Assessment of Student Learning (WASL)—to make high-stakes decisions about students or schools.

If we want to be accurate and fair, schools should use additional tests, classroom work and other methods to measure a child's academic progress. And when looking at a school's performance, we must take into consideration demographics, drop-out rates, graduation rates and other factors.

School accountability is a shared responsibility. Lawmakers, parents and voters must work with educators to ensure that all children meet the new higher academic standards.

Here's what's needed:

- More time to learn
- Small, manageable class sizes
- More time for teacher and staff planning and collaboration
- Community and parent support and involvement
- Training for teachers and other educators
- Competitive compensation to attract and retain high-quality school employees.

The need for better compensation is one area where the P-I got it right. Gov. Gary Locke and the Legislature once again failed to provide the pay and benefits that will allow our public schools to compete with higher-paying professions in the private sector and with schools in other states.

While they rush to demand school accountability, our state's elected leaders have refused to fully fund voter-mandated cost-of-living increases for public school employees.

As a result, teachers, parents and voters are being forced to sue the state over its lack of support for public schools. As student achievement continues to improve in our state, educators have proven their commitment to high-quality public schools.

Yet when it comes to providing the resources our students need to meet higher academic standards, who is holding our legislators accountable?

1. Considering Charles Hasse's commentary, what do you see as the most significant reform change from an external party (politicians, non-educators, etc.) at the federal level during your career? Describe the lasting effect(s) this has had on teachers within your school system.
2. What are the benefits and the limitations of having a federal system of education?
3. At the school level, what role do teachers and principals play in interpreting state and federal policy?
4. How would you describe the district-state-federal relations in the current accountability-based reform agenda?
5. What are the advantages and disadvantages to including external accountability measures for school district effectiveness? How does this add to, or subtract from, the level of effectiveness of internal accountability measures?

CHAPTER FIVE

Standards and Expectations

LEARNING OBJECTIVES_____

- Recognize that standards are essential operational components through which educational leaders can initiative changes to improve instructional practices by aligning curriculum, instruction, and assessment to meet increasingly high expectations.
- Explain the ways in which standards are designed and used to improve processes of teaching and learning.
- Provide examples of how standards function in states, including Illinois, Massachusetts, and Tennessee.
- Understand how leaders can assist teachers to align standards with curriculum, instruction, and student assessment.
- Present examples of strategies that educational leaders can use to successfully bring academic and performance standards into continuous dialogue throughout the school and district to transform instructional practices.

■ INTRODUCTION

Educational accountability may bring about significant improvements in student performance if educators throughout the system understand the way the reform proposes to bring about change and, in turn, effectively adopt the reform's mediating components. One of the primary theoretical assumptions of educational accountability is the establishment of clear academic and performance standards to improve student learning. Educators must design and implement high-quality standards systemwide based on results-driven goals that raise educational expectations for all students. However, the development of academic and performance standards at the district or state level will not improve student performance alone. Rather, educational leaders at each level of the system will need to ensure that mechanisms are in place to support the improvement of instructional practices. The design and implementation of high-quality standards cannot be isolated from effective instructional practices. Regrettably, the perception that standards-based reform and educational accountability will increase student learning through the mere development of high academic content standards and high-stakes testing has been prevalent. For example, Betts (1998) asserts:

> *Far and away the most important determinant of how quickly students learn is the effort of students themselves. It follows that an increase in schools' expectations of students could have important effects on the quality of public schooling. By establishing a rigorous set of educational standards, schools can create a set of incentives and rewards to promote student learning.* (p. 98)

While developing academic and performance standards to motivate students is one element of results-driven school improvement, the critical issue is that students need to be exposed to higher-order content and thinking skills in order to perform well in standards-based accountability systems. Smith and Desimone (2003) state, "many teachers use a 'traditional' model of teaching and learning that focuses heavily on memorization, without also emphasizing a deeper understanding of subject knowledge" (p. 119). Research suggests that teachers, on the other hand, who implement standards-based teaching practices at high levels, will contribute to the improvement of student achievement (Ross, McDougall, Hogaboam-Gray, & LeSage, 2003). Specifically, Ainsworth (2003) comments, "standards have the potential to significantly sharpen and focus curriculum, instruction, and assessment" (p. 3). For this reason, educational leaders will have to make considerable efforts to facilitate the process of aligning instructional practices with academic and performance standards to improve student learning.

The call for standards-based reform stems from shifting perceptions in the education community away from differentiated teaching and learning toward the belief that all students can perform well irrespective of background characteristics when held to high expectations and provided with appropriate instructional content and strategies. Sandholtz, Ogawa, and Scribner (2004) note, "the widespread enthusiasm for standards springs from the belief that they can contribute to improving and equalizing student achievement" (p. 1178). Of course, standards-based reform has not yet made the types of changes in the education system where we can make claims that students across the system are performing at high levels. Annual federal NCLB accountability reporting suggests that each year a large percentage of students and schools across the nation do not meet the level of proficiency on standards-based assessments. At the end of the 2002–2003 school year, 26,014 schools were identified across the nation as not meeting adequate yearly progress. In the 2003–2004 school year, 19,644 schools were identified as failing to make adequate yearly progress (Education Week, 2004; Education Week, 2005). Additionally, educators voice concern that accountability initiatives have the effect of standardizing and narrowing their instructional practices. If standards-based accountability mechanisms are to bring about improvements in student performance, educators will have to make certain that accountability encourages, rather than inhibits, innovative instructional practices. Darling-Hammond (1997) addresses the implementation of standards without the standardization of practices. "Standards and frameworks should identify fundamental concepts and relationships that structure a discipline and describe a common core of expectations for students . . . However, there must also be room for schools to teach what is important to the people in them" (p. 230). Accordingly, educational leaders must provide teachers with the resources to fundamentally change instructional practices by aligning curriculum, instruction, and assessment to high-quality standards in creative and effective ways in order to benefit student learning.

As standards are essential operational components of educational-accountability reform, this chapter focuses on explaining the ways standards are designed and used to improve processes of teaching and learning. First, we describe what academic and performance standards entail in systems of educational accountability. In particular, we provide examples of how standards function in states, including Illinois, Massachusetts, and Tennessee. Second, we address the key way that educational leaders can ensure that educational accountability is used to improve student performance; and that is by understanding how to assist teachers align standards with curriculum, instruction, and student assessment. We present examples of strategies that educational leaders can use to successfully bring academic and performance standards into continuous dialogue throughout the school to transform instructional practices. Educational leaders are critical to the alignment process in educational accountability as they will provide the vision, support, motivation, and incentives to keep teachers focused on high expectations and results-driven goals for all students. In turn, educational leaders must have the knowledge and skills about educational standards in order to facilitate improvements in the instructional core of schools.

■ EDUCATIONAL ACCOUNTABILITY: HOW STANDARDS FUNCTION

While the design of high-quality academic and performance standards must be a priority at the state and district levels when using educational-accountability reform, the mere development of standards will not bring about the type of improvements in student performance until educational leaders and educators understand the standards and effectively put them into daily practice. Dutro, Fisk, Koch, Roop, and Wixson (2002) comment, "standards must make sense to committed, strong practitioners or they may never become practice" (p. 307). Central to understanding and putting standards into practice is having educators engage in local discussions of how standards inform the processes of teaching and learning to benefit students. Valencia and Wixson (2001) state, "standards should offer midrange advice, specific enough to ensure that both curricula and assessment will work toward a common destination but broad enough to accommodate a wide range of strategies to fit different contexts" (p. 210). In turn, educational leaders will need to possess the knowledge and skills about academic and performance standards to guide teachers in their schools to productive conversations about standards that lead to continuous and substantial changes in instructional practices.

An essential component of leading educators toward understanding and adopting practices informed by academic and performance standards will be clearly distinguishing authentic standards-based initiatives from what Thompson (2001) identifies as "high-stakes, standardized, test-based reform" (p. 358). The former refers to using high-quality standards to expand and transform the instructional core of education, whereas the latter allows standardized tests to narrowly determine instructional practices based on the portions of subject areas that are tested. Some educators resist the standards component of educational accountability claiming that it forces them to limit content and curriculum and "teach to the test." When accountability is used in a high-stakes manner that creates more consequences and pressure than support, it should not be surprising that educators find unintended consequences of accountability such as narrowing of curriculum and content. Indeed, it may be the case that current education policy and legislation is structured in such a way that places strict sanctions on schools that result in teachers feeling obligated to focus on subjects covered in standardized tests. As long as the high-stakes legislative mandates remain in place, these will be valid concerns. However, educational accountability does not have to restrict or standardize the processes of teaching and learning. Regardless of legislative mandates, educational leaders, believing that educational accountability can improve student performance by making substantial changes to instructional practices, will have to address the challenges with vision, support, and resources. Educational leaders must demonstrate through knowledge, skills, and modeling processes of inquiry and collaboration that academic and performance standards can be used to facilitate exploration and understanding about the instructional practices that best improve student performance in their schools.

We do not intend to minimize the resolve and skill it will take from educational leaders to make educational accountability initiatives a success. Nonetheless, educational leaders committed to understanding how academic and performance standards function will be better prepared to contend with the challenges that may arise when implementing a large-scale school-improvement initiative. In turn, this section examines standards developed at the state level and highlight how they are designed to provide guidance on the issues of expectations for content coverage, indicators that assist students demonstrate learning accomplishments, and benchmarks for proficiency. While academic and performance standards are directly related to one another and work concurrently to comprise our notion of standards in educational accountability, we will attempt to parse out the individual aspects of each by describing them separately.

Academic Standards

Academic standards should provide clear and rigorous expectations for all students and educators with specific descriptions of the knowledge and skills that students are expected to have as they progress through school. Within educational accountability, academic standards are used to inform instructional practices by establishing high expectations for student learning. Reeves (2002) claims that academic standards should "be rigorous and challenging; be related to the technological forces that will mold the 21st century in which today's students will work; and provide a fair and equitable basis for education" (p. 7). While it is important that academic standards are designed to be challenging, they should also be reasonably attainable for all students (Linn, 2003). Discovering the appropriate balance between academic rigor and reasonable expectations is a difficult task for educational leaders given the responsibility of designing academic standards. Typically, systems of academic standards consist of separate standards for each of the subject areas, such as Language Arts, Mathematics, Science, and Social Studies. Within each subject area, objectives, indicators, and benchmarks for student progress are specified over a range of grade levels. We briefly describe objectives, indicators, and benchmarks and then return to them as we present examples of state systems of standards. Additionally, states may label their academic standards with different names, such as academic content standards, learning standards, achievement standards, or curriculum standards. We will use the term *academic standards* for consistency.

Objectives, indicators, and benchmarks function together to comprise our notion of academic standards. Objectives are the goals or learning expectations intended for the content areas within particular subject areas. For example, within the subject area of Language

Arts, Tennessee identifies reading, writing, and elements of language as content areas, whereas Massachusetts identifies language, reading and literature, composition, and media. In both Tennessee and Massachusetts, specific learning objectives are designated for the content areas within the given subject area. Indicators correspond with the objectives by providing examples of detailed tasks students should be able to accomplish. The indicators allow teachers to determine the skills and knowledge students should demonstrate in the classroom for each of the objectives. Benchmarks, on the other hand, organize indicators into a rubric of student performance to guide educators in determining the achievement level students should attain at a given grade level with academic standards. Benchmarks should be aligned with measures of student outcomes from teacher or state assessments.

Beginning in the 1990s, state departments and boards of education assumed the role of designing systemwide academic standards while state legislatures instituted them into law. Standards developed at the state level ensure consistent expectations throughout the state, as well as systematic frameworks for content coverage between grade levels and within subject areas. Many states treat the academic standards as minimum expectations for students and encourage local school districts to add to the standards in areas deemed important at the local level. This allows districts and schools to use processes of inquiry and collaboration to determine whether gaps need to be filled in the state standards in order to cover content that meets the needs of their students. In general, the process of writing academic standards at the state level includes the involvement of educators, researchers, business people, and the public. For example, in 1995 the Illinois State Board of Education (ISBE) established writing teams for each of the seven learning areas covered by the framework of academic standards. The writing teams adhered to the following criteria when developing the standards (Illinois State Board of Education, 2005):

- The standards and benchmarks must be clear and meaningful to students, parents, educators, business representatives and the community at large.
- The standards and benchmarks should include an appropriate combination of knowledge and skills, not just facts alone or skills alone.
- The standards and benchmarks should build upon and go beyond the basics within each of the academic disciplines.
- The standards and benchmarks should be specific enough to convey what students should learn, but broad enough to allow for a variety of approaches to teaching, curriculum, course design and assessment.
- The standards and benchmarks should be specific enough to be used in assessing progress and improving students' learning.

Once the writing teams drafted a set of academic standards, ISBE contracted with a local university to conduct surveys on public opinions of the standards. Subsequent refinement teams and a final external advisory committee revised the academic standards taking into consideration the public feedback. The revised academic standards have been passed by the Illinois state legislature. The process for designing and adopting academic standards in Illinois took over two years and represents a fairly typical course of action among the states.

As of December 2003, every state had developed a set of academic standards either in response to standards-based reform in the 1990s or in response to NCLB legislative mandates. While all states have designed systemwide academic standards, research suggests that academic standards may vary widely between states in terms of how challenging they are for students and in their specificity in design (Kingsbury, Olson, Cronin, Hauser,

& Houser, 2003; Linn, 2003). Kingsbury et al. (2003) find, "proficiency standards among states differ enough to cause substantial differences in the percentage of students categorized as proficient from one state to another, even if the students have exactly the same skills" (p. 26). Several organizations, including the newspaper *Education Week* and the nonprofit Thomas B. Fordham Foundation annually assess and rate state academic standards. Valencia and Wixson (2001) find that external grading systems reflect ideological and political beliefs about the role of standards in education policy. As long as it is understood that the ratings may represent fundamental beliefs about standards, the grades provide an opportunity to make comparisons between state systems of standards. In Table 5.1, we present the ratings assigned to state academic standards by *Education Week* and the Fordham Foundation for the 2003–2004 school year. The two organizations use different methods for ranking states, which accounts for large disparities between grades for a given state, such as Michigan or New York. *Education Week* calculates the number of established content area standards at the elementary, middle, and secondary levels and then weights the number with other components of accountability. The Fordham Foundation rates existing academic standards for intelligibility and coverage. Despite the different ways the organizations rank states, the grades from both organizations demonstrate the wide range of grades between states.

While there may be wide variations in state systems of academic standards, we give examples from states that have designed coherent systems where the objectives and indicators are clearly defined and presented in an accessible manner for educators to put them into practice. The examples provide assistance to educational leaders as they examine how their state academic standards operate and think about ways to use the standards to improve instructional practices. We begin with a set of mathematics standards in Massachusetts that received the highest rating from the Fordham Foundation for intelligibility and coverage and a high grade from *Education Week*. We then examine Tennessee's language arts standards that describe specific objectives and indicators and clearly links them with student performance benchmarks. The academic standards from these two states represent high-quality standards that should be used by educators to inform instructional practices to improve student performance.

Massachusetts has developed academic standards for eight subject areas including Language Arts, Mathematics, Science and Technology/Engineering, History and Social Sciences, Foreign Languages, Arts, and English Language Proficiency. The standards for mathematics are organized into five content strands: number sense and operations; patterns, relations, and algebra; geometry; measurement; and data analysis, statistics, and probability. Within each of the subject areas, the framework for academic standards begins with a set of guiding principles that underscore the importance of viewing curriculum, instruction, and assessment as part of a clear, coherent, and comprehensive enterprise that all educators must embrace to improve student performance. For mathematics, the guiding principles include (Massachusetts Department of Education, 2000, pp. 5–7):

Guiding Principle I: Learning

Mathematical ideas should be explored in ways that stimulate curiosity, create enjoyment of mathematics, and develop depth of understanding

Guiding Principle II: Teaching

An effective mathematics program focuses on problem solving and requires teachers who have a deep knowledge of mathematics as a discipline

TABLE 5.1   Grades for State Academic Standards, 2004

State	Education Week: Quality Counts 2004*	Thomas B. Fordham Foundation: Grading the Systems 2004†‡
Alabama	B−	3.6 (B−)
Alaska	C−	—
Arizona	B	3.4 (C+)
Arkansas	C+	2.3 (D+)
California	B	—
Colorado	B−	3.3 (C+)
Connecticut	B−	—
Delaware	B+	—
District of Columbia	D−	3.2(C)
Florida	A	—
Georgia	B+	3.6 (B−)
Hawaii	C+	2.3 (D+)
Idaho	C+	2.3 (D+)
Illinois	A−	—
Indiana	A−	—
Iowa	F	—
Kansas	B−	—
Kentucky	A	3.5 (C+)
Louisiana	A	—
Maine	C	2.5 (D+)
Maryland	A	—
Massachusetts	B+	4.7 (A−)
Michigan	B	2.3 (D+)
Minnesota	C	2.8 (C−)
Mississippi	B−	—
Missouri	B+	—
Montana	D−	2.2 (D)
Nebraska	D	—
Nevada	B	—
New Hampshire	C−	2.6 (C−)
New Jersey	B−	—
New Mexico	B	2.4 (D+)
New York	A	2.5 (D+)
North Carolina	B	3.4 (C+)
North Dakota	C−	2.5 (D+)
Ohio	A	4.0 (B)
Oklahoma	B+	—
Oregon	B−	—
Pennsylvania	B	3.5 (C+)
Rhode Island	D	1.5 (F)
South Carolina	A	—
South Dakota	C+	2.5 (D+)
Tennessee	B	—
Texas	C+	3.5 (C+)
Utah	C+	—
Vermont	C	2.2 (D)
Virginia	B	3.1 (C)
Washington	C+	2.2 (D)
West Virginia	A	3.3 (C+)
Wisconsin	C+	3.1 (C)
Wyoming	D	—

*Source: Education Week. (2004). *Quality counts 2004: Count me in: Special education in an era of standards.* Washington, DC: Editorial Projects in Education.

†Source: Cross, R. W., Rebarber, T., Torres, J., & Finn, C. E., Jr. (Eds.). (2004). *Grading the systems: The guide to state standards, tests, and accountability policies.* Washington, DC: The Thomas B. Fordham Foundation.

‡Note: The Fordham Foundation rating system ranges from 1 to 5. The grades in parentheses were calculated by the authors to assist in comparing the ratings with the *Education Week* grades.

TABLE 5.2 Massachusetts Mathematics Learning Standards for Measurement, Grades Pre-K–6

Grade Level		Learning Standards	NCTM Standard†	Examples of Activities and Problems
Pre-K–K	K.M.1	Recognize and compare the attributes of length, volume/capacity, weight, area, and time using appropriate language, e.g., longer, taller, shorter, same length; heavier, lighter, same weight; holds more, holds less, holds the same amount.	1	*Refers to standards K.M.1 and K.M.3* Students can use concrete materials such as pieces of ribbon or string, Popsicle sticks, or body parts to measure the height of their block constructions, the length or width of classroom materials, or the distance between objects.
	K.M.2	Make and use estimates of measurements from everyday experiences.	2	
	K.M.3	Use nonstandard units to measure length, area, weight, and capacity.	2	
1–2	2.M.1	Identify parts of the day (e.g., morning, afternoon, evening), days of the week, and months of the year. Identify dates using a calendar.	1	*Refers to standards 2.M.1 and 2.M.2* With the children's help, make a schedule of activities for the morning, recording times to the hour and half-hour. Set the alarms of both a digital clock and an analog clock to ring at the start of each new activity. Call on children to read the clocks to verify that they match the times in the schedules.
	2.M.2	Tell time at quarter-hour intervals on analog and digital clocks using a.m. and p.m.	1	
	2.M.3	Compare the length, weight, area, and volume of two or more objects by using direct comparison.	1	
	2.M.4	Measure and compare common objects using metric and English units of length measurement, e.g., centimeter, inch.	1	
	2.M.5	Select and correctly use the appropriate measurement tools, e.g., ruler, balance scale, thermometer.	1	
	2.M.6	Make and use estimates of measurement, including time, volume, weight, and area.	2	
3–4	4.M.1	Demonstrate an understanding of such attributes as length, area, weight, and volume, and select the appropriate type of unit for measuring each attribute.	1	*Refers to standards 4.M.1 and 4.M.4* Each □ is one square centimeter. What is the area of the shaded letter?
	4.M.2	Carry out simple unit conversions within a system of measurement, e.g., hours to minutes, cents to dollars, yards to feet or inches, etc.	1	
	4.M.3	Identify time to the minute on analog and digital clocks using a.m. and p.m. Compute elapsed time using a clock (e.g., hours and minutes since...) and using a calendar (e.g., days since...).	2	

	4.M.4	Estimate and find area and perimeter of a rectangle, triangle, or irregular shape using diagrams, models, and grids or by measuring.	
	4.M.5	Identify and use appropriate metric and English units and tools (e.g., ruler, angle ruler, graduated cylinder, thermometer) to estimate, measure, and solve problems involving length, area, volume, weight, time, angle size, and temperature.	2
5–6	6.M.1	Apply the concepts of perimeter and area to the solution of problems. Apply formulas where appropriate.	2
	6.M.2	Identify, measure, describe, classify, and construct various angles, triangles, and quadrilaterals.	2
	6.M.3	Solve problems involving proportional relationships and units of measurement, e.g., same system unit conversions, scale models, maps, and speed.	2
	6.M.4	Find areas of triangles and parallelograms. Recognize that shapes with the same number of sides but different appearances can have the same area. Develop strategies to find the area of more complex shapes.	2
	6.M.5	Identify, measure, and describe circles and the relationships of the radius, diameter, circumference, and area (e.g., $d = 2r$, $\pi = C/d$), and use the concepts to solve problems.	2
	6.M.6	Find volumes and surface areas of rectangular prisms.	2
	6.M.7	Find the sum of the angles in simple polygons (up to eight sides) with and without measuring the angles.	2

Refers to standard 6.M.6

Storage boxes are cube shaped and measure 4 inches on an edge. How many of these storage boxes are needed for 300 small cubes, 2 inches on an edge?

Refers to standard 6.M.7

Determine the sum of the measures of the angles of an equilateral triangle, a square, a regular pentagon, a regular hexagon, and a regular octagon.

†NCTM Standards:
1. Understand numbers, ways of representing numbers, relationships among numbers, and number systems
2. Understand meanings of operations and how they relate to one another
3. Compute fluently and make reasonable estimates
4. Analyze changes in various contexts

Source: Compiled by authors from, Massachusetts Department of Education. (2000). *Massachusetts mathematics curriculum framework.* Retrieved on June 5, 2005, from http://www.doe.mass.edu/frameworks/math/2000/final.pdf.

Guiding Principle III: Technology
Technology is an essential tool in a mathematics education

Guiding Principle IV: Equity
All students should have a high-quality mathematics program

Guiding Principle V: Assessment
Assessment of student learning in mathematics should take many forms to inform instruction and learning

The guiding principles are heavily influenced by the nationally recognized and developmentally appropriate content standards developed by the National Council of Teachers of Mathematics (NCTM). Massachusetts also uses the NCTM standards to guide specific objectives and indicators. For one example of the specific objectives and indicators of the five mathematics content strands, we turn to measurement.

The learning standards for measurement for grades Pre-K through six are displayed in Table 5.2 on pages 82–83. Massachusetts also has learning standards for measurement in grades six through 12 that are not presented in this table. If we take a look at the learning standards in the second column, we can see that they are clustered into two-year grade spans and presented in a consecutive manner so that educators can easily identify the standards students should know and be able to do from prior grade levels, as well as identify the standards that should be covered in the particular grade span. Students are held responsible for all learning standards in previous grades. It should be noted that in Massachusetts, objectives and indicators are combined in the learning standards. (In our example of academic standards from Tennessee, objectives and indicators will be more clearly distinguished from one another.) In the third column we have placed a number that corresponds with broad concepts of the NCTM standards. Throughout the mathematics academic standards, Massachusetts uses symbols to indicate the NCTM concept that each learning standard represents. For the content strand of measurement, only two of the NCTM concepts are covered. However, each of the four NCTM concepts are addressed when taking into consideration the other four content strands. Finally, in the fourth column are examples of problems and activities Massachusetts provides for teachers to use and adapt for their own students. The activities and problems linked to specific learning standards are intended to clarify how the learning standards can be put into practice. While we supply only one example per grade span, Massachusetts provides multiple examples for every cluster within each content strand. The learning standards are presented in the same way for the other four mathematics content strands.

The mathematics academic standards developed by Massachusetts are presented in a clear and coherent manner, providing educators with an organized framework of the knowledge and skills students should have as they progress through school. As the mathematical skills and knowledge represented in the learning standards build on previous objectives, educational leaders will need to make certain that teachers have the capacity to collaborate and communicate with each other about student progress. Additionally, the way the learning standards are grouped into two-year grade spans in the Massachusetts academic standards makes it necessary for educational leaders to ensure that teachers within grade-level clusters work together to increase continuity and avoid overlap in content coverage.

We now examine a set of academic standards from Tennessee. The state has done a good job at describing the objectives students should meet as well as the tasks students should be able to accomplish in order to demonstrate mastery of the particular objective. In addition, Tennessee clearly describes and organizes specific expectations for student performance in a set of benchmarks. In Appendix G we present Tennessee's eighth grade academic standards for language arts in the content area of reading. The Tennessee language arts academic standards begin with the same broad goal for students in kindergarten through eighth grade to guide educators in the content area of reading. "The student will develop the reading and listening skills necessary for word recognition, comprehension, interpretation, analysis, evaluation, and appreciation of print and non-print text" (Tennessee State Board of Education, 2001). In the first column of Appendix G we list the 13 learning expectations or objectives Tennessee identifies for mastery of the reading standard. The learning expectations are the same for grades four through eight, while kindergarten through third grade have a separate set of learning expectations for reading. For each learning expectation, Tennessee links a set of accomplishments that teachers can use to understand the type of student activities or knowledge that correspond with the learning expectations at that grade level. The accomplishments, or indicators of the objectives, are displayed in the second column. As the accomplishments are different for each grade level, educators can study the entire list of accomplishments for a particular learning expectation to determine what the student should be able to do from prior years and what the student should be prepared to do in subsequent years. This type of design of the academic standards should encourage educational leaders to facilitate teacher collaboration to make certain that students are achieving each of the learning expectations as they progress through school.

In addition to clearly describing objectives and indicators, the Tennessee academic standards provide educators with benchmarks that are aligned with state or teacher assessments and explain specific expectations for student performance that would display mastery of the standards. The state organizes the benchmarks into rubrics of student performance levels for each content area and for every grade level. The state creates separate performance rubrics for benchmarks aligned with state assessments and benchmarks aligned with teachers' own assessments of students. The performance rubric in Table 5.3 presents benchmarks aligned with the state assessment of students, the Tennessee Comprehensive Assessment Program (TCAP). Table 5.4 displays a set of performance benchmarks that the state encourages teachers to use in their classrooms through observation and other authentic assessments of student mastery of the standards. Each rubric is structured by three performance levels that each student is supposed to master by the end of the grade level. We describe the determination of the three performance levels in the next section on performance standards.

Tennessee has designed its academic standards for language arts to provide a comprehensive set of learning objectives, specific indicators, and benchmarks that determine student performance. While the Tennessee academic standards do not provide examples of activities and problems for teachers to use like Massachusetts, educational leaders can use time allotted for professional development or staff meetings as an opportunity for educators to collaborate and design their own activities that reflect the intent of the standards. Once educators become familiar with the learning expectations for reading and the other content areas within language arts, they can structure their instructional practices to incorporate the objectives and indicators. We provide examples of strategies for aligning the standards with curriculum, instruction, and assessment later in this chapter.

TABLE 5.3 Tennessee Eighth Grade Reading Performance Benchmarks, State Assessment

Below Proficient	Proficient	Advanced
At Level 1, the student is able to	At Level 2, the student is able to	At Level 3, the student is able to
8.1.spi.1. formulate appropriate questions during the reading of text	8.1.spi.10. recognize and use grade appropriate and/or content specific vocabulary	8.1.spi.23. determine the influence of culture and ethnicity on the themes and issues of literary texts
8.1.spi.2. choose the correct meaning/usage of multi-meaning words by replacing the word in context with an appropriate synonym or antonym	8.1.spi.11. determine an author's purpose for writing or a student's purpose for reading	8.1.spi.24. identify how the author reveals character (e.g., physical characteristics, dialog, what others say about him, what he does)
8.1.spi.3. locate information using available text features (e.g., maps, charts, graphics, indexes, glossaries, tables of contents, and appendices)	8.1.spi.12. identify an implied theme from a selection or related selections	8.1.spi.25. recognize literary elements that shape meaning within context (e.g., symbolism, foreshadowing, flashback, irony, mood and tone)
8.1.spi.4. identify on a graphic organizer the points at which various plot elements occur	8.1.spi.13. use text features (e.g., sidebars, footnotes, and endnotes) to determine meaning	8.1.spi.26. identify instances of bias and stereotyping in print and non-print contexts
8.1.spi.5. identify an appropriate title to reinforce the main idea of a passage or paragraph	8.1.spi.14. distinguish among different genres (e.g., poetry, drama, letters, ads, historical fiction, biographies, autobiographies, and essays) and their distinguishing characteristics	8.1.spi.27. recognize the effect of stressed and unstressed syllables to aid in identifying the meaning of multiple meaning words
8.1.spi.6. determine cause-effect relationships in context	8.1.spi.15. identify examples within context of similes, metaphors, alliteration, onomatopoeia, personification, and hyperbole	

8.1.spi.7. determine inferences from selected passages

8.1.spi.8. recognize a reasonable prediction of future events of a passage

8.1.spi.9. select information using keywords and headings

8.1.spi.16. choose a logical word or phrase to complete an analogy, using scrambled words and homophones in addition to previously learned analogies

8.1.spi.17. recognize and identify the techniques of propaganda (i.e., bandwagon, loaded words, and testimonials)

8.1.spi.18. recognize author's point of view (e.g., first person or third person, limited/ omniscient)

8.1.spi.19. determine how a story changes if the point of view is changed

8.1.spi.20. recognize commonly used foreign phrases (e.g., *bonjour, hasta la vista, bon voyage, mi casa es su casa, e pluribus unum, c'est la vie*)

8.1.spi.21. identify examples of sound devices within context (e.g., rhyme, alliteration, assonance, slant rhyme, repetition, internal rhyme)

8.1.spi.22. recognize and identify words within context that reveal particular time periods and cultures

Source: Compiled by authors from, Tennessee State Board of Education. (2001). *English/Language arts curriculum standards.* Retrieved on June 5, 2005, from http://www.state.tn.us/education/ci/cistandards2001/la/cilag8reading.htm.

TABLE 5.4 Tennessee Eighth Grade Reading Performance Benchmarks, Teacher Assessment

Below Proficient	Proficient	Advanced
At Level 1, the student is able to	At Level 2, the student is able to	At Level 3, the student is able to
8.1.tpi.1. decode unknown grade level words utilizing previously learned strategies to verify the word's meaning within the context of the selection	8.1.tpi.7. develop an awareness of literature that reflects a diverse society	8.1.tpi.18. define and apply internal (subjective) and external (objective) criteria in making critical evaluation of given statements
8.1.tpi.2. recognize various literary genres (e.g., short stories, novels, plays, legends, poetry, biographies, non-fiction)	8.1.tpi.8. read fluently basic grade appropriate selections	8.1.tpi.19. create an example of allusion
8.1.tpi.3. express reactions and personal opinions to a selection or relate the selection to a personal experience	8.1.tpi.9. create and deliver an organized oral presentation using multiple sources of information from any content area utilizing visual aids for contextual support	8.1.tpi.20. differentiate between internal and external conflict in a given passage
8.1.tpi.4. organize prior knowledge using a variety of strategies while reading (e.g., pausing, reading ahead, rereading, identifying miscues, and consulting other sources)	8.1.tpi.10. summarize, paraphrase, and evaluate selected passages	8.1.tpi.21. determine the significance/ meaning of a symbol in a print or non-print selection
8.1.tpi.5. preview the text to establish a purpose for reading, to activate prior knowledge, and to facilitate the reading process	8.1.tpi.11. develop and enhance vocabulary by reading from a wide variety of texts and literary genres	8.1.tpi.22. analyze literary elements
8.1.tpi.6. participate in creative responses to text (e.g., debates, dramatization, speeches)	8.1.tpi.12. make inferences and recognize unstated assumptions	8.1.tpi.23. evaluate reading selections and media sources to determine their applications to and effect on daily life
	8.1.tpi.13. make connections among the various literary genres, themes, and print and non-print texts with personal, historical, and cultural experiences	8.1.tpi.24. explore and distinguish between primary and secondary source documents
	8.1.tpi.14 demonstrate how time periods and cultures affect plots/characters in literature	
	8.1.tpi.15. recognize recurring themes in literature	
	8.1.tpi.16. distinguish between primary and secondary sources	
	8.1.tpi.17. identify instances of flashback and foreshadowing	

Source: Compiled by authors from, Tennessee State Board of Education. (2001). *English/Language arts curriculum standards.* Retrieved on June 5, 2005, from http://www.state.tn.us/education/ci/cistandards2001/la/cilag8reading.htm.

In this section we addressed the primary components of academic standards, including objectives, indicators, and benchmarks. By studying examples of academic standards in Massachusetts and Tennessee, it is clear that high-quality standards entail a comprehensive, clear, and logical framework for improving teaching and learning. Academic standards should be designed to make the process of transforming instructional practices as straightforward as possible. Furthermore, the academic standards we examined in this section do not limit content or instructional practices. Rather, the standards provide a framework to organize and prioritize content, as well as expand instructional practices. Academic standards should assist teachers in meeting the needs of students while avoiding low expectations (Sandholtz, Ogawa, & Scribner, 2004). As academic standards work hand in hand with performance standards in educational accountability, we now turn to describing the way performance standards function.

Performance Standards

While academic standards are used within educational accountability to establish expectations for what students should know and be able to do, performance standards determine expected levels of student performance outcomes. Linn (2000) comments that performance standards are "supposed to specify 'how good is good enough'" (p. 9). In other words, performance standards should be used to determine whether students and schools meet academic proficiency with the standards. Performance standards differ from traditional methods of assessing students that rely on norms of performance. Where normative assessments make comparisons between students based on a moving target of average student performance, performance standards allow educators to measure what students know and what they still need to learn to achieve proficiency with fixed learning standards (Izard, 2002; Linn, 2000; Reeves, 2002b). Unlike normative assessments that present student performance in bell-shaped curves suggesting that specific percentages of students should succeed and fail, performance standards are not competitive between students. Each and every student can achieve proficiency with high-quality academic standards without hindering another student's ability to achieve the same high outcomes. As a result, performance standards provide educators, students, and parents with more precise information regarding what students should know and be able to do as they progress through school.

Performance standards use indicators and benchmarks to indicate the expected level of achievement a student should attain at a particular grade level on the academic standards. Performance standards are typically defined by a relatively small number of performance levels. The NCLB legislation mandates that states develop performance or achievement standards aligned with the academic standards and arranged into three levels of achievement. Specifically, performance standards should include two levels of high achievement, such as advanced and proficient, that allow educators to determine how well students are mastering the academic standards. The third level of performance standards should indicate a basic level of achievement, such as below proficient, to provide information regarding the progress of low-performing students toward mastering proficient- and advanced-level achievement. While states have heeded the federal mandate for designing performance standards, there is some variation in the levels of achievement. As we demonstrated in the example of Tennessee's language arts academic standards, the state-designed rubrics of student performance that organize the benchmarks into three levels of performance similar to the federal mandate, including below proficient, proficient, and advanced (see Table 5.3 and Table 5.4). However, Florida's assessment, the Florida Comprehensive Assessment Test (FCAT), assigns five levels of academic achievement, numbered one through five with one being the lowest and five the highest. To meet federal demands for reporting student performance, Florida has renamed level one "Below Basic," level two "Basic," levels three and four "Proficient," and level five "Advanced." Once the performance standards have been aligned with academic standards and incorporated into assessments that measure student achievement on the standards, they are used in educational accountability to determine the percentage of students in a school who meet academic proficiency. Within educational accountability, schools that have a large percentage of students failing to meet proficiency should receive a combination of pressure and support to facilitate improvement.

While performance standards set necessary expectations for student attainment, questions remain regarding precisely when the performance benchmarks should be met. Fink and Thompson (2001) note, "if standards-based reform is to achieve its aim, we must transition from a system where time is the constant and results vary to one where standards are the constant and time varies" (p. 241). The issue at hand is in the way the education system uses discrete grade levels to determine expectations for academic development. Linn (2000) comments:

> *A reasonable question that generally goes unanswered is whether the intent is to aspire not just to high standards for all students, but to the same high standards for all students. And, more-over, to do so on the same time schedule for all students. It is quite possible to have high standards without the standards being common for all students.* (p. 10)

In a sense, the researchers claim that we may be setting some students up for failure if we maintain rigid expectations for when standards are to be attained. Linn (2000) and Fink and Thompson (2001) address an interesting concern in the way that we think about appropriate student development. However, it would be a disservice to students if educators suggest that simply because a student is currently identified as low-performing the student will not attain proficiency on the standards in a given period of time. This is where educational leaders must intervene and present new ways of thinking about the processes of teaching and learning. Certainly, students will not attain proficiency on the standards if educators continue to use the strategies that have failed in the past. Instead, the academic and performance standards should guide processes of inquiry about the instructional practices that will be effective in improving student performance. In our example of the academic standards in Massachusetts, the state-designed mathematics standards cover a two-year span of grade levels. By providing a larger window of opportunity for students to achieve the standards, education leaders can work with teachers to systematically deal with content coverage to meet the benchmarks set in the performance standards.

Performance standards perform an essential role in the process of development and adoption of high-quality academic standards to improve instructional practices and benefit student learning. In particular, performance standards provide valuable information for educators concerning whether students have attained the knowledge and skills associated with academic standards for their grade level. Rather than presenting teachers with a test score from a normative assessment that only indicates how well students test in relation to other students, performance standards are able to explicitly inform educators on how much students know and are able to do in relation to academic content of the standards. It is the role of educational leaders to provide the support and resources necessary to encourage educators throughout the school to use this knowledge to inform their instructional practices and meet the needs of every student.

■ ALIGNING STANDARDS WITH CURRICULUM, INSTRUCTION, AND ASSESSMENT

Once high-quality academic and performance standards have been designed at the state level, they must inform and impact instructional practices in order to improve student performance. Understanding how the standards operate in educational-accountability reform is the first step. Next, educators must make academic and performance standards part of their daily practice through inquiry, reflection, dialogue, and experimentation. However, the attention educators give to standards must be focused and purposeful. Valencia and Wixson (2001) state, "research and experience suggest that more time on standards and assessments alone will not improve learning. What is needed is a direct link between the components of standards-based reform (i.e., standards, assessment, accountability, and flexibility) and instructional improvement strategies" (p. 210). In effect, educational leaders will have to be familiar with strategies that assist teachers align curriculum, instruction, and assessment with academic and performance standards. Attempting the process of putting state academic and performance standards into practice may seem like an overwhelming endeavor for many educational leaders. Making use of standards-based instructional practices will undeniably be a challenge in schools dominated by traditional methods where teachers work in isolation. Research suggests, though, that the use of standards-based curriculum will improve student achievement (Reys, Reys, Lapan, Holliday, & Wasman, 2003). Educational leaders have to get directly involved in the technical core of schooling to ensure that instructional practices reflect the goals of results-driven, standards-based reform. In this section we address curriculum, instruction, and assessment individually and provide educational leaders with examples of specific alignment strategies for each of the instructional practices.

Aligning Standards with Curriculum

As curriculum encompasses all of the learning resources educators have at their disposal to use in their daily practices, the notion of aligning curriculum with academic standards may seem like a daunting task. On the other hand, using academic content standards to guide the selection of curriculum may remove a great deal of the uncertainty and inconsistency that takes place in schools on a regular basis. First, the traditional way where teachers design curriculum in isolation limits their ability to work within a consistent framework of curriculum. Teachers should be in continuous dialogue with other teachers in their school about curriculum coverage and student progress. Additionally, educators have generally relied on textbooks to provide relevant information and guide content coverage. While textbooks may supply a foundation of information, rarely will a textbook cover a content area in its entirety. If the textbook is incomplete, how do educators systematically find gaps in coverage and address them with supplemental resources? Certainly, good teachers have developed methods for providing their students with the appropriate curriculum to achieve at high levels, but these effective practices have been not been used consistently by educators throughout the education system. Accordingly, the alignment of curriculum with academic standards can restructure schools such that educators within and across grade levels know what is expected of students because they are all working with a clear and comprehensive curriculum framework. Moreover, aligning curriculum with academic standards will assist schools in systematically filling curriculum gaps and identifying redundancy in order to enhance students' learning experiences.

As in the examples from Massachusetts and Tennessee, high-quality academic standards are composed of clear, comprehensive, and consistent guidelines for academic content and student progress. Not only do the academic standards set expectations for what students should know and be able to do at a given grade level, they provide indicators of student mastery of standards across grade levels. In turn, academic standards can easily be used as a schoolwide framework to direct the selection of curriculum resources. Aligning curriculum with academic standards should begin by using the standards to develop a curriculum pacing guide. Pacing guides for curriculum group learning objectives into units, allocate time to the units, and sequence the units on an academic calendar (Rettig, McCullough, Santos, & Watson, 2004). In many cases, the district level of the education system has assumed responsibility for designing curriculum guides that align with academic standards. For example, the Spotsylvania County Schools district in Virginia has put together curriculum guides for ten subject areas from kindergarten through twelfth grade that are aligned with Virginia's academic standards. Table 5.5 lists the Virginia state academic standards for fifth grade science, which specify six content areas and seven objectives. The format of the academic standards does not differ significantly from Massachusetts or Tennessee. In Table 5.6, we present the curriculum guide developed by the Spotsylvania County school district to help teachers determine when to cover each of the science objectives over the course of an academic year. The year is split up into four nine-week grading periods. For example, the second column in the first grading period recommends that teachers cover objectives from the first and fifth content areas, or Scientific Investigation, Reasoning and Logic, and Living Systems, respectively. The curriculum guide details a set of activities that would be indicators of the content area, as well as examples of assessments. While this particular curriculum guide is relatively simple, pacing guides can become more comprehensive and move closer toward daily lesson plans as they detail content coverage in smaller units of time. In effect, curriculum guides are lesson plans that make certain each activity and material is linked to an academic standard.

The process of developing curriculum guides is often called curriculum mapping as it involves matching curriculum and materials with the academic content that should be covered in a given time period. While many districts assume the responsibility of designing curriculum guides, district guides may not completely meet the needs of individual schools (Fink & Thompson, 2001). As the curriculum guide in Table 5.6 demonstrates, the district may not provide detailed enough direction, which will require that educational leaders assist their teachers in covering the assignment. Jacobs (2004) identifies the following tasks as essential to curriculum mapping: "filling in the gaps, eliminating repetitions, seeking potential areas for integration, validating and integrating standards, and updating antiquated programs with timely curriculum" (p. 29). While we presented one subject area in one grade level in Table 5.6, curriculum mapping should entail a more comprehensive examination of the academic standards. With curriculum mapping, teachers should work with their subject-area colleagues throughout the school in addition to teachers in the same grade level to encourage within- and across-grade level inquiry and collaboration about curriculum alignment. If we take the curriculum guide for fifth grade science in Table 5.6 as a starting point, the next step for educators would be to thoroughly study the

TABLE 5.5   Virginia Academic Standards for Science, Fifth Grade

Content Areas	Objectives and Indicators
Scientific Investigation, Reasoning, and Logic	5.1 The student will plan and conduct investigations in which a) rocks, minerals, and organisms are identified using a classification key; b) estimations of length, mass, and volume are made; c) appropriate instruments are selected and used for making quantitative observations of length, mass, volume, and elapsed time; d) accurate measurements are made using basic tools (thermometer, meter stick, balance, graduated cylinder); e) data are collected, recorded, and reported using the appropriate graphical representation (graphs, charts, diagrams); f) predictions are made using patterns, and simple graphical data are extrapolated; g) manipulated and responding variables are identified; and h) an understanding of the nature of science is developed and reinforced.
Force, Motion, and Energy	5.2 The student will investigate and understand how sound is transmitted and is used as a means of communication. Key concepts include a) frequency, waves, wavelength, vibration; b) the ability of different media (solids, liquids, and gases) to transmit sound; and c) uses and applications (voice, sonar, animal sounds, and musical instruments). 5.3 The student will investigate and understand basic characteristics of visible light and how it behaves. Key concepts include a) the visible spectrum and light waves; b) refraction of light through water and prisms; c) reflection of light from reflective surfaces (mirrors); d) opaque, transparent, and translucent; and e) historical contributions in understanding light.
Matter	5.4 The student will investigate and understand that matter is anything that has mass, takes up space, and occurs as a solid, liquid, or gas. Key concepts include a) atoms, elements, molecules, and compounds; b) mixtures including solutions; and c) the effect of heat on the states of matter.
Living Systems	5.5 The student will investigate and understand that organisms are made of cells and have distinguishing characteristics. Key concepts include a) basic cell structures and functions; b) kingdoms of living things; c) vascular and nonvascular plants; and d) vertebrates and invertebrates.
Interrelationships in Earth/Space Systems	5.6 The student will investigate and understand characteristics of the ocean environment. Key concepts include a) geological characteristics (continental shelf, slope, rise); b) physical characteristics (depth, salinity, major currents); and c) biological characteristics (ecosystems).

continued

continued

Earth Patterns, Cycles, and Change	5.7 The student will investigate and understand how the Earth's surface is constantly changing. Key concepts include a) the rock cycle including identification of rock types; b) Earth history and fossil evidence; c) the basic structure of the Earth's interior; d) plate tectonics (earthquakes and volcanoes); e) weathering and erosion; and f) human impact.

Source: Compiled by authors from, Virginia Department of Education. (2003). *Standards of Learning.* Retrieved on June 5, 2005, from http://www.pen.k12.va.us/VDOE/Superintendent/Sols/science5.pdf.

indicators and locate curriculum resources and materials that align with the content standards. As it is unlikely that textbooks will be a perfect match to the content standards, educators will have to find or create supplemental materials to fill in gaps in content coverage. Educators collaborating together may want to keep an ongoing file of resources organized by content area and indicator. Educators can modify the curriculum guide by adding a column that specifies the textbook chapter or supplemental resource that matches with a given indicator. Additionally, if educators find that the academic standards omit content area that the school deems important for their students, they can adapt the curriculum guide by adding the content into the framework. Curriculum mapping can provide great detail on the timing of content coverage, as well as the materials used to help students meet the academic standards.

Aligning curriculum with academic standards should not be viewed as an overly difficult task or as a process that will narrow content coverage. Rather, aligning curriculum with academic standards encourages collaboration and provides educators with a school-wide framework for comprehensive and consistent content coverage. Developing detailed curriculum guides will give educators the opportunity to carefully examine the curriculum materials they use to make certain that they match with objectives, indicators, and benchmarks that will improve student performance.

Aligning Standards with Instruction

Identifying the components of high-quality instruction that will bring about success with educational accountability or any large school-reform initiative is a difficult endeavor. As students have a variety of learning styles, educators have to continuously adapt their instructional practices to meet the needs of the entire class, as well as the needs of each student. Educational leaders instinctively know good teaching when they see it. Nevertheless, educational leaders need to know how to assist every teacher in their school to develop good instructional practices. Thompson (2001) states, "If you want to improve student learning across the board, then you need to fundamentally improve the quality of instructional content and practice" (p. 359). At the heart of teaching there are essential acts, including "knowing their students, engaging them in learning, acting as models of a good life, assessing students' moral and intellectual growth, and reflecting on the arts of teaching that enable that growth" (Grant & Murray, 1999, p. 32). What we know about teachers who effectively use academic standards to inform instruction is that they engage

TABLE 5.6 Curriculum Guide of Virginia, Academic Standards for Science, Fifth Grade (Spotsylvania County Schools)

Nine-Weeks	Virginia Academic Standards: Content Areas	Indicators	Assessments
	Scientific Investigation, Reasoning, and Logic: • Measurement (5.1) • Classification (5.1) • Analyzing Data (5.1)	Scientific Investigation, Reasoning, and Logic: • Select and use appropriate instruments, and make accurate measurements • Use a classification key to organize organisms • Collect, record, and report data • Graph data using an appropriate type of graph • Recognize trends in data, and make predictions based on those trends • Estimate length, mass, and volume • Measure the mass and volume of an object and calculate its density	
1st	Living Systems: • Cells (5.5) • Using a microscope (5.5) • Classification of organisms (5.5)	Living Systems: • Describe and demonstrate proper techniques when using a microscope • Use a microscope to observe plant and animal cells • Draw and label basic structures of plant and animal cells; describe the function of each structure • Compare and contrast plant and animal cells • Compare and contrast the distinguishing characteristics of the six kingdoms of organisms	Living Systems: • Make an edible model of a cell and label the important parts of the cell • Use pictures of vertebrates and invertebrates from magazines to create a poster that illustrates the differences between the two • Make drawings of cells or one-celled organisms observed under magnification • Create an analogy between the parts of a cell and a factory or city

continued

TABLE 5.6 continued

Nine-Weeks	Virginia Academic Standards: Content Areas	Indicators	Assessments
		Classify common organisms: By kingdom As a vascular or a non-vascular plant As a vertebrates or non-vertebrates • Apply the 5.1 science skills in the context of the content of this topic	• Make a comparison chart to compare major characteristics of organisms in the six kingdoms
2nd	Scientific Investigation, Reasoning, and Logic: • Experimental design (5.1)	Scientific Investigation, Reasoning, and Logic: • Identify manipulated (independent) and responding (dependent) variables in a controlled experiment	
	Interrelationships in Earth/Space Systems: • Physical and biological oceanography (5.6) • Geology of the ocean floor (5.6) • Public policy regarding the oceans (5.6)	Interrelationships in Earth/Space Systems: • Create and interpret a model of the ocean floor • Describe how sonar (sound) is used to determine the depth of the ocean • Describe the variation in ocean depth • Describe the motion of a floating object as a wave passes • Design a model to illustrate the formation of waves and currents • Design an investigation to demonstrate how salinity and temperature affect the density of water, and relate density to the formation of underwater currents • Describe how pressure increases with depth and how organisms adjust to living in deep water • Interpret graphical data related to physical or biological characteristics of the ocean	Interrelationships in Earth/Space Systems: • Write a letter to your senator or congressman taking a position on an issue related to the oceans such as over fishing or pollution • Write an opinion essay on a marine issue • Make a model or drawing of the ocean floor that shows ocean floor features; label the features • Make a model of an ocean food chain or web • Create an imaginary animal that would be suited for living in a particular ocean environment (i.e., deep ocean, tidal pool, reef, etc.); explain how your animal is adapted to its environment

TABLE 5.6 continued

Nine-Weeks	Virginia Academic Standards: Content Areas	Indicators	Assessments
		• Explain the formation of ocean surface currents, and locate the Gulf Stream	
		• Analyze how physical characteristics of the ocean determine where organisms can live	
		• Create and interpret a model or diagram of a marine food web	
		• Describe important ocean resources, and tell what nations have done to conserve and protect the ocean environment	
		• Apply the 5.1 science skills in the context of the content of this topic	
3rd	Scientific Investigation, Reasoning, and Logic:	Scientific Investigation, Reasoning, and Logic:	Scientific Investigation, Reasoning, and Logic:
	• Classification keys (5.1)	• Identify rock samples using a classification key	• Identify common rocks using a classification key
	Earth Patterns, Cycles, and Change:	Earth Patterns, Cycles, and Change:	Earth Patterns, Cycles, and Change:
	• The rock cycle (5.7)	• Compare and contrast the origin of igneous, sedimentary, and metamorphic rocks	• Use a model to explain motion of plates at the three types of plate boundaries
	• Types of rocks (5.7)		
	• Earth's interior (5.7)	• Draw, label, and interpret the rock cycle	• Make and interpret a model of the rock cycle
	• Plate tectonics (5.7)		
	• Weathering and erosion (5.7)	• Make inferences about changes in the Earth's surface over time based on fossil evidence	• Make observations of erosion at home or school and describe how that erosion could be prevented or controlled
	• Human impact on the Earth's surface (5.7)		

continued

TABLE 5.6 continued

Nine-Weeks	Virginia Academic Standards: Content Areas	Indicators	Assessments
		• Model and describe the interior of the Earth • Model and differentiate between the three types of tectonic boundaries • Explain how moving plates change the surface of the Earth and the ocean floor • Use a model or diagram to explain earthquakes and volcanoes • Differentiate between weathering and erosion • Design an investigation to locate, chart and report erosion at home or at school; create a plan to solve erosion problem that might be found • Design an investigation to determine the amount and kinds of weathered rock material that may be found in soil • Describe how people change the Earth's surface and ways that negative changes can be controlled • Apply the 5.1 science skills in the context of the content of this topic	• Plot locations of earthquakes and/or volcanoes on the surface of the Earth; compare what you find to the locations of plate boundaries • Use pieces of cardboard to "act out" the different plate boundaries • Pretend you are making a journey through the rock cycle; write a story telling of your adventure • Make a model of the interior of the Earth • Explain why we don't have active volcanoes in Virginia
	Matter: • Atoms, molecules, elements and compounds (5.4) • Mixtures and solution (5.4) • Effects of temperature on the states of matter (5.4)	Matter: • Compare and contrast atoms and molecules • Compare and contrast elements, compounds, and mixtures including solutions; give examples of each • Given a mixture, design a procedure to separate the components and test your procedure	Matter: • Classify common substances as elements, compounds, or mixtures • Given a mixture, determine a method to separate the components • Make models of simple molecules with toothpicks and marshmallows or gumdrops

98

TABLE 5.6 continued

Nine-Weeks	Virginia Academic Standards: Content Areas	Indicators	Assessments
		• Design an investigation to determine how heat affects the state of water • Construct and interpret a sequence of models showing the activity of molecules in a solid, a liquid, and a gas • Apply the 5.1 science skills in the context of the content of this topic	• Have a scavenger hunt in your kitchen for elements, com-pounds, and mixtures
4th	Force, Motion, and Energy: • Waves (5.2, 5.3) • Sound (5.2) • Light (5.3)	Force, Motion, and Energy: • Describe a wave as a means of transmitting energy • Use a slinky to distinguish between a transverse and compressional (longitudinal) wave; describe the motion of particles of the material as a transverse or compressional wave passes through; make a draw-ing to represent each type of wave • Demonstrate that a sound is created when something vibrates, and explain why sound waves travel only where there is matter to transmit them • Classify sound as a compressional wave • Relate frequency of a sound to the pitch	Force, Motion, and Energy: • Make a musical instrument and describe how it works • Make a model showing a sound wave • Create tow pitch pipes; predict which will have the highest pitch • Explain how the eye is like a camera • Set up a mirror maze • Use a slinky to model types of waves and wave properties

continued

TABLE 5.6 continued

Nine-Weeks	Virginia Academic Standards: Content Areas	Indicators	Assessments
		• Design an experiment to determine what factors influence the pitch of the sound produced by vibrating strings	
		• Design an experiment to determine the effect of amount of water in a bottle on the pitch of the sound produced when the bottle is struck and when air is blown across the opening	
		• Compare the speed of sound passing through solids, liquid, and gases	
		• Compare and contrast the pitch of sounds that humans make and hear to those of other animals, and explain how animals use sound	
		• Classify light as a transverse wave	
		• Name the colors of the visible spectrum, and explain the relationship between wavelength and color	
		• Describe the visible spectrum as part of the electromagnetic spectrum	
		• Classify materials as transparent, translucent, or opaque	
		• Identify some common optical tools	
		• Describe contributions of Galileo, Hook, van Leeuwenhoek, and Newton in creating and using optical tools	
		• Apply the 5.1 science skills in the context of the content of this topic	

Source: Spotsylvania County Schools. (2004). *Curriculum Map.* Retrieved on June 5, 2005, from http://www.spotsylvania.k12.va.us/cmaps/pdf/science/Science%205.pdf.

students in active in-depth learning, emphasize authentic student performance, pay attention to student development, appreciate diversity, and institute structures for caring (Darling-Hammond, 1997).

While many educators perceive that academic standards force them into using drilling, memorization, and direct teaching to impart the basic learning skills that are assessed on high-stakes test, these practices do not engage students in critical thinking, which is the goal of standards-based reform (Sandholtz, Ogawa, & Scribner, 2004). Indeed, academic standards should "require students to utilize high-order thinking skills and integrate present learning with prior knowledge" (Ainsworth, 2003, p. 11). When aligned with high-quality academic standards, instruction can transform to meet the needs of all students. In research on standards-based mathematics teaching, Ross, McDougall, Hogaboam-Gray, and LeSage (2003) find:

> The high reform teachers used [the textbook] to amplify their implementation of standards-based teaching, compensating for the text's perceived inadequacies in ways consistent with the standards . . . They did not implement the text verbatim but drew from it an overview of the domain and used it as a source of materials to build their own ideas. The low reform teachers used the text to justify traditional practices modifying the text or replacing key sections to redirect its emphasis away from the standards. (p. 360)

The research suggests that the use of appropriate curriculum materials aligned with academic standards influences the quality of instruction. These findings correspond with the notion that what is taught is directly related to how well students perform. Teachers will develop varying strategies to match the needs of their students but the content is critical to improving student learning. Additionally, educational leaders can aid teachers in employing standards-based instruction by providing resources for teachers to observe exemplar teaching practices in other classrooms, encouraging collaboration around curriculum selection, requesting lesson plans linked with academic standards, and providing professional development around the issue of using student data to inform instruction.

Facilitating changes in teaching practices is a difficult process for even the most skilled educational leader. However, educational leaders can make it clear that aligning practices with academic standards is essential for improving student performance when they provide appropriate support and resources to assist teachers incorporate standards-based practices. The discussion of effective professional development activities in Chapter 9 provides further guidance for educational leaders in assisting teachers make changes in instructional practices.

Aligning Standards with Assessment

While there is merit in using student assessment data to make comparisons between students or schools, the primary purpose of assessment should be to improve the processes of teaching and learning. Whether the assessment data is from state tests or teacher assessments in their classrooms, assessments aligned with academic standards can help educators improve student performance by providing information regarding what students know and are able to do in a given subject area. Dorward, Hudson, Drickey, and Barta (2001) note, "teachers who use information from formative assessment practices, including standards-based criterion-referenced tests, can see measurable improvement in student achievement" (p. 248). As it will be imperative for educators to learn how to effectively use student assessment data to inform teaching practices, we cover this topic in great detail in

Chapter 8. In this section we focus on ways in which educators can ensure that assessments they use are aligned with academic standards.

In compliance with NCLB legislation, each state has developed state-level tests aligned with the academic standards. In most states, the standards-based tests focus on the subject areas of Language Arts, Mathematics, and Science. However, we are going to provide an example from Social Studies to illustrate how educators should be prepared to use alternative standards-based assessments besides the state tests in their classrooms to gauge student mastery of the academic standards. Illinois administers the Illinois Standards Achievement Test (ISAT) for Social Science in fourth and seventh grades. In Table 5.7, we present the academic standard for the content area of government within Social Studies along with several aligned sample test items. While results from ISAT will provide achievement information to teachers of fourth or seventh grade students who take the state assessment, teachers of students in the grade levels not tested will need to use classroom assessments aligned with the academic standards. Rettig, McCullough, Santos, and Watson (2004) claim that classroom assessment can be designed to provide meaningful information if it focuses on essential skills, assessment of unit goals, and mid-unit checkpoints. In effect, educators should plan curriculum and instruction that will support the success of standards-based assessments. The Illinois State Board of Education provides detailed examples of standards-based assessments teachers may find helpful for each of the content areas within Social Studies. In Table 5.8, we list the suggested classroom assessments aligned with the academic standards for each grade level. The examples of assessment include links to materials and performance rubrics for determining student mastery of the standards. Of course, the assessments provided by Illinois are examples and educators should collaborate within their school to develop additional assessments aligned with the academic standards to measure student progress.

While mandated testing that is associated with educational accountability may cause educators to feel pressured to focus on the content covered in the tests, standards-based student assessment should be used to gauge student progress and improve the processes of teaching and learning. Student assessments in educational accountability should not have the effect of narrowing the content educators cover. Rather, standards-based assessments should help educators identify areas where students may need further assistance in order to master the academic standards. The next chapter explains fundamental testing concepts and describes in fuller detail the different types of performance measures.

Summary

- Educational leaders are critical to the alignment process in educational accountability as they articulate the vision and provide the incentives to keep teachers focused on high expectations and results-driven goals for all students. In turn, educational leaders must have the knowledge and skills about educational standards in order to facilitate improvements in the instructional core of schools.
- Examples from several states show that high-quality academic standards comprise clear, comprehensive, and consistent guidelines for academic content and student progress.
- Not only do the academic standards set expectations for what students should know and be able to do at a given grade level, they provide indicators of student mastery of standards across grade levels. In turn, academic standards can easily be used as a schoolwide or districtwide framework to direct the selection of curriculum resources.

TABLE 5.7 Illinois Standards Achievement Test (ISAT) for Social Science, Sample Items, Fourth Grade

STATE GOAL 14: Understand political systems, with an emphasis on the United States.

Why This Goal Is Important: The existence and advancement of a free society depend on the knowledge, skills, and understanding of its citizenry. Through the study of various forms and levels of government and the documents and institutions of the United States, students will develop the skills and knowledge that they need to be contributing citizens, now and in the future.

B. Understand the structures and functions of the political systems of Illinois, the United States and other nations.

Sample items aligned with 14.B:

1. The U.S. Congress is a group of people who
   a. run the city.
   b. are soldiers.
   c. are lawyers.
   d. make laws.
2. If something happened to the president, who would take his or her place?
   a. Vice president
   b. Mayor
   c. Governor
   d. Senator
3. Why does the United States flag have 50 stars?
   a. Stars make a good design.
   b. There is one star for each state.
   c. The flag is 50 years old.
   d. There is one star for each president.
4. The United States Congress includes the
   a. president and the vice president.
   b. Supreme Court and the Appeals Court.
   c. House of Representatives and the Senate.
   d. Senate and the vice president.
5. If a stoplight is needed on a corner, what action should people in the area take?
   a. Pass petitions asking for a stoplight.
   b. Put up a barricade.
   c. Complain to the neighbors.
   d. Buy a stoplight.
6. U.S. citizens cast their votes by
   a. ballots.
   b. telephone.
   c. television.
   d. letters.

Source: Compiled by authors from, Illinois State Board of Education. (2003). *Illinois Standards Achievement Test sample social science materials.* Retrieved on June 5, 2005, http://www.isbe.net/assessment/PDF/2003SSSample.pdf.

Curriculum mapping can provide great detail on the timing of content coverage, as well as the materials used to help students meet the academic standards.

• Student assessments in educational accountability should not have the effect of narrowing the content educators cover. Rather, standards-based assessments can help educators identify areas where students may need further assistance in order to master the academic standards.

TABLE 5.8   Assessments Aligned with Illinois Academic Standards for Social Studies

STATE GOAL 14: Understand political systems, with an emphasis on the United States.				
Why This Goal Is Important: The existence and advancement of a free society depend on the knowledge, skills, and understanding of its citizenry. Through the study of various forms and levels of government and the documents and institutions of the United States, students will develop the skills and knowledge that they need to be contributing citizens, now and in the future. B. Understand the structures and functions of the political systems of Illinois, the United States and other nations.				
	Early Elementary	Late Elementary	Middle/Junior High School	Early High School	Late High School
Social Studies Content Standard	14.B.1 Identify the different levels of government as local, state, and national	14.B.2 Explain what government does at local, state, and national levels	14.B.3 Identify and compare the basic political systems of Illinois and the United States as prescribed in their constitutions	14.B.4 Compare the political systems of the United States to other nations	14.B.5 Analyze similarities and differences among world political systems (e.g., democracy, socialism, communism)
	1st grade, 14.B *Rules and Responsibilities:* Draw and label a picture of a rule/responsibility that students must follow at home, school, and in public places	4th grade, 14.B *Functions of the Three Branches of Government:* Illustrate and summarize the functions of the three branches of government	6th grade, 14.B *Responsibilities of Office:* Create an organizational chart that describes the roles, responsibilities, and relationships among the major offices of the executive branch of Illinois state government	9th & 10th grades, 14.B *"Motor-Voter" Registration Trends:* Examine attempts to increase voting registration through "Motor-Voter" registration	11th & 12th grades, 14.B *FDR-Hitler: Conflicting Political Systems:* Contrast the governments of Germany and the United States just before the outbreak of World War II
Assessments Aligned with the Academic Standards	2nd grade, 14.B *Who Are Our Leaders?:* Draw a picture of the president of the United States and a leader or official from their community, and describe the duties of the officials in a sentence	5th grade, 14.B *Treaties and Separation of Powers:* Make a diagram that identifies separation of powers by using a treaty the United States has signed with another country	7th grade, 14.B *Gulf of Tonkin Resolution:* Write an essay that analyzes the Gulf of Tonkin Resolution and the impact of the Vietnam War on American society		
	3rd grade, 14.B *Contributors to the Common Good:* Prepare a chart about an historical figure that includes major events, contributions and changes that person brought about		8th grade, 14.B *Comparing the House and Senate:* Construct a poster and write a description on the powers and responsibilities assigned to both houses of the U.S. Congress		

Source: Compiled by authors from, Illinois State Board of Education. (2005). *Illinois Learning Standards.* Retrieved on June 5, 2005, http://www.isbe.state.il.us/ils/Default.htm.

- Facilitating changes in teaching practices is a difficult process for even the most skilled educational leader. However, educational leaders can make it clear that aligning practices with academic standards is essential for improving student performance when they provide appropriate support and resources to assist teachers incorporate standards-based practices.

Article and Discussion Questions

The following article discusses the issue of states' implementation of NCLB testing requirements into their existing standardized testing structures. They must make sure that these additional tests complement those currently being administered. If this is not ensured, huge advancements or deficiencies may appear on concept knowledge from one year to the next when, in fact, what are being observed are discrepancies in content tested. To correct for such problems, states can adopt proficiency standards per grade based on content standards, test difficulty, and raw test score data. Also, it is important that committees are set up to analyze testing procedures and have the authority to adjust standards higher or lower.

States Confront Definition of "Proficient" as They Set the Bar for Lots of New Tests

By Lynn Olson
Education Week, December 14, 2005

As states add reading and math exams in previously untested grades to comply with the No Child Left Behind Act, they will have to determine the level of performance considered "proficient."

In particular, states must figure out how to make their achievement standards on the new tests mesh with those in the grades already being tested, so that the progression of growth expectations across grade levels is smooth. Otherwise, 4th graders who are rated proficient in mathematics one year may suddenly score below that level the next simply because the standard, or cut point, has shifted.

"I think it's causing some difficulties," Robert L. Linn, a professor of education emeritus at the University of Colorado at Boulder, said of state efforts to set performance standards.

The combination of new performance standards and tests will make it even harder to determine if schools are really improving, based on whether they have made adequate yearly progress under the federal law.

As states add performance standards or revise the scores students need to qualify as "proficient," it may be unclear if the bar has been raised, lowered, or kept largely the same.

COMPARISONS DIFFICULT

Figuring out the height of the bar is not easy, responses to the EPE Research Center survey show.

In Arizona, for example, officials held a series of meetings last May to set new achievement levels in reading, math, and writing for their state's tests in grades 3–8 and high school. State officials report that high school students now must answer a lower percentage of items correctly to meet the proficiency standard. But the tests also now contain more items, so students must show more knowledge to be rated proficient.

Arkansas also set new performance levels in 2005 for its reading and math exams. "On balance, the cut scores are generally comparable," a state education department official reported, "although at one particular grade or another, the cut score may be somewhat higher or lower.

"It is difficult to make an exact comparison," the Arkansas official continued, in response to the EPE Research Center survey, "since the content standards being measured have been revised and since the design of the literacy portion of the examination has changed."

What states want to avoid, said Scott Marion, a vice president of the Center for Assessment, a Dover, N.H.–based group that works with states to improve their testing-and-accountability systems, are erratic swings in performance from grade to grade because of where they've set the bar.

"If you have an assessment in grades 4, 8, and 11 and now you're going to fill in the rest of the grades, do you go back and completely revisit all your performance standards, which some folks are doing," Mr. Marion said, "or do you try and set new standards for the new tests and live with your old ones where they were?"

SEEKING CONSISTENCY

Some states, such as Arizona, have developed a single "vertical" scale that summarizes student achievement across grade levels, at least in grades 3–8.

Such scales, according to Robert W. Lissitz, a professor of education at the University of Maryland College Park, assume that tests at different grade levels focus on similar math or reading concepts even though they measure different content. Students are expected to improve on the scale each year as their math or reading skills increase.

But Mr. Lissitz and other assessment experts say that vertical scales are hard to construct and are based on questionable assumptions about how common the content really is across grades.

He and others advocate what they call "vertically articulated" or "vertically moderated" standards. Such methods rely on a combination of human judgment and statistical analyses. They consider both the content standards and test difficulty in each grade, along with data on how students actually perform, to set cutoff scores.

The assumption, said Mr. Marion of the Center for Assessment, is that if 50 percent of a state's 3rd graders are proficient in mathematics, "and you don't think 4th grade math is all that different, your best guess is 50 percent of the kids should be proficient in grade 4, too."

"That's not deterministic," he said. "It allows you to set a starting point."

"A PURPOSEFUL ACT"

In Michigan, for example, curriculum standards were revised in 2004, based on the NCLB testing requirements, so that grade-level expectations are now more rigorous and specific. The state not only added new tests in grades 3, 5, 6, 7, and 8, but also shifted from a spring to a fall testing date.

The state plans to set performance standards and cutoff scores for the new tests in late December and early January. As one step in that process, said Ed Roeber, the state's testing director, committees will review books in which test items are arranged in order of difficulty and determine where to set the proficiency bar.

Those books also will show where that bar would be placed to maintain a level of proficiency consistent with that in adjacent grades. What the committees decide from there is really unconstrained, Mr. Roeber said.

"Even at the grades where we've had tests, the committees could set standards higher or lower," he said. "We don't want them to do it by accident; we want it to be a purposeful act."

For now, said Mr. Lissitz, "nobody has a real solid answer" on the best method for making such judgments.

"It's a hard thing, because the models that we have are being developed as we speak," he said. "Right now, we have answers, but they're not as satisfactory as they will be in a couple of years.

1. In reference to Lynn Olson's article, to what extent has the No Child Left Behind Act changed standardized testing in your school system? If its requirements have forced your school system to add tests to previously non-tested gap years, how do these tests fit in to the previous testing system?
2. Using your own state or district as an example, can you identify the objectives, indicators, and benchmarks for student progress in the core subject areas?
3. Using your district or school as a case study, discuss the challenge of improving alignment between standards, curriculum, and instruction. What are the challenge in aligning academic standards and student assessment?
4. In your school system, can you identify the mechanisms that are put in place to support the improvement of instructional practices? Are these mechanisms evenly distributed across all the schools? How would you think about improving these support mechanisms?

CHAPTER SIX

Assessment and Measurement of Progress

LEARNING OBJECTIVES

- Recognize the central role of student assessments in educational-accountability reform.
- Understand the necessity to determine whether the intended purpose of assessments corresponds with what existing assessments are capable of measuring.
- Discuss the types of student assessments available for educators, including norm-referenced tests, criterion-referenced tests, tests aligned with academic standards, and formative assessments.
- Address the technical issues that are associated with testing, such as reliability and validity, that determine how effective the tests will be in assessing student learning and performance.
- Describe the ways assessments are used to measure changes in student performance. Educational leaders will need to have a good understanding of these fundamental testing issues in order to contend with the reporting and monitoring requirements of educational accountability that are discussed in the next chapter.

■ INTRODUCTION

While educators have always made use of some form of testing to measure student achievement, assessment in educational accountability serves a more fundamental and systematic purpose. First, educational accountability holds students to higher academic expectations in terms of content coverage and promotion of high-order thinking skills. In turn, educational accountability requires high-quality assessments capable of providing educators with reliable and valid information regarding student progress in attaining pertinent academic content and thinking skills. Second, based on outcomes from student assessments, educational accountability maintains that educators must change their instructional practices and make educational decisions that benefit student learning. For educators to make the improvements in instructional practices demanded by educational accountability, assessments will have to measure appropriate indicators of student performance. And third, educational accountability makes use of student assessment outcomes to assign rewards and consequences for student performance. If students and schools are to be held to high-stakes accountability based on outcomes from assessments, it is imperative that the assessments measure student performance with reliability and validity. Educational accountability will not succeed if educators believe that the work they put into providing students with high-quality learning opportunities is not reflected in student outcomes on assessments. In effect, whether we consider large-scale assessments or on-going evaluations that teachers use in their classrooms, educational accountability necessitates that the measurement of student performance is aligned with the purposes of education, including high-quality academic content and high-order thinking skills.

The demands that educational-accountability reform places on assessing student performance differ dramatically from the ways tests have typically been used in the education system. Assessments in educational accountability should be distinguished from our traditional conception of a single test determining student performance. Sirotnik and Kimball (1999) state, "a test is a single way of getting a sample (and thus a limited amount) of information about what a student knows or is able to do in reference to a specified domain of knowledge or behavior" (p. 210). There is an undeniable appeal in using tests to measure the effects of large-scale educational reform. Linn (2003) comments that tests are relatively inexpensive, can be externally mandated, can be implemented quickly, and provide visible results. However, the use of a single test is limited in its ability to provide adequate information about student performance. Alternatively, assessments require multiple measures of the indicators of student performance that determine student attainment of academic content standards and a frame of reference for interpreting and judging acceptable performance (Ryan, 2002).

Given the central role of student assessments in educational-accountability reform, it is necessary to determine whether the intended purpose of assessments corresponds with what existing assessments are capable of measuring. In this chapter, we first discuss the types of student assessments available for educators, including norm-referenced tests, criterion-referenced tests, and tests aligned with academic standards. Second, we address the technical issues of testing, such as reliability and validity that determine how effective the tests will be in assessing student performance. Finally, we describe the ways assessments are used to measure changes in student performance. Educational leaders will need to have a good understanding of these fundamental testing issues in order to contend with the reporting and monitoring requirements of educational accountability that we discuss in the next chapter.

In the era of results-driven goals and high expectations for students, educational leaders must have the knowledge and skills to lead their schools toward the effective use of student assessments. Making use of student assessments in educational accountability depends on educational leaders understanding how assessments function in order to gauge student progress toward academic standards. In addition, educational leaders will need the technical skills to translate student outcome data into appropriate decisions for their schools (Anthes, 2002). In this chapter, we provide educational leaders with information regarding effective student assessments that correspond with the goals of educational accountability.

▌ TYPES OF STUDENT ASSESSMENTS

Educational accountability demands that assessments be able to measure student progress in attaining academic standards, inform educators' instructional practices, and determine the assignment of sanctions. As educational accountability may entail severe consequences for many students and schools, it is imperative that assessments accurately reflect the work of educators and students in achieving the academic standards. In light of the nature of educational accountability, the question undoubtedly emerges as to whether existing assessments are capable of meeting the rigorous demands of educational accountability. More specifically, can assessments measure student attainment of academic standards and provide educators with information to make judgments regarding acceptable student performance? We can say for certain that one test alone will not realize the multipurpose nature of assessment in educational accountability. In particular, large-scale external assessments may be unable to measure the academic content and curriculum covered at the local level, while classroom-based assessments may be unable to systematically assess what students should know and be able to do concerning academic standards. However, the use of multiple indicators of student performance may provide enough pieces of information to gauge student performance in regards to the academic standards, as well as allow educators to make informed improvements in instructional practices (Linn, 2003; Sirotnik & Kimball, 1999; Thompson, 2001).

The types of large-scale tests available in the education system and the purposes of these tests have shifted dramatically over the years. Prior to the 1960s, large-scale testing was limited and functioned primarily to evaluate individual students and curricula with few systematic implications for poor performance (Hamilton & Koretz, 2002). With the enactment of the Elementary and Secondary Act (ESEA) of 1965 came the legislative mandate that Title I be continuously evaluated for program effectiveness. In turn, ESEA gave rise to the use of standardized or norm-referenced tests to measure student achievement (Linn, 2003). The standardized tests allowed for the comparison of students receiving compensatory educational services with a national sample of students. At the same time, the National Assessment of Educational Progress (NAEP), or the Nation's Report Card as it is referred to, was designed to conduct regular criterion-referenced assessments of what students know and can do in subject areas, including mathematics, reading, writing, science, geography, U.S. history, social studies, civics, and arts. In the 1970s, minimum-competency tests were advanced at the state level to contend with public opinion about dismal levels of performance in the public schools. The tests set out to establish levels of basic skills and create remediation mechanisms for poor performance (Marion & Sheinker, 1999). In addition, minimum-competency tests initiated the practice of measurement-driven instruction where large-scale tests provide information to educators to facilitate changes in instructional practices (Popham, Cures, Rankin, Sandifer, & Williams, 1985). While minimum-competency tests remain in many states in the form of assessments to determine academic promotion between grade levels and high school graduation or exit exams, researchers have found that the tests may contribute to students' decision to drop out of school (Griffin & Heidorn, 1996; Jacob, 2001; Roderick & Engel, 2001).

Large-scale standardized achievement tests have drawn criticism from educators and policymakers who believe that they should not be used to make high-stakes decisions because they are limited in their ability to measure student attainment of high-quality academic standards. Additionally, evidence from countries using curriculum-based external exams suggests that when assessments are based on academic content standards, they may improve the processes of teaching and learning (Bishop, 1996). As a result, the 1990s brought about the development of tests aligned to standards and curriculum. Hamilton and Koretz (2002) comment:

> *The use of test-score information in a standards-based system requires that performance be reported based on what students have accomplished rather than where they rank among their*

peers. It also requires that assessments accurately reflect what is communicated by the stan-
dards; in other words, that standards and tests be well aligned. (p. 22)

While tests that are aligned with academic standards are the most likely to meet the purposes of assessment in education accountability, the commonly administered norm-referenced tests will continue to be used to measure student performance. In addition, formative and alternative assessments in the classroom provide continuous information about student performance when aligned with the academic-content standards. Educational leaders should be familiar with the way each type of student assessment operates to determine the multiple indicators of student performance that will provide enough information to make improvements in instructional practices. In this section, we describe norm-referenced tests, criterion-referenced tests, and formative assessments.

Norm-Referenced Tests

Norm-referenced tests measure student performance on a broad range of academic content with test items that can differentiate between high and low achievers. Norm-referenced tests include the Iowa Test of Basic Skills (ITBS), the Stanford Achievement Test (SAT), and the California Achievement Test (CAT) including TerraNova. Academic content covered by the tests is typically taken from a selection of national textbooks rather than from content and curricula developed at the state or district level (Huitt, 1996). This may lead to a disconnection between what is taught and what is covered in the test, as well as the unintended consequence of teachers teaching to the content tested.

Norm-referenced tests are designed to provide student performance scores that can be compared and ranked with a sample of the target population, such as a national sample of the grade level tested. Testing organizations administer the test with a representative sample of students in each grade level and these students remain the normed group for five to seven years (Bond, 1996). Test questions are typically multiple-choice and selected from different difficulty levels to distribute students along a normal, or bell, curve so that most students score around the average while fewer students score at the top or the bottom of the curve (Popham, 1975). Moreover, normally distributed curves indicate that half of students score below the average while half of the students score above the average (see Figure 6.1).

Raw test scores from norm-referenced tests provide the number of questions answered correctly by a student. However, a raw norm-referenced test score does not provide information about what a student knows or is able to do. The raw score has to be converted into a derived score corresponding with the normal distribution curve in order to give the test score meaning. In turn, representative samples of students provide a frame of reference for norm-referenced test scores. How much a student knows is determined by the student's ranking in relation to a representative group. The derived test scores are reported with percentile ranks, grade equivalents, standard scores, and stanines. Percentile ranks range from 1 to 99 and represent a score that tells the student what percentage of students in a representative group scored lower on the same test. For example, a student in third grade with a national percentile rank of 81 scored higher than 81 percent of third grade students in the nation. Table 6.1 illustrates national percentile rank scores at the state, district, and school levels for third grade mathematics and reading on the Iowa Test of Basic Skills (ITBS). The results indicate that third grade students in the state and the district scored higher than a national sample of third grade students in both reading and

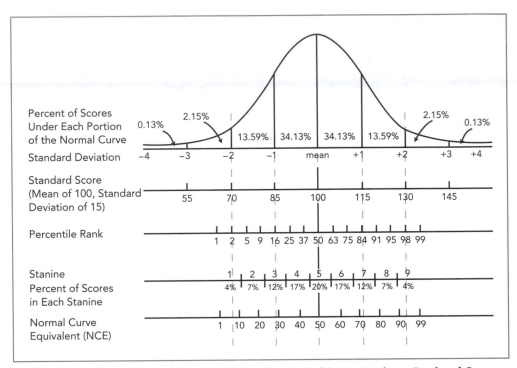

FIGURE 6.1   The Normal Curve and Its Relationship to Various Derived Scores

mathematics. At the school level, though, third graders' percentile rank scores suggest that students scored lower than 50 percent of the nation's third graders in mathematics and reading between 2001 and 2003. As the normed national group may change between years, we cannot make inferences about changes in percentile ranks over time.

Grade-equivalent scores are based on a developmental scale that report student performance in a decimal number representing the grade level and month of a typical student with the same performance. For example, a fifth grade student with a grade equivalent score of 7.3 indicates that the student has the same level of performance as the median seventh grader in the third month of a ten-month academic year. While grade equivalent scores measure developmental growth by suggesting that a student would increase by 1.0 each year, students with high grade-equivalent scores for their grade level reflect high levels of performance rather than the recommendation that the student should be moved to another grade level.

In norm-referenced tests, standard scores use the normal curve to report student performance in terms of how many standard deviations the test score is from the mean test score (Hamilton & Koretz, 2002). Standard scores can be in the form of z scores (mean = 0, standard deviation = 1), standard score scale (mean = 100, standard deviation = 15), or normal curve equivalents (mean =.50, standard deviation = 21.06). A student has the same standard score with a z score of 1, a standard score scale of 115, and a normal curve equivalent score of 71.06. In addition, this standard score equates to a percentile rank of 84 (see Figure 6.1). Stanine scores also correspond with the normal curve. Stanines represent nine broad intervals and can be used as rough indicators of student performance.

TABLE 6.1   Iowa Test of Basic Skills (ITBS) National Percentile Rank, 3rd Grade Reading and Mathematics

| | Reading | | | Mathematics | | | | Reading/ |
| | | | | Concepts & | Problems/ Data | | | Math |
	Vocabulary	Comprehension	Total	Estimation	Interpretation	Computation	Total	Composite
National								
	50	50	50	50	50	50	50	50
State								
2000			56				63	60
2001	56	58	57	62	66	61	64	61
2002			57				66	62
2003			58				67	63
2004			58				67	63
2005			58				66	62
District								
2000	66	69	68	75	79	69	77	73
2001	64	67	65	77	79	71	77	71
2002	64	66	65	76	80	66	76	71
2003	67	68	67	77	80	66	77	72
2004	67	67	67	78	80	70	78	73
2005	68	68	68	78	82	71	79	74
School								
2000	48	57	53	54	61	59	60	57
2001	36	42	39	40	48	52	47	43
2002	43	47	43	53	58	38	51	47
2003	48	46	47	52	52	38	48	48
2004	49	52	50	56	57	48	55	53
2005	53	53	52	57	65	58	60	56

Source: Compiled by authors from, Bellevue School District. (2005). *State third grade testing program*. Retrieved on June 5, 2005 from, http://www.bsd405.org/ITBS3.pdf.

Norm-referenced tests are limited in that they cannot provide adequate information to educators about individual student performance in any particular subject area or academic standard. In addition, educators need to be mindful that norm-referenced tests are susceptible to test biases. In order to create a set of test items capable of discriminating between high and low achievers, norm-referenced tests may select questions that bias against certain groups of students by covering culturally partial content or skills attained at home rather than in school. Moreover, students can take advantage of norm-referenced tests by learning test-taking skills and memorizing key content. Given the limitations of norm-referenced tests, though, they should not be used to determine if students have met the academic standards of educational accountability.

Criterion-Referenced Tests

Criterion-referenced tests are designed to measure and provide outcome data on how well a student has learned a specified set of knowledge and skills. Criterion-referenced tests are standards-based when the content on the test is appropriately aligned with the learning expectations of high-quality academic standards. Reeves (2002b) comments, "standards-based performance assessments force educators to come to grips with this central question: What do we expect of our students?" (p. 40). The National Assessment of Education Progress (NAEP) is an example of a standards-based, criterion-referenced test. In response to the standards-based reform movement and federal legislation, each state has adopted standards-based, criterion-referenced tests, such as the Florida Comprehensive Assessment Test (FCAT), the California Standards Test (CST), and the Idaho Standards Achievement Tests (ISAT). In addition, independent testing organizations like the Northwest Evaluation Association (NWEA) are providing school systems with criterion-referenced tests aligned with state academic standards. As criterion-referenced tests are intended to measure whether students have learned specific knowledge and skills, they differ from norm-referenced tests in terms of the content covered, the design of test items, and the interpretation of test scores (Huitt, 1996).

While the content covered by norm-referenced tests is generally broad and detached from curriculum and instruction at the local level, criterion-referenced tests can be designed to reflect the knowledge and skills students should know and be able to do in order to display mastery of the academic content. However, unless a district contracts with a testing organization to design criterion-referenced tests for their local content and instructional goals, criterion-referenced tests are being adopted at the state level to match state academic standards. To meet the demands of educational accountability, educational leaders at the district and school levels will have to make certain that the state tests have not omitted academic content deemed important at the local level. As it is likely that the state standards-based tests will not cover all of the pertinent academic content, educational leaders will have to assist teachers to develop classroom level assessments to fill in the gaps.

With regard to test questions, criterion-referenced tests design and administer an adequate number of test items to ensure that the test can reliably report on individual student achievement in each academic content area. In addition, test items are not designed so that only a small portion of students will be able to answer the items correctly. Instead, test items for each academic area are similar in the level of difficulty to provide an accurate index of individual mastery of the content. As a result, criterion-referenced tests do not place students in competition with one another. Criterion-referenced tests allow for all students to achieve high levels.

Rather than interpreting the meaning of test scores by comparing them to test scores from a representative group of students, criterion-referenced tests report student performance in terms of predetermined levels of performance and cut scores. For standards-based tests, the levels of performance correspond with fixed levels of performance standards, such as basic, proficient, and advanced. For example, we list the levels of performance NAEP has established for each subject area tested in Table 6.2. In Table 6.3 we present a rubric NAEP has designed to describe how students will meet the expectations of the performance levels for the subject area of reading in grades four and eight. The table also includes cut scores established by NAEP for each of the levels of performance at each grade level. As test scores for NAEP range between 0 and 500 with an average score of 250 anchored at grade eight, cut scores determine the range of test scores that corresponds with each performance level. For example, the cut point for the basic performance level in fourth grade reading is 208. This means that students with test scores

TABLE 6.2   NAEP Achievement-Level Definitions

Basic	Partial mastery of prerequisite knowledge and skills that are fundamental for proficient work at each grade.
Proficient	Solid academic performance for each grade assessed. Students reaching this level have demonstrated competency over challenging subject matter, including subject-matter knowledge, application of such knowledge do real-world situations, and analytical skills appropriate to the subject matter.
Advanced	Superior performance.

Source: Compiled by authors from, National Center for Education Statistics, http://nces.ed.gov/nationsreportcard/.

below 208 are identified as below basic on the criterion-referenced test, whereas students with scores between 208 and 238 have achieved the basic level of performance. In turn, test scores in criterion-referenced tests can be interpreted in terms of the knowledge and skills students have attained based on expected levels of performance.

Criterion-referenced test scores can also be used to assess trends and measure achievement gaps over time. Figure 6.2 and Figure 6.3 present the long-term trends in NAEP scale scores by race/ethnicity for reading and mathematics, respectively. If we take a look at the trends in reading, it is evident that each student group has made gains in average scale scores over the years. However, the cut score for proficiency in fourth grade reading is 238, which is well above the scale scores for white, black, and Hispanic students. In terms of achievement gaps, black and Hispanic students have made improvements in their average scale scores and reduced the achievement gap with white students. For example, the gap between black and white students was 35 scale-score points in 1999 and that has been reduced to 26 scale-score points in 2004. Hispanic students have reduced the scale-score difference from 28 points in 1999 to 21 points in 2004. For fourth grade NAEP mathematics, the basic level of academic performance has a cut score of 214, while proficiency is 249 and advanced is 282. If we look at Figure 6.3, it is evident that white students on average are approaching the proficiency level of performance in mathematics with a scale score of 247 in 2004. Black and Hispanic students are also making gains in average scale scores toward proficiency, as well as reducing the achievement gap with white students. Examining criterion-referenced test scores in this manner can provide information for making comparisons between students and identifying areas where educators need to make improvements in instructional practices.

While individual test scores from a criterion-referenced test provide educators with specific information regarding student progress toward attaining academic content, test scores can also be expressed as the percentage of students in a school, district, state, or the nation who meet each of the performance levels. NAEP allows us to look at data from students across the nation, though similar strategies can be used with state, district, or school level data. Figure 6.4 and Figure 6.5 display the percentage of students at or above each of the performance levels for reading and mathematics, respectively. If we take a look at the percent of students who attained proficiency in reading, we can see that between 1992 and 2003 roughly 30% of students in fourth and eighth grade achieve at the proficient or advanced levels of performance. The NAEP data indicate the troubling finding that for over a decade 70% of our nation's students have failed to attain proficiency in the knowledge

TABLE 6.3   NAEP Performance Levels and Cut Scores, Reading

Grade 4	Basic (208)	Fourth-grade students performing at the *Basic* level should demonstrate an understanding of the overall meaning of what they read. When reading text appropriate for fourth-graders, they should be able to make relatively obvious connections between the text and their own experiences and extend the ideas in the text by making simple inferences.
	Proficient (238)	Fourth-grade students performing at the *Proficient* level should be able to demonstrate an overall understanding of the text, providing inferential as well as literal information. When reading text appropriate to fourth grade, they should be able to extend the ideas in the text by making inferences,drawing conclusions, and making connections to their own experiences. The connection between the text and what the student infers should be clear.
	Advanced (268)	Fourth-grade students performing at the *Advanced* level should be able to generalize about topics in the reading selection and demonstrate an awareness of how authors compose and use literary devices. When reading text appropriate to fourth grade, they should be able to judge text critically and, in general, to give thorough answers that indicate careful thought.
Grade 8	Basic (243)	Eighth-grade students performing at the *Basic* level should demonstrate a literal understanding of what they read and be able to make some interpretations. When reading text appropriate to eighth grade, they should be able to identify specific aspects of the text that reflect overall meaning, extend the ideas in the text by making simple inferences, recognize and relate interpretations and connections among ideas in the text to personal experience, and draw conclusions based on the text.
	Proficient (281)	Eighth-grade students performing at the *Proficient* level should be able to show an overall understanding of the text, including inferential as well as literal information. When reading text appropriate to eighth grade, they should be able to extend the ideas in the text by making clear inferences from it, by drawing conclusions, and by making connections to their own experiences—including other reading experiences. *Proficient* eighth-graders should be able to identify some of the devices authors use in composing text.
	Advanced (323)	Eighth-grade students performing at the *Advanced* level should be able to describe the more abstract themes and ideas of the overall text. When reading text appropriate to eighth grade, they should be able to analyze both meaning and form and support their analyses explicitly with examples from the text; they should be able to extend text information by relating it to their experiences and to world events. At this level, student responses should be thorough, thoughtful, and extensive.

Source: Compiled by authors from, National Center for Education Statistics, http://nces.ed.gov/nationsreportcard/.

and skills of reading based on high-quality academic content standards. While the fourth and eighth grade students who demonstrated proficiency in mathematics in 1990 was at a dismal low of 15%, the percent of students attaining proficiency has since increased to around 30% in 2003. As a criterion-referenced test, NAEP is able to inform educators

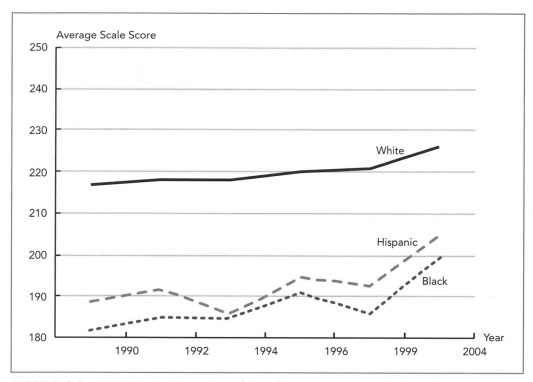

FIGURE 6.2   NAEP Long-Term Trend Reading, Average Scale Score by Student Group, Grade 4

Source: Compiled by authors from, National Center for Education Statistics, http://nces.ed.gov/nationsreportcard/.

that students are not mastering the knowledge and skills that correspond with high-quality academic standards.

Of course, criterion-referenced tests are based on the content and performance levels from academic standards in question and the quality of those academic standards can vary widely (Linn, 2000; Kingsbury, Olson, Cronin, Hauser, & Houser, 2003). Recent research from RAND suggests that performance levels for proficiency on academic standards may not be as challenging as performance levels from NAEP academic standards (McCombs, Kirby, Barney, Darilek, & Magee, 2004). In Figure 6.6 we present findings from the RAND study that indicate the percentage of students meeting proficiency on state standards-based assessments is much higher than those meeting proficiency on NAEP for fourth grade reading. The range in differences in percent proficient ranges from seven percentage points in South Carolina to as high as 69 percentage points in Mississippi. Even in states where the highest percentages of students meet proficiency in reading on NAEP, such as Connecticut, Massachusetts, New Jersey, and Colorado, the percentage point differences are 26, 50, 40, and 50, respectively. In turn, while criterion-referenced tests are better equipped to provide information to educators regarding student progress toward

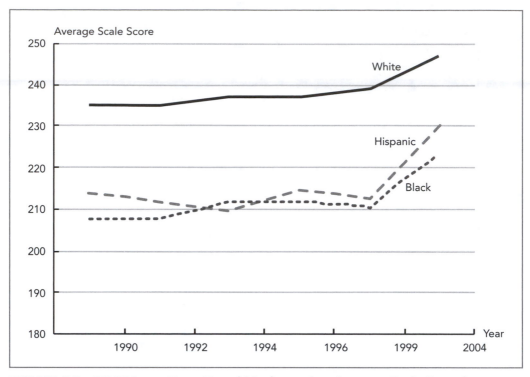

FIGURE 6.3   NAEP Long-Term Trend Mathematics, Average Scale Score by Student Group, Grade 4

Source: Compiled by authors from, National Center for Education Statistics, http://nces.ed.gov/nationsreportcard/.

academic standards, the content and performance levels that provide the basis of criterion-referenced tests need to be at a level of quality that will produce useful results for educational accountability.

The way in which criterion-referenced tests are designed allows for the measurement of student accomplishments toward specified academic content. As the tests are based on academic and performance standards, they encourage educators to reference student progress in terms of what is expected of students rather than merely making comparisons with other students. However, criterion-referenced tests still do not entirely fulfill the requirements for assessments in educational accountability. If tests are administered at the end of an academic year, they will not provide information to educators throughout the year to improve instructional practices. Criterion-referenced tests may indicate students' overall progress toward meeting academic standards, but educations will need to develop and adopt standards-based assessments at the classroom level to conduct on-going evaluations of student progress. Additionally, like any large-scale assessment, criterion-referenced tests can be limited by issues of reliability and validity. Later in the chapter we address the reasons why reliability and validity are so important to developing assessments for educational accountability.

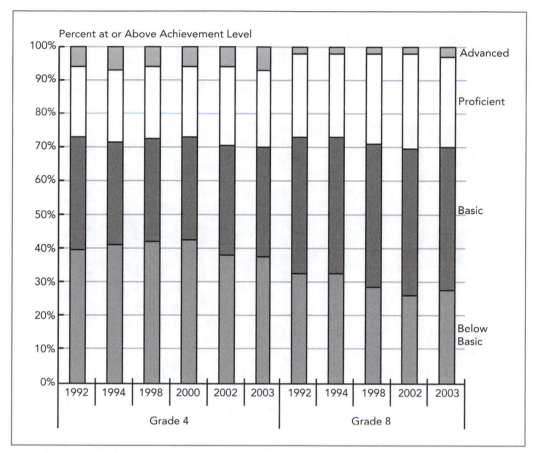

FIGURE 6.4   NAEP Performance Levels, Reading

Source: Compiled by authors from, National Center for Education Statistics, http://nces.ed.gov/nationsreportcard/.

Formative Assessments

Unlike norm-referenced or criterion-referenced tests that may only be administered once or twice a school year, formative assessments in the classroom allow for frequent and continuous assessment of student progress. On-going evaluations in the classroom or the school allow educators the opportunity to identify student needs and make adjustments to instructional practices on a more regular basis. While educators can administer formative assessments as often as they wish, developing effective assessments that support the efforts of educational-accountability reform require purposeful planning and decision making. Stiggins and Conklin (1992) comment:

> *Each investigation of the teaching process arises out of a model or conceptualization of teaching and learning. Every model of effective teaching requires that teachers base their instructional decisions on some knowledge of student characteristics. We begin to comprehend the complexity*

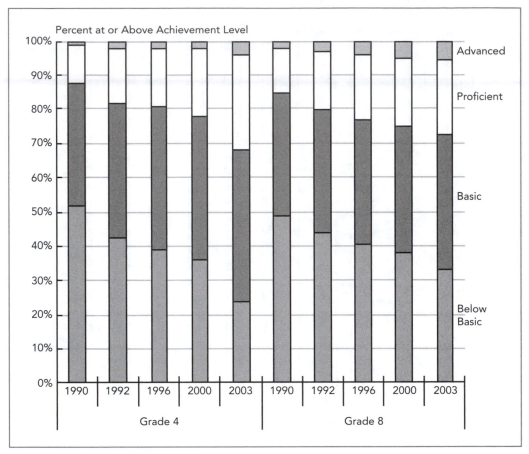

FIGURE 6.5   NAEP Performance Levels, Mathematics

Source: Compiled by authors from, National Center for Education Statistics,
http://nces.ed.gov/nationsreportcard/.

> *of classroom assessment as we explore the amount of assessment, the range and frequency of teachers' decisions and the plethora of student characteristics teachers must consider in making those decisions. (p. 20)*

The strength of formative assessment rests in its ability to provide frequent information regarding student progress. The reality that educators are inundated by instructional decisions suggests that formative assessments in educational-accountability reform will be most useful when they are aligned with the academic content standards.

In addition to providing ongoing feedback on student learning, formative assessments allow for multiple indicators of student performance. Multiple indicators provide more accurate measures of student progress by permitting students additional chances to demonstrate their understanding. Formative assessments that use multiple, *authentic* indicators

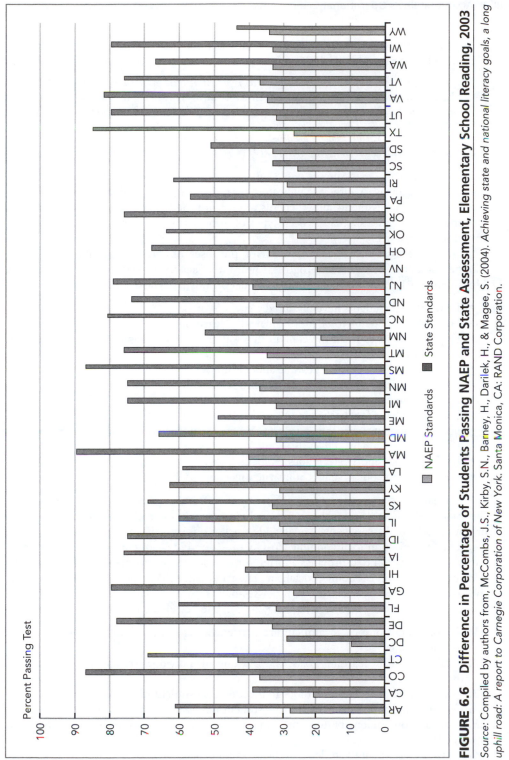

FIGURE 6.6   Difference in Percentage of Students Passing NAEP and State Assessment, Elementary School Reading, 2003

Source: Compiled by authors from, McCombs, J.S., Kirby, S.N., Barney, H., Darilek, H., & Magee, S. (2004). *Achieving state and national literacy goals, a long uphill road: A report to Carnegie Corporation of New York.* Santa Monica, CA: RAND Corporation.

of student learning greatly expand the diagnostic possibilities of assessments. Darling-Hammond, Ancess, and Falk (1995) state:

> *[Authentic assessments] are designed to be truly representative of performance in the field . . . The tasks are contextualized, complex intellectual challenges involving the student's own research or use of knowledge in "ill-structured" tasks requiring the development and use of meta-cognitive skills. They also allow appropriate room for student learning styles, aptitudes, and interests to serve as a source for developing competence and for the identification of (perhaps previously hidden) strengths. (pp. 11–12)*

Criterion-referenced assessments based on academic standards are unable to match formative assessments with authentic indicators for measuring what students know. However, standards-based assessments allow schools to measure the progress of all students toward meeting the academic standards. Both types of information are necessary for making instructional decisions.

Formative assessments can be used for purposes besides the specific question of whether students have made progress toward the academic standards. For example, McMillan (2001) identifies a list of the potential purposes of classroom assessment:

- To identify if students have mastered a concept or skill
- To motivate students to be more engaged in learning
- To get students to learn the content in a way that stresses application and other reasoning skills
- To help develop a positive attitude about a subject
- To communicate to parents what students know and can do
- To communicate expectations to students
- To give students feedback about what they know and can do
- To show students what they need to focus on to improve their understanding
- To encourage student self-evaluation
- To determine report card grades
- To evaluate the effectiveness of instructional approaches (p. 5)

Formative assessments may be formal or informal, depending on the purpose (Foriska, 1998). Formal assessments may include a quiz, homework assignments, or a journal entry. Informal assessments may include teacher observations or interviews.

The Organisation for Economic Co-Operation and Development (OECD), an international organization that provides a forum for democratic governments to compare policies and practices on economic, social, and environmental challenges conducted an extensive review of research on formative assessments in the classroom and designed a framework with six key elements (OECD, 2005). The key elements include:

1. Establishment of a classroom culture that encourages interaction and the use of assessment tools
2. Establishment of learning goals, and tracking of individual student progress toward those goals
3. Use of varied instruction methods to meet diverse student needs
4. Use of varied approaches to assessing student understanding
5. Feedback on student performance and adaptation of instruction to meet identified needs
6. Active involvement of students in the learning process (pp. 46–51)

These elements of formative assessment identified by OECD are entirely compatible with the intentions of educational accountability to improve the practices of teaching and learning. When educators use formative assessment together with standards-based assessments, they will be better prepared to make informed instructional decisions.

■ TESTING ISSUES: RELIABILITY AND VALIDITY

In order to make use of student assessments to inform instructional practices and assign high-stakes accountability consequences, the tests must demonstrate reliability and validity. Test reliability indicates the internal consistency of tests and provides information about how well test scores remain stable from one testing instance to another. Reliability is desirable since we want test scores to be constant measures of student performance over time. Test validity, on the other hand, denotes the extent to which test items reflect a specified content domain. Evidence of validity demonstrates that the content covered reflects the knowledge and skills of the academic standard that the test is supposed to measure. While reliability and validity are necessary components of student assessments when using tests to make consequential decisions, one test alone will not have high enough levels of validity and reliability to justify high-stakes decisions (Thompson, 2001). Rather, high-stakes decisions should be made based on multiple tests and indicators of student performance to increase levels of reliability and validity. In this section, we describe factors that have an effect on the levels of reliability and validity on student assessments.

Reliability

The rationale underlying reliability is that a test should produce the same score even if the student takes the test on a different day or is administered a version of the test with a different sample of test items. In other words, chance effects should not have a significant influence on test scores (Le & Klein, 2002). Le and Klein (2002) identify four factors that can reduce test reliability, including item sampling, transitory variables, rater agreement, and test length and format. Testing organizations typically develop a bank of questions where each test item is supposed to be comparable in measuring student knowledge and ability in a given content area. When samples of test items are selected for different versions of a test, item sampling can reduce reliability if a student does better on one set of questions over another set. Transitory variables are one-time factors independent of the sample of test items that may attenuate reliability and impact test scores. Kane, Staiger, and Geppert (2002) refer to transitory variables as nonpersistent changes that occur as a result of factors such as the time of day the test was administered, disruptive students in the classroom, fire drills, or the weather. Reliability depends on how disturbing the transitory variables are to students. Rater agreement refers to the degree to which test scores on open-ended questions and essays are subject to differences in opinion regarding student performance. Inter-rater reliability can be enhanced when effective performance and scoring rubrics are adopted and raters are trained to use them. With test length, longer tests with a larger number of test items will produce more reliable test scores since students have more opportunities to demonstrate mastery of the knowledge and skills being measured. In terms of test formats, multiple-choice tests will produce more consistent results. However, open-ended questions or essays are capable of assessing knowledge and skills that multiple-choice questions measure, which suggests that reducing reliability will have to be weighted against other aspects of testing, such as appropriately measuring indicators of student performance.

The dependability of test scores can be estimated through the use of several reliability tests (Le & Klein, 2002). Reliability can be examined through parallel forms reliability by administering a student two or more forms of the test and correlating the scores to see if they are highly related with one another. Alternatively, the same test can be given to a student on two occasions and those test scores can be tested for correlation, which is called test-retest reliability. Finally, the test items within a single version of the test can be assessed for internal consistency by determining correlations between test items, such as by using Cronbach's coefficient alpha or latent variable modeling. For each of the reliability estimates, the coefficient of reliability is determined by variability in what the test items measure and measurement error (DeVellis, 2003). Reliability increases as variability and measurement error in test items are diminished.

Validity

While reliability refers to whether test scores are constant indicators of student performance, validity signifies the degree to which the test items reflect the specified content domain. In regards to validity and the academic content domain, Baker and Linn (2002) ask, "Is the definition of the content domain to be assessed adequate and appropriate? Does the test provide an adequate representation of the content domain the test is intended to measure?" (p. 6). The adequacy and appropriateness of the content domain are of concern for validity as the more specific and concrete the academic content standards are, the easier it will be to develop corresponding test items. In turn, broadly defined academic standards will reduce test validity. Additionally, if the selection of academic constructs influences instruction, it is important that tests measure high-quality academic standards (Linn, 2000). The extent to which test items represent the academic content becomes a critical issue when test scores are used to make consequential decisions from inferences about student progress. The validity of test scores can be tested for convergent validity, which determines how well test items measure the same content domain, and discriminant validity, which provides evidence that test items measure different concepts (Crocker & Algina, 1986; Loehlin, 2004). In effect, test validity becomes an issue of fairness as students and schools should only be held accountable for academic content that has been well-defined and measured by valid assessments.

Reliability and validity are testing issues that establish the underlying usefulness of student assessments in making high-stakes accountability decisions. Long, multiple-choice tests may produce more reliable test scores, whereas open-ended or essay questions will provide greater validity in covering content. As it is unlikely that one test will have suitable levels of reliability and validity to make high-stakes decisions; using test scores from multiple tests may meet the assessment demands of educational accountability. Multiple indicators of student performance will provide more generalizable and accurate information to make decisions about instructional practices and assign rewards and consequences.

■ MEASURING CHANGE IN STUDENT PERFORMANCE

While measuring student progress toward meeting high-quality academic standards in the course of an academic year with reliability and validity provides relevant information for making changes to instructional practices, high-stakes decisions in educational accountability operate by assessing change in student performance over time. In turn, it is important for educational leaders to understand that there are different methods for measuring change in student performance that vary in terms of comparing average achievement year-to-year or gains in achievement over time. Furthermore, the methods can be distinguished by the unit of analysis. Specifically, changes in student performance can be aggregated to the school level or disaggregated to the grade, subgroup, or individual level. In this section, we discuss the features, including the benefits and limitations of using the different methods for measuring change in student performance.

Measuring Change in Average Achievement

The most common method used to measure change in student performance is to examine changes in average achievement scores from one academic year to the next. This method is referred to as a status model and it uses a longitudinal cross-sectional approach in which the average achievement of a cohort of students is compared to the average achievement of the same cohort composed of different students in the following year. The cohort of students can include all students in a school, students in a fixed grade level, or students in a subgroup, such as race/ethnicity, eligible for free/reduced-price lunch, or English language learner. In educational accountability, the status model is used to compare the percentage of students in a fixed grade level or subgroup who meet proficiency on the standards-based assessment year to year. For example, a school may compare the percentage of students in fourth grade who achieve proficiency on the standards-based assessment to fourth graders in the next academic year. The grade level in the comparison stays the same while the students are different. While most states are using the status model to make high-stakes decisions about schools under NCLB, the status model uses an imperfect measure of change in student performance that may produce a set of unintended consequences, such as misidentifying schools as failing to meet specified levels of improvement in student performance. The primary concerns with the status model include sampling variation when comparing different students each year, aggregate achievement scores unadjusted for student demographics, and the inability to distinguish improvement that occurred in the academic year from cumulative educational experiences.

First, the status method for measuring changes in student performance places too much emphasis on single-year changes in average achievement that are susceptible to volatility in test scores due to sampling variation and nonpersistent one-time factors (Kane & Staiger, 2002). The issue with sampling variation is that when the sample of students in a fixed grade level differs from year to year, it creates nonrandom fluctuations in tests scores that increase the volatility of the school's average achievement score. Most educators have had experience with cohorts of students differing year to year as a result of a variety of factors, such as heterogeneous student population, attitudes toward school, teacher-student dynamics, and high rates of residential mobility. Moreover, sampling variation and testing fluctuation within a school is heightened when student sample sizes are small. The nonpersistent factors we described earlier in this chapter, such as a fire alarm, the time of day the test is administered, and disruptive students, can also affect fluctuations in average achievement scores. While average achievement at the school level in an individual academic year can be measured with a high degree of reliability, Kane and Staiger (2002) find that when measuring changes in average achievement year-to-year, nonpersistent factors account for 58% of the variation in test scores from small schools and 29% of the variation in test scores from large schools. In turn, it is not difficult to imagine how high-stakes decisions in educational accountability that are based on changes in a school's average achievement may misclassify schools as failing to make improvements in student performance.

The second issue with the status model is that it fails to adjust for student demographic variables, such as previous academic achievement and socioeconomic status. Educational accountability theory promotes the notion that all students can learn and their background characteristics should not be used as excuses for lower academic expectations. Hanushek and Raymond (2002) discuss how the theory of educational accountability has been put into practice:

> In reaction, explicit goals of narrowing and eliminating the existing gaps have been translated into status accountability models built on unadjusted aggregate scores. This confuses goals with the incentives of accountability systems, because each school finds that incentives include aspects of performance that it does not control. Put another way, if one school has students who come to school with poorer preparation than another, that school must meet a higher standard in terms of its value-added to student learning. (p. 11)

While educators should not hold low-achieving or disadvantaged students to lower academic expectations, student demographic variables should not be ignored when making comparisons in student performance. Even with status models, adjustments for student background variables will give educators a clearer picture about student progress and the impact of instructional practices on students over the course of an academic year.

The final concern with status models for measuring changes in student performance is that a comparison of average achievement does not allow educators to determine the source of the change. Changes in average achievement from one year to the next could be the result of the different samples of students, the instructional practices, or some unknown factor. For example, a change in the percentage of fifth grade students in a given school who meet proficiency could be due to the school hiring a new fifth grade teacher, or maybe the fourth grade team of teachers made significant improvements in their teaching practices so that the second cohort of fifth graders were better prepared when they started the academic year. However, it is not possible with status models to distinguish between the possible causes of the change in average achievement, which, in turn, means that educators will not have adequate information to make good instructional decisions to improve student learning.

While many states are using status models to measure changes in the percentage of students who meet academic proficiency from one academic year to the next, status models will not provide educators with the information necessary to make effective instructional decisions to improve student performance. Furthermore, high-stakes accountability decisions that are based on status models of measurement may misidentify schools as failing to meet performance standards. Several states and districts have adopted alternative methods for measuring changes in student performance that allow for an examination of gains in academic achievement between school years. We discuss the models that measure gains in achievement in the following section.

Measuring Gains in Achievement

In contrast to status models that examine changes in average achievement in successive cohorts at the school or grade level, methods for measuring gains in achievement assess the progress of individual students over time. In order to measure gains in achievement, students will need to be tested annually and be given individual identifying codes to track test scores longitudinally. As states now have to annually test students for educational accountability, this requirement is not as much of a burden as was a decade ago. With the gains in achievement method, educators can determine how much an individual student has progressed toward academic standards over the course of an academic year rather than simply knowing whether the student met academic proficiency. In addition, as students are compared with their own achievement in previous academic years, educators can distinguish between prior learning and the learning that occurred in the given school year (Thum, 2003). Thum and Bryk (1997) claim that the principal advantage to measuring gains in achievement is "that for a range of intra-individual variation, the student *acts as his or her own control*. Properly adjusted, the student gain score measures the amount of learning added during the period of instruction (or schooling) between testing" (p. 107). In turn, measuring academic gains presents educators with information that can effectively inform instructional practices to improve student learning.

While measuring gains in achievement provides educators with clear data on student-level progress toward academic standards, the individual student gains in achievement can be aggregated to the grade or school level for more accurate reflections of changes in student achievement than what the status method provides. Hanushek and Raymond (2002) comment, "This approach provides the highest level of precision because it controls for family differences and differences in student body composition, and it isolates the year-over-year contribution of schools to student performance" (p. 15). Measuring individual student gains in achievement and aggregating the results to the school level captures the most information about what occurs in the school over time.

While all states currently use the status model to determine student progress toward meeting academic standards under NCLB legislative mandates, several states have submitted proposals to the U.S. Department of Education to use growth models instead, including Massachusetts, Oklahoma, Minnesota, and Tennessee (Olson, 2005a). In general, these states want to provide alternative opportunities for schools to demonstrate improvement in student performance, particularly in schools with a large percentage of low performing students.

As states move closer to using achievement gains to measure student progress, there are limitations to the method. Ballou (2002) describes several limiting factors when using achievement gains analysis in accountability systems. First, measuring achievement gains does not completely control for measurement error and the statistical processes for estimating the measurement error complicates the transparency of the data. Second, achievement gains analysis is biased toward large amounts of data, which favors gains in large schools over small schools. Third, factors beyond school quality, such as student background characteristics may still impact growth rates in the progress of student learning. And fourth, making comparisons between gains in student learning is limited by determining the differences in difficulty between test items. In addition, it may take considerable explanation to clarify the meaning of measuring achievement gains to significant stakeholders, such as educators and parents.

Measuring gains in student achievement is an improvement on the status method for measuring change in student performance that the federal level requires states use to make high-stakes educational accountability decisions. While the technical methods for measuring achievement gains need to be further improved, data from achievement gains provide information to educators that reflect what occurs in schools and classrooms over an academic year. Educators can use this information to understand what students know and are able to do and then to make significant improvements in their instructional practices to improve student learning.

Summary

- In the era of results-driven goals and high expectations for students, educational leaders must have the knowledge and skills to lead their schools toward the effective use of student assessments.
- Making use of student assessments in educational accountability depends on educational leaders understanding how assessments function in order to gauge student progress toward academic standards. In addition, educational leaders will need the technical skills to translate student outcome data into appropriate strategies and policy decisions to support school and district improvement.

Editorial and Discussion Questions

The following editorial discusses the introduction of a longitudinal study of Coloradoan public school students as the next education reform step now that they are reaching set standardized test score levels. The legislation requires all school systems to participate in tracking students using randomly assigned student identification numbers so that they can be tracked from one school to the next. It enables a more long-term and accurate study of student progress through grades as long as experts correctly set advancement standards. With this data, parents and teachers can assess where their students stand and how they have attained knowledge over the years. Also, it shows how effective individual schools are.

Stay on Reform Track

Editorial
The Denver Post, January 13, 2002

Like *The Little Engine That Could*, education reform in Colorado has been chugging up the mountain, headed for designated peaks.

With each milepost passed—state standards, state tests, school accountability reports—the train has come closer and closer to one of its key destinations.

Now it has reached the critical point. It's time for Colorado to get on board with longitudinal tracking—measuring each student's academic growth year to year. That valuable data can be mined to diagnose student needs and gauge teacher and school effectiveness.

Current measurements—of a school's third-grade reading scores one year vs. its third-grade scores the next year—are a futile exercise, comparing entirely different sets of kids. With longitudinal tracking, each pupil would be followed from third to fourth grade to determine whether he actually attained a year's worth of academic growth.

Such tracking has been the target from the start. But it's tricky business. It can't come soon enough—and it mustn't be done too quickly.

The solution to that conundrum already has been crafted, however, by state Rep. Keith King, R-Colorado Springs. He will introduce legislation to create a pilot project for longitudinal tracking. Schools could participate voluntarily until 2005–06, when the program would become mandatory.

The beauty of the pilot project is that it will buy the state time to work out all the inevitable bugs of this mammoth undertaking.

For example, a system of student identifiers must be created, assigning each student a secret code that allows individualized tracking in and out of any school yet ensures complete confidentiality.

Also, experts must determine what constitutes a year's growth. Kids with unsatisfactory achievement may progress dramatically, while advanced kids likely won't. So someone must determine appropriate growth for each level of student, then adjust state ratings accordingly.

King would have the Colorado Department of Education review proposals, then contract with outside experts to annually calculate each student's growth in reading, writing and math.

For parents and teachers, this means learning where your kid stands today—and how much growth has been attained. For all citizens, it means getting ratings on where schools stand—and whether they've improved or declined.

Such specifics would greatly enrich Colorado's school accountability reports, and they would give teachers the diagnostic tools to help students.

Myriad experts—in the education department, school districts and higher education—eagerly anticipate the onset of tracking, and they salute King for tapping their expertise. We salute him, too. State leaders would be crazy not to take the next positive step in education reform.

1. In reference to the *Denver Post* editorial, does your school system accumulate longitudinal data on its students? What do you see the significance of collecting, analyzing, and providing such data to teachers and administrators to be within your school system?
2. From the perspective of school leadership, what are the benefits and limitations of the norm-referenced and the criterion-referenced tests?
3. What accounts for the differences between proficiency on NAEP and student proficiency on state standards-based assessments?
4. What is your view on the "status model" for measuring changes in average student achievement?
5. In your current responsibility, how do you plan to use information on achievement gains and achievement gaps?

Reporting, Monitoring, and Consequences in Systems of Educational Accountability

LEARNING OBJECTIVES

- Understand that in the U.S. education system, states and districts have only recently begun to implement educational accountability systems designed to address the intricate relationships between reporting, monitoring, and consequences.
- Recognize that the federal No Child Left Behind (NCLB) legislation has driven the development of educational accountability systems across the nation. There is a need for educational leaders to comprehend the structure of accountability systems as prescribed by NCLB legislative mandates.
- Pay attention to the federal provision in disaggregating and reporting school-level data for subgroups including economically disadvantaged students, students from major racial and ethnic groups, students with disabilities, and limited english proficiency (LEP) students.
- Discuss the minimum percent-proficient targets that states must develop for each content area, participation in assessments, attendance rates, and graduation rates.
- Understand how indicators of annual progress, such as dropout rates and school report cards indicate whether students at the school level, as well as each of the subgroups within a school, have made progress toward academic proficiency, which is called adequate yearly progress (AYP).
- Examine how states determine a monitoring approach for guaranteeing 100% proficiency in the 12 years before the 2014 deadline under NCLB. In general, the states have chosen from three methods to ensure that students reach proficiency: equal yearly goals, steady stair-step, and accelerating curve.

■ INTRODUCTION

Although educational accountability is commonly viewed as a reform that places severe sanctions on low-performing schools in order to facilitate change, the threat of consequences alone will not improve instructional practices nor bring about significant increases in student performance. Using pressure to motivate change in schools is a fundamental component of educational accountability only when it is used in combination with high-quality academic and performance standards, assessment tools that accurately measure school quality, autonomy and flexibility for educational leaders, and most importantly, sufficient support to make improvements in processes of teaching and learning. In effect, we need to move away from thinking about educational accountability as a mechanism for punishing low-performing schools. Instead, educational accountability should provide educators with a framework that sets high academic expectations and guides the process of making changes to instructional practices to benefit student learning. While some educational leaders and schools may be able to develop and adopt their own systems of internal accountability to improve student performance, large-scale improvement in the education system will entail a broader system for ensuring that schools respond to the demands of educational accountability. Specifically, systems of educational accountability are designed to evaluate school progress toward meeting academic standards and implement a set of pressure and support mechanisms in schools identified as struggling to meet the needs of their students. The processes of reporting and monitoring school progress should function as the infrastructure for assigning incentives, rewards, and sanctions.

Federal education legislation prior to NCLB had established many of the reporting and monitoring instruments that are associated with the NCLB legislation for holding schools receiving Title I funds accountable, including the development of school report cards, adequate yearly progress, and stages of school improvement. However, state-level compliance with the legislation prior to NCLB was uneven and often lax in terms of making sure that all students were included and identifying schools who failed to meet adequate yearly progress after two consecutive years. Mintrop and Trujillo (2005) suggest that states failed to embrace accountability mechanisms before they became compulsory with NCLB due to the responsibility and political costs that accompany sanctions, as well as the possibility that severe consequences do not motivate educators as intended. For example, severe sanctions that are not balanced with corresponding support may put too much pressure on schools that are already struggling to secure principal and teacher commitment. Instead of motivating educators to improve practices, severe sanctions may lead to low morale, dissatisfaction, or educators leaving the school. Moreover, Mintrop and Trujillo (2005) comment, "identifying low performing schools has put the spotlight on glaring capacity deficits in these schools that a motivation strategy alone cannot remedy. This in turn brings issues of fairness and attribution to the fore" (p. 10). The concerns regarding sanctions in educational accountability are indeed warranted when the system for reporting, monitoring, and assigning rewards and sanctions is not linked directly with the provision of adequate support to help low-performing schools make significant improvements. As systems of educational accountability are now compulsory with NCLB and apply to both Title I and non–Title I schools, educational leaders at each level of the education system have the responsibility to make certain that sufficient support is available for low-performing schools to meet the pressures and demands of educational accountability.

In this chapter we describe how educational accountability systems operate in terms of reporting academic achievement, monitoring school progress, and assigning rewards and sanctions for improvements in student performance. The critical issue for systems of educational accountability is making sure that the mechanisms for reporting and monitoring are capable of detecting when educators make improvements in their instructional practices that lead to improvements in student learning. For educational accountability to motivate educators to make substantial and sustained improvements in the processes of teaching and learning, educators must see a direct relationship between their practices for improving student performance and relief from the sanctions of accountability. Baker and Linn (2002) note that accountability must "ensure that changes in performance (the proverbial bottom-line) are real, are due to quality instruction plus motivation, are sustainable, and can be attributed to the system itself" (p. 4). In effect, reporting, monitoring, and implementing consequences must be sensitive to improvements in the quality of instruction and the effort of students.

The federal education system, states, and districts have only recently begun to implement educational accountability systems designed to address the intricate relationships between reporting, monitoring, and consequences. NCLB legislation has driven the development of educational accountability systems across the nation. In turn, we will primarily discuss the structure of accountability systems as prescribed by NCLB legislative mandates given that these are the systems educational leaders need to be familiar with. However, it is important to keep in mind that the systems of accountability that have emerged from the NCLB legislation may not be perfect examples of how accountability systems should function. Educational leaders will need to be familiar with the assumptions and goals of educational accountability in order to determine whether the systems of educational accountability will provide enough of an incentive for schools to change their instructional practices. For example, the NCLB legislation has been very specific about how to report and monitor school progress, as well as the benchmarks for applying rewards and sanctions. However, NCLB is less specific about informing schools about the best practices for making significant improvements in student learning. Educational leaders at the district and school levels will be responsible for filling in the gaps of the systems of educational accountability with knowledge and skills about effective practices for low-performing schools, as well as high-quality professional development in order to significantly improve the processes of teaching and learning. Only when sanctions are matched with adequate support will educational accountability work to improve student learning.

■ ACCOUNTABILITY SYSTEMS: REPORTING

Systems of educational accountability rely on accurate and frequent reports of results from student assessments in order to provide information for a variety of educational decisions. For example, educational leaders and teachers need reports of the progress in student achievement to make decisions regarding instructional practices that meet the specific needs of their students. District- and state-level administrators need reports of each school's progress toward meeting the academic standards in order to assign sanctions and rewards and to determine which schools will require additional support and assistance. Additionally, parents need reports of student and school outcomes to select the school where they will send their children. As a result, accountability systems must establish the frequency of data collection, as well as the level of the education system at which data will be collected and reported (Adams & Kirst, 1999). In general, the state, district, and schools all collect data on various indicators of student progress toward meeting the academic standards. It is the responsibility of the state to use the data collected from each level to develop annual school report cards that indicate the status of each school in meeting annual objectives toward proficiency on the academic standards. In this section we describe the process of reporting and the information it provides in systems of educational accountability.

Academic Standards, Performance Standards, and Assessments

The reporting component of educational accountability operates by providing clear, frequent, and accurate information to educators about students' progress toward achieving proficiency on academic standards. For this reason, the impact of reporting hinges on the development of high-quality academic and performance standards, as well as student assessments that measure what students know and are able to do. Unless reporting is based on academic standards that reflect high expectations for all students and assessments that are able to measure student progress toward attaining the standards, the reporting process will not produce information that can be beneficial for educators as they make decisions about their instructional practices. While it may seem obvious that reporting depends on the quality of standards and assessments, we stress the intricate interrelationship between components of educational accountability to underscore what it will take to make educational accountability successful in bringing about improvements in student learning.

Reporting begins with the state's academic and performance standards. Every school must annually report the percentage of students who attain the performance level of proficiency in the content areas of language arts and mathematics. By the 2007–2008 school year, schools will also have to report the percentage of students meeting proficiency in science. As we discussed in Chapter 6, standards-based assessments should be designed to measure student progress toward attaining proficiency with the academic standards. According to NCLB, states are expected to produce individual, diagnostic, descriptive, and interpretive reports for schools based on student-level achievement from the standards-based assessments. The state-level reports should provide individual student test scores for the content areas and each of their subcategories. Test scores from standards-based assessments correspond with predetermined levels of performance, or proficiency levels. In turn, data from the state reports can be used to determine the percentage of students within a school who meet proficiency.

In addition to the individual student reports of academic achievement, the state, or the district in some cases, produce annual school report cards that compare the aggregated percentage of students in each school who achieve proficiency on standards-based assessments with a state target for proficiency. The school report cards also include minimum targets for attendance rates, as well as graduation and dropout rates for high schools. If a school meets all of the state targets for proficiency, it will not be identified as in need of improvement. However, if a school misses one or more of the state's minimum targets for proficiency, it will be identified as in need of school improvement. The annual school report cards must be made publicly available and accessible for parents and the community.

The primary purpose of the school report cards is to provide academic achievement and attendance data that is used to assign accountability-based awards and sanctions. The reports provide supplementary pieces of information that are not used for determining accountability consequences. Rather, the additional information is intended to assist educators in the process of making changes in instructional practices. These data include percentages of students who achieve each level of proficiency at each grade level.

The state reports provide specific information on student progress toward proficiency on academic standards, but as a single indicator of student achievement, they are limited. For one, results from the standards-based assessments are reported once, maybe twice, in an academic year to reduce the testing burden for students and teachers. Educators will need to use their own ongoing student assessments to supplement the reports from the state. Specifically, data from the state reports should be integrated by educators with local measures of student achievement to inform instructional decisions that address the academic needs of students. Additionally, the timing of when state standards-based assessments are administered creates a tradeoff between providing schools with student-level data in a time frame that will be useful and having enough time in the school year to cover the academic content on the assessments. For example, if a state administers the test early in the academic year in order to prepare individual reports that can be used to inform academic decisions before the school year ends, students may not show as much progress toward meeting the standards simply because they did not have a full academic year to prepare. On the other hand, if tests are administered later in the academic year to provide additional instructional time for content coverage, educators may not receive the individual reports until the summer and in turn, not be able to use them to make academic decisions until the following school year. For these reasons, individual reports of student achievement from the state provide valuable information about student progress, but they will need to be supplemented by teacher assessments to ensure that the types of improvements in instructional practices that educational accountability entails are carried out. We discuss the use of individual student reports to make educational decisions further in Chapter 8.

Aggregated and Disaggregated Data

Each school receives individual student standards-based assessment reports from the state to inform decisions on instructional practices. However, the unit of analysis for assigning awards and sanctions in educational accountability is not the student, but rather the school. Educational accountability decisions for rewards and sanctions are based on school-level data including the percent of students proficient in each content area, student participation in testing, attendance rates, graduation rates, and dropout rates. Additionally, schools must report the progress of students in the following subgroups: economically disadvantaged students, students from major racial and ethnic groups, students with disabilities, and limited english proficiency (LEP) students. In turn, student-level data must be aggregated to the school level and then disaggregated from the school level to subgroups for the purposes of educational accountability reporting.

To aggregate student level data to the school level, the number of students who attain proficiency is divided by the number of students in the grade levels tested. For example, a K–8 school must test all students in grades three through eight in the content areas of language arts and mathematics. If the school has 50 students per grade level, 300 of the 450 students at the school should be tested. If 30 students per grade level meet proficiency in math, then 180 students meet proficiency in this content area at the school-level. We divide 180 by 300 to get the percentage of students who attain proficiency, or 60%. The state's minimum target for proficiency in mathematics might be 75% indicating that the school with 60% of its students attaining proficiency would not meet the state target. Since the school missed at least one of the state's targets for proficiency, it would be identified as in need of school improvement.

Although many states had been generating school report cards prior to NCLB, the federal legislation enacted a fairly groundbreaking policy mandate in terms of disaggregating and reporting school-level data for subgroups including economically disadvantaged students, students from major racial and ethnic groups, students with disabilities, and LEP students. In effect, schools must show the percentage of students in each subgroup who attain proficiency in the academic content areas tested. The policy intends to provide more specific information to educators regarding how students are doing in their school. Moreover, disaggregating school-level data by the subgroups may serve to highlight acute gaps in achievement within schools. Hall, Wiener, and Carey (2003) report that they have found schools identified as academically successful under educational accountability policies before NCLB that would no longer be considered successful due to severe gaps in academic proficiency between subgroups within the schools. For example, the researchers point to a middle school in Florida that received an "A" under the state accountability system prior to NCLB because roughly half of the students across the school were proficient in reading and mathematics. The school was made up of 31% white, 59% black, and 57% low-income students. While 90% of the white students achieved proficiency in reading and mathematics, the black and low-income students achieved around 22% in reading and 15% in mathematics. These findings demonstrate the potential for large achievement gaps between subgroups within a school.

According to both NCLB and the Individual with Disabilities Act Amendments of 1997 (IDEA), students with disabilities are required to participate in district and state assessments. Support for the inclusion of students with disabilities in large-scale assessments has come from parents, policymakers, and researchers. In particular, researchers found that many students were being excluded from assessments that they could participate in if given accommodations, such as braille or sign language, testing in multiple sessions or in small-group or individual sessions, flexible scheduling, and extended time (Olson & Goldstein, 1997). Typically, the students' individual education plan (IEP) will designate whether the student takes the assessment with no accommodations, with accommodations, or with an alternative assessment (Roeber, 2002). The test scores of students with disabilities are aggregated and included in the school level determination of AYP.

Included in the reporting of disaggregated data by subgroups is the mandate that 95% of students in each subgroup be tested on the state standards-based assessments. NCLB does not require that disaggregated data be reported in schools in which the number of students in a subgroup is insufficient to yield statistically reliable information or if the results would reveal personally identifiable information about a student. States are left to determine the minimum number of students, or minimum "n", in a subgroup needed to meet these guidelines. Not surprisingly, states have interpreted and responded to the guidelines in different ways. Selecting a minimum number of students for the reporting of subgroups can be complicated as it involves both statistical and political issues. States must decide whether to set a high minimum "n" that will guarantee statistical significance, but place the accountability burden on large schools, or set a low minimum "n" that will result in unreliable outcomes, but identify more schools and subgroups (CCSSO, 2002).

In general, states are using three approaches to determine the minimum "n" for subgroup size (Pierce, 2003). The first approach identifies a fixed minimum number that will apply to all subgroups in all schools across the state. For example, Florida has established the minimum subgroup size at 30 students. The fixed minimum numbers range from five in Maryland to 100 in California (Pierce, 2003). The second method sets a desired statistical confidence interval such as 95% or 99%, which then allows the minimum number to vary based on the size of the subgroup within each school. Montana sets its confidence interval at 95% rather than determine a fixed number for the subgroup. The third approach combines the first two methods, such that a fixed minimum number is selected, but it will be tested to make sure that it fits within a statistically significant confidence interval. For example, Utah sets the minimum subgroup size at 10 students, but also uses a confidence interval of 99% to ensure statistical significance. In general, the states are evenly split between the first and third approach. Montana is the only state to only use confidence intervals exclusively (Pierce, 2003).

Reporting in systems of educational accountability require that student-level data be aggregated to the school-level, as well as disaggregated to critical subgroups within the school. Student-level data is aggregated to the school-level because accountability rewards and sanctions are based on overall school performance. However, school-level data is disaggregated to subgroups within the school to ensure that average schoolwide test scores, testing participation, attendance rates, and graduation rates do not conceal the performance of students who have not traditionally done well in our education system. More importantly, disaggregated data provides strong evidence to educators about the status of each subgroup within the school, which can emphasize areas that need to be targeted for improvements in instructional strategies.

Adequate Yearly Progress

The minimum targets that states must develop for percent proficient in each of the content areas, participation in assessments, attendance rates, graduation rates, and dropout rates are indicators of annual progress. The measurable objectives of annual progress are reported in school report cards to indicate whether students at the school level, as well as each of the subgroups within a school, have made progress toward academic proficiency, which is called adequate yearly progress (AYP). According to the legislative intent of NCLB, minimum targets should be designed in annual, incremental increases to guarantee that schools reach 100% academic proficiency over twelve years, or by 2014. In developing minimum targets, states are required to identify a starting point of percent proficient and establish the annual increments it will take for schools to reach proficiency. Schools are allowed to average the percent proficient for each subgroup over two consecutive academic years, as well as over all grade levels tested in the school to calculate whether the school has made adequate yearly progress.

The process of identifying schools that do not make adequate yearly progress is regarded as a status model for measuring progress since it relies on absolute changes in proficiency levels, rather than considering gains in student achievement. For example, a student could make achievement gains equaling a grade level of improvement or more and still be below proficient. In this case, the improvement the student made over the course of the academic year would not count toward the determination of adequate yearly progress because the student is still below proficient. The U.S. Department of Education has granted waivers to several states to experiment with growth models for determining adequate yearly progress (Olson & Hoff, 2005). Growth models would give schools credit for student improvement over time by tracking individual student achievement year to year.

By and large, the reporting of adequate yearly progress is intended to make certain that schools, districts, and states systematically monitor student proficiency on the academic content standards. We further detail the process for measuring and determining adequate yearly progress when we describe how monitoring is used in systems of educational accountability.

School Report Cards

As we have discussed, school report cards are used within systems of educational accountability to present clear and pertinent information regarding the progress of students and schools in attaining proficiency on academic standards. In Table 7.1 we present a portion of the information provided in a school report card prepared for elementary schools in Illinois. The Illinois school report card displays school demographic information, a matrix for determining AYP, and data on the percentage of students in each grade level and subgroup who achieve at the different performance levels on the state standards-based assessment, the Illinois Standards Achievement Test (ISAT). The elementary school enrolls 709 students in pre-kindergarten through sixth grade. The school is composed of a diverse student population with 19.2% white, 57.5% black, 7.3% Hispanic, and 15.5% Asian/Pacific Islander students. Compared to the district and state student population, the school has a relatively small percentage of low-income students at 30.6%. For the purposes of reporting, it is important to know the number of students in the school who were tested. In this elementary school, a combined number of 211 students in grades three, four, and five were tested by the state standards-based assessment. According to the system of educational accountability designed by the state of Illinois, a subgroup at the school level must have a minimum of 40 students for statistical significance purposes in order to be held accountable for meeting adequate yearly progress. As we can see from Table 7.1, in this elementary school only the subgroups of black and low-income students have the minimum number of 40 students tested at the school level to be included in the determination of AYP. However, for simple reporting purposes, the state specifies the percentage of students by grade level and subgroup who achieve at different performance levels with a minimum of 10 students. In the third panel of data in Table 7.1 we can see that the majority of the subgroups had a minimum of ten students in each of the three grade levels tested.

Looking at Table 7.1 we find out how well this elementary school did in making adequate yearly progress toward meeting proficiency on the state academic standards. The highlighted row displays the minimum targets the state establishes for making adequate yearly progress. In both reading and mathematics, 95% of students in the grade levels tested must participate and 40% of the students must meet academic proficiency on the assessments. Additionally, students in elementary schools in Illinois must meet a minimum target of 89% for their attendance rate. Minimum targets for academic proficiency will increase every year until schools meet 100% proficiency for each subgroup. If we first examine the data aggregated to the school level, 99.5% of students tested in grades three, four, and five participated in the reading and mathematics assessments. In reading, 65% of the students tested met the performance level of academic proficiency or advanced. In mathematics, 79.3% of the students attained academic proficiency. The students had an attendance rate of 96%. At the school level, the students exceeded each of the five minimum targets for adequate yearly progress.

Looking at the two subgroups that have the minimum number of 40 students necessary to be held accountable we see that the black students have a testing participation rate of 99.2% for both the reading and mathematics assessments, while the low-income students have 100% participation. On the reading assessment, 54.9% of black students and 50.7% of low-income students meet or exceed proficiency on the academic standards. In terms of mathematics, 72.1% of black students and 68.5% of low-income students meet or exceed proficiency. For both reading and mathematics, students in the subgroups exceed

TABLE 7.1 Illinois Elementary School Report Card, 2003–2004

Demographic Variables

	White	Black	Hispanic	Asian/Pacific Islander	Native American	Low-Income	Limited-English Proficient	High School Dropout	Chronic Truancy	Mobility	Attendance	Total Enrollment
# Tested	36	127	14	33	1	76	21					211
% School	19.2	57.7	7.3	15.5	0.3	30.6	8.7		0.2	13.5	96.0	709
% District	9.1	49.7	37.6	3.3	0.2	85.2	14.1		3.6	24.4	92.3	420,322
% State	57.7	20.8	17.7	3.6	0.2	39.0	6.7		2.1	16.8	94.2	2,060,048

School AYP Report Card

	Percent Tested on State Tests				Percent Meeting/Exceeding Standards						Other Indicators			
	Reading		Mathematics		Reading			Mathematics			Attendance		Graduation Rate	
	%	Met AYP	%	Met AYP	%	Safe Harbor Target	Met AYP	%	Safe Harbor Target	Met AYP	%	Met AYP	%	Met AYP
State AYP Minimum Target	95.0		95.0		40.0			40.0			89.0		66.0	
All	99.5	Yes	99.5	Yes	65.0		Yes	79.3		Yes	96.0	Yes		
White														
Black	99.2	Yes	99.2	Yes	54.9		Yes	72.1		Yes				
Hispanic														
Asian/Pacific Islander														
Native American														
LEP														
Students with Disabilities														
Low-Income	100.0	Yes	100.0	Yes	50.7		Yes	68.5		Yes				

Percentage of Student Scores in Each Performance Level

Grade	Performance Levels	Reading 1	Reading 2	Reading 3	Reading 4	Mathematics 1	Mathematics 2	Mathematics 3	Mathematics 4	Science 1	Science 2	Science 3	Science 4
3th Grade	Overall	6.4	25.5	39.4	28.7	8.5	10.6	45.7	35.1				
	White	0.0	13.3	46.7	40.0	6.7	0.0	26.7	66.7				
	Black	10.7	35.7	33.9	19.6	12.5	16.1	57.1	14.3				
	Hispanic												
	Asian/Pacific Islander	0.0	0.0	47.1	52.9	0.0	0.0	23.5	76.5				
	Native American												
	IEP	26.7	53.3	6.7	13.3	40.0	6.7	40.0	13.3				
	Non-IEP	2.5	20.3	45.6	31.6	2.5	11.4	46.8	39.2				
	Free/Reduced Price Lunch	9.4	37.5	40.6	12.5	12.5	21.9	53.1	12.5				
	Not Eligible Free/Reduced	4.8	19.4	38.7	37.1	6.5	4.8	41.9	46.8				
4th Grade	Overall	0.0	36.3	35.3	28.4	2.0	21.6	53.9	22.5	0.0	29.7	56.3	14.1
	White	0.0	30.0	15.0	55.0	5.0	15.0	40.0	40.0	0.0	0.0	46.2	53.8
	Black	0.0	44.3	42.9	12.9	1.4	27.1	62.9	8.6	0.0	39.5	58.1	2.3
	Hispanic												
	Asian/Pacific Islander												
	Native American												
	IEP									0.0	36.4	45.5	18.2
	Non-IEP									0.0	28.3	58.5	13.2
	Free/Reduced Price Lunch									0.0	26.7	66.7	6.7
	Not Eligible Free/Reduced									0.0	30.6	53.1	16.3
5th Grade	Overall	0.0	78.9	15.8	5.3	10.5	63.2	26.3	0.0				
	White	0.0	26.5	39.8	33.7	0.0	12.0	60.2	27.7				
	Black	0.0	48.7	28.2	23.1	0.0	28.2	59.0	12.8				
	Hispanic												
	Asian/Pacific Islander												
	Native American												
	IEP												
	Non-IEP												
	Free/Reduced Price Lunch												
	Not Eligible Free/Reduced	0.0	28.6	39.7	31.7	3.2	17.5	50.8	28.6				

Source: Compiled by authors from, Illinois State Board of Education. (2005). Illinois state report cards. Retrieved on June 5, 2005 from: http://statereportcards.cps.k12.il.us/.

the 40% minimum target for academic proficiency. The students in this elementary school meet adequate yearly progress on each of the indicators for students overall, as well as the subgroups. As a result of meeting the schoolwide measurable objectives and the subgroup targets, this school would not be identified for school improvement by the state.

While the determination of adequate yearly progress is an important component to assigning accountability rewards and sanctions, the aggregated data is averaged across grade levels and over two academic years, which does not provide educators with specific enough information for making instructional decisions. In turn, many states include supplementary data disaggregated to the grade level that is not used for making AYP decisions. For example, the grade-level data will indicate the percentage of students who score at the different performance levels on the standards-based assessment. The supplementary data is incorporated into the school report cards to better inform educators about the progress of students within their school. The data should be used to assist in making instructional decisions throughout the school. In the third panel of Table 7.1, the school report card presents the percentage of students in the grade levels tested who achieve at each of the performance levels. In Illinois, level 1 corresponds with academic warning, level 2 with below standards, level 3 with meets standards, and level 4 with exceeds standards. Students who achieve at level 3 or level 4 are considered proficient on the academic standards for that subject area. Students in grades three and five are tested in reading, mathematics, and writing, while fourth graders are tested in science and social studies. NCLB requires that students in grades three through eight be tested annually in mathematics and language arts. Illinois received permission from the U.S. Department of Education to begin testing fourth graders in math and reading in spring 2006. In turn, Table 7.1 includes science, achievement data for grade four. Data from the writing and social studies assessments are not included in the table.

Looking at the data from the reading assessments, 68.1% of third graders and 63.7% of fifth graders in the school meet or exceed proficiency on the standards. We calculate the percentage meeting proficiency by adding the percentages achieving at levels 3 and 4. If we want to take a look at the subgroups within grade levels, Illinois reports the status of subgroups with a minimum of 10 students. In this elementary school, Hispanic and Native American students are not reported for third grade because there are fewer than 10 students from these subgroups in the grade level. In the fourth and fifth grades, Hispanic, Asian/Pacific Islander, and Native American students are not reported. All of the subgroups with data reported in third and fifth grades, except for students with disabilities who are categorized as having Individualized Education Plans (IEP), exceed the minimum target of 40% proficient. Nearly 80% of the IEP students in third and fifth grades fail to meet proficiency on the reading assessment. If this elementary school had more than 40 students with disabilities, the percentage proficient would be reported by subgroup for determining AYP. The data from the grade-level disaggregation suggests that this elementary school would fail to meet AYP if it had more than 40 students with disabilities. However, because this school has fewer than 40 students with disabilities schoolwide, the state only reports the information by grade level and subgroup for the purpose of improving instructional strategies in the school.

Looking at the percentage of students who meet proficiency in mathematics, we see a similar situation. All of the subgroups, except for students with disabilities in fifth grade, attain academic proficiency in math. If we look at fourth graders and their proficiency in science, we see that all of the subgroups meet the 40% minimum target set by the state.

Given the data reported in the school report card in Table 7.1, this elementary school should consider putting additional resources into instructional strategies that assist students with disabilities in reading and mathematics. Additionally, schools will want to look at the subgroups that barely meet the minimum target for academic proficiency in each of the content areas. For example, 48.7% of students identified as low income in fifth grade failed to meet academic proficiency on the reading assessment. While the low-income subgroup met the state's minimum target of 40% proficient for the academic year being reported, the school will want to pay attention to the low-income subgroup as the minimum target for proficiency will increase incrementally toward 100% in subsequent years. The low-income subgroup may have met proficiency on this report card, but if the school does not do more to improve student learning among this subgroup, the subgroup may not meet AYP when the minimum target is 50% or 60%. In the case of low-income students, the school should be receiving Title I funds to address the needs of this subgroup. In order to improve the performance of low-income students, the school may have to rethink the way that Title I resources are utilized throughout the school. In many schools Title I funds are targeted to the lower grade levels. This school may need to consider reallocating the resources to focus on the upper grade levels where low-income students are struggling.

The Illinois report card, in this example, demonstrates that states include information above what is necessary to determine whether a school has met proficiency for accounting purposes. Indeed, the disaggregated data will be of use to school leaders as they determine how to improve instructional practices to enhance student learning. However, reporting is only one component of the systems of educational accountability. States and districts are required to use the data included in school reports to monitor schools' progress toward attaining academic proficiency. In the next section we describe the process of monitoring in educational accountability.

■ ACCOUNTABILITY SYSTEMS: MONITORING

The reporting of school-level aggregated data, as well as subgroup and student-level disaggregated data is imperative to systems of accountability in order to provide school leaders and educators with information on student progress toward attaining proficiency on academic standards. While some schools have the capacity to use the data and implement internal accountability mechanisms to motivate and sustain improvements in instructional practices, systems of educational accountability function to provide the necessary incentives, goals, benchmarks, and support for schools who have not traditionally been able to substantially improve student learning. The process of monitoring schools works in conjunction with reporting of data to create a signaling system that indicates the progress schools have made in meeting academic proficiency. Specifically, states have the responsibility of designing their own systems of monitoring to provide guidelines to districts and schools for how adequate yearly progress will be determined. In this section we discuss in detail how states determine the starting points for minimum targets. We will also examine how states systematically increase minimum targets over time to meet the NCLB goal of 100% proficiency by 2014. Additionally, we describe safe harbor provisions that permit schools to meet adequate yearly progress even if they have not met all of the minimum targets for academic proficiency in an academic year.

Starting Points

The process of monitoring within systems of educational accountability relies on states developing appropriate baselines for academic proficiency that can be subsequently increased in increments to create benchmarks and guidelines for assessing adequate yearly progress toward 100% proficiency. The first year of legislative accountability mandates under NCLB is the 2002–2003 school year. As part of educational accountability under NCLB, each state was required to put together an accountability plan establishing statewide starting points that indicate the percent of students who reached proficiency in the 2002–2003 school year in language arts and mathematics. These starting points for language arts and mathematics specify how far schools within the state have to go over the course of 12 years of accountability in order to reach 100% academic proficiency by 2013–2014. In selecting a starting point, states were permitted to choose between the percent of students proficient on the state standards-based assessment in the lowest performing subgroup and the percent of students proficient in the school at the 20th percentile in the state, whichever was higher (P.L. No. 107-110, section 1111[b][2][E]). Each state found that the 20th percentile method produced the higher percentage of proficient students in language arts and mathematics.

Several states make use of the following procedure in their accountability plans to determine the school at the 20th percentile in terms of the percent of student proficient. They rank all public schools in order according to the percent of students who scored at the proficient level or above in reading in spring 2003. The same process is used to calculate the starting point for mathematics. In a table similar to Table 7.2, they record the total students in the enrollment records for each school after they have been ordered based on the percent of students who scored at the proficient level or above. Beginning with the school with the smallest percent of proficient students in reading, the cumulative enrollment is calculated. Multiply the total student enrollment for public schools (top cumulative enrollment number) by 20 percent (.20) to find 20 percent of the total student enrollment. In Table 7.2 for example, 20 percent of 1,619 is 323.8. Rounding yields 324. Count up from the school with the smallest percent of students proficient in reading to identify the public schools whose combined school populations represent 20 percent of the total student enrollment (cumulative enrollment). From Table 7.2, 20 percent of the total student enrollment is 324. To reach this number, the student populations from School X,

TABLE 7.2 Calculating the Starting Point with the 20th Percentile Method

School Name	Percent of Students Proficient in Reading and Math	Total Students in Enrollment Records	Cumulative Enrollment
School A	54%	235	1,619 (1,384 + 235)
School B	40%	400	1,384 (984 + 400)
School W	38%	587	984 (397 + 587)
School X	30%	132	397 (265 + 132)
School Y	29%	65	265 (200 + 65)
School Z	20%	200	200
Total			

School Y, and School Z are combined. The cumulative enrollment for School X is 397 (200 [School Z] + 65 [School Y] + 132 [School X]). So this is the school at the 20th percentile. Using the percent of students who scored at the proficient level in reading and mathematics from the identified public school. This percent is the minimum starting point for reading and mathematics. In Table 7.2, the minimum starting point is 30 percent (the percent of proficient students at School X).

In Table 7.3 we present the starting points states have established in their accountability plans submitted to the U.S. Department of Education. Even though all of the accountability plans have been approved, there are several states waiting for additional student achievement data in order to calculate their starting points. States decided whether to set the same starting points for all grade levels in the state or establish separate baselines for different grade levels. While the starting points may vary by content area and grade level, they are not permitted to vary by subgroups of students. For example, Florida set the starting point for all grade levels at 30.68% and 37.54% for language arts and math, respectively. Michigan, on the other hand, has determined separate starting points for elementary, middle, and high school grades in both language arts and math. It is evident from the data in Table 7.3 that there is significant variability in the starting points states determined from the proficiency of schools at the 20th percentile in each state. States like Arizona, Arkansas, Hawaii, and South Carolina have low starting points compared to states like Colorado, Georgia, and Tennessee. This means that on average, schools in the states with low starting points have to make substantially more improvement on their standards-based assessments in order to meet 100% proficiency by the 2013–2014 school year.

Intermediate Goals

Once a state has established its starting point for academic proficiency in language arts and mathematics, it must determine a monitoring approach for guaranteeing 100% proficiency in the twelve years before the 2014 deadline under NCLB. The NCLB law provides flexibility to the states to select intermediate goals for annual improvements toward proficiency. In general, the states have chosen from three methods to ensure that students reach proficiency: equal yearly goals, steady stair-step, and accelerating curve. In the equal yearly goals approach, the percent of students meeting proficiency increases in equal increments every year until the 2014 deadline for 100% proficiency. Annual equal increments are calculated by subtracting the starting point proficiency from 100 and then dividing by 12. The steady stair-step approach requires that the percent of students meeting proficiency will increase incrementally every two or three years to meet the 2014 deadline. In the third approach, states create an accelerating curve for improvement where the percent of students meeting proficiency will increase slowly in the initial years with greater gains occurring closer to the 2014 deadline. Table 7.3 indicates the approaches states selected for establishing intermediate goals in their accountability plans. Of the states that have indicated which approach they have chosen, 13 states use the equal yearly goals, 24 states use the steady stair-step, and six states use the accelerating curve.

Figure 7.1 illustrates the three approaches that are used to determine adequate yearly progress (we have diagramed the steady stair-step for both two and three years). Each of the approaches is graphed for a hypothetical state that establishes its starting point for academic proficiency at 30%. As the figures demonstrate, the approaches will have different implications for identifying schools that fail to made adequate yearly progress. With the

TABLE 7.3   2002–2003 Starting Points and Intermediate Goals

State	Intermediate Goals	Grade	Language Arts	Math
			Starting Points	
Alabama	Equal Yearly Goals	NA	NA	NA
Alaska	Equal Yearly Goals	3–10	64.03%	54.86%
Arizona	Steady Stair-Step (Two Year Increments)	3	44%	32%
		5	32%	20%
		8	31%	7%
		High School	23%	10%
Arkansas	Equal Yearly Goals	K–5	31.8%	28.2%
		6–8	18.1%	15.3%
		9–12	19.0%	10.4%
California	Equal Yearly Goals	2–8	13.6%	16.0%
		High School	11.2%	9.6%
Colorado	Steady Stair-Step (Three Year Increments)	Elementary	77.5%	79.5%
		Middle	74.6%	60.7%
		High School	80.3%	50.5%
Connecticut	Steady Stair-Step (Three Year Increments)	Elementary/Middle	55%	64%
		High School	62%	59%
Delaware	Equal Yearly Goals	All	53.9%	30.0%
Florida	Steady Stair-Step (Three Year Increments)	All	30.68%	37.54%
Georgia	Steady Stair-Step (Three Year Increments)	Elementary/Middle	60%	50%
		High School	88%	81%
Hawaii	Steady Stair-Step (Three Year Increments)	3, 5, 8, 10	30%	10%
Idaho	Equal Yearly Goals	NA	NA	NA
Illinois	Equal Yearly Goals	3	62.2%	74.2%
		5	59.1%	62.8%
		8	68.0%	52.5%
		High School	58.2%	53.6%
Indiana	Steady Stair-Step (Two Year Increments)	NA	NA	NA
Iowa	Steady Stair-Step (Three Year Increments) & Equal Goals from 2011–2014	3–5	65%	64%
		6–9	61%	63%
		10–12	69%	69%
Kansas	Steady Stair-Step (Three Year Increments)	K–8	51.2%	46.8%
		9–12	44%	29.1%
Kentucky	Equal Yearly Goals	Elementary	47.5%	22.73%
		Middle	45.6%	16.51%
		High School	19.26%	19.84%
Louisiana	Steady Stair-Step (Three Year Increments) & Equal Goals from 2011–2014	All	36.9%	30.1%
Maine	Steady Stair-Step (Three Year Increments)	NA	NA	NA
Maryland	Steady Stair-Step (Three Year Increments)	NA	NA	NA
Massachusetts	Steady Stair-Step (Two Year Increments)	All	39.7%	19.5%

State	Intermediate Goals	Starting Points		
		Grade	Language Arts	Math
Michigan	Steady Stair-Step (Three Year Increments) & Accelerating Curve from 2010–2014	Elementary Middle High School	38% 31% 42%	47% 31% 33%
Minnesota	Equal Yearly Goals	3 5	62.75% 66.17%	69.89% 65.35%
Mississippi	Steady Stair-Step (Three Year Increments)	3 4 5 6 7 8 9 10 11 12	51% 49% 43% 35% 30% 27% NA 16% NA NA	72% 49% 35% 39% 19% 23% 13% 5% 0% 0%
Missouri	Equal Yearly Goals	All	18.4%	8.3%
Montana	Steady Stair-Step (Two to Three Year Increments)	4, 8, 10	55%	40%
Nebraska	Steady Stair-Step (Three Year Increments)	4 8 11	62% 61% 66%	65% 58% 62%
Nevada	Steady Stair-Step (Three Year Increments) & Equal Goals from 2011–2014	Elementary Middle High School	32.4% 37% 91%	37.3% 38% 58%
New Hampshire	Steady Stair-Step (Three Year Increments)	3–8 High School	60% 70%	64% 52%
New Jersey	Steady Stair-Step (Three Year Increments)	4 8 11	68% 58% 73%	53% 39% 55%
New Mexico	Equal Yearly Goals	All	37%	16%
New York	Steady Stair-Step (Three Year Increments)	4 8 11	123 Annual Measurable Objective (AMO) 107 AMO 142 AMO	136 AMO 81 AMO 132 AMO
North Carolina	Steady Stair-Step (Three Year Increments)	3–8 10	69% 52%	75% 55%
North Dakota	Equal Yearly Goals	4 8 12	65.1% 61.4% 42.9%	45.7% 33.3% 24.1%
Ohio	Steady Stair-Step (Three Year Increments) & Equal Goals from 2010–2014	All	40%	40%
Oklahoma	Steady Stair-Step (Three Year Increments)	All	622 (API) Academic Performance Index, 1500 is 100%	648 API, 1500 is 100% proficient

continued

continued

State	Intermediate Goals	Starting Points		
		Grade	Language Arts	Math
Oregon	Steady Stair-Step (Three Year Increments)	All	40%	39%
Pennsylvania	Steady Stair-Step (Three Year Increments)	All	45%	35%
Rhode Island	Steady Stair-Step (Three Year Increments) & Equal Goals from 2010–2014	Elementary Middle School High School	73% 66% 60%	61% 44% 45%
South Carolina	Steady Stair-Step (Three Year Increments)	3–8	17.6%	15.5%
South Dakota	Steady Stair-Step (Three Year Increments)	K–8 9–12	65% 50%	45% 60%
Tennessee	Steady Stair-Step (Three Year Increments)	Elementary/Middle High School	77% 86%	72% 65%
Texas	Equal Yearly Goals	All	46.8%	33.4%
Utah	Steady Stair-Step (Two Year Increments)	3–8 10	65% 64%	57% NA
Vermont	Steady Stair-Step (Three Year Increments)	2, 4 8 10	385 (AMO), 500 is 100% proficient 342 AMO 345 AMO	314 AMO 287 AMO 268 AMO
Virginia	Steady Stair-Step (Two Year Increments)	All	60.7%	58.4%
Washington	Equal Yearly Goals	4 7 10	53.8% 30.8% 49.5%	30.3% 17.6% 25.4%
West Virginia	Equal Yearly Goals	NA	NA	NA
Wisconsin	Steady Stair-Step (Three Year Increments) & Equal Goals from 2010–2014	All	61%	37%
Wyoming	Steady Stair-Step (Three Year Increments) & Accelerating Curve from 2011–2014	4 8 11	30.2% 34.5% 48.4%	23.8% 25.3% 35.8%

Source: Compiled by authors from the 2003 Approved State Accountability Plans, http://www.ed.gov/admins/lead/account/stateplans03/index.html.

equal yearly goals approach, schools will have to make annual and steady gains in the percent of students who meet academic proficiency. Researchers have questioned whether it is feasible for schools to demonstrate improvement in equal annual increments (Elmore, 2003; Thum, 2003). As a result, the equal yearly goals approach may lead to more schools being identified as in need of improvement. The steady stair-step approach for two and three year increments of change presents an alternative to making adequate yearly progress decisions based on annual gains in proficiency. With the steady stair-step approach, schools will have either two or three years to meet the next increase in the benchmark for percent proficient. However, schools will have to make larger improvements at each increase in the benchmark. The reasoning behind the accelerated curve approach is that

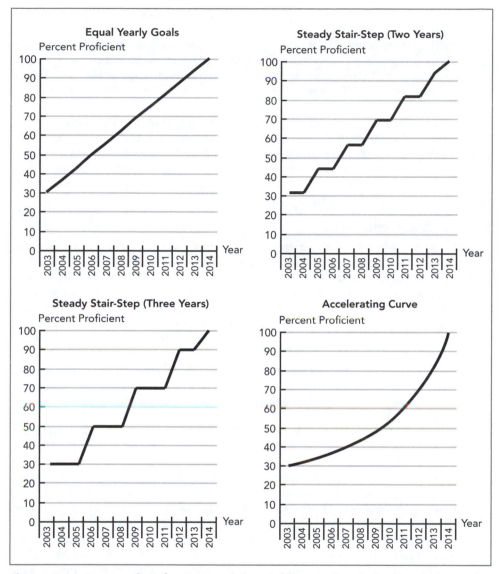

Figure 7.1   Approaches for Determining Adequate Yearly Progress through Intermediate Goals

schools will need a period of time for adjustment into the reform strategies of educational accountability before significant improvements in student performance will be demonstrated. In turn, schools in states using the accelerated curve approach may have less of a chance of being identified as in need of improvement during the early years of reform. In the later years of reform, though, schools will have to show large increases in the percent of students who attain proficiency. States may consider this approach if they believe that the educational programs, professional development, and testing mandates that will be implemented as a part of educational accountability will improve instructional practices and student learning over time.

The three approaches we discussed that set intermediate goals for determining adequate yearly progress are status models that permit states to monitor changes in the percent of students who attain academic proficiency. However, the approaches do not indicate the amount of academic improvement students in a school may make over the course of an academic year. For schools that have a low percentage of students meeting proficiency, the status model for monitoring adequate yearly progress may seem unrealistic and demoralizing. Waivers from the U.S. Department of Education that permit states to use growth models will relieve some of the burden on low-performing schools by giving them credit for gains in student academic achievement. In addition, the safe harbor provision in the NCLB law may be used by low-performing schools during the process of monitoring to review adequate yearly progress determinations.

Safe Harbor Provision

In order to make adequate yearly progress, a school must meet or exceed the minimum targets for proficiency in each of the academic content areas, as well as for the other indicators such as participation in testing, attendance, and graduation rates. The determination of adequate yearly progress also includes the safe harbor provision, which states that a school will make adequate yearly progress even if one or more of its subgroups fails to meet the minimum targets for academic proficiency if each of the subgroups that failed to meet the minimum targets have reduced failure rates by 10 percent from the preceding academic year and the subgroups have made progress on the additional indicators (P.L. No. 107-110, Section 111[b][2][I]). The safe harbor provision is applied only when a school fails to make adequate yearly progress. The safe harbor provision provides the opportunity for schools to present evidence for review after being identified as in need of improvement.

In Table 7.4 we present an example of a school that fails to meet adequate yearly progress in the 2003–2004 and 2004–2005 school year because one of its subgroups, the low-income subgroup, does not meet the state's minimum target for percent proficient in reading. This school would want to have their data reviewed by the state under the safe harbor provision. In the 2003–2004 school year, 20% of the low-income subgroup attain academic proficiency in reading, which means that 80% of the students in this subgroup failed to meet adequate yearly progress. The subgroup failed to meet the state's minimum target for proficiency is 30%. In the 2003–2003 school year, 30% of the low-income subgroup are proficient and 70% fail to meet the minimum target. The state uses a steady stair-step approach with two year increments so the minimum target is 43% in 2004–2005. The subgroup again fails to meet adequate yearly progress. However, if we calculate the decrease in the percentage of students in the low-income subgroup who fail to meet proficiency, we find that the low-income students made a 12.5% gain between academic years ($[80 - 70]/80 = 12.5\%$). If the subgroup met the minimum targets for participation in testing and attendance, then this school would make adequate yearly progress.

The safe harbor provision creates opportunities for schools that have been identified as in need of improvement to review their adequate yearly progress status. While our example included only one content area, schools will have to show that a subgroup decreases the percent failing to meet proficiency in each content area. The safe harbor provision makes meeting adequate yearly progress attainable for schools that are making significant improvements in student performance among low-performing subgroups.

TABLE 7.4   Example of School Meeting AYP with the Safe Harbor Provision

Year	Subgroup	Target Proficiency*
2003–2004	White	45%
	Black	35%
	Latino	33%
	LEP	31%
	Low-Income	20%
2004–2005	White	49%
	Black	44%
	Latino	43%
	LEP	43%
	Low-Income	30%

*State's minimum target for percent proficient in 2004 is 30%. State's minimum target for percent proficient in 2005 is 43%.

■ ACCOUNTABILITY SYSTEMS: CONSEQUENCES

The third component of systems of educational accountability is developing and implementing consequences for schools that fail to make adequate yearly progress. While educational accountability should include both rewards and sanctions for school improvement, it is the sanctions that receive the most attention. In fact, there is little discussion in state and federal responses to NCLB legislation about the types of rewards schools will receive for making significant improvements in student performance beyond being exempt from sanctions. The lack of concrete and attractive rewards for significant improvements in instructional practices and student learning contributes to the belief that district and state involvement in schools is undesirable and to be avoided at all costs. The mentality that external involvement in local schools should be avoided runs counter to the goals of educational accountability. The types of instructional changes that educational accountability calls for require that states, districts, and schools continuously work together to improve the environments of student learning with high quality professional development and effective educational programs. The schools that meet adequate yearly progress should be positively recognized with rewards besides being excused from sanctions. However, even schools that are meeting the annual minimum targets for academic proficiency will need technical assistance and support from the district and state to sustain improvement efforts. In effect, sanctions should work to motivate and support schools in improving instructional practices, but external assistance should not be viewed as a stigma for schools if educational accountability is to significantly improve student performance.

The mechanism for applying consequences to low-performing schools in systems of accountability follows a series of school-improvement processes. Throughout the stages of school improvement, progress toward academic proficiency is monitored and schools continue to the next stage of improvement if they fail to meet minimum targets or schools are removed from identification of in need of improvement if minimum targets are met in consecutive academic years. Figure 7.2 displays the full series of school-improvement stages. A school must fail to make adequate yearly progress for two consecutive academic years to be identified as in need of school improvement and begin the stages of school improvement. In the following sections we describe the consequences associated with each stage of school improvement.

School Improvement

The 2002–2003 school year was the first academic year states monitored under NCLB to determine whether schools had made adequate yearly progress by meeting all of the state's minimum targets for academic proficiency, test participation, attendance rates, graduation rates, and dropout rates. If a school received its report card in the summer of 2003 and found out that it failed to make adequate yearly progress over the last academic year, it did not immediately receive sanctions. The school would have to fail to meet adequate yearly progress again in the 2003–2004 school year to be identified by the state as in need of school improvement. It takes two consecutive academic years to be identified for improvement to give schools a chance to make necessary changes.

For example, a school may have failed to meet adequate yearly progress because it did not meet the minimum target for the percent of students participating in testing for one subgroup. As the process of determining adequate yearly progress is a signaling system, the school would know its area of weakness and could improve it in the next academic year in order to avoid being identified for school improvement. If the school made adequate yearly progress by meeting all of the minimum targets after the first year of failing, it would be removed from identification. Of course, in systems of educational accountability, schools' progress toward meeting academic proficiency is continuously monitored. Even if a school is removed from identification after the second year, in the third year the minimum targets may be increased such that the school fails to meet the minimum target for a different subgroup. In turn, this school would return to the classification of the first year of identification and would have one year to make changes before being identified as in need of improvement.

If a school fails to make adequate yearly progress for two consecutive academic years, it is classified as in year one of *school improvement*. Schools in year one of school improvement must offer public school choice to all students in the school and develop a two-year school-improvement plan (SIP). Offering public school choice to students in schools that fail to make adequate yearly progress is one of the more significant school-reform changes brought about by NCLB. However, there are certain conditions limiting the scope of school choice. Schools are required to offer school choice only if they are Title I schools. Students are only allowed to transfer to a public or charter school within their district that has not also been identified for school improvement. Additionally, the district must give priority for school choice transfers to low-performing students from low-income families. The district is responsible for paying for student transportation to the new school. If the student's original school meets adequate yearly progress for two consecutive years and is removed from school improvement, the student may return to the original school or remain at the new school until the completion of the last grade level in the new school. However, the district is not required to pay for transportation to the new school once the original school is removed from school improvement.

The second element of year one of school improvement is developing a two-year school-improvement plan (SIP). NCLB legislation stipulates that the SIP be composed of ten components. The SIP must address the specific academic issues that caused the school

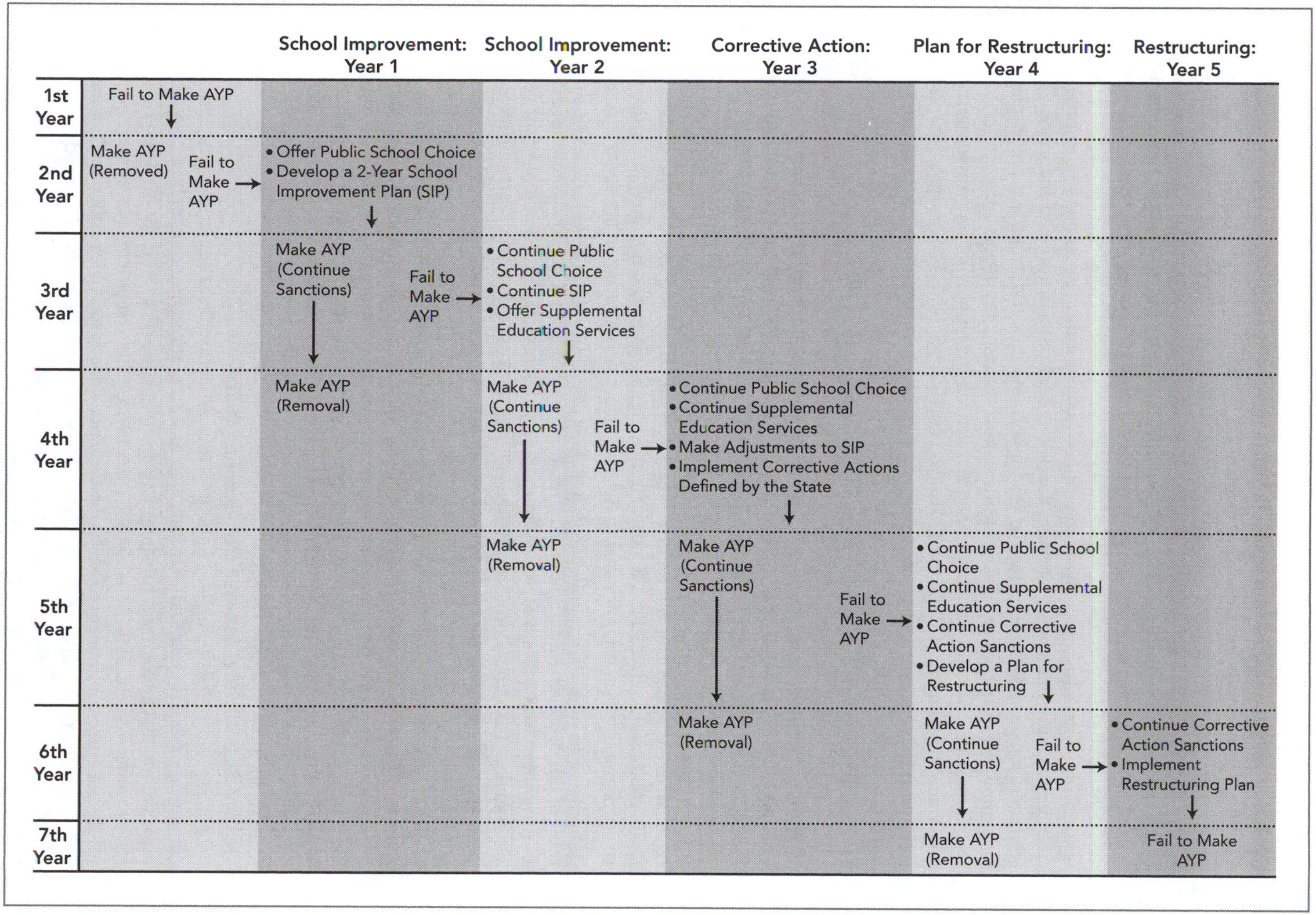

	School Improvement: Year 1	School Improvement: Year 2	Corrective Action: Year 3	Plan for Restructuring: Year 4	Restructuring: Year 5
1st Year	Fail to Make AYP ↓				
2nd Year	Make AYP (Removed) Fail to Make AYP →	• Offer Public School Choice • Develop a 2-Year School Improvement Plan (SIP) ↓			
3rd Year	Make AYP (Continue Sanctions) ↓	Fail to Make AYP →	• Continue Public School Choice • Continue SIP • Offer Supplemental Education Services		
4th Year	Make AYP (Removal)	Make AYP (Continue Sanctions) Fail to Make AYP →	• Continue Public School Choice • Continue Supplemental Education Services • Make Adjustments to SIP • Implement Corrective Actions Defined by the State ↓		
5th Year		Make AYP (Removal)	Make AYP (Continue Sanctions) Fail to Make AYP →	• Continue Public School Choice • Continue Supplemental Education Services • Continue Corrective Action Sanctions • Develop a Plan for Restructuring ↓	
6th Year			Make AYP (Removal)	Make AYP (Continue Sanctions) Fail to Make AYP →	• Continue Corrective Action Sanctions • Implement Restructuring Plan ↓
7th Year				Make AYP (Removal)	Fail to Make AYP

Figure 7.2   Stages of School Improvement

to be identified for school improvement with effective strategies; adopt policies and practices for the core academic areas that will ensure that all subgroups of students meet academic proficiency; develop professional development opportunities that directly address the academic achievement problems that caused the school to be identified for school improvement; describe how professional development funds will used to remove the school from school improvement; establish annual and measurable objectives for sustained progress by each subgroup toward attaining academic proficiency; describe how the school will provide written notice to all parents about the school's identification as in need of improvement; specify the responsibilities of the state, district, and school in improving the school; include strategies for promoting effective parental involvement; and develop a teacher mentoring program. The district must review and approve the school's two-year SIP.

In year one of school improvement, the district is responsible for providing technical assistance and support to the school. Mintrop and Trujillo (2005) comment, "high-quality support and oversight need to be an integral part of a low-performing schools program in both the school improvement and corrective action stages. The need for strong support grows in proportion to performance demands" (p. 22). The district must assist schools in this stage of school improvement in analyzing data to identify and address problems in instruction. Strategies may include the areas of curriculum alignment, classroom instruction, and test preparation. The district must also support the school in determining appropriate professional development that addresses the use of effective instructional practices for improvements in student learning.

Table 7.5 presents estimates of the number of schools by state that failed to make adequate yearly progress and the number of schools identified for school improvement in the 2002–2003, 2003–2004, and 2004–2005 school years. Even though the 2002–2003 school year was the first year schools failed to meet adequate yearly progress under NCLB, the legislation stipulates that schools identified by previous state accountability mechanisms as in need of improvement would move through the stages of school improvement more quickly. In turn, there were schools identified in the first year of NCLB as in need of improvement.

It takes two consecutive academic years of making adequate yearly progress for a school to be removed from school improvement for the same reasons that it takes two consecutive years to be identified as in need of school improvement. Schools must show evidence that improvement is sustained for more than one school year. After year one of school improvement, states monitor school progress and determine whether the school made adequate yearly progress during the first year of school improvement. As Figure 7.2 indicates, even if the school makes adequate yearly progress after the first year of being identified for school improvement, the school continues to undergo sanctions. However, the subsequent stage of improvement is delayed and the school remains under the sanctions of the present stage. Only if the school makes adequate yearly progress a second consecutive time will it be removed from identification.

If the school fails to make adequate yearly progress after the first year of being identified, the school is classified as in year two of school improvement. In year two of school improvement, schools must continue to offer school choice and follow through with the school-improvement plan. In addition, schools must offer supplemental education services to all students. Supplemental educational services are tutoring or other enrichment programs that are provided in addition to instruction in the regular school day and composed of effective strategies designed to increase academic achievement of the students involved. Schools are required to offer supplemental services if they are Title I. As with school choice,

TABLE 7.5   Schools Failing to Make AYP and Schools Identified for School Improvement

State	2002–2003*		2003–2004†		2004–2005‡	
	Fail to Make AYP	Identified for School Improvement	Fail to Make AYP	Identified for School Improvement	Fail to Make AYP	Identified for School Improvement
Alabama	71	46	1,042	83	653	472
Alaska	282	58	205	179	205	190
Arizona	351	226	319	184	270	174
Arkansas	208	126	298	305	—	271
California	3,220	925	3,213	1,626	3,504	1,752
Colorado	817	87	382	129	414	99
Connecticut	157	8	187	134	220	176
Delaware	86	12	44	43	52	42
District of Columbia	29	15	117	79	113	72
Florida	2,525	48	2,349	965	2,193	1,097
Georgia	776	258	416	413	366	345
Hawaii	199	84	133	138	187	136
Idaho	217	42	113	71	286	100
Illinois	1,718	581	—	694	1,152	725
Indiana	442	117	438	77	764	96
Iowa	145	11	115	66	134	89
Kansas	175	30	102	21	127	14
Kentucky	470	26	288	130	356	151
Louisiana	17	69	116	75	243	197
Maine	124	10	132	50	152	53
Maryland	511	131	277	256	341	246
Massachusetts	256	208	476	381	800	446
Michigan	535	410	826	450	464	503
Minnesota	144	79	472	48	284	87
Mississippi	250	7	210	71	99	81
Missouri	1,536	0	464	132	791	158
Montana	159	34	—	40	60	77
Nebraska	269	6	—	—	—	—
Nevada	146	22	210	122	289	158
New Hampshire	140	11	125	71	—	—
New Jersey	531	265	944	520	947	607
New Mexico	164	73	249	124	431	244
New York	893	715	990	713	903	813
North Carolina	1,195	35	662	160	949	203
North Dakota	47	23	45	21	47	21
Ohio	829	191	662	487	921	499
Oklahoma	337	51	—	146	54	125
Oregon	365	8	303	328	392	319
Pennsylvania	1,076	299	566	333	606	415
Rhode Island	98	22	—	39	—	—
South Carolina	652	87	455	208	578	164
South Dakota	238	32	159	106	117	110
Tennessee	711	0	235	165	115	148
Texas	1,000	13	—	199	1,020	235
Utah	246	6	142	16	115	9
Vermont	29	10	39	28	—	—

continued

continued

State	2002–2003[*]		2003–2004[†]		2004–2005[‡]	
	Fail to Make AYP	Identified for School Improvement	Fail to Make AYP	Identified for School Improvement	Fail to Make AYP	Identified for School Improvement
Virginia	732	43	460	113	353	111
Washington	436	51	326	166	448	202
West Virginia	295	33	200	37	128	38
Wisconsin	110	68	108	51	44	44
Wyoming	55	0	30	15	76	15
U.S. Total	26,014	5,712	19,644	11,008	22,763	12,329

Source: Education Week. (2004). Quality counts 2004: Count me in: Special education in an era of standards. Washington, DC: Editorial Projects in Education.

†*Source: Education Week.* (2005). Quality counts 2005: No small change: Targeting money toward student performance. Washington, DC: Editorial Projects in Education.

‡*Source: Education Week.* (2006). Quality counts at 10: A decade of standards based education. Washington, DC: Editorial Projects in Education.

priority will be given to the lowest achieving students from low-income families in the schools identified for year two of school improvement. States are responsible for developing criteria for identifying qualified supplemental educational services providers based on a demonstrated record of improving academic achievement. The states must also maintain a list of approved providers accessible to districts, schools, and parents. The district is responsible for notifying parents of eligibility to receive supplemental educational services. The district must inform parents about the services offered by each provider and their demonstrated impact on academic achievement. Districts must provide the information about providers located within the district, as well as providers located in neighboring districts.

Corrective Action

After two years in school improvement the school will be monitored to determine whether it makes adequate yearly progress. If the school makes adequate yearly progress after year two of school improvement, the school will not move forward to the next stage of improvement, but will continue to face the sanctions of the present stage. However, if the school meets adequate yearly progress in two consecutive years after being identified for year two of school improvement, the school will be removed from identification. If the school fails to meet adequate yearly progress after year two of school improvement, the school will be classified as in *corrective action*. The NCLB legislation states that schools identified in the stage of corrective action show consistent academic failure and may have underlying problems in staffing and curriculum.

In corrective action, schools must continue to offer school choice options and supplemental educational services. In addition, the district must take one of the following corrective actions against the school:

- Replace the school staff who are relevant to the failure of the school to make adequate yearly progress;

- Institute and fully implement a new curriculum based on research on effective practices;
- Significantly decrease management authority at the school level;
- Appoint an outside expert to advise the school on its progress toward making adequate yearly progress;
- Extend the school year or school day for the school; or
- Restructure the internal organizational structure of the school.

While the district is given the responsibility of selecting a corrective action strategy, the state may intervene at any point.

As of the 2004–2005 school year, very few schools have been identified as being in the corrective stage under NCLB mostly as a function of the amount of time that has passed since the legislation was passed. However, many states and districts had implemented similar sets of corrective action consequences for low-performing schools prior to NCLB. It is likely that schools that reach this stage of school improvement were involved in previous cycles of corrective action. In turn, leaders at the district- and state-levels will have to be mindful that schools may not be new to reform efforts. From their examination of corrective action strategies implemented prior to NCLB, Mintrop and Trujillo (2005) note:

> NCLB *interventions will increasingly look like a déjà vu to affected schools unless states design intervention approaches that are truly different from "all the other things" a school has already tried. Such approaches need to decrease turbulence, rather than add to it. Thus, instead of rigid staging, states and districts need flexibility in designing measures that are appropriate to the developmental needs of a given school. (p. 15)*

The comment is worth emphasizing since schools that reach corrective action will likely be the lowest-performing schools in the education system and have struggled academically prior to NCLB. Corrective action strategies must be relevant to the context of the school in order to make significant improvements in instructional practices and student learning. When school improvement reaches this stage, it becomes even more critical that the state and district provide sufficient support to schools so that the sanctions do not become harsh and ineffective strategies for bringing about substantial change in the school. The state, district, and school need to be able to work together to critically assess the status of the school and design mechanisms for improvement. This is the stage where not only the assumptions of educational accountability for improving student performance will be tested, but also educational leadership.

Restructuring

If after one year of corrective action the school makes adequate yearly progress, the school's progression through the stages of improvement will be delayed and the school will continue with the sanctions of corrective action. If the school makes adequate yearly progress for two consecutive years after being identified as in corrective action, the school will be removed from identification as in need of improvement. However, if the school fails to make adequate yearly progress after the stage of corrective action, it will continue into the *plan for restructuring* stage. In the first year after corrective action, the school will continue the sanctions involved in corrective action, including school choice, supplemental educational services, and the corrective action mechanism selected by the district. In addition, the district will develop a plan for restructuring the school. Consistent with state law, the district must make arrangements to implement one of the following alternative governance structures:

- Reopen the school as a public charter school;
- Replace all or most of the school staff (including the principal) who are relevant to the failure to meet adequate yearly progress;
- Enter into a contract with a private management company, with a demonstrated record of effectiveness, to operate the public school;
- Turn the operation of the school over to the state; or
- Any other restructuring arrangement that makes fundamental reforms to improve student academic achievement.

If the school again fails to make adequate yearly progress two years after being identified in the corrective action stage, the school will phase into the restructuring stage. Schools that have made it to this stage of school improvement have failed to make adequate yearly progress six times and have been through five years of school improvement without making significant improvements in meeting academic proficiency. In turn, the district will implement its selected alternative governance structure in the school. At this point in the stages of school improvement, the state may intervene to reform the school.

When the system of educational accountability reaches the point at which schools are completely restructured in order to make improvements in instructional practices and student learning, the state and district must be careful not to demoralize the community or diminish the school's remaining social capital. There will be schools in our education system that reach this point in the stages of school improvement and educational leaders need to be acutely aware of the context of the school and effective instructional practices that can be used to improve student performance. In the beginning of this section we noted that states have not fully defined the rewards that will be given to schools for school improvement. Schools that reach restructuring will need a wide set of incentives and motivators in order to do the work necessary to improve student performance. In turn, as the sanctions get more severe, rewards and support for improvements will become more important to the educators in these schools.

Summary

- While NCLB may not reflect the theory of educational accountability in its entirety, the federal policy has driven accountability practices across the country. Educational leaders should be familiar with the specifics of the policy to determine if there are areas that need to be changed to better reflect the intentions of educational-accountability reform.
- The chapter begins with a discussion on the mechanisms for reporting and monitoring school progress toward meeting academic proficiency in systems of educational accountability.
- The third component of systems of educational accountability is developing and implementing consequences for schools that fail to make adequate yearly progress.
- While educational accountability should include both rewards and sanctions for school improvement, it is the sanctions that receive the most public attention. In fact, there is little discussion in state and federal responses to NCLB legislation about the types of rewards schools will receive for making significant improvements in student performance beyond being exempt from sanctions.

- If a school fails to make adequate yearly progress for two consecutive academic years, it is classified as in year one of *school improvement*. Schools in year one of school improvement must offer public school choice to all students in the school and develop a two-year school-improvement plan (SIP). Offering public school choice to students in schools that fail to make adequate yearly progress is one of the more significant school-reform changes brought about by NCLB.
- If the school fails to meet adequate yearly progress after year two of school improvement, the school will be classified as in *corrective action*. The NCLB legislation stipulates that schools identified in the stage of corrective action show consistent academic failure and may have underlying problems in staffing and curriculum.

Commentary and Discussion Questions

The following commentary discusses how the No Child Left Behind Act (NCLB) may have the undesirable consequence of keeping schools segregated through its requirement of tracking the performance of certain subgroups of students. As schools integrate they much constantly monitor and report their racial make-up and "race gaps" whereas segregated schools have consistent racial profiles, that is, all-white and all-black schools. In this respect, NCLB is creating an undue burden on such schools. In addition, new accountably measures exist that track minority students without such tracking for white students. Here is a situation that creates extra administrative work for urban schools while the majority of suburban and rural school districts can use that time and those resources differently.

Subgroup Reporting and School Segregation: An Unhappy Pairing in the No Child Left Behind Equation
By Amy Ellen Schwartz, Leanna Stiefel, and Colin Chellman
Education Week, March 23, 2005

One of the more prominent features of the federal No Child Left Behind Act is the requirement that schools and districts track the performance of subgroups of students. While the law identifies several subgroups, including low-income and English-language learners, the low-performance of black and Hispanic students should be of particular concern. Ironically, because of the way the law is written, the schools and districts that could end up being most heavily penalized are those that are the most heavily integrated.

The impact of these new subgroup-reporting provisions will be felt most keenly where there is new information and new sanctions. While the provisions of the No Child Left Behind law will require some states to create accountability systems from scratch, prior to the federal legislation many states already publicly reported school performance, and many also imposed some type of sanctions on low-performing schools. So then, where will the new subgroup reporting yield new information? Only in integrated schools, which, of course, are the only ones to have racial subgroups. And where will there be new sanctions? Only in integrated schools that are performing adequately but have sizable subgroups that are not, or in integrated schools that are only occasionally performing below par, but have subgroups that are persistently performing inadequately. Unfortunately, there will be no new information based on subgroup reporting in segregated schools. New accountability for a "race gap" in performance is limited to a subset of integrated schools and districts. The law brings little additional pressure to bear on the significant gap in performance between schools that are racially segregated, at least in the early years before strict sanctions take place.

But this is far from being just a theoretical reporting problem. Our research in New York state reveals that the problem is large indeed. More than 40 percent of New York state schools with 4th graders served only white students in 2001–2002, and over 20 percent served only nonwhite students, meaning that less than 35 percent of the state's schools served both white and nonwhite students. Schools with 8th grades were not much different. Over a third of the state's elementary and middle schools were essentially all-white in 4th and 8th grades and would be exempt from having any racial subgroup to report.

Making matters worse, we found that the biggest gaps in test scores are between schools that only serve white students and those that do not serve any white students. And well over half the 4th grades fell into these groups. In segregated white 4th grades, 74 percent of students passed the reading test; in segregated nonwhite schools, 40 percent of the students passed; in integrated 4th grades, 75 percent of white and 55 percent of nonwhite students passed. Strikingly, white performance did not vary much across types of schools, but nonwhite performance was much worse in all-nonwhite grades.

Will reporting at the district level remedy the problem? Not much. At the district level, nearly a quarter of schools with 4th grades and more than one-third of schools with 8th grades served segregated populations.

Moreover, new accountability for the performance of minority students will be unevenly distributed across districts, falling disproportionately on urban schools, and substantially ignoring rural and suburban schools. And whatever thresholds individual states use to determine whether there are "enough" students in the subgroup to provide statistically reliable subgroup-performance scores, schools—and perhaps districts—will face an incentive to stay below the threshold to avoid the increased pressure of No Child Left Behind subgroup accountability. The end result? Schools and school districts could actually benefit from segregation.

So what can be done? In our opinion, the glare of public reporting is a good tool to help solve the problem of racial test-score disparities. Since school and district subgroup reporting will not be entirely effective because of segregated schools and districts, individual states are going to need to step in. Perhaps high-performing schools could each adopt an all-nonwhite school for reporting and remedy. Or maybe states, or even the federal government itself, could be held accountable for racial test-score gaps.

Of course, there might be a far more basic solution: Work harder to integrate our schools.

1. In reference to the Schwartz, Stiefel, and Chellman commentary, is your school required to report racial subgroup data according to NCLB? Do you see such a reporting system as providing proper attention to educational factors associated with race, or do you see it as an added hindrance to such schools?
2. Do your state and district provide clear, frequent, and accurate information to parents and educators about student academic progress?
3. What can you lean about subgroup performance from the disaggregated data in your school/district report cards?
4. What is your view on the AYP requirement? Are there changes to the AYP requirement you would like to put in place?

CHAPTER EIGHT

Using Student- and School-Performance Indicators

LEARNING OBJECTIVES

- Describe the process of decision making that will bring about significant school improvement through the critical assessment of student and school performance indicators.
- Discuss the conditions that should be in place in schools in order to make the most of the decision-making process toward school improvement.
- Illustrate and explain the components of the process for using performance indicators to improve the practices and teaching and learning.
- Provide strategies for using data to make instruction-driven decisions that educational leaders can use to lead their schools through educational accountability school improvement.

■ INTRODUCTION

Perhaps the most important reform tool educational leaders and educators can possess is the capacity to use student- and school-performance indicators to make decisions that significantly improve student learning. Accordingly, educational accountability requires that educational leaders know how to analyze and employ the results from multiple assessments of student and school performance to make sustained improvements. Certainly, educational accountability is most frequently associated with the application of pressure and motivation to improve schools. In previous chapters we discuss how educational accountability uses reporting, monitoring, and consequences as a system for signaling that low-performing schools need to receive a combination of pressure and support to make changes in instructional practices. However, unless school leaders create a school environment that fosters collaborative inquiry and reflection in order to make use of performance indicators to improve instructional quality, sanctions and incentives will just be empty reform mechanisms that fail to bring about large-scale school improvement.

Concerns have been raised regarding educational accountability as a school-reform strategy because it does not specifically identify educational programs that have a demonstrated record of improving student academic achievement. For example, Ryan (2002) writes:

> *While the primary goal of these systems is to* improve *education, these systems do not provide information to administrators, teachers, parents, or students about* what to do and how to improve *performance. The standards-based, large scale assessments identify students who exceed, meet, or fail to meet the learning standards with minimal diagnostic information that might provide this kind of guidance. The treatment is testing—the idea is that educational assessments can themselves be the key to improving student achievement by directing teaching and learning. (p. 458)*

Ryan (2002) is not unfounded in commenting that educational accountability reforms, such as NCLB, failed to name educational programs that may be effective in improving student academic achievement in its inception. However, in 2002 the U.S. Department of Education established the What Works Clearinghouse (WWC) to provide information on education programs that are supported by scientifically based research. WWC has identified a handful of educational programs that meet its selection criteria.

Even with a clearinghouse that identifies and lists evidence-based educational practices, concerns similar to Ryan (2002) fail to recognize that educational accountability is a process-oriented school-reform strategy. Significant school reform will not occur by prescribing one-size-fits-all educational programs. Instead, educational leaders must make certain that they have the knowledge and skills to lead their schools through the processes of identifying the needs of their school, setting school-improvement goals, developing learning goals, and guiding teachers in tailoring instruction to individual student needs. Selecting evidence-based educational programs is an effective strategy when part of a larger reform effort to meet the needs of struggling students. In effect, school leaders must make the school environment conducive for the use of student and school performance indicators to make significant changes in instructional practices. Schlechty (2002) comments, "creating the capacity to assess results by which one can lead and by which decisions can be disciplined is an essential prerequisite to the systematic restructuring of schools" (p. 198). School reform must be thought about in the context of the schools' needs and the conditions necessary for successful improvements in student learning.

Using student- and school-performance indicators throughout the processes of educational-accountability reform will provide educational leaders and educators with the information for deciding "what to do and how to improve performance." The list of evidence-based educational practices is a great resource for schools, but educational leaders still need to have the skills to guide their schools through the processes of analyzing and interpreting results to make instruction-driven decisions that improve student performance. In this chapter we describe the process of decision making that will bring about significant school improvement through the critical assessment of student- and school-performance indicators. We begin by discussing the conditions that should be in place in schools in order to make the most of the decision-making process. We then illustrate and explain the components of the process for using performance indicators to improve the practices and teaching and learning. This chapter provides strategies for using data to make instruction-driven decisions that educational leaders can use to lead their schools through educational accountability school improvement.

■ CONDITIONS NECESSARY FOR MAKING EFFECTIVE SCHOOL-IMPROVEMENT DECISIONS

Making educational decisions that have a positive impact on student achievement are critical to educational-accountability reform. However, the conditions in many schools and districts will limit the ability of schools to effectively match their educational decisions with the needs of the school. Schools where teachers work in isolation are not likely to have the capacity to engage in the processes necessary, such as collaborative inquiry and reflection, to use data to make significant improvements in student performance. Likewise, schools where principals do not share leadership responsibilities with educators throughout the school, or where the school leaders do not take part in thinking about the core practices of teaching and learning, will find it difficult to find success with data-driven decisions. Additionally, if schools do not receive substantial and reliable resources from the district and state levels of the education system, they may find the process for making effective instruction-driven decisions too overwhelming. Consequently, there are certain conditions that must be met in order to make effective school-improvement decisions. The primary condition educational leaders should be thinking about is how they can work to create an environment conducive to collaborative inquiry and reflection. While the most important condition is building capacity within the school to make instruction-driven decisions, educational leaders must also think systematically about the types of decisions they have to make. Selecting appropriate educational programs and instructional practices that improve student academic achievement are not easy tasks. However, educational leaders who facilitate collaboration and reflection for the systematic use of data and understand the nature of the decisions will lead schools that are able to identify strategies and practices suitable for the context of their schools.

Environment Conducive to Inquiry and Reflection

When we described the shift in expectations for educational leaders toward leading by results, we noted the centrality of collaborative inquiry and reflective practices for making significant changes to instruction and student performance. Inquiry and reflection thrive in educational environments where curiosity is valued, mutual respect is embraced, and there are protocols established for ongoing dialogue around instructional practices. Using collaborative inquiry and reflection to inform instructional practices will bring about improvements in student learning. The importance of collaborative inquiry and reflection is evident when we consider what it takes for educators to experiment with instructional practices to meet the individual needs of students. Reeves (2004) comments:

> *Reflection, therefore, requires not only the analytical task of reviewing one's own observations but also the more challenging task of listening to colleagues and comparing notes. The reflective process is at the very heart of accountability. It is through reflection that we distinguish between the popularity of teaching techniques and their effectiveness. The question is not "Did I like it?" but rather "Was it effective?" (p. 52)*

Certainly there are teachers who are able to adapt their instructional practices within the confines of their classroom and make gains in student performance without much collaboration. However, if we want to obtain large-scale school-improvement results, we cannot rely on the possibility that individuals will take it upon themselves to use data-driven decision making. The entire school community must work together to make cohesive and comprehensive changes in school practices that meet the goals of educational accountability.

Creating professional norms for collaboration and group reflection around instructional practices can be difficult to implement when educators are used to working by themselves and not used to having their practices examined by other educators on a regular basis. There may even be a fear among teachers that exposing their instructional practices will become an evaluation of their teaching that could result in negative consequences. It is the responsibility of the educational leader to establish a structure that specifies the ways in which collaboration and reflection will work in the school, emphasizing that the process of sharing teaching practices will not be used for evaluative purposes. In terms of putting inquiry into action, the Annenberg Institute for School Reform's guide for school improvement states:

> *It is important to build a community of adult learners who share a common interest in creating a stronger school. Because of the emphasis on the whole school, a review or self-study does not target any individual or single classroom within the building. Rather, it targets how to improve current practices and policies that stand in the way of student learning. (Barnes, 2004, p. 2)*

The processes of collaboration and reflection should be positive experiences that improve the practices of teaching and learning throughout the school rather than single out any individual educator. Collaborative inquiry and reflection present opportunities for the entire school community to focus their efforts toward the common goal of improving instructional practices. Educational leaders will have to underscore the need for schools to change the ways in which they have gone about the business of educating students by appealing to a collective curiosity regarding the way in which students learn. When this happens, the school will have the ability to truly meet the individual learning needs of every student.

Part of the task of ensuring that professional norms for collaboration and reflection are embraced by the school community is providing the support necessary to assist educators properly make use of student and school performance indicators. Research indicates that the meaningfulness of performance indicators will vary with the ability of educators to make sense of the information (Baker & Linn, 2002; O'Day, 2002). If school leaders are not proficient in guiding the use of data to make school-improvement decisions, then they should seek out assistance from the district or an external organization, such as a local university, a regional educational laboratory, or an education consulting agency. Organizations like the Coalition for Essential Schools have expert facilitators who guide schools through the data-driven school-improvement process.

Critical to the process is developing a protocol for how the reflective conversation around instructional practices will work. Protocols are not prescribed for collaborative inquiry and reflection. Rather, protocols consist of guidelines that participants agree on that promote in-depth conversations about instructional practices. The National School Reform Faculty (2005) finds that protocols promote the following processes:

- A protocol creates a structure that makes it safe to ask challenging questions of each other; it also ensures that there is some equity and parity in terms of how each person's issues are attended to. The presenter has the opportunity not only to reflect on and describe an issue or a dilemma, but also to have interesting questions asked of him or her, and to gain differing perspectives and new insights. Protocols build in a space for listening, and often give people a license to listen, without having to continually respond.

- In schools, many people say that time is of the essence, and time is the one resource that no one seems to have enough of. Protocols are a way to make the most of the time people do have.
- Finally, it is important to remember that the point is not do the protocol well, but to have an in-depth, insightful, conversation about teaching and learning.

These guidelines for protocols address concerns about how educators will interact with one another when using the strategies of collaborative inquiry and reflection. In some schools, intensive conversations about the practices of teaching and learning will challenge assumptions about how schools function. However, change may be necessary and the processes that support the identification of sound educational practices will improve student performance.

The findings about protocols also raise the important issue of creating the time within the school day for educators to meet and engage in data-based decisions for school improvement. Educational leaders must make sure that educators throughout the school have sufficient time to work with one another. Collaborative inquiry and reflective practices that significantly improve instructional practice will not occur if teachers do not have the opportunity to meet on a regular basis. In regards to the process of using data to make decisions, Learning Point Associates (2004) state:

> The process requires time—time during the day and the week to involve teachers; always a challenge. Schools that are committed to using data to guide their work allocate time for teachers to meet, discuss, reflect upon data, and make informed instructional decisions. Schools identify the need for this time, then find it through a combination of creative scheduling (e.g., having all first-grader teachers share student data while students attend "specials" such as art and music), and priority setting (e.g., using weekly faculty meetings to analyze student data). (p. 2)

Educational leaders are in the position to make certain that teachers have time to meet with one another to examine and reflect on data. The key is that priorities are established such that teachers meet on a regular basis and the time is spent working on instruction-driven reflection. New and pressing issues will always arise in schools. The time for making school-improvement decisions should be nonnegotiable.

As with all elements of educational-accountability reform initiatives, support from the district and state are important in the process of creating an educational environment conducive for collaborative inquiry and reflection. The American Association of School Administrators (2002) comments, "in data-driven districts, superintendents work side by side with other administrators, teachers, principals and parents to ensure all children achieve. Everyone strives toward common goals" (p. 1). Districts and states should be engaging in their own data-driven decision-making processes for educational improvement, but they must also aid schools in obtaining adequate resources to make educational accountability a success. Specifically, district and state leaders can provide schools with financial resources, technical assistance, training, and moral support.

Portin and Knapp (2001) compile a list of the dimensions of school readiness central to using data to make educational decisions:

- A cadre of teacher leaders in the school who have the time, capacity, and inclination to assume responsibility for a self-reflective process and the planning and action that come from it.
- A principal who is supportive and involved at some level.

- Sufficient building-level autonomy and/or district support to engage in a self-reflective improvement process, as a way to realize district priorities, as well as priorities set by the school.
- Available resources for supporting this process from within the school or district and from the external environment.
- A history of experience with school change and improvement processes in the school that encourages staff to consider new challenges.
- Some familiarity with self study data, or ways to gain this familiarity (p. 122).

The dimensions of readiness are consistent with our notion that schools must create an environment conducive for collaborative inquiry and reflection in that they reflect the need for commitment and support for practices that focus on improving instructional practices. School leaders should keep these dimensions in mind and recognize that they will have to be considerably involved in the process of using data for analysis, reflection, and change in their school. Crow, Hausman, and Scribner (2002) comment, "as instructional leaders, effective principals rely on empirical rather than anecdotal data to facilitate curricular and instructional decisions" (p. 203). Using empirical data simply requires that educational leaders meet the conditions for effective data-driven school-improvement decisions.

Types of Data-Driven Decisions

A further condition for making school-improvement decisions is thinking systematically about the types of decisions that have to be made in the school as a function of the different levels where educational decisions are made. There are educational decisions that will affect the whole school, while others are necessary across grade levels, and still others impact specific subject areas. In addition, the educational decisions that take place on a daily basis within individual classrooms constitute a critical level of decision-making within the school. In turn, the level of the decision will greatly impact the type of student and school performance indicators necessary to make significant educational improvements, as well as who in the school community should participate in the particular decision-making process (Schmoker, 2003).

Schoolwide decisions impact teachers and students in the aggregate, such as whether to change the schedule of the school day to block scheduling or deliberations around no-tolerance policies for school violence. As a result, schoolwide decisions require data aggregated to the school-level. School leaders may want to also have the schoolwide data broken down by subgroups of students, but in general, schoolwide decisions are made by taking into account the needs of the school as a whole. When making schoolwide decisions, educational leaders may want to make use of results from standards-based assessments, as well as data on attendance rates, student delinquency, demographic information, and financial reports. While much of the data already exists in some format or another at the school, educational leaders may want to collect additional data on topics such as parent involvement and satisfaction or school community indicators.

Decisions at the classroom level will primarily focus on student understanding and performance. When decisions are made at the grade level, subject area, or within a classroom, educators should use data from standards-based assessments, but also make use of data from formative assessments that allow for more frequent feedback and information on the progress of student learning. In educational-accountability reform, many of the educational decisions are based on academic content standards. Using the goals of the academic content standards, educators can make decisions regarding curriculum and instruction based on the process of backward mapping where instructional units are developed with the standards and final assessment in mind.

Educational leaders should be thinking about the various decisions that occur in their schools as a launching point for discussing the process of making school-improvement decisions. The process can be used at any level of decision making. Educational leaders will just want to keep in mind that different levels within the school will have different instruction-based questions that will require different types of indicators of performance.

■ DECISION-MAKING PROCESS FOR SCHOOL IMPROVEMENT

Within the theory of educational accountability, data-driven decision making is an iterative tool schools use to make certain that performance indicators are used to improve instructional practices. Figure 8.1 illustrates the process for using performance indicators to make school-improvement decisions. As an iterative process, data-driven decision making is a continual cycle of strategies where data is used throughout and the stages inform one another. The strategies include collecting data from multiple sources, conducting needs-assessments, setting goals for improvement, adapting instructional practices, and evaluating the impact of decisions on outcomes. As we mentioned in the previous section, the process for making data-driven decisions can and should be used for educational improvement decisions at every level of the school.

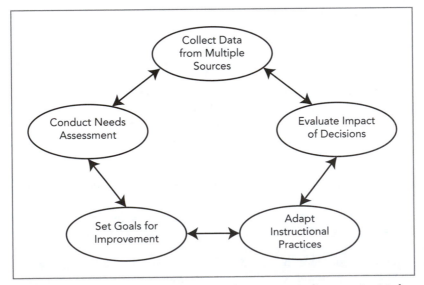

FIGURE 8.1   Process for Using Performance Indicators to Make School-Improvement Decisions

Collect Data from Multiple Sources

The types of performance indicators educators use to make school-improvement decisions will depend on a range of issues. There are no firm rules that require the use of particular sets of data or preclude the use of others. Rather, determining the appropriate student- and school-performance indicators to make educational decisions should follow the particular needs of the school. Nonetheless, given that standards-based assessments are developed within systems of accountability to align with academic content standards and are used to monitor schools' progress toward meeting proficiency, schools should make certain that the results from these assessments are incorporated into school-improvement decisions. There are some general guidelines that educational leaders should abide by when making data-driven decisions. The central principle is that multiple sources of data should be used for any decision for the reason that one indicator of performance is rarely an adequate measure of the issue in question. Additionally, data should be selected based on the level at which the decision is being made, the purpose and feedback frequency needs of the educational decision, and the quality of the measurement.

Under the conditions necessary for making effective data-driven educational decisions, we addressed the issue that data should be selected as a function of the level of the school where the decision is made. Educators making schoolwide decisions will want to use aggregated student and teacher performance indicators, while decisions made closer to the individual student will want to supplement standards-based assessment results with more authentic ongoing assessments. This leads directly into the purpose of the decision and the frequency at which feedback is needed. As we discuss in Chapter 6, large-scale, standards-based assessments provide outcome results once or twice per year. In turn, these performance indicators should not be used for day-to-day instructional decisions. Instead, educators will want to develop their own assessments of student performance that indicate mastery of the academic content. In general, standards-based assessment results will be better suited for making trend-based decisions. For example, a school may receive its report card from the state and find out from the data that fourth graders are not meeting proficiency on the mathematics standards. The data could then be used to make decisions about whether to increase the teacher-pupil ratios in fourth grade math classes, or the school may want to consider developing professional development that targets mathematics instructional practices. Fourth- and fifth-grade teachers could also use the results from the standards-based assessment to group students for extra instructional assistance. In this scenario, educators would also want to collect supplementary indicators of performance to confirm that students in fourth-grade mathematics are not performing well. Supplementary indicators could also point to intervention strategies that the results from standards-based assessments do not provide.

Educational leaders and educators engaging in data-driven decision making should be concerned about the quality of the performance indicators they use to make decisions (Baker & Linn, 2002). Results from standards-based assessments should be checked against alternative performance indicators. Assessments developed by teachers for day-to-day evaluations of students should be examined in a collaborative manner with teachers in the same grade level or subject area. An alternative way to monitor the quality of student- and school-performance indicators is to review research on the educational focus determining whether the indicators are appropriate for answering the question. The U.S. Department of Education has developed the What Works Clearinghouse to systematically review research on education and provide assessments of effective educational strategies. This tool would be a good source for access to high-quality education research.

Collecting multiple sources of data to make educational decisions will make for better decisions. Additionally, the other stages of the school-improvement decision process may lead educators to identify new sources of data that should be considered to make significant changes in instructional practices.

Conduct Needs Assessment

In the cycle of making instruction-driven decisions, educators have to identify areas in the school where improvements can be made to increase student performance. In essence, assessments of the needs of the school result in the purpose of the particular decision-making process. Needs assessments should take place at every level of the school where educational decisions are being made. Given the levels of the school and the different issues that schools face, educators should be engaging in on-going needs assessments. Because there are so many directions the needs assessments can go, educational leaders may want to formulate groups of educators from the school community that focus on particular areas of concern. For example, a group of educators may work together to determine if there are gaps between the academic standards and instruction, curriculum, and assessments within the school. This group may examine the state academic standards for science and recognize that teachers in sixth grade do not have the content knowledge necessary to ensure that students will meet proficiency. Additionally, in the process of examining the academic standards, the group realizes that the textbooks do not cover the academic content for sixth-grade science. In turn, these are weaknesses that should be identified and made the purpose of subsequent stages of the decision-making process. In the case of identifying gaps between the academic standards and the strengths of teachers and materials, the purpose of improvement decisions becomes making sure that the teachers receive training and additional resources to meet the academic needs of students.

Some educational problems in the school will be striking and easy to identify as areas in need of improvement. However, there will be problems that hinder the school's ability to significantly improve student performance that educators in the school may not be willing to recognize (Johnson, 2002). For example, teachers in a high school may be unwilling to recognize that their reliance on teacher-directed, whole classroom instruction is a potential limitation to meeting the educational needs of students. In every school there may be problems that neither the school leaders nor teachers recognize. In turn, educators may have to use the processes of collaborative inquiry and reflection to think critically about the problems that face the school. The problem may not be one that is easy to tackle. Identifying the problems that obstruct improvements in student performance is a critical task and one that should be used frequently.

Set Goals for Improvement

Once a needs assessment has been conducted and a problem has been identified, educators will have to design goals for improvement. The goals for improvement will depend on the context and extent of the issue at hand. Improvement goals should consist of measurable objectives and benchmarks so that educators can determine whether the changes they make in instructional practices impact the identified problem. If the identified educational problem is considerable—such as finding that there are achievement gaps between subgroups of white and black students in the content area of reading across all grade levels in the school—the goals for improvement will have to be extensive but also realistic. While educators will want to correct the significant problems they identify during the needs assessment as quickly as possible, consideration must be taken regarding what it will reasonably take to make significant improvements. In the case of large academic-achievement gaps, the improvement goals will have to be multifaceted and long-term in nature. In fact, a problem as large as schoolwide achievement gaps in reading may have to be broken down into more manageable issues in order to develop measurable objectives and benchmarks. In turn, educators should return the issue to the needs-assessment stage of the decision making cycle and reexamine it for specific underlying problems.

Adapt Instructional Practices

Based on the improvement goals that are established for the educational problem identified in the needs-assessment stage of the cycle for school-improvement decisions, educators must decide how to adapt instructional practices to address the issue. It should be noted that when we refer to adapting instructional strategies, we have in mind all educational practices that impact student learning. Instructional practices are not limited to teaching strategies. Rather, they include a range of activities from deciding how to allocate resources throughout the school to vertical alignment of the curriculum to identifying students for remedial assistance. The range of instructional practices that can be adapted in order to meet the improvement goals is quite large and will be determined by the nature of the problem and demonstrated evidence of strategies effective for improving student performance.

While collaborative inquiry and reflection should be a part of each of the stages, professional norms for these practices need to be in place in this stage in particular so that educators can work together to examine and experiment with instructional practices. Additionally, this stage makes the iterative process of the cycle clear as educators will likely have to go back and forth between collecting data, examining data, assessing needs, evaluating impact, and making changes in instructional practices in order to find strategies suitable for meeting the learning needs of students. The decision-making process cannot come to an end once an instructional strategy is selected. Instead, dialogue must continue between educators to monitor the impact of the instructional strategy in improving student performance.

Evaluate Impact of Decisions

The final element of the cycle of data-driven decision making, though not the end of the process, is evaluating the impact of decisions made through the process on instructional practices and outcomes relevant to the identified problem. As the overarching goal of educational accountability is to improve student performance, student performance indicators will likely be the outcome measure that educators monitor. However, there could be other outcome measures, such as a school community index, if educators in the school decide that a particular instructional strategy is an intermediary goal toward improving student learning. In the case of school community, educators may believe that if their school has a strong sense of community, it will raise student performance. In the end, it is likely that student performance indicators will be the primary outcome educators will need to look at to assess whether the practices they have adopted are effective. If the practices do not bring about desired changes in student performance, then educators will have to move through the cycle again to identify strategies that will meet the needs of students in the school.

It should be evident from the cycle of decision making that this important data-driven tool is a process that will have to be understood and embraced by educators throughout the school system. If a school has an environment conducive to productive collaborative inquiry and reflection practices, this process should adapt nicely to the professional norms established in the school.

Summary

- Data-driven decision making is a continual cycle of strategies where data is used throughout and the stages inform one another.
- Key strategies include collecting data from multiple sources, conducting needs assessments, setting goals for improvement, adapting instructional practices, and evaluating the impact of decisions on outcomes.
- The process for making data-driven decisions can and should be used for educational improvement decisions at every level of the school policy organization. The process needs to be understood and embraced by educators throughout the school system, particularly in low-performing schools.

Article and Discussion Questions

The following article discusses the use and implementation of "benchmark assessments" in schools, which are used in addition to yearly ones that attempt to monitor the amount of education absorbed over a long period of time. There are several ways such assessments can be implemented, so one must be cautious not to lump them all together. Some benchmark assessments look at the overall content students are supposed to master through specific curricula (formative assessments), while others test in the fashion of year-end statewide/national tests (benchmark assessments). Though both have their pros and cons, what is important is that teachers and school administrators are trained, competent, and willing to use the data gleaned from such tools.

Benchmark Assessments Offer Regular Checkups on Student Achievement

By Lynn Olson
Education Week, November 30, 2005

School districts worried about how students will perform on end-of-the-year state tests are increasingly administering "benchmark assessments" throughout the year to measure students' progress and provide teachers with data about how to adjust instruction.

Most benchmark assessments take one hour each for reading and mathematics, but may include other subjects. Extensive reporting systems break down test results by the same student categories required under the federal No Child Left Behind Act, such as by race, income, disability, and English proficiency, in addition to providing individual progress reports at the district, school, classroom, and student levels.

"I do believe that three years from now, certainly five years from now, no one will remember a time when there weren't benchmarks," said Robert E. Slavin, the director of the Center for Data-Driven Reform in Education, at Johns Hopkins University.

SKIMMING THE SURFACE?

Lorrie A. Shepard, the dean of the school of education at the University of Colorado at Boulder, voices caution about the trend.

While "not all formal benchmarking systems are bad," she said, she worries about the effects of using 15- or 20-item multiple-choice tests that mirror the format of state exams to drive classroom instruction.

Previous research by Ms. Shepard and others has found that students who do well on one set of standardized tests do not perform as well on other measures of the same content, suggesting that they have not acquired a deep understanding.

"The data-driven-instruction fad means earlier and earlier versions of external tests being administered at quarterly or monthly intervals," Ms. Shepard said. "The result is a long list of discrete skill deficiencies requiring inexperienced teachers to give 1,000 mini-lessons."

Good benchmark assessments, she suggested, should include rich representations of the content students are expected to master, be connected to specific teaching units, provide clear and specific feedback to teachers so that they know how to help students improve, and discourage narrow test-preparation strategies.

Rather than trying to assess everything, added Douglas B. Reeves, the founder of the Center for Performance Assessment, the best benchmark tests focus on the most important state or district content standards. And they provide results almost immediately, in simple, easy-to-use formats, he said.

The National Center for Educational Accountability stresses that good benchmark assessments measure performance "on the entire curriculum at a deep level of understanding." They also begin before grade 3 in both reading and math and provide a process to ensure that data on student performance are reviewed and acted upon by both districts and schools, the center says. In addition to such tests, it adds, districts may provide unit or weekly assessments that principals and teachers can use to monitor student progress.

APPROACHES DIFFER

But in talking about benchmark assessments, not everyone means the same thing.

According to Mr. Slavin, some benchmark tests, like 4Sight, are designed primarily to predict students' performance on end-of-the-year state exams. They measure the same set of knowledge and skills at several points during the school year to see if students are making progress and to provide an early warning of potential problems.

Other benchmarks are tied more closely to the curriculum, and to the knowledge and skills students are supposed to have learned by a particular time. For example, a skill-by-skill benchmark series in math might focus on fractions in November, decimals in January, geometry in March, and problem-solving in May, rather than testing all skills at the same time, Mr. Slavin said.

Such benchmarks serve as pacing guides for teachers and schools, providing information on whether students have learned the curriculum they've just been taught. Some companies claim their tests serve both purposes, predicting students' ultimate success on state tests and gauging how they're progressing through the curriculum.

Historically, vendors would design one set of benchmark tests for the entire country. Now they craft tests for each state, starting with the larger ones.

Many companies also work with districts to design the districts' own assessments, tied to state and district standards, or permit districts and schools to modify previously formatted exams. Some vendors provide large, computerized pools of item banks that teachers and schools can use to create their own classroom tests and check students' progress on state standards.

Stuart R. Kahl, the president of Measured Progress, a Dover, N.H.–based testing company, says that while item banks hold great promise, because they permit teachers to design tests that can be used during the ongoing flow of instruction, one issue is whether teachers are prepared to use them appropriately.

"Now we're putting individual items in the hands of teachers," he said, "saying, 'You construct the test; make it as long or as short as you want.' Do we think they have the understanding to know how much stock they can put in the generalizations they make from such exams?"

Some also worry that as vendors have rushed in, quality has not kept pace. The Eduventures report noted that many vendors have marketed formative assessments "on the basis of the quantity of exam items, as opposed to those items' quality." For example, companies may tout having tens of thousands of exam items, it said, although many of the items have not been extensively field-tested or undergone a rigorous psychometric review.

"I think vendors in our space have found it challenging," said Marissa A. Larsen, the senior product manager for assessment at the Bloomington, Minn.–based Plato Learning Inc., whose eduTest online assessment system is now used in more than 3,000 schools.

While districts sometimes apply the same psychometric standards to benchmark tests that are applied to high-stakes state exams, she said, "in many cases, that's not what vendors in this space are trying to do. If we did that, it would be well beyond what districts could afford to buy for formative systems."

Critics also say that even the best benchmark assessments are more accurately described as "early warning" or "mini-summative" tests, rather than as true "formative" assessments, which are meant to help adjust teaching and learning as it's occurring. In contrast, summative tests are designed to measure what students have learned after instruction on a subject is completed.

"Formative assessments are while you're still teaching the topic, providing on-the-spot corrections," said Mr. Kahl. "With benchmark assessments, you're finished. You've moved on. Not that you don't get individual student information, but at that stage, it's remediation."

WHAT IS "FORMATIVE"?

Yet Eric Bassett, the research director for Eduventures, said the terms formative and benchmark assessments are often used interchangeably in the commercial education market.

And that, some critics say, is precisely the problem.

"I recognize that I've lost the battle over the meaning of the term 'formative assessment,'" said Dylan Wiliam, a senior researcher at the Educational Testing Service, based in Princeton, N.J.

In the 1990s, he wrote an influential review that found that improving the formative assessments teachers used dramatically boosted student achievement and motivation. Now that same evidence, he fears, is being used to support claims about the long-term benefits of benchmark assessments that have yet to be proven. "There's a lack of intellectual honesty there," Mr. Wiliam said. "We just don't know if this stuff works."

He and others say the money, time, and energy invested in benchmark assessments could divert attention from the more potent lever of changing what teachers do in classrooms each day, such as the types of questions they ask students and how they comment on students' papers.

"If you're looking, as you should be, at the full range of development that you want kids to engage in, you're going to have to look at their work products, their compositions, their math problem-solving, their science and social-studies performance," said Mr. Slavin of Johns Hopkins.

Mr. Wiggins of Authentic Education said that while some commercially produced benchmark assessments are far from ideal, they're better than nothing. "I would rather see a district mobilizing people to analyze results more frequently," he said. "That's all to the good."

The key point, he and others stress, is what use is made of the data.

"It's only a diagnosis," Mr. Slavin said. "If you don't do anything about it, it's like going to the doctor and getting all the lab tests, and not taking the drug."

1. In reference to Lynn Olson's article, has your school and/or school system implemented "benchmark" or "formative" assessments in addition to what your state already requires? What do you see as the advantages and disadvantages of such an assessment scheme if applied to your school system's student and teacher populations?
2. Does your school have the capacity to engage in the practices of collaborative inquiry and reflection to make school-improvement decisions? Please describe what this looks like.
3. In which levels of your school are important educational decisions occurring that could benefit from the use of data? What might the capacity look like in practice?
4. Think of an educational problem in your school that could be tackled with the process for school-improvement decision making. Then explain how you would tackle this problem with the improvement process.

CHAPTER NINE

Professional Development and Educational Accountability

LEARNING OBJECTIVES

- Discuss the problems schools and districts have experienced with traditional professional development.
- Examine research on effective professional-development strategies.
- Focus on professional-development activities that promote accountability and alignment of assessment, curriculum, and instruction.
- Understand the importance and challenges of teacher collaboration.
- Conduct in-depth examination on professional learning communities and peer coaching as strategies to improve teaching and learning for all students.

■ INTRODUCTION

The changes to instructional practices that educational accountability entails—such as aligning instruction, curriculum, and assessment with high academic standards or using student-performance data to make decisions regarding practices—will require that educational leaders use effective professional-development strategies. In the theory of educational accountability, professional development functions is an iterative tool that schools should employ to facilitate the alignment of standards and the use of assessments to inform educational decisions. The goal of professional development should be improving instructional practices to increase student achievement. Recent research on the relationship between educational accountability and professional development suggests that few schools are offering teachers high-quality professional development (Berry, Turhci, & Johnson, 2003). In order for educational accountability to make significant improvements in student performance, educational leaders and teachers must make changes in the instructional practices that have proven to be ineffective. Professional development should serve the purpose of aiding in adjustments to the processes of teaching and learning; needs that are neither small nor easy to put into practice.

Educational accountability calls for teachers to concentrate on higher-order content and thinking skills aligned to structured standards and assessment systems (Cohen & Hill,

2000; Smith & Desimone, 2003; Wang & Odell, 2003). Smith and Desimone (2003) find, "although teachers generally support high standards for teaching and learning, many are not prepared to implement teaching practices based on the integration of high academic standards" (p. 119). As a gap between educational accountability policy and instructional practices may exist, educational leaders need to ensure that high-quality professional development is central to reform initiatives (Cohen & Hill, 2000; Dutro, Fisk, Koch, Roop, & Wixson, 2002). Moreover, academic content and performance standards should guide educational leaders as they design and implement professional development activities. Desimone, Porter, Birman, Garet, and Yoon (2002) claim:

> State and district standards and assessments provide a vehicle for unifying reforms and professional development. Thus, one method of designing and developing a program of professional development is to align the activities, pedagogy, and curriculum with standards and assessments adopted by the state or district and to coordinate funding with other programs in the state and district to develop a coherent professional development reform strategy. (p. 1269)

Professional development activities should be consistent, coherent, and intensive throughout the entire education system, especially between districts and schools to transform instructional practices (Fink & Thompson, 2001). It is the responsibility of educational leaders to make certain that school leaders and teachers have the knowledge and skills necessary to improve student performance. However, teachers have the reciprocal responsibility to take advantage of professional development opportunities (Marks & Printy, 2003). Ultimately for educational accountability, as Grogan and Andrews (2002) note, "the value of staff development will be determined by whether it brings about changes in teacher behavior that are beneficial for students" (p. 243).

As the design and implementation of high-quality professional development activities is critical to improving student performance with educational accountability, we discuss research on professional development strategies that have been effective in assisting educational leaders and teachers change their practices to improve teaching and learning for all students. We begin by discussing the problems schools have experienced with traditional professional development. Next, we present research on effective professional development strategies that should be implemented in a consistent and systematic manner between districts and schools. Finally, we focus on professional development activities that may promote the components of educational accountability by increasing opportunities for teachers to collaborate in order to make changes to instructional practices. Collaboration between teachers that is focused on aligning instruction, curriculum, and assessment with academic standards is essential for making significant improvements in student performance. The professional-development activities we will discuss include professional-learning communities and peer coaching.

Educational accountability requires significant transformations in the processes of teaching and learning. In previous chapters we discuss the components of educational accountability educational leaders will need to become proficient with, such as standards alignment, use of student test data, and responding to accountability consequences. As accountability may have the unintended consequence of making it more difficult for low-performing schools to attract high-quality teachers, schools will have to make certain that professional development is in place that will encourage broad improvements in effective instructional practices (Ladd & Zelli, 2002). Educational leaders at the district and school levels who are able to put in place high-quality professional development will provide school leaders and teachers with the necessary knowledge and skills, as well as appropriate setting for reflective dialogue and collaboration to make large improvements in student performance. When embarking on educational-accountability reform, educational leaders should not overlook the way effective professional development can fill in the gap between policy and practice by facilitating reflection and experimentation with effective teaching practices.

▪ EFFECTIVE PROFESSIONAL-DEVELOPMENT STRATEGIES

Many educational leaders and teachers may be familiar with the traditional form of professional development where teachers are released for a day of in-service on topics chosen by the district that usually have little if any relevance to the daily practices of teachers. Teachers attend the sessions because they are required to, but the professional development rarely makes an impact on teaching practices. In general, traditional professional development has not provided authentic learning opportunities for teachers to reflect on their instructional practices and experiment with different strategies to improve student performance. In this section we will discuss the problems with traditional professional development. If traditional professional development is allowed to be the dominant form of training in the school system, it will impede schools' ability to make significant improvements in student performance with educational accountability. There is no reason traditional professional-development approaches should continue. Research suggests that strategies defined by coherent and consistent activities focused on subject-matter content with high levels of participation and grounded in new curriculum and standards produce positive impacts on student learning and performance (Cohen & Hill, 2000; DuFour, 1991; Garet, Porter, Desimone, Birman, & Yoon, 2001; Kennedy, 1998; Newmann, King, & Youngs, 2000; Porter, Garet, Desimone, & Birman, 2003). In turn, resources need to be made available at the federal, state, and district levels to increase the development and use of effective professional-development strategies to make changes in instructional practices required by educational accountability. This chapter presents educational leaders with the knowledge on effective professional-development approaches.

Problems with Traditional Professional Development

Attitudes and views toward professional development in the education system have not always positive or productive. In many cases, educational leaders and teachers merely go through the motion with traditional professional development treating it as a necessary condition to meet certification requirements rather than an opportunity for growth and reflection on instructional practices. Schlechty (2002) comments, "teachers and administrators should be expected to participate in continuing education because it is part of their job, not because it is a requirement to keep their certificates or licenses current" (p. 196). However, if professional development is not designed in an intensive, consistent, and relevant manner, educators cannot be blamed for giving it little attention.

Districts and schools have made an effort to use professional-development strategies to impart new teaching techniques and curriculum as well as to facilitate changes in teacher practices. In spite of this, typical professional development has not addressed the alignment of academic and performance standards with curriculum, instruction, and assessment due to its limited nature of one-shot workshops consisting of guest speakers on discrete topics of content and instructional strategies (Cohen & Hill, 2000; Desimone, Porter, Garet, Yoon, & Birman, 2002; Kennedy, 1998). Traditional professional development is rarely connected to high-quality content and standards that teachers will need to improve student performance. Kelleher (2003) notes:

> *Traditional professional development activities, such as teacher workshops and faculty meetings with guest speakers, have been criticized as "adult pull-out programs." These activities, which may or may not be connected to a particular school or district goal and often have no follow-up, tend to amount to a series of disjointed experiences that do not necessarily have any observable effect on education. (p. 751)*

As teachers are regularly pressed for time, they are seldom able to put into practice the new strategies covered in professional development when the practices are not part of a comprehensive improvement plan. Generally, schools do not have the capacity to monitor whether new instructional practices are being effectively used or used at all by teachers. Additionally, many educators expect to receive easy answers about effective instructional practices during professional development, rather than using the time and resources to ask questions and reflect on the most useful practices for their students (Neuman & Pelchat, 2001). Consequently, traditional professional development has not been used as an opportunity for teachers to transform and align their teaching practices with academic standards.

Correspondingly, traditional professional development is based on what Richardson (2003) describes as a "cultural norm of individualism" in the education system where teachers are allowed and even encouraged to work in isolation. In this way, traditional professional development is infrequently presented in a manner that suggests teachers work together to share and reflect on instructional practices guided by a common school goal. Instead, teachers are left to voluntarily implement new teaching practices based on personal preferences. Additionally, Boone and Kahle (1997) find that while implementing standards-based reform initiatives, school leaders tend to focus on the easier task of supplying teachers with new physical supplies, rather than supporting the process of collaboration and observation of exemplary teaching practices. While physical supplies may be a practical need for many teachers, they will not bring about significant improvements in student performance. If the promises of educational-accountability reform are to be realized, the norm of individualism in schools has to be discarded. Educational-accountability reform entails educators in a school work together to change instructional practices and as such, professional development should be used within a framework of common goals and collaboration.

As traditional professional development does not fit the needs of educational-accountability reform in creating consistent and relevant learning opportunities for educators, the use of discrete sessions ought to be limited. In its place, educational leaders should take advantage of research on effective professional development strategies to design and implement activities that will aid in the improvement of instructional practices. In the next section, we describe the characteristics and components that have emerged in research on effective professional development.

Research on Effective Professional-Development Strategies

Traditional professional-development strategies have not demonstrated that they use consistent, coherent, or relevant strategies that help bring about necessary changes in the processes of teaching and learning. Fortunately, recent research has identified professional-development strategies proven to be effective in transforming instructional practices to benefit student performance. The effective strategies that have emerged from the research correspond with the demands and theoretical components of educational-accountability reform in that they encourage schools to design comprehensive approaches for improvement that are guided by results-driven goals and that make time and resources available for productive collaboration and processes of inquiry. Spillane and Seashore Louis (2002) comment:

> *Professional growth requires that staff be able to engage in serious discussions about the fundamental aspects of their teaching (reflective dialogue and sharing of practice), with at least a minimal level of agreement about the purposes of teaching and learning in their school (goal consensus). (p. 93)*

Educational leaders who successfully implement educational accountability will have to manage a delicate balance between setting up a results-driven accountability framework for school improvement and creating an environment conducive for collaboration through professional development. While collaboration and processes of inquiry are essential to accountability, teachers may respond to educational-accountability reform with resistance and attempts to retain isolation in order to wait out what may be viewed as just another wave of reform. Effective professional development used to support educational accountability should demonstrate that collaboration and reflection on teaching practices are not reform fads, but rather good educational practices essential to improving the way in which educators think about the process of teaching and learning.

There are consistent characteristics of professional development activities that promote the use of new instructional strategies in the classroom, as well as increase student-learning opportunities. The following components have been identified in the research on effective professional-development strategies (Cohen & Hill, 2000; Desimone, Porter, Garet, Yoon, & Birman, 2002; Kelleher, 2003; Kennedy, 1998; Richardson, 2003):

- Focus is content-based, grounded in curriculum and connected to instruction and assessment
- Provides active learning opportunities for educators
- Aligns with academic and performance standards
- Functions through inquiry-based processes
- Provides occasion for teachers to assume leadership responsibilities
- Continues with intensity over an extended duration
- Becomes embedded in daily practices of all educators in the school
- Encourages the collective and collaborative participation of all educators through school-, grade-, or department-level activities

When taken together to design professional development activities, these elements comprise a truly powerful framework for engaging educators in the process of changing instructional strategies with the purpose of improving student performance. The critical issue with effective professional development is that it incorporates and balances all of the characteristics to present successful strategies for educators. The components of effective professional development are noticeably different from traditional staff development. Where traditional professional development lacked a coherent or results-driven purpose and relevant knowledge, effective professional development provides educators with the proper tools to work together to bring about important changes.

Educational leaders play an essential role in the use of effective professional-development strategies. Not only must leaders manage and participate in the design of intense and integrated professional development activities, educational leaders must sustain the common objective of improvements in instructional practices through collaboration and processes of inquiry on a regular basis. The research on effective professional development suggests that the main purpose of any activity should be to focus efforts on teacher competency in subject-matter knowledge and the ways in which students successfully learn subject matter. As we discuss in Chapter 5, educators must work to ensure that the standards are aligned with curriculum, instruction, and assessment. Linking professional development to academic and performance standards will provide necessary guidance on appropriate content knowledge for grade levels and departments. Educational leaders can use staff meetings and scheduled professional-development time as opportunities to not only collaborate on instructional practices, but also to monitor and handle issues that may arise in the process of aligning the process of teaching and learning with high-quality standards (Rettig, McCullough, Santos, & Watson, 2004).

Although the specific professional development strategies adopted by one district or school may not be exactly the same as another, districts and schools should design their professional development plans around the characteristics of effective practices. Dorward, Hudson, Drickey, and Barta (2001) present an example of professional development designed to provide the rationale and strategies to increase teacher understanding of student assessment and transform instructional practices. Before educators in a school can begin to use student assessment to adjust teaching practices, they must collectively address and come to agreement on the content that should be covered in a particular grading period. As the content to be covered should come from high-quality academic content standards, school leaders need to organize schedules so that teachers in the same grade levels or content areas will be able to work together. From there, the professional development is designed to assist teachers work together to develop assessments that have the capability of diagnosing student need and that can be used to determine whether re-teaching of the content is necessary. The process of addressing content coverage, designing suitable assessment, diagnosing student performance, and determining a need for re-teaching should be incorporated into daily practices and repeated for each educational unit. Dorward et al. (2001) comment that professional development created in this way can "increase teacher use of instruction, diagnostic, and remediation strategies appropriate for the development, background, and interests of their students" (p. 249). In addition to focusing on academic content and alignment with standards, it is evident that this approach integrates all of the components of effective professional development including collective participation, inquiry-based procedures, embedded practices, and long-term processes. Shared leadership between school leaders and teachers can occur within this approach by designating lead teachers by grade level or subject area.

Effective professional development activities are complex and dynamic interactions between educators, content knowledge, curriculum, instructional strategies, and student assessment. Educational leaders who successfully use effective practices for professional development will have to integrate numerous components in an intensive, coherent, and relevant manner. However, in doing so, educational leaders create the potential for significant learning opportunities for both teachers and students. Moreover, the use of effective professional development will provide the backbone for realizing improvements in student performance through educational accountability.

System-Wide Professional Development

The problems that have arisen with traditional professional-development activities originate to some extent from disconnect between activities at the district and school levels. In many cases, district and school leaders do not communicate effectively regarding the types of professional-development strategies that will be offered at each level. In turn, teachers are left with professional development that lacks relevancy and consistency. Rather than continue the pattern of detached activities between the district and school levels, educational leaders need to collectively work toward determining the professional-development approaches each level will focus on, as well as how to combine efforts to improve the impact on changing instructional practices. Fink and Thompson (2001) state, "a blended approach opens the way for custom-designed professional development to meet the needs of individual teachers and individual schools, something that does not happen under a strictly centralized approach" (p. 242). Professional development at the school level may entail more day-to-day strategies such as using staff and grade level meetings on a regular basis to collaborate on results-driven approaches for improving student performance and observing exemplar teachers to share instructional practices. In contrast, professional development at the district level may be conducted less frequently, but focus on broad yet important topics of how to align instructional practices with the standards and using student data to make instructional decisions. Districts and schools will have to determine the suitable professional-development activities each level will administer based on resources, time, and expertise.

In an analysis of district spending on professional development, Hornbeck (2003) finds that many districts spend more on professional development than they think. However, the funding is seldom used in a coherent or systematic manner to meet the strategic-instructional goals of the district. In order to assess the way in which districts allocate funds to professional development, Hornbeck suggests that districts address the following questions (p. 30):

1. How much is the district spending on professional development, broadly defined?
2. What key initiatives are going to be counted as part of the inventory and analysis of professional-development spending?
3. Who actually manages or controls the professional development resources?
4. What does current spending buy (stipends, substitutes, travel, registration, tuition, teacher time, expert consulting support, staff, materials)?
5. How is it funded (federal, state, local, union, or private sources)?
6. How is it delivered (professional-development academy, external whole-school model, school-based coaching, lead teachers, coursework, mentors, summer institute, etc.)?
7. Who is targeted to receive professional development (individuals, teams of subject-area or grade-level teachers, or whole schools)?
8. What is the purpose of the professional development (for individuals: induction, continuing education, remediation, or leadership) (for teams or schools: school restructuring, content support, support for special populations, etc.)?
9. What is the topic of the spending (literacy, math, science, etc.)?
10. What strategy or focus does the current professional-development spending and activities imply?

TABLE 9.1   Estimate District-Level Spending on Professional Development

Professional Development Initiative or Program Name (Describe in as Much Detail as Possible)	Total Dollar Amount with Benefits	Spending Purpose (What Money Is Used For)	Funding Source	Name of Manager of Line Item	Topic of Focus of Professional Development Activity
Literacy coaches	1.				
Math coaches	2.				
New teacher mentors	3.				
Professional development days for new teachers only	4.				
Comprehensive school-reform models	5.				
Locally developed whole-school reform models	6.				
Principal leadership academy	7.				
Lead teacher training program	8.				
Support/formative intervention for low-performing schools	9.				
Departmental, content-related or signature instructional initiative	10.				
Other	11.				
Other	12.				
TOTAL A: Spending on professional development (Add together the amounts 1–12)					
Number of calendar days or equivalent days designated for professional development					
Salary costs for one day of teacher time for all teachers					
TOTAL B: Cost of professional development days (Multiply previous two rows)					
TOTAL C: Total of professional development spending and professional development days (Add Total A and Total B)					
TOTAL D: Total operating budget not including capital spending					
% of total operating budget committed to professional development, including professional development days (Divide Total C by Total D)					

Source: Hornbeck, M. (2003). What your district's budget is telling you. *Journal of Staff Development, 24*(3), p. 31.

Additionally, districts can use the resource in Table 9.1 to estimate district-level spending on professional development. Once a district understands where resources are being allocated for professional development, strategies can be designed to design consistent and system-wide professional development that is aligned with high-quality academic standards and instructional goals to improve student performance.

Recent research on district-wide urban school reform in San Diego presents an example of system-wide professional-development initiatives. Hightower and McLaughlin (2005) find that in the San Diego City school district the "primary focus has been on upgrading the skills and knowledge of teachers, principals, and district leaders through intense systemwide professional development" (p. 71). As the San Diego City school district believes that the principal is the key agent of changes to instructional practices, district professional development was designed to increase school principals' learning and leadership skills with "tightly connected, interactive, and thoughtfully sequenced" activities, such as helping principals develop a sound pedagogical base in content areas, creating a centralized institute for learning, assigning district instructional mentors, and encouraging principals to network with other school leaders (p. 72). The district reduced the number of district-level workshops available to teachers. As Hightower and McLaughlin (2005) explain, "district leaders felt that these centralized courses had served their purpose and were less necessary in a system where school were increasingly the locus of professional learning" (p. 86). The remaining district-level professional development activities for teachers centered on describing and providing assistance in teaching practices endorsed by the district. A further component of the systemwide professional development in San Diego was the establishment of an onsite peer coach or staff developer at every school to assist teachers with instructional issues. The district created this position with the intention of supporting principals in their professional development efforts. The reform undertaken by the San Diego City school district provides insight into the functioning of a systemwide professional-development program. The example highlights the magnitude of political will, coherency, and resources that may be necessary to establish effective professional development throughout the education system. However, as professional development is key to closing the gap between educational accountability policy and practice, educational leaders throughout the education system should take the necessary steps toward making system-wide professional development a reality.

Other districts and states across the nation have used professional development grant money to create similar learning institutes for educational leaders. For instance, in 2000 Peabody College of Vanderbilt received a state challenge grant from the Gates Foundation to partner with the Office of Professional Development for School Improvement in the Tennessee Department of Education and establish an Institute for School Leaders (ISL) that provides professional development to principals and superintendents statewide. Over three years, ISL worked with 1,800 educational leaders in Tennessee on effective teaching and learning practices. Through a three-day intensive workshop, ISL uses rigorous and coherent content as well as an instructional framework that is "(1) learner centered, (2) community centered, (3) assessment centered, and (4) knowledge centered" (Goldring, Rowley, & Sims, 2005, p. 7). ISL is one example of expanding system-wide professional development to include external partners who have expertise and experience, such as local universities, to improve professional-development opportunities for school leaders. The ISL program also shows that the state level can get involved in systemwide professional development by tapping into Title II funds through NCLB or other grants.

In the next sections we focus our attention on professional-development strategies that are consistent with educational accountability demands that teachers have opportunities to collaborate and use processes of inquiry to change instructional practices. These professional development strategies, including professional-learning communities and peer coaching, integrate the characteristics of effective professional development while ensuring that teachers share processes of teaching and learning to improve student performance.

■ PROFESSIONAL DEVELOPMENT AND EDUCATIONAL ACCOUNTABILITY: CREATE OPPORTUNITIES FOR TEACHER COLLABORATION

Educational accountability requires that educators throughout the school system focus attention on changing instructional practices to achieve results-driven goals for student performance. High-quality interactions among educators through professional development are critical to bridging the gap between educational accountability policy and practice. Specifically, educators who share their teaching practices and reflect on the processes of teaching and learning with their colleagues are more likely to make changes in their practices that benefit student performance. Spillane and Seashore Louis (2002) state:

> *Teachers who have found a network of colleagues with whom they can discuss their professional practice—either inside or outside their school—are more likely to be engaged in improving their practice in ways that have the potential to affect student learning. (p. 93)*

Furthermore, in research on teacher responses to educational accountability, Sunderman, Tracey, Kim, and Orfield (2004) find that teachers would prefer school leaders reallocate time and resources for collaboration with other teachers, rather than offer more traditional professional-development activities. In the study, teachers also highlight their preference for working with experienced teachers and administration in school-reform initiatives. The findings indicate that necessary changes in instructional practices will not occur without making resources available for team-based structures and environments conducive to collaborative processes of inquiry. In this section we will describe two forms of professional development that create opportunities for teacher collaboration. In particular, professional learning communities and peer coaching are consistent with the research on effective professional-development strategies and compatible with bringing about educational-accountability reform.

Professional Learning Communities

Professional learning communities are being used in schools choosing to abandon traditional knowledge-sharing organizational structures in which administrators maintain hierarchical authority and teachers work in isolation from one another. As a professional development and school restructuring strategy, professional learning communities derived from the school-reform literature on schools as communities (Bryk & Driscoll, 1988; Coleman & Hoffer, 1987; Hoban, 2002) and organizational learning within schools (Cook & Yanow, 1993; Darling-Hammond, 1996; Leithwood, Leonard, & Sharratt, 1998; Marks & Seashore Louis, 1999). By building on these two school-reform components, professional learning communities address the intrinsic social nature of interactions within schools and the importance of individual and organizational learning for school change. Bryk and Schneider (2002) explain the dynamic interplay of social interactions and organizational learning for school improvement:

> *The nature of these social exchanges, and the local cultural features that shape them, condition a school's capacity to improve. Designing good schools requires us to think about how to best organize the work of adults so that they are more likely to fashion together a coherent environment for the development of children. (p. 5)*

The rationale of the professional learning community initiative is that the use of school capacity building strategies, such as creating opportunities for teacher collaboration, will foster normative changes to teaching practices that will in turn improve student learning.

Professional learning communities are designed to promote school improvement and change through shared leadership, a common vision focused toward student learning, regular interaction among teachers and administrators, collaborative work by way of reflective dialogue, and shared learning (Educational Research Service, 2003; Hord, 1997; Westheimer, 1999). In particular, professional learning communities demonstrate the following five critical elements for school and teacher functioning: reflective dialogue, deprivatization of practice, collective focus on student learning, collaboration, and shared norms and values (Kruse, Seashore Louis, & Bryk, 1994). The theoretical components of professional learning communities mirror the goals of educational accountability for improvements in student performance and correspond with the elements of effective professional development.

In professional learning communities, reflective dialogue is part of the process of continuous inquiry that builds on naturalistic elements of changing teaching practices through constructivist theories of learning and teacher expertise (Richardson, 2003). As reflective dialogue requires that teachers and administrators conduct conversations around tough questions, challenged assumptions, and disagreements over practices in an environment of trust and mutual support, the capacity to develop productive reflective dialogue occurs gradually. Little, Gearhart, Curry, and Kafka (2003) identify a set of challenges to implementing reflective dialogue, including the necessary time and effort to introduce the strategy, concern for personal comfort and collegial relationships, productive use of time, and the ability to identify the critical issues to be brought up through the practice (p. 191). If teachers have traditionally developed their teaching practices autonomously, what mechanisms must schools put in place to encourage reflective dialogue and processes of inquiry on teaching practices? Educational leaders who want to make use of reflective dialogue in their schools may need the assistance of trained facilitators and well-designed conversation protocols.

Little et al. (2003) assess the tools and resources of three organizations, including Harvard Project Zero, the Coalition for Essential Schools, and the Academy for Educational Development that provide technical assistance to schools for examining student work. The researchers find commonalities between the three projects and the practice of sharing student work. First, each of the technical assistance providers brings teachers together to focus on student learning and teaching practices. In other words, teachers in the schools participating in the school improvement have time reserved during their regular schedules to engage in reflective practices. Principals are critical in this process by restructuring school schedules to create time for collaborative team work between teachers in subject area departments or grade levels. Second, the technical assistance providers supported teachers in "getting student work on the table and into the conversation" (p. 187). The school-improvement efforts created expectations that the practice of sharing student work is important by developing systematic and structured events. The principals in this study take the importance of implementing structured procedures for reflective practices seriously and make it part of daily school practice. And third, the technical assistance providers helped teachers structure their conversations when examining student work. Each of the programs has particular protocols with guidelines, procedures, and group norms to facilitate conversations and structure teacher participation. In addition, Little et al. (2003) find that the use of skilled instructional facilitators is critical to building group dynamics and deepening the conversations on student learning (p. 190). In this way, school leaders must recognize that they may have to restructure school practices to incorporate qualified instructional facilitators into the school-improvement plan to effectively implement reflective dialogue practices for professional learning communities.

The de-privatization of practice refers to attempts to "break down patterns of teacher isolation stemming from the 'cellular' form of organizations of schools" (Rowan, 1990, p. 374). Rather than accepting the traditional premise that teachers be left alone to resolve instructional, curricular, and management problems that arise, the de-privatization of practice in professional learning communities suggests that teachers share, observe, and discuss one another's teaching practices. At the heart of the de-privatization of practice rests the notion of "new professionalism" that regards teaching as a part of a communal and collaborative endeavor (Goldring & Greenfield, 2002, p. 11). Sharing teaching practices follows a process of observation, feedback, and discussion (Seashore Louis & Kruse, 1995). Discarding the practice of teacher isolation within professional learning communities is particularly relevant to the demands of educational accountability as educators must be comfortable in discussing and sharing strategies in order to change instructional practices.

In terms of a collective focus on student learning, professional learning communities establish clear and common goals about the purpose and methods of learning, as well as concentrate on student outcome results. In order to develop a clear vision on student learning, DuFour (2004) raises a set of questions that should guide professional learning communities (p. 7):

- What do we want each student to learn?
- How will we know when each student has learned it?
- How will we respond when a student experiences difficulty in learning?

The critical issue is that educators develop collective and reciprocal responsibility for student learning, which includes high expectations for all students and the belief that each teacher has the capacity to teach all students (Teddlie & Reynolds, 2000). Similar to our discussion in Chapter 8, conversations concerning student learning and outcomes within professional learning communities must be data driven (Strahan, 2003).

The professional learning component of collaboration between teachers builds on reflective dialogues and the de-privatization of practice. As we elaborated in our discussion of effective professional development strategies, when teachers in a school are able to engage in reflection and collaboration about the processes of teaching and learning grounded in standards-based and results-driven goals, teachers will develop a strong professional community (Spillane & Seashore Louis, 2002). Collaboration depends on the presence of supportive school conditions such as shared planning time, reduced isolation between teachers, mechanisms for effective communication, high levels of trust and respect between colleagues, adequate cognitive and skill levels among teachers to promote high-quality learning environments, and a process for socializing newcomers to the school environment (Hord, 1997).

The final element of professional learning communities is the development of shared norms and values. Building and sustaining shared norms and values necessitates supportive leadership and school structures that allow the school community to come to consensus regarding critical issues facing the organization (Copland, 2003). In particular, professional learning communities increase teacher participation in school decision making in order to identify shared norms and values. Hord (1997) finds that principals in schools practicing learning communities are supportive, share decision-making authority, advance professionalism among teachers, and encourage teachers to question, investigate, and seek solutions to challenges for school improvement.

The use of professional learning communities may present unintended consequences and barriers for educational leaders to manage. Scribner, Hager, and Warne (2002) note, "as interaction with others increases, the potential for conflict also increases" (p. 49). In turn, the role of educational leaders becomes critical in mediating tensions. Scribner, Hager, and Warne find that when faced with barriers of interpersonal conflicts, school leaders with inclusive and open styles of leadership are able to maintain respect among teachers and pursue school-improvement efforts. Additionally, as a result of school leaders determination to compel teachers to take ownership of the professional learning community initiative, "teachers worked with administration to integrate curriculum, develop interdisciplinary teams, and develop new curriculum strands (e.g., conflict mediation to meet student needs) and other initiatives that brought teachers together to solve problems of practice" (2002, p. 73). Overall, the researchers find that what matters most to teachers is the principal's willingness to trust and involve them in important school-reform decisions.

In determining whether professional learning communities may be developed and sustained in schools with varying contexts, Bryk, Camburn, and Seashore Louis (1999) find that the characteristics of professional learning communities identified in the literature can exist in a broad scale in urban elementary schools. Specifically, Bryk, Camburn, and Seashore Louis (1999) comment, "perhaps the most important and hopeful conclusion to be drawn from this research is that a professional community can exist in very ordinary urban schools. Moreover, positive teacher reports about professional community came from a wide cross-section of schools" (p. 772). Furthermore, the findings suggest that professional learning community initiatives provide an environment conducive for instructional innovation.

In terms of the impact of professional learning communities on student performance, Bryk and Schneider (2002) consider the impact of relational trust in schools on student learning. For Bryk and Schneider (2002), relational trust facilitates a school's ability to implement school-reform initiatives, such as professional learning communities, that require mutual support and coordinated efforts among leadership, teachers, and other community members (p. 106). Trends in levels of trust for improving student learning suggest that schools with positive trust levels are more likely to be categorized as improving in reading and mathematics than schools with weak trust reports. Hence, professional learning communities may be a good option for educational leaders looking for a comprehensive professional development approach to create opportunities for teacher collaboration.

Peer Coaching

Peer coaching emerged in the early 1980s as a strategy to improve the degree of implementation of new curriculum and instructional techniques in the classroom. Showers and Joyce (1996) write that early research showed "teachers who had a coaching relationship—that is, who shared aspects of teaching, planned together, and pooled their experiences—practiced new skills and strategies more frequently and applied them more appropriately than did their counterparts who worked alone to expand their repertoires" (p. 14). Peer coaching has typically operated as a process of collaborative planning, observation, and feedback, rather than functioning as a formal evaluation or review, in order to increase the level of implementation of instructional techniques and curriculum (Ackland, 1991; Odell, 1990; Perkins, 1998; Showers & Joyce, 1996). This section reviews the common elements of peer-coaching programs and then examine its impact on the process of changing teaching practices.

A number of strategies are used by peer-coaching programs and the approaches found in the literature can be classified into three broad categories of practice: (1) building instructional capacity, (2) development of a professional culture, and (3) supporting a process of ongoing observation and feedback (see Table 9.2).

In terms of building instructional capacity, peer coaching focus on improving instructional techniques and teacher interactions with students in the classroom. In general, coaches should attempt to assist teachers in linking new information to existing knowledge, experience, and values. Wildman, Magliaro, Niles, and Niles (1992) find that peer coaches tend to provide instructional support in the form of sharing materials, lesson plans, and "specific intact products and procedures designed for immediate use with a specific problem" (p. 210). Peer coaches should also encourage reflection through observations and feedback, as well as regularly model or demonstrate effective teaching practices. Perkins

TABLE 9.2   Peer-Coaching Strategies

	Peer Coaching Strategies
Building Instructional Capacity	Provide training for coaches Determine logistics, such as incentives and class coverage Establish an ongoing process supported by modeling, coaching, collaboration, and problem solving Focus on linking new information to existing knowledge, experience, and values Coaches give advice about instructional content and strategies Coaches share new ideas on curriculum and instruction Coaches demonstrate classroom instruction
Development of a Professional Culture	Establish rationale for peer-coaching program at school Set criteria for the selection of coaches Redesign the workplace of a school for collaboration and team planning Establish a coaching culture that values collegial interaction and professionalism among participants Define the roles of mentor and mentoree: reciprocal or expert coaching Have all teachers agree to participate in peer coaching
Ongoing Support for Evaluation	Make peer coaching distinct from teacher evaluation Coaches observe classroom instruction regularly Coaches provide support and companionship Coaches consult about lesson plans and objectives Coaches provide feedback and assistance through analysis of teacher application of strategies Allow for experimentation of teaching strategies Encourage reflection on the teaching and learning process Evaluate the peer-coaching program to determine the impact of the initiative on students and teachers

(1998) identifies specific speech and agenda skills peer coaches should use to effectively encourage instructional capacity building. In the speech acts of evaluation, reactions, questions and requests, peer coaches should use open-ended questions, paraphrases, probes, positive presuppositions, and descriptive reports of data (p. 242). For the agenda skills, Perkins (1998) suggests that peer coaches set goals with the teacher prior to the observation and then follow-up with a summary of impressions, comparison of goals to the reality of the situation, and inferring lessons for future practice (p. 243). Overall, building instructional capacity is the essential component of peer coaching in order to bring about changes in teaching practices.

Peer-coaching strategies can assist schools develop a professional culture by redesigning the workplace and using professional-development time for collaboration and team building. Peer coaching can be used to encourage teachers to exchange advice and reflect on teaching practices and student learning in a comfortable and collegial fashion. Furthermore, peer coaching is designed to implement and facilitate an environment of ongoing feedback and observation of teaching practices and student learning. The literature is resolute that the peer-coaching processes consist of nonevaluative communication, observation, and feedback (Ackland, 1991; Becker, 1996; Perkins, 1998; Showers & Joyce, 1996). In order for peer coaches to maintain levels of trust and the support necessary to impact teaching practices, the peer-coaching process should remain distinct and separate from evaluation. However, peer-coaching programs should be continually evaluated to determine their impact on teaching practices and student learning.

Peer coaches should be chosen through a combination of professional and personality characteristics to match the roles they will have to assume. As peer coaching involves highly dynamic and personal interactions based on the context of the school, the roles of coaches may not be able to be rigidly defined. However, peer coaches should be identified as highly competent educators, possess expertise in teaching and content-specific areas, be able to clearly articulate intricacies of their teaching, and have routinized their daily practices in order to demonstrate strategies to fellow teachers (Enz, 1992, p. 67). The effective personal characteristics of peer coaches may consist of thoughtful reflectors, facilitative initiators and maintainers of the relationships, and capable of building relationships built on trust and respect (Enz, 1992, pp. 65–67). Ackland (1991) makes an important distinction between two types of coaching roles:

> The programs could be divided into two basic forms: (a) coaching by experts (specially trained teachers with an acknowledged expertise who observe other teachers to give them support, feedback, and suggestions), and (b) reciprocal coaching (teachers observe and coach each other to jointly improve instruction). (p. 24)

Reciprocal coaching would categorize informal mentoring relationships among teachers, while expert coaching is the strategy that encompasses effective professional development strategies to help teachers align content-specific standards with instruction and student learning. Wang and Odell (2002) comment, "in particular, mentors need to know how to support novices in posing problems for current teaching practice, uncovering assumptions underlying current practice, and constructing and reconstructing the curriculum and teaching practice in the unique context of teaching" (p. 489). Peer coaches should be chosen based on their knowledge- and context-based characteristics and integrate their practices with the large-scale reform initiatives of the school, such as educational accountability.

Peer-coaching programs experience many of the same limitations that transpire in other school-reform programs, such as insufficient training, limited resources, and lack of evaluation (Evertson & Smithey, 2000). In an evaluation of peer coaching, Grimmert (1987) finds that "time constraints, peer incompatibility, professional threat, and interpersonal defensiveness had, in most cases, essentially rendered their participation in the peer coaching process minimal" (pp. 236–237). The findings suggest that dynamic interactions between teachers, administrators, and coaches in peer-coaching programs can create challenging circumstances. In order to overcome these challenges and positively impact the improvement of teaching practices, peer coaches will have to provide concrete and usable remedies for instructional problems (Gersten, Morvant, & Brengelman, 1995). Additionally, Kohler, Crilley, Shearer, and Good (1997) find that peer-coaching strategies must be feasible and effective for teachers to use so that teachers can use, refine, and sustain the use of the instructional activities and impact student learning. In a review of research on peer-coaching and mentoring programs, Wang and Odell (2002) find:

> *Mentor teachers who effectively help novices to learn standards-based teaching are ones who work directly with novices on the content and processes of learning in light of the principles and assumptions of such teaching practice. They help novices to identify assumptions about teaching and learning in specific contexts and develop reasonable and effective solutions necessary for learning standards-based teaching. They treat novices as active learners and facilitate their construction and reconstruction of the meanings of specific but crucial events and situations of teaching and learning rather than simply offering suggestions and solutions. (p. 524)*

In turn, peer coaches may be used by educational leaders during educational-accountability reform as agents of professional development to bring about changes in instructional practices. However, effective peer coaches will need quality training in order to develop the knowledge and skills necessary to assist teachers in productive manners that correspond with the goals of educational accountability.

Summary

- Recent research has identified professional development strategies proven to be effective in transforming instructional practices to benefit student performance.
- Effective strategies encourage schools and districts to design comprehensive approaches for improvement that are guided by results-driven goals and that make time and resources available for productive collaboration and processes of inquiry.
- Effective strategies also make sure that teachers have opportunities to collaborate and use processes of inquiry to change instructional practices.
- Among the promising professional-development strategies include professional learning communities and peer coaching. These strategies integrate the characteristics of effective professional development while ensuring that teachers share processes of teaching and learning to improve student performance.

Commentary and Discussion Questions

The following commentary discusses teacher supply and retention issues in urban contexts, specifically Boston. Issues around traditional school reform and accountability are debated while alluding to the fact that, ultimately, "good teachers make good schools." Ideas such as paid internships, alternative certification options, school loan forgiveness, and so on, could attract people into the profession who would normally seek other employment options. As the population of urban teachers gets closer to retirement age, not only are such teacher-employment reforms desirable, they are necessary. The authors argue for a reprofessionalization of teachers due to their innumerable tasks and that the future of the traditional urban public school rests on their work.

To Improve Schools, Focus on Teachers

A Commentary by Jesse Solomon and Richard Weissbourd
The Boston Globe, January 14, 2001

As Massachusetts enters the eighth year of education reform, what's to show for all the fuss? Progress has been slight. A majority of eighth-graders failed the MCAS last spring. Moreover, this spring the stakes will rise. For the first time the MCAS will be tied to a high school diploma.

While there has been no shortage of reform initiatives, not nearly enough attention has been given to an alarmingly simple idea: Good teachers make good schools. Research shows that the reform most important to student success is improving teacher quality.

As much as half of the achievement gap between poor students and others results not from poverty or family circumstances but from differences in teacher effectiveness. Hotly debated reforms such as high-stakes testing, school choice, and smaller class size consume air time, but each will have little positive impact without high-quality teachers.

In his State of the City Address, Mayor Menino laid a strong foundation for a campaign to recruit and prepare excellent teachers. The mayor was being proactive. This country will need to fill an estimated 2.5 million vacancies over the next 10 years; in Boston, nearly half the teachers will retire in the next five years.

The mayor also took up the other end of the battle: retaining teachers. Up to half of all new teachers leave urban schools in their first five years, while many of the best veteran teachers pursue other careers.

The challenge will be to assure that this campaign does not become another quick education fix, tinkering with a system that needs overhauling. What will it take to recruit, prepare, and keep qualified teachers in our classrooms?

We need to focus on recruiting top-notch candidates. There are a great number of potential teachers graduating at the top of their classes at our nation's best colleges, working in other professions, who are discouraged from teaching by unnecessary barriers. It doesn't have to be this way. Innovations such as paid internships, alternative routes to certification, and loan and tuition forgiveness can help bring talented people into teaching.

Next, we need to stop underestimating what it takes to be a good teacher. Teaching ninth-grade algebra in a typical urban classroom where the average student has sixth-grade math skills and many children struggle with emotional and cognitive difficulties is no less complex or demanding than surgery or engineering.

Yet we ask new teachers to take the toughest assignments with irrelevant or insufficient preparation and without support.

There is another way. There are successful programs in Boston and around the state where teachers, like medical residents, are apprenticed to a veteran professional during their first years on the job. These professionals challenge them, model strategies, provide immediate feedback, and push them to examine rigorously their own practice. It is through this kind of mentoring that teachers learn the nuts-and-bolts lessons of teaching. They encounter the complexity of both remediating and accelerating students, of identifying cognitive and emotional delays, of engaging uninvolved parents, of managing time effectively and preparing students for standardized, high-stakes tests.

We need to strengthen and expand these kinds of preparation and induction programs.

To retain our best teachers, we need to make fundamental changes. As it stands, a teacher has few ways to diversify her career path. Her job looks the same as it did on the day she began. What if it was common practice for teachers to serve as researchers, to take sabbaticals or job-share with professionals in their field without leaving teaching?

What if we changed the teaching culture so teachers could learn by observing one another and consulting with one another and a range of skilled professionals? What if we supported teachers getting strong academic results to write about and disseminate what they have learned?

These reforms could remake the profession and solve several problems at once. New teachers could flourish because they were truly learning how to teach and were energized by exciting learning environments and real success. Older teachers could be invigorated by the opportunity to mentor.

We need to make widespread changes. The effort will require a focus of resources and attention rare in education, but the result will stand a far greater chance of fulfilling the promise of education reform.

1. In reference to Jesse Solomon's and Richard Weissbourd's commentary and considering your school system, which of the following do you see as the best innovation to attract talented people into the teaching profession: providing an apprenticeship year when first year teachers co-teach in with the most senior and talented teachers; alternative routes to certification; or loan and tuition forgiveness? Why?
2. How can professional development fill the gap between policy goals and classroom practices?
3. In your professional experience, have you encountered a "cultural norm of individualism"? If so, how did you address it?
4. Do you see a tension between professional collaboration and results-driven accountability for school performance? Explain the specific aspects of the tension and how you might develop strategies to address the challenge.
5. Given the current level of resources in your school and district, how do you design a systemwide professional-development initiative? What are some of the core components of such an initiative?

No Child Left Behind Act of 2001

ELEMENTARY & SECONDARY EDUCATION

■ PART A—IMPROVING BASIC PROGRAMS OPERATED BY LOCAL EDUCATIONAL AGENCIES

Subpart 1 — Basic Program Requirements

SEC. 1111. STATE PLANS.

(a) PLANS REQUIRED—

(1) IN GENERAL—For any State desiring to receive a grant under this part, the State educational agency shall submit to the Secretary a plan, developed by the State educational agency, in consultation with local educational agencies, teachers, principals, pupil services personnel, administrators (including administrators of programs described in other parts of this title), other staff, and parents, that satisfies the requirements of this section and that is coordinated with other programs under this Act, the Individuals with Disabilities Education Act, the Carl D. Perkins Vocational and Technical Education Act of 1998, the Head Start Act, the Adult Education and Family Literacy Act, and the McKinney-Vento Homeless Assistance Act.

(2) CONSOLIDATED PLAN—A State plan submitted under paragraph (1) may be submitted as part of a consolidated plan under section 9302.

(b) ACADEMIC STANDARDS, ACADEMIC ASSESSMENTS, AND ACCOUNTABILITY—

(1) CHALLENGING ACADEMIC STANDARDS—

(A) IN GENERAL—Each State plan shall demonstrate that the State has adopted challenging academic content standards and challenging student academic achievement standards that will be used by the State, its local educational agencies, and its schools to carry out this part, except that a State shall not be required to submit such standards to the Secretary.

(B) SAME STANDARDS—The academic standards required by subparagraph (A) shall be the same academic standards that the State applies to all schools and children in the State.

(C) SUBJECTS—The State shall have such academic standards for all public elementary school and secondary school children, including children served under this part, in subjects determined by the State, but including at least mathematics, reading or language arts, and (beginning in the 2005–2006 school year) science, which shall include the same knowledge, skills, and levels of achievement expected of all children.

(D) CHALLENGING ACADEMIC STANDARDS—Standards under this paragraph shall include—

(i) challenging academic content standards in academic subjects that—

(I) specify what children are expected to know and be able to do;

(II) contain coherent and rigorous content; and

(III) encourage the teaching of advanced skills; and

(ii) challenging student academic achievement standards that—

(I) are aligned with the State's academic content standards;

(II) describe two levels of high achievement (proficient and advanced) that determine how well children are mastering the material in the State academic content standards; and

(III) describe a third level of achievement (basic) to provide complete information about the progress of the lower-achieving children toward mastering the proficient and advanced levels of achievement.

(E) INFORMATION—For the subjects in which students will be served under this part, but for which a State is not required by subparagraphs (A), (B), and (C) to develop, and has not otherwise developed, such academic standards, the State plan shall describe a strategy for ensuring that students are taught the same knowledge and skills in such subjects and held to the same expectations as are all children.

(F) EXISTING STANDARDS—Nothing in this part shall prohibit a State from revising, consistent with this section, any standard adopted under this part before or after the date of enactment of the No Child Left Behind Act of 2001.

(2) ACCOUNTABILITY—

(A) IN GENERAL—Each State plan shall demonstrate that the State has developed and is implementing a single, statewide State accountability system that will be effective in ensuring that all local educational agencies, public elementary schools, and public secondary schools make adequate yearly progress as defined under this paragraph. Each State accountability system shall—

(i) be based on the academic standards and academic assessments adopted under paragraphs (1) and (3), and other academic indicators consistent with subparagraph (C)(vi) and (vii), and shall take into account the achievement of all public elementary school and secondary school students;

(ii) be the same accountability system the State uses for all public elementary schools and secondary schools or all local educational agencies in the State, except that public elementary schools, secondary schools, and local educational agencies not participating under this part are not subject to the requirements of section 1116; and

(iii) include sanctions and rewards, such as bonuses and recognition, the State will use to hold local educational agencies and public elementary schools and secondary schools accountable for student achievement and for ensuring that they make adequate yearly progress in accordance with the State's definition under subparagraphs (B) and (C).

(B) ADEQUATE YEARLY PROGRESS—Each State plan shall demonstrate, based on academic assessments described in paragraph (3), and in accordance with this paragraph, what constitutes adequate yearly progress of the State, and of all public elementary schools, secondary schools, and local educational agencies in the State, toward enabling all public elementary school and secondary school students to meet the State's student academic achievement standards, while working toward the goal of narrowing the achievement gaps in the State, local educational agencies, and schools.

(C) DEFINITION—Adequate yearly progress' shall be defined by the State in a manner that—

(i) applies the same high standards of academic achievement to all public elementary school and secondary school students in the State;

(ii) is statistically valid and reliable;

(iii) results in continuous and substantial academic improvement for all students;

(iv) measures the progress of public elementary schools, secondary schools and local educational agencies and the State based primarily on the academic assessments described in paragraph (3);

(v) includes separate measurable annual objectives for continuous and substantial improvement for each of the following:

(I) The achievement of all public elementary school and secondary school students.

(II) The achievement of—

(aa) economically disadvantaged students;

(bb) students from major racial and ethnic groups;

(cc) students with disabilities; and

(dd) students with limited English proficiency;

except that disaggregation of data under subclause

(II) shall not be required in a case in which the number of students in a category is insufficient to yield statistically reliable information or the results would reveal personally identifiable information about an individual student;

(vi) in accordance with subparagraph (D), includes graduation rates for public secondary school students (defined as the percentage of students who graduate from secondary school with a regular diploma in the standard number of years) and at least one other academic indicator, as determined by the State for all public elementary school students; and

(vii) in accordance with subparagraph (D), at the State's discretion, may also include other academic indicators, as determined by the State for all public school students, measured separately for each group described in clause (v), such as achievement on additional State or locally administered assessments, decreases in grade-to-grade retention rates, attendance rates, and changes in the percentages of students completing gifted and talented, advanced placement, and college preparatory courses.

(D) REQUIREMENTS FOR OTHER INDICATORS—In carrying out subparagraph (C)(vi) and (vii), the State—

(i) shall ensure that the indicators described in those provisions are valid and reliable, and are consistent with relevant, nationally recognized professional and technical standards, if any; and

(ii) except as provided in subparagraph (I)(i), may not use those indicators to reduce the number of, or change, the schools that would otherwise be subject to school improvement, corrective action, or restructuring under section 1116 if those additional indicators were not used, but may use them to identify additional schools for school improvement or in need of corrective action or restructuring.

(E) STARTING POINT—Each State, using data for the 2001–2002 school year, shall establish the starting point for measuring, under subparagraphs (G) and (H), the percentage of students meeting or exceeding the State's proficient level of academic achievement on the State assessments under paragraph (3) and pursuant to the timeline described in subparagraph (F). The starting point shall be, at a minimum, based on the higher of the percentage of students at the proficient level who are in—

(i) the State's lowest achieving group of students described in subparagraph (C)(v)(II); or

(ii) the school at the 20th percentile in the State, based on enrollment, among all schools ranked by the percentage of students at the proficient level.

(F) TIMELINE—Each State shall establish a timeline for adequate yearly progress. The timeline shall ensure that not later than 12 years after the end of the 2001–2002 school year, all students in each group described in subparagraph (C)(v) will meet or exceed the State's proficient level of academic achievement on the State assessments under paragraph (3).

(G) MEASURABLE OBJECTIVES—Each State shall establish statewide annual measurable objectives, pursuant to subparagraph (C)(v), for meeting the requirements of this paragraph, and which—

(i) shall be set separately for the assessments of mathematics and reading or language arts under subsection (a)(3);

(ii) shall be the same for all schools and local educational agencies in the State;

(iii) shall identify a single minimum percentage of students who are required to meet or exceed the proficient level on the academic assessments that applies separately to each group of students described in subparagraph (C)(v);

(iv) shall ensure that all students will meet or exceed the State's proficient level of academic achievement on the State assessments within the State's timeline under subparagraph (F); and

(v) may be the same for more than 1 year, subject to the requirements of subparagraph (H).

(H) INTERMEDIATE GOALS FOR ANNUAL YEARLY PROGRESS—Each State shall establish intermediate goals for meeting the requirements, including the measurable objectives in subparagraph (G), of this paragraph and that shall—

(i) increase in equal increments over the period covered by the State's timeline under subparagraph (F);

(ii) provide for the first increase to occur in not more than 2 years; and

(iii) provide for each following increase to occur in not more than 3 years.

(I) ANNUAL IMPROVEMENT FOR SCHOOLS—Each year, for a school to make adequate yearly progress under this paragraph—

(i) each group of students described in subparagraph (C)(v) must meet or exceed the objectives set by the State under subparagraph (G), except that if any group described in subparagraph (C)(v) does not meet those objectives in any particular year, the school shall be considered to have made adequate yearly progress if the percentage of students in that group who did not meet or exceed the proficient level of academic achievement on the State assessments under paragraph (3) for that year decreased by 10 percent of that percentage from the preceding school year and that group made progress on one or more of the academic indicators described in subparagraph (C)(vi) or (vii); and

(ii) not less than 95 percent of each group of students described in subparagraph (C)(v) who are enrolled in the school are required to take the assessments, consistent with paragraph (3)(C)(xi) and with accommodations, guidelines, and alternative assessments provided in the same manner as those provided under section 612(a)(17)(A) of the Individuals with Disabilities Education Act and paragraph (3), on which adequate yearly progress is based (except that the 95 percent requirement described in this clause shall not apply in a case in which the number of students in a category is insufficient to yield statistically reliable information or the results would reveal personally identifiable information about an individual student).

(J) UNIFORM AVERAGING PROCEDURE—For the purpose of determining whether schools are making adequate yearly progress, the State may establish a uniform procedure for averaging data which includes one or more of the following:

(i) The State may average data from the school year for which the determination is made with data from one or two school years immediately preceding that school year.

(ii) Until the assessments described in paragraph (3) are administered in such manner and time to allow for the implementation of the uniform procedure for averaging data described in clause (i), the State may use the academic assessments that were required under paragraph (3) as that paragraph was in effect on the day preceding the date of enactment of the No Child Left Behind Act of 2001, provided that nothing in this clause shall be construed to undermine or delay the determination of adequate yearly progress, the requirements of section 1116, or the implementation of assessments under this section.

(iii) The State may use data across grades in a school.

(K) ACCOUNTABILITY FOR CHARTER SCHOOLS—The accountability provisions under this Act shall be overseen for charter schools in accordance with State charter school law.

(3) ACADEMIC ASSESSMENTS—

(A) IN GENERAL—Each State plan shall demonstrate that the State educational agency, in consultation with local educational agencies, has implemented a set of high-quality, yearly student academic assessments that include, at a minimum, academic assessments in mathematics, reading or language arts, and science that will be used as the primary means of determining the yearly performance of the State and of each local educational agency and school in the State in enabling all children to meet the State's challenging student academic achievement standards, except that no State shall be required to meet the requirements of this part relating to science assessments until the beginning of the 2007–2008 school year.

(B) USE OF ASSESSMENTS—Each State educational agency may incorporate the data from the assessments under this paragraph into a State-developed longitudinal data system that links student test scores, length of enrollment, and graduation records over time.

(C) REQUIREMENTS—Such assessments shall—

(i) be the same academic assessments used to measure the achievement of all children;

(ii) be aligned with the State's challenging academic content and student academic achievement standards, and provide coherent information about student attainment of such standards;

(iii) be used for purposes for which such assessments are valid and reliable, and be consistent with relevant, nationally recognized professional and technical standards;

(iv) be used only if the State educational agency provides to the Secretary evidence from the test publisher or other relevant sources that the assessments used are of adequate technical quality for each purpose required under this Act and are consistent with the requirements of this section, and such evidence is made public by the Secretary upon request;

(v)(I) except as otherwise provided for grades 3 through 8 under clause vii, measure the proficiency of students in, at a minimum, mathematics and reading or language arts, and be administered not less than once during—

(aa) grades 3 through 5;

(bb) grades 6 through 9; and

(cc) grades 10 through 12;

(II) beginning not later than school year 2007–2008, measure the proficiency of all students in science and be administered not less than one time during—

(aa) grades 3 through 5;

(bb) grades 6 through 9; and

(cc) grades 10 through 12;

(vi) involve multiple up-to-date measures of student academic achievement, including measures that assess higher-order thinking skills and understanding;

(vii) beginning not later than school year 2005–2006, measure the achievement of students against the challenging State academic content and student academic achievement standards in each of grades 3 through 8 in, at a minimum, mathematics, and reading or language arts, except that the Secretary may provide the State 1 additional year if the State demonstrates that exceptional or uncontrollable circumstances, such as a natural disaster or a precipitous and unforeseen decline in the financial resources of the State, prevented full implementation of the academic assessments by that deadline and that the State will complete implementation within the additional 1-year period;

(viii) at the discretion of the State, measure the proficiency of students in academic subjects not described in clauses (v), (vi), (vii) in which the State has adopted challenging academic content and academic achievement standards;

(ix) provide for—

(I) the participation in such assessments of all students;

(II) the reasonable adaptations and accommodations for students with disabilities (as defined under section 602(3) of the Individuals with Disabilities Education Act) necessary to measure the academic achievement of such students relative to State academic content and State student academic achievement standards; and

(III) the inclusion of limited English proficient students, who shall be assessed in a valid and reliable manner and provided reasonable accommodations on assessments administered to such students under this paragraph, including, to the extent practicable, assessments in the language and form most likely to yield accurate data on what such students know and can do in academic content areas, until such students have achieved English language proficiency as determined under paragraph (7);

(x) notwithstanding subclause (III), the academic assessment (using tests written in English) of reading or language arts of any student who has attended school in the United States (not including Puerto Rico) for three or more consecutive school years, except that if the local educational agency determines, on a case-by-case individual basis, that academic assessments in another language or form would likely yield more accurate and reliable information on what such student knows and can do, the local educational agency may make a determination to assess such student in the appropriate language other than English for a period that does not exceed two additional consecutive years, provided that such student has not yet reached a level of English language proficiency sufficient to yield valid and reliable information on what such student knows and can do on tests (written in English) of reading or language arts;

(xi) include students who have attended schools in a local educational agency for a full academic year but have not attended a single school for a full academic year, except that the performance of students who have attended more than 1 school in the local educational agency in any academic year shall be used only in determining the progress of the local educational agency;

(xii) produce individual student interpretive, descriptive, and diagnostic reports, consistent with clause (iii) that allow parents, teachers, and principals to understand and address the specific academic needs of students, and include information regarding achievement on academic assessments aligned with State academic achievement standards, and that are provided to parents, teachers, and principals, as soon as is practicably possible after the assessment is given, in an understandable and uniform format, and to the extent practicable, in a language that parents can understand;

(xiii) enable results to be disaggregated within each State, local educational agency, and school by gender, by each major racial and ethnic group, by English proficiency status, by migrant status, by students with disabilities as compared to nondisabled students, and by economically disadvantaged students as compared to students who are not economically disadvantaged, except that, in the case of a local educational agency or a school, such disaggregation shall not be required in a case in which the number of students in a category is insufficient to yield statistically reliable information or the results would reveal personally identifiable information about an individual student;

(xiv) be consistent with widely accepted professional testing standards, objectively measure academic achievement, knowledge, and skills, and be tests that do not evaluate or assess personal or family beliefs and attitudes, or publicly disclose personally identifiable information; and

(xv) enable itemized score analyses to be produced and reported, consistent with clause (iii), to local educational agencies and schools, so that parents, teachers, principals, and administrators can interpret and address the specific academic needs of students as indicated by the students' achievement on assessment items.

(D) DEFERRAL— A State may defer the commencement, or suspend the administration, but not cease the development, of the assessments described in this paragraph, that were not required prior to the date of enactment of the No Child Left Behind Act of 2001, for 1 year for each year for which the amount appropriated for grants under section 6113(a)(2) is less than—

(i) $370,000,000 for fiscal year 2002;

(ii) $380,000,000 for fiscal year 2003;

(iii) $390,000,000 for fiscal year 2004; and

(iv) $400,000,000 for fiscal years 2005 through 2007.

(4) SPECIAL RULE—Academic assessment measures in addition to those in paragraph (3) that do not meet the requirements of such paragraph may be included in the assessment under paragraph (3) as additional measures, but may not be used in lieu of the academic assessments required under paragraph (3). Such additional assessment measures may not be used to reduce the number of or change, the schools that would otherwise be subject to school improvement, corrective action, or restructuring under section 1116 if such additional indicators were not used, but may be used to identify additional schools for school improvement or in need of corrective action or restructuring except as provided in paragraph (2)(I)(i).

(5) STATE AUTHORITY—If a State educational agency provides evidence, which is satisfactory to the Secretary, that neither the State educational agency nor any other State government official, agency, or entity has sufficient authority, under State law, to adopt curriculum content and student academic achievement standards, and academic assessments aligned with such academic standards, which will be applicable to all students enrolled in the State's public elementary schools and secondary schools, then the State educational agency may meet the requirements of this subsection by—

(A) adopting academic standards and academic assessments that meet the requirements of this subsection, on a statewide basis, and limiting their applicability to students served under this part; or

(B) adopting and implementing policies that ensure that each local educational agency in the State that receives grants under this part will adopt curriculum content and student academic achievement standards, and academic assessments aligned with such standards, which—

(i) meet all of the criteria in this subsection and any regulations regarding such standards and assessments that the Secretary may publish; and

(ii) are applicable to all students served by each such local educational agency.

(6) LANGUAGE ASSESSMENTS—Each State plan shall identify the languages other than English that are present in the participating student population and indicate the languages for which yearly student academic assessments are not available and are

needed. The State shall make every effort to develop such assessments and may request assistance from the Secretary if linguistically accessible academic assessment measures are needed. Upon request, the Secretary shall assist with the identification of appropriate academic assessment measures in the needed languages, but shall not mandate a specific academic assessment or mode of instruction.

(7) ACADEMIC ASSESSMENTS OF ENGLISH LANGUAGE PROFICIENCY—Each State plan shall demonstrate that local educational agencies in the State will, beginning not later than school year 2002–2003, provide for an annual assessment of English proficiency (measuring students' oral language, reading, and writing skills in English) of all students with limited English proficiency in the schools served by the State educational agency, except that the Secretary may provide the State 1 additional year if the State demonstrates that exceptional or uncontrollable circumstances, such as a natural disaster or a precipitous and unforeseen decline in the financial resources of the State, prevented full implementation of this paragraph by that deadline and that the State will complete implementation within the additional 1-year period.

(8) REQUIREMENT—Each State plan shall describe—

(A) how the State educational agency will assist each local educational agency and school affected by the State plan to develop the capacity to comply with each of the requirements of sections 1112(c)(1)(D), 1114(b), and 1115(c) that is applicable to such agency or school;

(B) how the State educational agency will assist each local educational agency and school affected by the State plan to provide additional educational assistance to individual students assessed as needing help to achieve the State's challenging academic achievement standards;

(C) the specific steps the State educational agency will take to ensure that both schoolwide programs and targeted assistance schools provide instruction by highly qualified instructional staff as required by sections 1114(b)(1)(C) and 1115(c)(1)(E), including steps that the State educational agency will take to ensure that poor and minority children are not taught at higher rates than other children by inexperienced, unqualified, or out-of-field teachers, and the measures that the State educational agency will use to evaluate and publicly report the progress of the State educational agency with respect to such steps;

(D) an assurance that the State educational agency will assist local educational agencies in developing or identifying high-quality effective curricula aligned with State academic achievement standards and how the State educational agency will disseminate such curricula to each local educational agency and school within the State; and

(E) such other factors the State educational agency determines appropriate to provide students an opportunity to achieve the knowledge and skills described in the challenging academic content standards adopted by the State.

(9) FACTORS AFFECTING STUDENT ACHIEVEMENT—Each State plan shall include an assurance that the State educational agency will coordinate and collaborate, to the extent feasible and necessary as determined by the State educational agency, with agencies providing services to children, youth, and families, with respect to local educational agencies within the State that are identified under section 1116 and that request assistance with addressing major factors that have significantly affected the academic achievement of students in the local educational agency or schools served by such agency.

(10) USE OF ACADEMIC ASSESSMENT RESULTS TO IMPROVE STUDENT ACADEMIC ACHIEVEMENT—Each State plan shall describe how the State educational agency will ensure that the results of the State assessments described in paragraph (3)—

(A) will be promptly provided to local educational agencies, schools, and teachers in a manner that is clear and easy to understand, but not later than before the beginning of the next school year; and

(B) be used by those local educational agencies, schools, and teachers to improve the educational achievement of individual students.

(c) OTHER PROVISIONS TO SUPPORT TEACHING AND LEARNING—
Each State plan shall contain assurances that—

(1) the State educational agency will meet the requirements of subsection (h)(1) and, beginning with the 2002–2003 school year, will produce the annual State report cards described in such subsection, except that the Secretary may provide the State educational agency 1 additional year if the State educational agency demonstrates that exceptional or uncontrollable circumstances, such as a natural disaster or a precipitous and unforeseen decline in the financial resources of the State, prevented full implementation of this paragraph by that deadline and that the State will complete implementation within the additional 1-year period;

(2) the State will, beginning in school year 2002–2003, participate in biennial State academic assessments of 4th and 8th grade reading and mathematics under the National Assessment of Educational Progress carried out under section 411(b)(2) of the National Education Statistics Act of 1994 if the Secretary pays the costs of administering such assessments;

(3) the State educational agency, in consultation with the Governor, will include, as a component of the State plan, a plan to carry out the responsibilities of the State under sections 1116 and 1117, including carrying out the State educational agency's statewide system of technical assistance and support for local educational agencies;

(4) the State educational agency will work with other agencies, including educational service agencies or other local consortia, and institutions to provide technical assistance to local educational agencies and schools, including technical assistance in providing professional development under section 1119, technical assistance under section 1117, and technical assistance relating to parental involvement under section 1118;

(5)(A) where educational service agencies exist, the State educational agency will consider providing professional development and technical assistance through such agencies; and

(B) where educational service agencies do not exist, the State educational agency will consider providing professional development and technical assistance through other cooperative agreements such as through a consortium of local educational agencies;

(6) the State educational agency will notify local educational agencies and the public of the content and student academic achievement standards and academic assessments developed under this section, and of the authority to operate schoolwide programs, and will fulfill the State educational agency's responsibilities regarding local educational agency improvement and school improvement under section 1116, including such corrective actions as are necessary;

(7) the State educational agency will provide the least restrictive and burdensome regulations for local educational agencies and individual schools participating in a program assisted under this part;

(8) the State educational agency will inform the Secretary and the public of how Federal laws, if at all, hinder the ability of States to hold local educational agencies and schools accountable for student academic achievement;

(9) the State educational agency will encourage schools to consolidate funds from other Federal, State, and local sources for schoolwide reform in schoolwide programs under section 1114;

(10) the State educational agency will modify or eliminate State fiscal and accounting barriers so that schools can easily consolidate funds from other Federal, State, and local sources for schoolwide programs under section 1114;

(11) the State educational agency has involved the committee of practitioners established under section 1903(b) in developing the plan and monitoring its implementation;

(12) the State educational agency will inform local educational agencies in the State of the local educational agency's authority to transfer funds under title VI, to obtain waivers under part D of title IX, and, if the State is an Ed-Flex Partnership State, to obtain waivers under the Education Flexibility Partnership Act of 1999;

(13) the State educational agency will coordinate activities funded under this part with other Federal activities as appropriate; and

(14) the State educational agency will encourage local educational agencies and individual schools participating in a program assisted under this part to offer family literacy services (using funds under this part), if the agency or school determines that a substantial number of students served under this part by the agency or school have parents who do not have a secondary school diploma or its recognized equivalent or who have low levels of literacy.

(d) PARENTAL INVOLVEMENT—Each State plan shall describe how the State educational agency will support the collection and dissemination to local educational agencies and schools of effective parental involvement practices. Such practices shall—

(1) be based on the most current research that meets the highest professional and technical standards, on effective parental involvement that fosters achievement to high standards for all children; and

(2) be geared toward lowering barriers to greater participation by parents in school planning, review, and improvement experienced.

(e) PEER REVIEW AND SECRETARIAL APPROVAL—

(1) SECRETARIAL DUTIES—The Secretary shall—

(A) establish a peer-review process to assist in the review of State plans;

(B) appoint individuals to the peer-review process who are representative of parents, teachers, State educational agencies, and local educational agencies, and who are familiar with educational standards, assessments, accountability, the needs of low-performing schools, and other educational needs of students;

(C) approve a State plan within 120 days of its submission unless the Secretary determines that the plan does not meet the requirements of this section;

(D) if the Secretary determines that the State plan does not meet the requirements of subsection (a), (b), or (c), immediately notify the State of such determination and the reasons for such determination;

(E) not decline to approve a State's plan before—

(i) offering the State an opportunity to revise its plan;

(ii) providing technical assistance in order to assist the State to meet the requirements of subsections (a), (b), and (c); and

(iii) providing a hearing; and

(F) have the authority to disapprove a State plan for not meeting the requirements of this part, but shall not have the authority to require a State, as a condition of approval of the State plan, to include in, or delete from, such plan one or more specific elements of the State's academic content standards or to use specific academic assessment instruments or items.

(2) STATE REVISIONS—A State plan shall be revised by the State educational agency if it is necessary to satisfy the requirements of this section.

(f) DURATION OF THE PLAN—

(1) IN GENERAL—Each State plan shall—

(A) remain in effect for the duration of the State's participation under this part; and

(B) be periodically reviewed and revised as necessary by the State educational agency to reflect changes in the State's strategies and programs under this part.

(2) ADDITIONAL INFORMATION—If significant changes are made to a State's plan, such as the adoption of new State academic content standards and State student achievement standards, new academic assessments, or a new definition of adequate yearly progress, such information shall be submitted to the Secretary.

(g) PENALTIES—

(1) FAILURE TO MEET DEADLINES ENACTED IN 1994—

(A) IN GENERAL—If a State fails to meet the deadlines established by the Improving America's Schools Act of 1994 (or under any waiver granted by the Secretary or under any compliance agreement with the Secretary) for demonstrating that the State has in place challenging academic content standards and student achievement standards, and a system for measuring and monitoring adequate yearly progress, the Secretary shall withhold 25 percent of the funds that would otherwise be available to the State for State administration and activities under this part in each year until the Secretary determines that the State meets those requirements.

(B) NO EXTENSION—Notwithstanding any other provision of law, 90 days after the date of enactment of the No Child Left Behind Act of 2001 the Secretary shall not grant any additional waivers of, or enter into any additional compliance agreements to extend, the deadlines described in subparagraph (A) for any State.

(2) FAILURE TO MEET REQUIREMENTS ENACTED IN 2001—If a State fails to meet any of the requirements of this section, other than the requirements described in paragraph (1), then the Secretary may withhold funds for State administration under this part until the Secretary determines that the State has fulfilled those requirements.

(h) REPORTS—

(1) ANNUAL STATE REPORT CARD—

(A) IN GENERAL—Not later than the beginning of the 2002–2003 school year, unless the State has received a 1-year extension pursuant to subsection (c)(1), a State that receives assistance under this part shall prepare and disseminate an annual State report card.

(B) IMPLEMENTATION—The State report card shall be—

(i) concise; and

(ii) presented in an understandable and uniform format and, to the extent practicable, provided in a language that the parents can understand.

(C) REQUIRED INFORMATION—The State shall include in its annual State report card—

(i) information, in the aggregate, on student achievement at each proficiency level on the State academic assessments described in subsection (b)(3) (disaggregated by race, ethnicity, gender, disability status, migrant status, English proficiency, and status as economically disadvantaged, except that such disaggregation shall not be required in a case in which the number of students in a category is insufficient to yield statistically reliable information or the results would reveal personally identifiable information about an individual student);

(ii) information that provides a comparison between the actual achievement levels of each group of students described in subsection (b)(2)(C)(v) and the State's annual measurable objectives for each such group of students on each of the academic assessments required under this part;

(iii) the percentage of students not tested (disaggregated by the same categories and subject to the same exception described in clause (i));

(iv) the most recent 2-year trend in student achievement in each subject area, and for each grade level, for which assessments under this section are required;

(v) aggregate information on any other indicators used by the State to determine the adequate yearly progress of students in achieving State academic achievement standards;

(vi) graduation rates for secondary school students consistent with subsection (b)(2)(C)(vi);

(vii) information on the performance of local educational agencies in the State regarding making adequate yearly progress, including the number and names of each school identified for school improvement under section 1116; and

(viii) the professional qualifications of teachers in the State, the percentage of such teachers teaching with emergency or provisional credentials, and the percentage of classes in the State not taught by highly qualified teachers, in the aggregate and disaggregated by high-poverty compared to low-poverty schools which, for the purpose of this clause, means schools in the top quartile of poverty and the bottom quartile of poverty in the State.

(D) OPTIONAL INFORMATION—The State may include in its annual State report card such other information as the State believes will best provide parents, students, and other members of the public with information regarding the progress of each of the State's public elementary schools and public secondary schools. Such information may include information regarding—

(i) school attendance rates;

(ii) average class size in each grade;

(iii) academic achievement and gains in English proficiency of limited English proficient students;

(iv) the incidence of school violence, drug abuse, alcohol abuse, student suspensions, and student expulsions;

(v) the extent and type of parental involvement in the schools;

(vi) the percentage of students completing advanced placement courses, and the rate of passing of advanced placement tests; and

(vii) a clear and concise description of the State's accountability system, including a description of the criteria by which the State evaluates school performance, and the criteria that the State has established, consistent with subsection (b)(2), to determine the status of schools regarding school improvement, corrective action, and restructuring.

(2) ANNUAL LOCAL EDUCATIONAL AGENCY REPORT CARDS—

(A) REPORT CARDS—

(i) IN GENERAL—Not later than the beginning of the 2002–2003 school year, a local educational agency that receives assistance under this part shall prepare and disseminate an annual local educational agency report card, except that the State educational agency may provide the local educational agency 1 additional year if the local educational agency demonstrates that exceptional or uncontrollable circumstances, such as a natural disaster or a precipitous and unforeseen decline in the financial resources of the local educational agency, prevented full implementation of this paragraph by that deadline and that the local educational agency will complete implementation within the additional 1-year period.

(ii) SPECIAL RULE—If a State educational agency has received an extension pursuant to subsection (c)(1), then a local educational agency within that State shall not be required to include the information required under paragraph (1)(C) in such report card during such extension.

(B) MINIMUM REQUIREMENTS—The State educational agency shall ensure that each local educational agency collects appropriate data and includes in the local educational agency's annual report the information described in paragraph (1)(C) as applied to the local educational agency and each school served by the local educational agency, and—

(i) in the case of a local educational agency—

(I) the number and percentage of schools identified for school improvement under section 1116(c) and how long the schools have been so identified; and

(II) information that shows how students served by the local educational agency achieved on the statewide academic assessment compared to students in the State as a whole; and

(ii) in the case of a school—

(I) whether the school has been identified for school improvement; and

(II) information that shows how the school's students achievement on the statewide academic assessments and other indicators of adequate yearly progress compared to students in the local educational agency and the State as a whole.

(C) OTHER INFORMATION—A local educational agency may include in its annual local educational agency report card any other appropriate information, whether or not such information is included in the annual State report card.

(D) DATA—A local educational agency or school shall only include in its annual local educational agency report card data that are sufficient to yield statistically reliable information, as determined by the State, and that do not reveal personally identifiable information about an individual student.

(E) PUBLIC DISSEMINATION—The local educational agency shall, not later than the beginning of the 2002–2003 school year, unless the local educational agency has received a 1-year extension pursuant to subparagraph (A), publicly disseminate the information described in this paragraph to all schools in the school district served by the local educational agency and to all parents of students attending those schools in an understandable and uniform format and, to the extent practicable, provided in a language that the parents can understand, and make the information widely available through public means, such as posting on the Internet, distribution to the media, and distribution through public agencies, except that if a local educational agency issues a report card for all students, the local educational agency may include the information under this section as part of such report.

(3) PREEXISTING REPORT CARDS—A State educational agency or local educational agency that was providing public report cards on the performance of students, schools, local educational agencies, or the State prior to the enactment of the No Child Left Behind Act of 2001 may use those report cards for the purpose of this subsection, so long as any such report card is modified, as may be needed, to contain the information required by this subsection.

(4) ANNUAL STATE REPORT TO THE SECRETARY—Each State educational agency receiving assistance under this part shall report annually to the Secretary, and make widely available within the State—

(A) beginning with school year 2002–2003, information on the State's progress in developing and implementing the academic assessments described in subsection (b)(3);

(B) beginning not later than school year 2002–2003, information on the achievement of students on the academic assessments required by subsection (b)(3), including the disaggregated results for the categories of students identified in subsection (b)(2)(C)(v);

(C) in any year before the State begins to provide the information described in subparagraph (B), information on the results of student academic assessments (including disaggregated results) required under this section;

(D) beginning not later than school year 2002–2003, unless the State has received an extension pursuant to subsection (c)(1), information on the acquisition of English proficiency by children with limited English proficiency;

(E) the number and names of each school identified for school improvement under section 1116(c), the reason why each school was so identified, and the measures taken to address the achievement problems of such schools;

(F) the number of students and schools that participated in public school choice and supplemental service programs and activities under this title; and

(G) beginning not later than the 2002–2003 school year, information on the quality of teachers and the percentage of classes being taught by highly qualified teachers in the State, local educational agency, and school.

(5) REPORT TO CONGRESS—The Secretary shall transmit annually to the Committee on Education and the Workforce of the House of Representatives and the Committee on Health, Education, Labor, and Pensions of the Senate a report that provides national and State-level data on the information collected under paragraph (4).

(6) PARENTS RIGHT-TO-KNOW—

(A) QUALIFICATIONS—At the beginning of each school year, a local educational agency that receives funds under this part shall notify the parents of each student attending any school receiving funds under this part that the parents may request, and the agency will provide the parents on request (and in a timely manner), information regarding the professional qualifications of the student's classroom teachers, including, at a minimum, the following:

(i) Whether the teacher has met State qualification and licensing criteria for the grade levels and subject areas in which the teacher provides instruction.

(ii) Whether the teacher is teaching under emergency or other provisional status through which State qualification or licensing criteria have been waived.

(iii) The baccalaureate degree major of the teacher and any other graduate certification or degree held by the teacher, and the field of discipline of the certification or degree.

(iv) Whether the child is provided services by paraprofessionals and, if so, their qualifications.

(B) ADDITIONAL INFORMATION—In addition to the information that parents may request under subparagraph (A), a school that receives funds under this part shall provide to each individual parent—

(i) information on the level of achievement of the parent's child in each of the State academic assessments as required under this part; and

(ii) timely notice that the parent's child has been assigned, or has been taught for four or more consecutive weeks by, a teacher who is not highly qualified.

(C) FORMAT—The notice and information provided to parents under this paragraph shall be in an understandable and uniform format and, to the extent practicable, provided in a language that the parents can understand.

(i) **PRIVACY**—Information collected under this section shall be collected and disseminated in a manner that protects the privacy of individuals.

(j) **TECHNICAL ASSISTANCE**—The Secretary shall provide a State educational agency, at the State educational agency's request, technical assistance in meeting the requirements of this section, including the provision of advice by experts in the development of high-quality academic assessments, the setting of State standards, the development of measures of adequate yearly progress that are valid and reliable, and other relevant areas.

(k) **VOLUNTARY PARTNERSHIPS**—A State may enter into a voluntary partnership with another State to develop and implement the academic assessments and standards required under this section.

(l) **CONSTRUCTION**—Nothing in this part shall be construed to prescribe the use of the academic assessments described in this part for student promotion or graduation purposes.

(m) **SPECIAL RULE WITH RESPECT TO BUREAU-FUNDED SCHOOLS**—In determining the assessments to be used by each operated or funded by BIA school receiving funds under this part, the following shall apply:

(1) Each such school that is accredited by the State in which it is operating shall use the assessments the State has developed and implemented to meet the requirements

of this section, or such other appropriate assessment as approved by the Secretary of the Interior.

(2) Each such school that is accredited by a regional accrediting organization shall adopt an appropriate assessment, in consultation with and with the approval of, the Secretary of the Interior and consistent with assessments adopted by other schools in the same State or region, that meets the requirements of this section.

(3) Each such school that is accredited by a tribal accrediting agency or tribal division of education shall use an assessment developed by such agency or division, except that the Secretary of the Interior shall ensure that such assessment meets the requirements of this section.

A Nation at Risk

THE NATIONAL COMMISSION ON EXCELLENCE IN EDUCATION, APRIL 1983

All, regardless of race or class or economic status, are entitled to a fair chance and to the tools for developing their individual powers of mind and spirit to the utmost. This promise means that all children by virtue of their own efforts, competently guided, can hope to attain the mature and informed judgment needed to secure gainful employment, and to manage their own lives, thereby serving not only their own interests but also the progress of society itself.

Our Nation is at risk. Our once unchallenged preeminence in commerce, industry, science, and technological innovation is being overtaken by competitors throughout the world. This report is concerned with only one of the many causes and dimensions of the problem, but it is the one that undergirds American prosperity, security, and civility. We report to the American people that while we can take justifiable pride in what our schools and colleges have historically accomplished and contributed to the United States and the well-being of its people, the educational foundations of our society are presently being eroded by a rising tide of mediocrity that threatens our very future as a Nation and a people. What was unimaginable a generation ago has begun to occur—others are matching and surpassing our educational attainments.

If an unfriendly foreign power had attempted to impose on America the mediocre educational performance that exists today, we might well have viewed it as an act of war. As it stands, we have allowed this to happen to ourselves. We have even squandered the gains in student achievement made in the wake of the Sputnik challenge. Moreover, we have dismantled essential support systems which helped make those gains possible. We have, in effect, been committing an act of unthinking, unilateral educational disarmament.

Our society and its educational institutions seem to have lost sight of the basic purposes of schooling, and of the high expectations and disciplined effort needed to attain them. This report, the result of 18 months of study, seeks to generate reform of our educational system in fundamental ways and to renew the Nation's commitment to schools and colleges of high quality throughout the length and breadth of our land.

That we have compromised this commitment is, upon reflection, hardly surprising, given the multitude of often conflicting demands we have placed on our Nation's schools and colleges. They are routinely called on to provide solutions to personal, social, and political problems that the home and other institutions either will not or cannot resolve. We must understand that these demands on our schools and colleges often exact an educational cost as well as a financial one.

On the occasion of the Commission's first meeting, President Reagan noted the central importance of education in American life when he said: "Certainly there are few areas of American life as important to our society, to our people, and to our families as our schools and colleges." This report, therefore, is as much an open letter to the American people as it is a report to the Secretary of Education. We are confident that the American people, properly informed, will do what is right for their children and for the generations to come.

■ RECOMMENDATIONS

In light of the urgent need for improvement, both immediate and long term, this Commission has agreed on a set of recommendations that the American people can begin to act on now, that can be implemented over the next several years, and that promise lasting reform. The topics are familiar; there is little mystery about what we believe must be done. Many schools, districts, and States are already giving serious and constructive attention to these matters, even though their plans may differ from our recommendations in some details.

We wish to note that we refer to public, private, and parochial schools and colleges alike. All are valuable national resources. Examples of actions similar to those recommended below can be found in each of them.

We must emphasize that the variety of student aspirations, abilities, and preparation requires that appropriate content be available to satisfy diverse needs. Attention must be directed to both the nature of the content available and to the needs of particular learners. The most gifted students, for example, may need a curriculum enriched and accelerated beyond even the needs of other students of high ability. Similarly, educationally disadvantaged students may require special curriculum materials, smaller classes, or individual tutoring to help them master the material presented. Nevertheless, there remains a common expectation: We must demand the best effort and performance from all students, whether they are gifted or less able, affluent or disadvantaged, whether destined for college, the farm, or industry.

Our recommendations are based on the beliefs that everyone can learn, that everyone is born with an urge to learn which can be nurtured, that a solid high school education is within the reach of virtually all, and that life-long learning will equip people with the skills required for new careers and for citizenship.

■ RECOMMENDATION A: CONTENT

We recommend *that State and local high school graduation requirements be strengthened and that, at a minimum, all students seeking a diploma be required to lay the foundations in the Five New Basics by taking the following curriculum during their 4 years of high school: (a) 4 years of English; (b) 3 years of mathematics; (c) 3 years of science; (d) 3 years of social studies; and (e) one-half year of computer science. For the college-bound, 2 years of foreign language in high school are strongly recommended in addition to those taken earlier.*

Whatever the student's educational or work objectives, knowledge of the New Basics is the foundation of success for the after-school years and, therefore, forms the core of the modern curriculum. A high level of shared education in these Basics, together with work in the fine and performing arts and foreign languages, constitutes the mind and spirit of our culture. The following Implementing Recommendations are intended as illustrative descriptions. They are included here to clarify what we mean by the essentials of a strong curriculum.

■ IMPLEMENTING RECOMMENDATIONS

1. The teaching of *English* in high school should equip graduates to: (a) comprehend, interpret, evaluate, and use what they read; (b) write well-organized, effective papers; (c) listen effectively and discuss ideas intelligently; and (d) know our literary heritage and how it enhances imagination and ethical understanding, and how it relates to the customs, ideas, and values of today's life and culture.

2. The teaching of *mathematics* in high school should equip graduates to: (a) understand geometric and algebraic concepts; (b) understand elementary probability and statistics; (c) apply mathematics in everyday situations; and (d) estimate, approximate, measure, and test the accuracy of their calculations. In addition to the traditional sequence of studies available for college-bound students, new, equally demanding mathematics curricula need to be developed for those who do not plan to continue their formal education immediately.

3. The teaching of *science* in high school should provide graduates with an introduction to: (a) the concepts, laws, and processes of the physical and biological sciences; (b) the methods of scientific inquiry and reasoning; (c) the application of scientific knowledge to everyday life; and (d) the social and environmental implications of scientific and technological development. Science courses must be revised and updated for both the college-bound and those not intending to go to college. An example of such work is the American Chemical Society's "Chemistry in the Community" program.

4. The teaching of *social studies* in high school should be designed to: (a) enable students to fix their places and possibilities within the larger social and cultural structure; (b) understand the broad sweep of both ancient and contemporary ideas that have shaped our world; and (c) understand the fundamentals of how our economic system works and how our political system functions; and (d) grasp the difference between free and repressive societies. An understanding of each of these areas is requisite to the informed and committed exercise of citizenship in our free society.

5. The teaching of *computer science* in high school should equip graduates to: (a) understand the computer as an information, computation, and communication device; (b) use the computer in the study of the other Basics and for personal and work-related purposes; and (c) understand the world of computers, electronics, and related technologies.
In addition to the New Basics, other important curriculum matters must be addressed.

6. Achieving proficiency in a *foreign language* ordinarily requires from 4 to 6 years of study and should, therefore, be started in the elementary grades. We believe it is desirable that students achieve such proficiency because study of a foreign language introduces students to non-English-speaking cultures, heightens awareness and comprehension of one's native tongue, and serves the Nation's needs in commerce, diplomacy, defense, and education.

7. The high school curriculum should also provide students with programs requiring rigorous effort in subjects that advance students' personal, educational, and occupational goals, such as the fine and performing arts and vocational education. These areas complement the New Basics, and they should demand the same level of performance as the Basics.

8. The curriculum in the crucial eight grades leading to the high school years should be specifically designed to provide a sound base for study in those and later years in such areas as English language development and writing, computational and problem solving skills, science, social studies, foreign language, and the arts. These years should foster an enthusiasm for learning and the development of the individual's gifts and talents.

9. We encourage the continuation of efforts by groups such as the American Chemical Society, the American Association for the Advancement of Science, the Modern Language Association, and the National Councils of Teachers of English and Teachers of Mathematics, to revise, update, improve, and make available new and more diverse curricular materials. We applaud the consortia of educators and scientific, industrial, and scholarly societies that cooperate to improve the school curriculum.

■ RECOMMENDATION B: STANDARDS AND EXPECTATIONS

We recommend *that schools, colleges, and universities adopt more rigorous and measurable standards, and higher expectations, for academic performance and student conduct, and that 4-year colleges and universities raise their requirements for admission. This will help students do their best educationally with challenging materials in an environment that supports learning and authentic accomplishment.*

■ IMPLEMENTING RECOMMENDATIONS

1. Grades should be indicators of academic achievement so they can be relied on as evidence of a student's readiness for further study.

2. Four-year colleges and universities should raise their admissions requirements and advise all potential applicants of the standards for admission in terms of specific courses required, performance in these areas, and levels of achievement on standardized achievement tests in each of the five Basics and, where applicable, foreign languages.

3. Standardized tests of achievement (not to be confused with aptitude tests) should be administered at major transition points from one level of schooling to another and particularly from high school to college or work. The purposes of these tests would be to: (a) certify the student's credentials; (b) identify the need for remedial intervention; and (c) identify the opportunity for advanced or accelerated work. The tests should be administered as part of a nationwide (but not Federal) system of State and local standardized tests. This system should include other diagnostic procedures that assist teachers and students to evaluate student progress.

4. Textbooks and other tools of learning and teaching should be upgraded and updated to assure more rigorous content. We call upon university scientists, scholars, and

members of professional societies, in collaboration with master teachers, to help in this task, as they did in the post-Sputnik era. They should assist willing publishers in developing the products or publish their own alternatives where there are persistent inadequacies.

5. In considering textbooks for adoption, States and school districts should: (a) evaluate texts and other materials on their ability to present rigorous and challenging material clearly; and (b) require publishers to furnish evaluation data on the material's effectiveness.

6. Because no textbook in any subject can be geared to the needs of all students, funds should be made available to support text development in "thin-market" areas, such as those for disadvantaged students, the learning disabled, and the gifted and talented.

7. To assure quality, all publishers should furnish evidence of the quality and appropriateness of textbooks, based on results from field trials and credible evaluation. In view of the enormous numbers and varieties of texts available, more widespread consumer information services for purchasers are badly needed.

8. New instructional materials should reflect the most current applications of technology in appropriate curriculum areas, the best scholarship in each discipline, and research in learning and teaching.

■ RECOMMENDATION C: TIME

We recommend *that significantly more time be devoted to learning the New Basics. This will require more effective use of the existing school day, a longer school day, or a lengthened school year.*

■ IMPLEMENTING RECOMMENDATIONS

1. Students in high schools should be assigned far more homework than is now the case.

2. Instruction in effective study and work skills, which are essential if school and independent time is to be used efficiently, should be introduced in the early grades and continued throughout the student's schooling.

3. School districts and State legislatures should strongly consider 7-hour school days, as well as a 200- to 220-day school year.

4. The time available for learning should be expanded through better classroom management and organization of the school day. If necessary, additional time should be found to meet the special needs of slow learners, the gifted, and others who need more instructional diversity than can be accommodated during a conventional school day or school year.

5. The burden on teachers for maintaining discipline should be reduced through the development of firm and fair codes of student conduct that are enforced consistently, and by considering alternative classrooms, programs, and schools to meet the needs of continually disruptive students.

6. Attendance policies with clear incentives and sanctions should be used to reduce the amount of time lost through student absenteeism and tardiness.

7. Administrative burdens on the teacher and related intrusions into the school day should be reduced to add time for teaching and learning.

8. Placement and grouping of students, as well as promotion and graduation policies, should be guided by the academic progress of students and their instructional needs, rather than by rigid adherence to age.

■ RECOMMENDATION D: TEACHING

This recommendation *consists of seven parts. Each is intended to improve the preparation of teachers or to make teaching a more rewarding and re-spected profession. Each of the seven stands on its own and should not be considered solely as an implementing recommendation.*

1. Persons preparing to teach should be required to meet high educational standards, to demonstrate an aptitude for teaching, and to demonstrate competence in an academic discipline. Colleges and universities offering teacher preparation programs should be judged by how well their graduates meet these criteria.
2. Salaries for the teaching profession should be increased and should be professionally competitive, market-sensitive, and performance-based. Salary, promotion, tenure, and retention decisions should be tied to an effective evaluation system that includes peer review so that superior teachers can be rewarded, average ones encouraged, and poor ones either improved or terminated.
3. School boards should adopt an 11-month contract for teachers. This would ensure time for curriculum and professional development, programs for students with special needs, and a more adequate level of teacher compensation.
4. School boards, administrators, and teachers should cooperate to develop career ladders for teachers that distinguish among the beginning instructor, the experienced teacher, and the master teacher.
5. Substantial nonschool personnel resources should be employed to help solve the immediate problem of the shortage of mathematics and science teachers. Qualified individuals, including recent graduates with mathematics and science degrees, graduate students, and industrial and retired scientists could, with appropriate preparation, immediately begin teaching in these fields. A number of our leading science centers have the capacity to begin educating and retraining teachers immediately. Other areas of critical teacher need, such as English, must also be addressed.
6. Incentives, such as grants and loans, should be made available to attract outstanding students to the teaching profession, particularly in those areas of critical shortage.
7. Master teachers should be involved in designing teacher preparation programs and in supervising teachers during their probationary years.

■ RECOMMENDATION E: LEADERSHIP AND FISCAL SUPPORT

We recommend *that citizens across the Nation hold educators and elected officials responsible for providing the leadership necessary to achieve these reforms, and that citizens provide the fiscal support and stability required to bring about the reforms we propose.*

■ IMPLEMENTING RECOMMENDATIONS

1. Principals and superintendents must play a crucial leadership role in developing school and community support for the reforms we propose, and school boards must provide them with the professional development and other support required to carry out their leadership role effectively. The Commission stresses the distinction between leadership skills involving persuasion, setting goals and developing community consensus behind them, and managerial and supervisory skills. Although the latter are necessary, we believe that school boards must consciously develop leadership skills at the school and district levels if the reforms we propose are to be achieved.

2. State and local officials, including school board members, governors, and legislators, have *the primary responsibility* for financing and governing the schools, and should incorporate the reforms we propose in their educational policies and fiscal planning.

3. The Federal Government, in cooperation with States and localities, should help meet the needs of key groups of students such as the gifted and talented, the socioeconomically disadvantaged, minority and language minority students, and the handicapped. In combination these groups include both national resources and the Nation's youth who are most at risk.

4. In addition, we believe the Federal Government's role includes several functions of national consequence that States and localities alone are unlikely to be able to meet: protecting constitutional and civil rights for students and school personnel; collecting data, statistics, and information about education generally; supporting curriculum improvement and research on teaching, learning, and the management of schools; supporting teacher training in areas of critical shortage or key national needs; and providing student financial assistance and research and graduate training. We believe the assistance of the Federal Government should be provided with a minimum of administrative burden and intrusiveness.

5. The Federal Government has *the primary responsibility* to identify the national interest in education. It should also help fund and support efforts to protect and promote that interest. It must provide the national leadership to ensure that the Nation's public and private resources are marshaled to address the issues discussed in this report.

6. This Commission calls upon educators, parents, and public officials at all levels to assist in bringing about the educational reform proposed in this report. We also call upon citizens to provide the financial support necessary to accomplish these purposes. Excellence costs. But in the long run mediocrity costs far more.

Colorado Legislation to Provide Exemptions for No Child Left Behind Assessments

Second Regular Session
Sixty-fifth General Assembly
STATE OF COLORADO

REENGROSSED
This Version Includes All Amendments
Adopted in the House of Introduction
HOUSE BILL 06-1289

LLS NO. 06-0376.01 Julie Pelegrin

HOUSE SPONSORSHIP
Solano, Benefield, Lindstrom, Merrifield, Pommer, and Todd
SENATE SPONSORSHIP
Williams, and Shaffer

House Committees   **Senate Committees**
Education

A BILL FOR AN ACT
101 **CONCERNING ELIMINATING PENALTIES ARISING FROM A PARENT'S**
102 **CHOICE REGARDING STUDENT PARTICIPATION IN STATEWIDE**
103 **ASSESSMENTS.**

Bill Summary

(Note: This summary applies to this bill as introduced and does not necessarily reflect any amendments that may be subsequently adopted.)

Recognizes the importance of parental choice in a child's education, including the choice of whether the child should participate in statewide assessments. Requires the department of education ("department") to request from the federal government a waiver of the requirements pertaining to the level of student participation in statewide assessments under the federal "No Child Left Behind Act of 2001".

Directs the department to report to the education committees concerning the status and determination of the waiver application.

Requires the department to exclude students who do not finish a statewide assessment due to absence or parental choice from the calculations of a school's academic performance rating and academic growth of students rating, and specifies that the department shall not place the students at a proficiency level in any academic area.

Prohibits a school district from imposing any form of penalty on a student who does not take a statewide assessment due to absence or parental choice.

Be it enacted by the General Assembly of the State of Colorado:

SECTION 1. Legislative declaration.

(1) The general assembly hereby finds that:

(a) Parental choice in education has been a guiding tenet in education policy in this state for several years and is a core value of the statewide system of public education in Colorado;

(b) Parents are in the best position to decide what is best and appropriate for their children's education, whether the decision pertains to the educational setting in which the child should be placed, the educational services the child should receive, or the types of testing in which the child should participate;

(c) The recent enactment of the federal "No Child Left Behind Act of 2001", 20 U.S.C. sec. 6301 et seq., imposes federal mandates on states, school districts, public schools, and parents that require, among other things, all children, regardless of their circumstances, annually to participate in a series of standardized tests, implemented in this state as the Colorado student assessment program;

(d) For many children, especially children with disabilities or other learning challenges, participating in the Colorado student assessment program creates an extremely high level of frustration;

(e) Because of the federal test participation mandate, a parent cannot choose whether participating in the tests is actually in his or her child's best interests without having to consider the negative consequences that may be imposed on the child's school and school district and the state as a result of the child's nonparticipation;

(f) A parent who would like to exercise choice and keep his or her child at home during the testing period often experiences great pressure from the school district to comply with the testing requirement and may feel responsible for the penalties imposed on the child's school in the form of lower academic performance ratings as a result of the child's nonparticipation;

(g) Under current state law, a school receives a weighting factor of -0.5 for each child who does not participate in a statewide assessment, and the school fails to make adequate yearly progress under the federal "No Child Left Behind Act of 2001", 20 U.S.C. sec. 6301 et seq., if more than five percent of the students do not participate in the statewide assessment;

(h) Thus, the only way a parent can exercise choice with regard to whether his or her child participates in the Colorado student assessment program, without harming the child's school or school district, is to withdraw the child from public school, even though the parent must continue paying taxes in support of the public school system.

(2) The general assembly, therefore, declares that schools should not be punished for the choices made and actions taken by parents with regard to participation by their children in the Colorado student assessment program.

SECTION 2. 22-7-604, Colorado Revised Statutes, is amended BY THE ADDITION OF A NEW SUBSECTION to read: 22-7-604. Academic performance—academic growth of students—rating—designation and methodology.

(9) Notwithstanding any provision of this section to the contrary, if a student does not participate in an assessment due to absence or the choice of the student's parent, the student shall not be included in any of the calculations required pursuant to this section or in the total number of students taking the assessments or the curriculum-based, achievement college entrance exam, and the student shall not be placed at a proficiency level for an academic area.

SECTION 3. Article 32 of title 22, Colorado Revised Statutes, is amended BY THE ADDITION OF A NEW SECTION to read: 22-32-137. Colorado student assessment program—student participation—no penalty.

(1) Each school district shall provide information to the parents of students enrolled in the school district regarding each parent's ability to exercise choice over whether his or her child participates in the statewide assessments administered pursuant to section 22-7-409. A school district or a public school shall not encourage parents to remove their children from participating in the statewide assessments.

(2) A school district or a public school shall not penalize a student for failure or refusal to participate in an assessment administered pursuant to section 22-7-409 as a result of absence or the choice of the student's parent. For purposes of this section, a penalty shall include, but need not be limited to:

(a) withholding of credits toward graduation or denying a student the ability to graduate or receive a diploma;

(b) denying a student the opportunity to participate in an educational program or an extracurricular activity;

(c) denying a student the ability to advance to a subsequent grade level.

(3) The provisions of this section shall not be interpreted to prohibit a school district from enforcing compulsory attendance requirements as provided in the school district attendance policy adopted pursuant to article 33 of this title.

SECTION 4. Safety clause. The general assembly hereby finds, determines, and declares that this act is necessary for the immediate preservation of the public peace, health, and safety.

School Leaders Licensure Assessment (1010)

■ MODULE I: EVALUATION OF ACTIONS I AND II

Evaluation of Actions I

All ten exercises in the Evaluation of Actions I section are scored on a three-point scale, with 2 the highest possible score and 0 the lowest.

Sample Exercise

Read the vignette below and briefly and specifically answer the question that follows:

It is early December and the students in an elementary school are practicing for the annual holiday concert. A parent phones the school to insist that her child not be required to sing any of the Christmas songs. The principal excuses the child from participation in the music practice.

Do you agree with the principal's action? Give a rationale, citing factors that are relevant to a principal's decisions in such situations.

Relevant ISLLC Standards

Standards 2, 4, and 5

General Scoring Guide

The following general scoring guide is used to score all responses in the Evaluation of Actions I Module

Score: 2

A score of 2 presents a reasoned response based on a clear understanding and application of the underlying standards.

A typical response in this category

- demonstrates a clear understanding of the standards applicable to the vignette
- applies the appropriate standards in a manner that is consistent with the intent and spirit of the standards
- provides a clear and specific answer to the question asked
- provides a logical and reasonable rationale for answers when requested

Score: 1

A score of 1 presents a response based on a general understanding and application of the underlying standards, but may also be uneven in its presentation.

A typical response in this category

- demonstrates a general understanding of the standards applicable to the vignette
- applies the standards in a manner that is supportive of the intent and spirit of the standards
- provides a general or uneven answer to the question
- provides an acceptable rationale for answers when requested

Score: 0

A score of 0 may demonstrate some competence in responding to the question, but is clearly limited or flawed.

A typical response in this category

- demonstrates a weak understanding of the standards applicable to the vignette
- does not apply appropriate standards or applies standards in opposition to the intent and spirit of the standards
- provides a vague or inappropriate answer to the question
- provides a weak, inappropriate, or illogical rationale or does not provide a rationale when one is requested

Sample Responses

The following are examples of actual responses (transcribed with errors) given by principal candidates to the sample exercise from Evaluation of Actions I. The score assigned to each is written above the response. An italicized explanation of how the score was derived is included below the response. Two examples are provided at each score point.

Sample Response 1 (Score = 2)

Yes, I agree with the principal's actins. First of all, parents have rights related to religious issues, and since this is a "holiday" concert, the principal should be sensitive to the parent's concerns. I think the principal should also ask the teachers to examine the program carefully, to be sure it is not advocating any one religion or that it would not be offensive to any group of students. Also, perhaps the principal should suggest some alternative activity for the student so the student will not feel left out.

Commentary: This reasoned response clearly cites several factors that are relevant to the principal's decision, such as the parent's/student's rights, examining the content of the concert to determine its appropriateness for all students, and finding an alternative activity for the student. Each of the rationales provided demonstrates an understanding of how the appropriate standards should be applied.

Sample Response 2 (Score = 2)

Before removing the child from the school activity, I would discuss with the parent the scope and purpose of the concert. In these days, very few concerts have "religious" songs in them in public schools. I would explain the cultural intent of the concert, and the need the children have to be part of such school activities. However, if the parent still wants the student excluded, I would excuse the child, because parents do have legal rights.

Commentary: This response presents clear reasoning in identifying relevant factors such as acknowledging the parent's/students' rights and meeting with the parent to discuss the objectives. The rationales provided are logical and reasonable, as well as based on the application of appropriate standards. While the response suggests trying to convince the parent, it is still respectful of the parent's point of view and legal rights.

Sample Response 3 (Score = 1)

The parent has the legal right to have the child removed from the activity if the content is objectionable from a religious point of view. Although I might want the parent to go ahead and allow the student to be involved, I would honor the parent's right to have the student excluded.

Commentary: By acknowledging the parent's/students' rights, this response identifies one factor the principal should consider, but it misses other important factors that would also be relevant in making a decision. While this response demonstrates some understanding of the standards and provides an acceptable response to the question, it is not as fully reasoned and the rationale is not as developed as a response scored a '2'.

Sample Response 4 (Score = 1)

I would allow the student to not participate, but I would work with the teacher to find another activity for the student to develop some of the same performance skills that would be learned by participating in the concert.

Commentary: Even though this response appropriately suggests an alternative activity for the student, by not recognizing the rights of the parent/student, it misses a factor central to demonstrating a clear understanding and application of the standards. As such, the response demonstrates a general understanding of the standards and suggests actions that are supportive of but not fully consistent with the underlying standards.

Sample Response 5 (Score = 0)

The principal did not do the right thing. The concert is an official part of the school curriculum, and if the principal begins making exceptions for one parent, the principal will have to make exceptions for every parent who wants something, and then the school will no longer have a standard curriculum.

Commentary: This response is clearly limited. While it provides a clear and specific response to the question, it is not sensitive to the parent's concerns and does not suggest a problem-solving approach. The approach provided in the response is inappropriate for the situation, does not demonstrate an understanding of the standards or the law, and actually violates the general sense of the ISLLC Standards.

Interstate Leaders Licensure Consortium (ISLLC) Indicators

■ STANDARD 1

Knowledge

The administrator has knowledge and understanding of:

- learning goals in a pluralistic society
- the principles of developing and implementing strategic plans
- systems theory
- information sources, data collection, and data-analysis strategies
- effective communication
- effective consensus-building and negotiation skills

Disposition

The administrator believes in, values, and is committed to:

- the educability of all
- a school vision of high standards of learning
- continuous school improvement
- the inclusion of all members of the school community
- ensuring that students have the knowledge, skills, and values needed to become successful adults
- a willingness to continuously examine one's own assumptions, beliefs, and practices
- doing the work required for high levels of personal and organization performance

Performance

The administrator facilitates processes and engages in activities ensuring that:

- the vision and mission of the school are effectively communicated to staff, parents, students, and community members
- the vision and mission are communicated through the use of symbols, ceremonies, stories, and similar activities

- the core beliefs of the school vision are modeled for all stakeholders
- the contributions of school community members to the realization of the vision are recognized and celebrated
- progress toward the vision and mission is communicated to all stakeholders
- the school community is involved in school improvement efforts
- the vision shapes the educational programs, plans, and activities
- the vision shapes the educational programs, plans, and actions
- an implementation plan is developed in which objectives and strategies to achieve the vision and goals are clearly articulated
- assessment data related to student learning are used to develop the school vision and goals
- relevant demographic data pertaining to students and their families are used in developing the school mission and goals
- barriers to achieving the vision are identified, clarified, and addressed
- needed resources are sought and obtained to support the implementation of the school mission and goals
- existing resources are used in support of the school vision and goals
- the vision, mission, and implementation plans are regularly monitored, evaluated, and revised

■ STANDARD 2

Knowledge

The administrator has knowledge and understanding of:

- student growth and development
- applied learning theories
- applied motivational theories
- curriculum design, implementation, evaluation, and refinement
- principles of effective instruction
- measurement, evaluation, and assessment strategies
- diversity and its meaning for educational programs
- adult learning and professional-development models
- the change process for systems, organizations, and individuals
- the role of technology in promoting student learning and professional growth
- school cultures

Disposition

The administrator believes in, values, and is committed to:

- student learning as the fundamental purpose of schooling
- the proposition that all students can learn
- the variety of ways in which students can learn
- life long learning for self and others
- professional development as an integral part of school improvement
- the benefits that diversity brings to the school community
- a safe and supportive learning environment
- preparing students to be contributing members of society

Performance

The administrator facilitates processes and engages in activities ensuring that:

- all individuals are treated with fairness, dignity, and respect
- professional development promotes a focus on student learning consistent with the school vision and goals
- students and staff feel valued and important
- the responsibilities and contributions of each individual are acknowledged
- barriers to student learning are identified, clarified, and addressed
- diversity is considered in developing learning experiences
- life long learning is encouraged and modeled
- there is a culture of high expectations for self, student, and staff performance
- technologies are used in teaching and learning
- student and staff accomplishments are recognized and celebrated
- multiple opportunities to learn are available to all students
- the school is organized and aligned for success
- curricular, co-curricular, and extra-curricular programs are designed, implemented, evaluated, and refined
- curriculum decisions are based on research, expertise of teachers, and the recommendations of learned societies
- the school culture and climate are assessed on a regular basis
- a variety of sources of information is used to make decisions
- student learning is assessed using a variety of techniques
- multiple sources of information regarding performance are used by staff and students
- a variety of supervisory and evaluation models is employed
- pupil personnel programs are developed to meet the needs of students and their families

Knowledge

The administrator has knowledge and understanding of:

- theories and models of organizations and the principles of organizational development
- operational procedures at the school and district level
- principles and issues relating to school safety and security
- human resource management and development
- principles and issues relating to fiscal operations of school management
- principles and issues relating to school facilities and use of space
- legal issues impacting school operations
- current technologies that support management functions

▪ STANDARD 3

Disposition

The administrator believes in, values, and is committed to:

- making management decisions to enhance learning and teaching
- taking risks to improve schools
- trusting people and their judgments

- accepting responsibility
- high-quality standards, expectations, and performances
- involving stakeholders in management processes
- a safe environment

Performance

The administrator facilitates processes and engages in activities ensuring that:

- knowledge of learning, teaching, and student development is used to inform management decisions
- operational procedures are designed and managed to maximize opportunities for successful learning
- emerging trends are recognized, studied, and applied as appropriate
- operational plans and procedures to achieve the vision and goals of the school are in place
- collective bargaining and other contractual agreements related to the school are effectively managed
- the school plant, equipment, and support systems operate safely, efficiently, and effectively
- time is managed to maximize attainment of organizational goals
- potential problems and opportunities are identified
- problems are confronted and resolved in a timely manner
- financial, human, and material resources are aligned to the goals of schools
- the school acts entrepreneurially to support continuous improvement
- organizational systems are regularly monitored and modified as needed
- stakeholders are involved in decisions affecting schools
- responsibility is shared to maximize ownership and accountability
- effective problem-framing and problem-solving skills are used
- effective conflict resolution skills are used
- effective group-process and consensus-building skills are used
- effective communication skills are used
- there is effective use of technology to manage school operations
- fiscal resources of the school are managed responsibly, efficiently, and effectively
- a safe, clean, and aesthetically pleasing school environment is created and maintained
- human resource functions support the attainment of school goals
- confidentiality and privacy of school records are maintained

■ STANDARD 4

Knowledge

The administrator has knowledge and understanding of:

- emerging issues and trends that potentially impact the school community
- the conditions and dynamics of the diverse school community
- community resources
- community relations and marketing strategies and processes
- successful models of school, family, business, community, government and higher education partnerships

Disposition

The administrator believes in, values, and is committed to:

- schools operating as an integral part of the larger community
- collaboration and communication with families
- involvement of families and other stakeholders in school decision-making processes
- the proposition that diversity enriches the school
- families as partners in the education of their children
- the proposition that families have the best interests of their children in mind
- resources of the family and community needing to be brought to bear on the education of students
- an informed public

Performance

The administrator facilitates processes and engages in activities ensuring that:

- high visibility, active involvement, and communication with the large community is a priority
- relationships with community leaders are identified and nurtured
- information about family and community concerns, expectations, and needs is used regularly
- there is outreach to different business, religious, political, and service agencies and organizations
- credence is given to individuals and groups whose values and opinions may conflict
- the school and community serve one another as resources
- available community resources are secured to help the school solve problems and achieve goals
- partnerships are established with area businesses, institutions of higher education, and community groups to strengthen programs and support school goals
- community youth family services are integrated with school programs
- community stakeholders are treated equitably
- diversity is recognized and valued
- effective media relations are developed and maintained
- a comprehensive program of community relations is established
- public resources and funds are used appropriately and wisely
- community collaboration is modeled for staff
- opportunities for staff to develop collaborative skills are provided

Knowledge

The administrator has knowledge and understanding of:

- the purpose of education and the role of leadership in modern society
- various ethical frameworks and perspectives on ethics
- the values of the diverse school community
- professional codes of ethics
- the philosophy and history of education

■ STANDARD 5

Disposition

The administrator believes in, values, and is committed to:

- the ideal of the common good
- the principles of the Bill of Rights
- the right of every student to a free, quality education
- bringing ethical principles to the decision-making process
- subordinating one's own interests to the good of the school community
- accepting the consequences for upholding one's principles and actions
- using the influence of one's office constructively and productively in the service of all students and their families
- development of a caring school community

Performance

The administrator facilitates processes and engages in activities ensuring that:

- examines personal and professional values
- demonstrates a personal and professional code of ethics
- demonstrates values, beliefs, and attitudes that inspire others to higher levels of performance
- serves as a role model
- accepts responsibility for school operations
- considers the impact of one's administrative practices on others
- uses the influence of the office to enhance the educational program rather than for personal gain
- treats people fairly, equitable, and with dignity and respect
- protects the rights and confidentiality of students and staff
- demonstrates appreciation for and sensitivity to the diversity in the school community
- recognizes and respects the legitimate authority of others
- examines and considers the prevailing values of the diverse school community
- expects that others in the school community will demonstrate integrity and exercise ethical behavior
- opens the school to public scrutiny
- fulfills legal and contractual obligations
- applies laws and procedures fairly, wisely, and considerately

■ STANDARD 6

Knowledge

The administrator has knowledge and understanding of:

- principles of representative governance that undergird the system of American schools
- the role of public education in developing and renewing a democratic society and an economically productive nation

- the law as related to education and schooling
- the political, social, cultural, and economic systems and processes that impact schools
- models and strategies of change and conflict resolution as applied to the larger political, social, cultural, and economic contexts of schooling
- global issues and forces affecting teaching and learning
- the dynamics of policy development and advocacy under our democratic political system
- the importance of diversity and equity in a democratic society

Disposition

The administrator believes in, values, and is committed to:

- education as a key to opportunity and social mobility
- recognizing a variety of ideas, values, and cultures
- importance of a continuing dialogue with other decision makers affecting education
- actively participating in the political and policy-making context in the service of education
- using legal systems to protect student rights and improve student opportunities

Performance

The administrator facilitates processes and engages in activities ensuring that:

- the environment in which schools operate is influenced on behalf of students and their families
- communication occurs among the school community concerning trends, issues, and potential changes in the environment in which schools operate
- there is ongoing dialogue with representatives of diverse community groups
- the school community works within the framework of policies, laws, and regulations enacted by local, state, and federal authorities
- public policy is shaped to provide quality education for students
- lines of communication are developed with decision makers outside the school community

Source: Council of Chief State School Officers. (1996). *Interstate school leaders licensure consortium (ISLLC): Standards for school leaders.* Washington, DC: Author. Retrieved February 1, 2005, from http://www.ccsso.org/content/pdfs/isllcstd.pdf.

NEA Lawsuit against Unfunded Mandates of No Child Left Behind

05-2708

IN THE UNITED STATES COURT OF APPEALS FOR THE SIXTH CIRCUIT

No. 05-2708

SCHOOL DISTRICT OF THE CITY OF PONTIAC, ET AL.,

Plaintiffs-Appellants

v.

SECRETARY OF U.S. DEPARTMENT OF EDUCATION,

Defendant-Appellee

ON APPEAL FROM THE UNITED STATES DISTRICT COURT FOR THE EASTERN DISTRICT OF MICHIGAN

AMICI CURIAE BRIEF OF THE STATES OF CONNECTICUT, DELAWARE, ILLINOIS, MAINE, OKLAHOMA, WISCONSIN, AND THE DISTRICT OF COLUMBIA

■ STATEMENT OF THE AMICI CURIAE

The sovereign States of Connecticut, Delaware, Illinois, Maine, Oklahoma, Wisconsin, and the District of Columbia, (collectively, the "Amici States") through their respective Attorneys General, submit this brief as amici curiae in support of the plaintiffs-appellants in this matter. Pursuant to Fed. R. App. P. 29(a), the Amici States are permitted to file this brief without the consent of the parties or leave of the Court.

The Amici States have a significant interest in the outcome of this case. Education historically has been the exclusive realm of the states. As the Supreme Court has repeatedly recognized, education is "perhaps the most important function of state and local governments," Honig v. Doe, 484 U.S. 305, 309 (1988), quoting Brown v. Board of Education, 347 U.S.

483, 493 (1954), and is committed to state and local control. <u>Board of Curators v. Horowitz</u>, 435 U.S. 78, 91 (1978); <u>Epperson v. Arkansas</u>, 393 U.S. 97, 104 (1968). Although educational rights are conspicuously absent from the federal constitution, nearly every state constitution requires the state to provide its children with an education.

Before passage of the No Child Left Behind ("NCLB") Act, Pub. L. 107-110 in 2002, the federal government's role in education generally was limited to providing supplemental resources to targeted groups of disadvantaged students, generally "Title I" students (with the most economic disadvantages, such as high poverty and homelessness) and special education students. By contrast, the ten Titles of the 670-page NCLB Act affect *all* students in the Nation's public schools, not only special education students or those in public schools that qualify for and receive Title I funding. Although the federal government provides only 5% to 8% of total educational funding, through the NCLB Act the federal government is now dictating educational policy on a wide variety of educational issues, from teacher qualifications to the timing of annual student assessments.

The Amici States respectfully disagree with the district court's determination that the Unfunded Mandates Provision of the NCLB Act, NCLB Act § 9527(a), 20 U.S.C. § 7907(a), merely means that the federal officials at the U.S. Department of Education cannot act *ultra vires* and add additional obligations beyond the requirements of the NCLB Act. *See* <u>Pontiac v. Spellings</u>, 2005 U.S. Dist. LEXIS 29253, *11-12 (E.D. Mich., November 23, 2005) ("District Court decision"). Certainly, that is not what Amici States understood when they opted to participate in the NCLB programs. Rather, Amici States understood, based on the plain language and statutory context of the Unfunded Mandates Provision, that neither states nor local school districts would be required to spend their own funds to comply with the NCLB mandates. The states' understanding of the plain meaning of the Unfunded Mandates Provision is significant, and should be given effect by this Court in order to avoid the considerable constitutional difficulties raised by construing the NCLB in a manner that undermines the states' settled expectations.

■ ARGUMENT

The Unfunded Mandates Provision means that the federal government must pay the costs imposed upon the states and local school districts by the NCLB Act and that the Secretary and her staff cannot implement the NCLB Act's requirements in a manner that requires any state or local school district to "spend any funds" or to "incur any costs not paid for under this Act."

Ignoring the plain meaning of the Unfunded Mandates Provision, the repeated use of the verb "mandate" elsewhere in the Act, and the legislative intent behind the enactment of the Provision, the district court reduced the Unfunded Mandates Provision to a meaningless tautology: it posits that the Provision means the Secretary cannot act outside her statutory authority even though prior to the passage of the Provision, as a creature of statute, the Secretary never had any authority to act beyond those statutory boundaries.

Given that the states understood the Unfunded Mandates Provision to mean what it says, an interpretation at odds with the plain language raises constitutional concerns, for the constitutional restrictions upon Congress' spending power authority requires that "Congress speak with a clear voice." *See* <u>Pennhurst State School & Hospital v. Halderman</u>, 451 U.S. 1, 17–18 (1981).

The district court's interpretation of the NCLB Act's Unfunded Mandates Provision renders it a nullity and should be rejected.

Tennessee Language Arts Curriculum Standards for Reading, Eighth Grade

■ CONTENT STANDARD: 1.0

The student will develop the reading and listening skills necessary for word recognition, comprehension, interpretation, analysis, evaluation, and appreciation of print and non-print text.

Learning Expectations	Accomplishments
1.01 Continue to develop oral language and listening skills	a. Continue to model active listening in both formal and informal settings b. Continue to adhere to rules for public conversations c. Continue to formulate and respond to questions from teachers and classmates d. Continue to organize and share information, stories, experiences, ideas, and feelings with others in both formal and informal situations e. Participate in creative responses to text (e.g., debates, dramatizations, speeches). f. Deliver a focused, well-organized oral presentation, using multiple sources of information from any content area utilizing visual aids for contextual support g. Incorporate into oral reading, discussions, and presentations the use of correct stress, pitch, and juncture h. Analyze a variety of non-verbal communication techniques and how they impact the audience and speaker
1.02 Develop an understanding of the concepts of print	a. Recognize the defining characteristics of a variety of texts (e.g., identify differences between poetry and narration, between plays and essays, between biography and historical fiction) b. Approach texts according to their type using appropriate skills and prior knowledge (e.g., read poetry aloud, bring

continued

continued

	knowledge of history to a reading of biography, provide "between the lines" information in drama, determine how the form/genre informs meaning)
	c. Recognize the structure and organization of various text features to locate information (e.g., sidebars, questions at the end of chapter/unit, footnotes, endnotes)
1.03 Expand reading skills through phonemic awareness	a. Continue to develop an awareness of the sounds of language through repeated exposure to a variety of auditory experiences (e.g., poems, music lyrics, books on tape, read alouds)
	b. Evaluate patterns of rhyme and rhythm and how they affect understanding
	c. Evaluate the effects of sound in language (e.g., alliteration [assonance and consonance], onomatopoeia, slant rhyme, internal rhyme, accent, repetition)
1.04 Use decoding strategies to read unfamiliar words	a. Recognize and identify the base/root word from words having affixes
	b. Determine the meaning of prefixes and suffixes through identification and usage
	c. Use context clues to determine multiple meaning words
	d. Decode unknown grade level words utilizing previous learned strategies and verify the word's meaning within the context of the selection
1.05 Read to develop fluency, expression, accuracy, and confidence	a. Demonstrate the ability to read fluently with expression, accuracy, and poise from a variety of texts (e.g., paired reading, choral reading, and read alongs)
	b. Continue to participate in guided readings
	c. Continue to read using appropriate pronunciations, expression, and rate
	d. Continue to adjust speed based on the purpose for reading
	e. Continue to read independently on a daily basis
1.06 Expand reading vocabulary	a. Build vocabulary by listening to literature, viewing films and documentaries, participating in class discussions, and reading self-selected and assigned texts
	b. Build vocabulary by reading and viewing from a wide variety of print and non-print texts, literary and media genres and modes
	c. Analyze word meanings using roots, prefixes, and suffixes
	d. Continue to determine the meaning of unfamiliar words using context clues, dictionaries, electronic sources, glossaries, and other resources
	e. Evaluate the use of synonyms, antonyms, homonyms, and multiple meaning words, and determine how they assist with understanding
	f. Continue to foster word consciousness (e.g., word play, word walls, graphic organizers, nuances of words, power words)
	g. Analyze and use useful mnemonic devices (e.g., rhyming words, vocabulary cartoons, kinesthetic) to acquire new vocabulary
	h. Select the correct word or phrase to complete an analogy

i. Recognize the historical influences on and changes to the English language

j. Consider word etymology and semantic change as part of vocabulary study

k. Recognize and interpret widely used foreign phrases (e.g., *e pluribus unum, c'est la vie*)

l. Use connotation and denotation for vocabulary studies

m. Recognize that word choices create a mood to set a tone

n. Discover ways by which a language acquires new words (e.g., brand names, acronyms)

o. Identify words and phrases that serve as clues to reveal time periods, cultures and regions represented (e.g., use of vocabulary associated with a particular time period, region, or country)

1.07 Employ pre-reading strategies to facilitate comprehension

a. Continue to establish a purpose for reading and viewing (e.g., to understand, to interpret, to enjoy, to solve problems, to answer specific questions, to discover information/facts, to discover models of writing)

b. Continue to utilize reference sources to build background knowledge for reading

c. Continue to use previously learned strategies to front load text (e.g., skimming and scanning, connecting to prior knowledge)

d. Preview text, using supports such as illustrations/pictures, captions, graphs, diagrams, headings, subheadings, and footnotes

e. Relate the importance and the significance of the reading, listening, and viewing selections to learning and life

f. Analyze significant words to be encountered in the text

g. Make predictions about print and non-print text

h. Relate print and non-print text to prior personal experiences or opinions, historical knowledge, current events and cultural background as well as previously read print and non-print texts

1.08 Use active comprehension strategies to derive meaning while reading and to check for understanding after reading

a. Derive meaning while reading by
   1. continuing to formulate clarifying questions
   2. evaluating predictions made in prereading and making adjustments
   3. continuing to predict outcomes, state reasonable generalizations, and draw conclusions based on prior knowledge and information gained while reading
   4. using metacognitive and self-monitoring strategies while reading (e.g., pausing, rereading, consulting other sources, reading ahead, asking for help)
   5. engaging in reading between the lines (i.e., changing perspective among characters to determine thoughts, imagining parallel events, stating implied information)
   6. continuing to create mental pictures from abstract information.
   7. continuing to relate text to prior personal experiences or opinions as well as previously read print and non-print texts

continued

continued

	8. making inferences and recognizing unstated assumptions.
	9. verifying or modifying pre-reading purpose as additional information is obtained
	10. exploring ways to interact with text (e.g., mark the text, use post-it notes, ask questions and make comments within the text)
	b. Derive meaning after reading by
	1. indicating, analyzing, and evaluating the sequence of events
	2. recognizing and stating the main idea/central element in a given reading selection, noting details that support the main idea/central element
	3. identifying the author's purpose and analyzing to determine if purpose is met
	4. discussing similarities and differences in events and characters using evidence cited from the text or various texts
	5. analyzing and evaluating the text to find contextual support for responses to questions, for assistance in formulating ideas and opinions, and for supporting personal responses
	6. assessing the accuracy and appropriateness of an author's details to support claims and assertions, noting instances of bias and stereotyping
	7. evaluating cause and effect relationships
	8. evaluating statements as fact or opinion
	9. analyzing the use of figurative language (idioms, similes, metaphors, personification, imagery, puns)
	10. analyzing themes, whether stated or implied.
	11. evaluating and reflecting upon comprehension strategies utilized to make meaning from texts
	12. making connections among various print and non-print texts
	13. making connections among the various literary genres and themes with personal, historical, and cultural experiences
	14. evaluating reading selections for their application to daily life (e.g., extend and apply meaning derived from text to different situations)
1.09 Refine study skills and develop methods of research to enhance learning	a. Determine appropriate reference sources in various formats (e.g., encyclopedias, card/electronic catalogs, almanacs, periodicals, Internet)
	b. Use media (e.g., films, video, the visual and performing arts, on-line catalogs, non-fiction books, encyclopedias, CD-ROMs, references, Internet) to view, read, and represent information
	c. Use current technology (e.g., the Internet, CD-ROMs, online catalogs) as a research communication tool
	d. Analyze a variety of reference sources (e.g., biographical sketches, letters, diaries, encyclopedias, periodicals)

	e. Distinguish between and use primary and secondary source documents
	f. Evaluate resources for validity and reliability
	g. Continue to refine skimming and scanning skills
	h. Retrieve, organize, represent, analyze, and evaluate information to demonstrate knowledge effectively acquired
	i. Develop and use notes that include important concepts, summaries, and identification of reference sources
	j. Investigate and evaluate the impact of bias/persuasive devices on daily life
	k. Recognize and identify a statement as an example of persuasive and/or propaganda techniques (e.g., false generalizations, loaded words, snob appeal, name-calling, bandwagon, testimonials, and inconsistencies of logic)
	l. Use and evaluate a variety of sources to prepare a research paper that includes a title page, outline, notes, and a bibliography
	m. Define and apply internal (subjective) and external (objective) criteria in making critical evaluations of given statements
1.10 Develop skills to facilitate reading in the content areas	a. Expand and maintain vocabulary specific to content areas and to current events
	b. Continue to locate information using available text features (e.g., maps, charts, timelines, graphics, indexes, glossaries, footnotes, author's biography, and tables of content)
	c. Apply, analyze, and evaluate comprehension skills and strategies used to obtain meaning from informational text in the content areas
	d. Continue to use self-correction strategies while reading (e.g., pausing, rereading, consulting other sources)
	e. Continue to interact with the text and analyze its effectiveness
	f. Determine the reliability of sources by exploring the author's background, intentions and motives
1.11 Read independently for a variety of purposes	a. Read for literary experience
	b. Read to gain information
	c. Read to perform a task
	d. Read for enjoyment
	e. Read to expand vocabulary
	f. Read to build fluency
1.12 Experience and explore the elements of various literary and media genres	a. Continue to read, view, and recognize various literary (e.g., novels, science fictions, plays, suspense, poetry, autobiographies/biographies, non-fiction of high interest) and media (e.g., music, films, videos, documentaries, the visual and performing arts) genres
	b. Recognize and analyze the elements of various literary and media genres
	c. Explore the elements that determine types of fiction (e.g., suspense/mystery, comedy/humor, drama, historical fiction, romance, legends and myths)

continued

continued

	d. Identify and evaluate stated or implied themes and connect recurring themes to previously read materials and current readings
	e. Evaluate how the author develops characters (e.g., through words, speech, action, thoughts, narrator, interaction, motivation) and evaluate whether the characters are stereotypical or realistic
	f. Evaluate words, phrases, and other devices used by authors to create mood to establish a tone
	g. Determine the elements of the plot and trace them using graphic organizers (i.e., exposition, rising action, climax, falling action, resolution/denouement)
	h. Distinguish among varying types of conflict (i.e., man v. man, man v. nature, man v. himself)
	i. Explore subplots in literary selections and films
	j. Compare and contrast between or among stories/events the elements of the plot
	k. Determine the narrator's/author's point of view (i.e., first person, third person, limited or omniscient)
	l. Explore and explain how a story changes or an event is perceived if the point of view is changed
	m. Summarize, paraphrase, and evaluate selected passages for discussion and/or written assignments or presentations
	n. Make inferences about print and non-print text
	o. Use deductive reasoning to facilitate and to extend understanding of texts
	p. Determine the differences among non-fiction materials (e.g., letters, memoirs, diaries, journals, documentaries, autobiographies, biographies, and educational, informational and technical texts)
	q. Demonstrate knowledge of similes, metaphors, personification, symbolism, idioms, puns, hyperbole, flashback, foreshadowing, and irony
	r. Explore the concept of allusion
1.13 Develop and sustain a motivation for reading	a. Visit libraries/media centers, book fairs, bookstores, and other print rich environments to explore books
	b. Use personal criteria to select reading material (e.g., personal interest, knowledge of authors, text difficulty, text genres, recommendation of others)
	c. Read daily from self-selected materials
	d. Relate literary experiences (e.g., book discussions, literary circles, writing, oral presentations, artistic expressions)
	e. Experience and develop an awareness of literature that reflects a diverse society
	f. Maintain a personal reading list/or reading log/journal to reflect reading gains and accomplishments

Source: Compiled by authors from, Tennessee State Board of Education. (2001). *English/Language arts curriculum standards.* Retrieved on June 5, 2005, from http://www.state.tn.us/education/ci/cistandards2001/la/cilag8reading.htm.

Glossary

A Nation at Risk (NAR)   A report released by the National Commission on Excellence in Education (NCEE) in 1983. In response to evidence of lagging U.S. student performance, the report recommended high-quality academic content standards, instruction, and standardized tests.

Academic Press   A term used to describe a combination of high-quality course content, assignments, and teacher expectations to improve student performance.

Academic Proficiency   A performance standards level of achievement indicating that students have demonstrated competency over challenging academic content standards.

Academic Standards   Provide clear and rigorous expectations for all students with specific descriptions of the knowledge, concepts, and skills students are expected to know and be able to do as they progress through school. Academic standards comprise objectives, indicators, and benchmarks. Academic standards may alternatively be called academic content standards, learning standards, achievement standards, or curriculum standards.

Accelerating Curve   A strategy for determining annual improvements toward academic proficiency. The percent of students meeting proficiency will increase slowly in the initial years with greater gains occurring closer to the 2014 deadline.

Achievement Gap   Differences in academic achievement between students of different racial/ethnic backgrounds, socioeconomic statuses, cultures, and first languages.

Adequate Yearly Progress (AYP)   State-developed minimum targets for the percent proficient in each of the academic content areas, participation in assessments, attendance rates, graduation rates, and dropout rates.

Aggregated Data   Data reported at the federal-, district-, school- or grade-level that has not been broken down by subgroup (e.g., gender, race/ethnicity, special education, free- or reduced-price lunch).

Alignment   The educational practice of connecting academic standards with curriculum, instruction, and assessment.

Alternative Assessments   A form of assessment where students are asked to create their own responses to a question or task rather than choosing the response from a given list of options (e.g., multiple-choice tests). Essays, short-answer questions, portfolios, and presentations are examples of alternative assessments.

Assessments   Instruments that measure and evaluate a range of student learning outcomes.

Authentic Assessments   A form of assessment that presents contextualized and intellectually complex tasks that are representative of performance in the real world and in school. The process of accomplishing the task in an authentic assessment is valued as highly as the finished product.

Authority Power that is handed over to educational leaders to make necessary improvements in student performance. Authority may be given over budgeting, resource allocation, hiring practices, curriculum development, and governance structures.

Autonomy Independence that is given to educational leaders to release them from bureaucratic constraints with the purpose of making improvements in student performance. In educational accountability, autonomy is linked with accountability for results.

Benchmark Assessments A form of assessment aligned to academic standards that are administered on a regular basis. Benchmark assessments may be used to determine whether students have mastered the knowledge and skills of a particular curriculum. Alternatively, benchmark assessments may be used to predict how well students will do on end-of-year standards-based assessments.

Benchmarks Examples of performance levels against which student academic achievement on standards-based assessments can be measured.

Building Instructional Capacity The process-oriented strategy of improving instructional practices to increase student performance. Educators should work to link new information on effective instructional practices with existing knowledge, experience, and values. Educators should work together collaboratively to encourage reflection through observations and feedback on instructional practices.

Bureaucratic Accountability Type of accountability that functions through the roles of hierarchy and control in the education system and the provision of rules and regulations for fiscal and compliance audits.

Capacity Building Process that supports the improvement of instructional practices that leads to increases in student performance. Capacity building includes setting clear educational goals, using effective communication strategies, valuing each individual within the school, creating opportunities for collaboration, and ensuring organizational stability.

Categorical Programs Federal and state educational programs created to serve the special needs of students. Categorical programs are directed by rules and regulations that restrict their use to specific groups of students.

Causality The direct relationship between cause and effect. When educators are held accountable for student improvement, it is important to identify causality, that is, whether particular educational practices lead to improvement.

Classroom Assessments A form of assessment that teachers use in their classrooms to frequently and continuously evaluate student progress. Classroom assessments allow educators the opportunity to identify student needs and make adjustments to instructional practices on a more regular basis than end-of-year standards-based assessments.

Collaboration The act of working together on a cooperative intellectual effort. Collaboration between educators on the development and evaluation of instructional practices is critical to large-scale student performance.

Collaborative Inquiry and Reflection Process-oriented strategies that encourage educators to work together to develop the instructional practices that will bring about desired improvements in student performance.

Compensatory Education Programs Federal and state education programs that provide extra services and resources to students identified as disadvantaged. The federal Title I program is the largest compensatory education program.

Consequences Pressure and sanctions used within educational accountability systems to motivate educators to improve instructional practices and student performance.

Content Coverage The curriculum that will be covered during a particular instruction period. In educational accountability, the academic standards should guide content coverage.

Convergent Validity A test used to determine how well different test items measure the same content domain by examining the relationship between items.

Core Technology of Schooling A term used to refer to the teaching and learning processes.

Corrective Action A stage of NCLB school improvement applied to low-performing schools after failing to make adequately yearly progress for three consecutive years. Corrective action may include replacing staff, implementing a new curriculum, decreasing leadership authority, appointing outside experts, extending the school calendar, or restructuring the internal organization of the school.

Criterion-Referenced Tests Tests designed to measure and provide outcome data on how well a student has learned a specified set of knowledge and skills. Criterion-referenced tests do not score students' achievement in relation to other students. Criterion-referenced tests are standards-based when the content on the test is appropriately aligned with the learning expectations of high-quality academic standards.

Critical Thinking Process of actively and skillfully conceptualizing, applying, analyzing, synthesizing, or evaluating information. Critical thinking differs from processes of rote memorization of knowledge and skills by facilitating students learning how to use evidence to make logical conclusions.

Cultural Norm of Individualism Result of the traditional, hierarchical structure of the education system where educators are encouraged to work in isolation.

Curriculum Mapping Strategy used to align curriculum, instruction, and assessment with the academic standards. Curriculum mapping involves working with colleagues to fill in gaps, eliminate vertical and horizontal repetition, and match suitable resources and materials to the academic standards.

Curriculum Pacing Guides Resource that aligns curriculum, instruction, and assessment with the academic standards. Curriculum pacing guides use the academic standards to group learning objectives into units, allocate time to the units, and sequence the units on an academic calendar.

Cut Scores Provide information about the range of test scores that corresponds with each performance level on large-scale assessments.

Data-Driven Decision Making The use of data to identify strengths and weaknesses in instructional practices and student learning. Educational accountability relies on data-driven decisions being made throughout the education system to inform educational practices from instructional practices to technical assistance to professional development.

De-Privatization of Practice An approach that supports teachers in sharing, observing, and discussing their teaching practices with one another. The de-privatization of practice attempts to transform the traditional educational practice of teachers being left alone to resolve instructional, curricular, and management issues.

Differentiated Curriculum Tracks Separate curricular tracks with vocational or college preparatory focuses. Differentiated curriculum tracks were initially proposed to meet the individual needs of students. However, research suggests that differentiated curriculum tracks contributed to discrimination based on race, gender, and socioeconomic status.

Disaggregated Data Data broken down by subgroups of students (e.g., gender, race/ethnicity, special education, free- or reduced-price lunch) to show the percentage of students in each subgroup who attain proficiency in the academic content areas tested.

Discriminant Validity A test used to determine whether test items measure different concepts by examining the relationship between items.

Distributed Leadership An educational leadership theory that recommends leaders seek out the ideas, insights, and expertise of teachers and incorporate them into the operation of the school. In addition, educational leaders are encouraged to share leadership responsibility with teachers.

Educational Accountability Education theory for improving student performance by directing all attention and support within the education system at improving instructional practices by influencing roles and responsibilities, academic standards, assessments, and accountability mechanisms.

Educational Accountability Systems Component of educational accountability that is designed to evaluate school progress toward meeting academic standards and implement a set of pressure and support mechanisms in schools identified as struggling to meet the needs of their students.

Educational Leaders Includes individuals at the district and school levels of the education system responsible for providing guidance and support that properly match the school-improvement needs of individual schools, teachers, and students.

Equal Yearly Goals A strategy for determining annual improvements toward academic proficiency. The percent of students meeting proficiency increases in equal increments every year until the 2014 deadline for 100% proficiency. Annual equal increments are calculated by subtracting the proficiency starting point from 100 and then dividing by 12 (for the 12 years of NCLB reform).

Evidence-Based Practices Educational programs or practices deemed to be supported by evidence must show effectiveness based on the quality of the research design used to evaluate the program and the quantity of studies supporting the positive impact of the program.

Experimentation The process by which educators experiment with new instructional practices. Experimentation is critical to school improvement and educational accountability when the process is based on collaborative inquiry, needs-assessments, evidence-based practices, and ongoing evaluation.

External Accountability Policies created and administered from outside of the school that hold educators responsible for student academic performance.

Filling in the Gaps A strategy used to align instruction, curriculum, and assessment with academic standards. The process involves examining existing textbooks, materials, and resources to determine where additional resources are needed to meet the demands of the academic standards.

First-Order and Second-Order Changes Characterizations of the organizational change necessary to successfully implement a reform initiative. First-order changes involve minimal disruption as they coincide with norms and values present in the school. The changes can be realized with existing knowledge and skills. Second-order changes, on the other hand, are considered disruptive when there is not consensus about the reform's likely success.

Flexibility   A strategy assigned to educational leaders in educational accountability to make necessary improvements in student performance. Flexibility allows educational leaders to be responsive to change in exchange for results.

Formative Assessments   A form of assessment that supports frequent and continuous evaluation of student progress. Formative assessments allow educators to collect multiple indicators of performance to identify student needs and make adjustments to instructional practices on a more regular basis.

Grade Equivalents   Test scores based on a developmental scale that report student performance in a decimal number representing the grade level and month of a typical student with the same performance.

High-Order Thinking Skills   Learning theory that suggests students who learn the skills to analyze, synthesize, and evaluate information will experience greater learning outcome gains.

Highly Qualified Teachers   A federal definition of teachers who have a bachelor's degree, full state certification or licensure, and proof that they know each subject they teach.

High-Stakes Tests   Scores from these assessments are used to make education decisions, such as academic promotion, graduation, or school improvement sanctions.

Indicators   Examples of detailed tasks students should be able to accomplish to meet the learning objectives of the academic standards. Indicators allow teachers to determine the skills and knowledge students should demonstrate in the classroom for each of the learning objectives of the academic standards.

Individual Education Plan (IEP)   A plan developed by the student's parents and teachers that outlines the student's academic goals, methods to attain these goals, and particular education services the student will receive.

Innovation   The practice of experimenting with new instructional practices to improve student learning and performance.

Inquiry-Based Practices   Instructional strategies that are designed through a process of identifying needs, gathering resources to address needs, using the resources to improve practice, and evaluating the effectiveness of the resources.

Instructional Leadership   An educational-leadership theory that recommends school leaders promote quality instruction, supervise and evaluate instruction, allocate and protect instructional time, coordinate the curriculum, promote content coverage, and monitor student progress.

Intergovernmental Education System   The U.S. education system is a multilevel system divided into federal, state, and local levels. While each level has designated roles and responsibilities, a significant degree of interaction between the levels of government is needed to secure efficient operation.

Intermediate Goals   Annual school-improvement targets that are used to ensure that school meet 100% proficiency within the allotted time.

Internal Accountability   Policies created and administered within the school that hold educators responsible for student academic performance.

Lead by Results   Educational leadership method that includes obtaining and adopting knowledge and skills about effective instructional practices, building school capacity, establishing norms of collaborative inquiry and reflection, and sharing leadership.

Legal Accountability   Type of accountability that operates through contractual obligations where a legal overseer, such as the federal legislature or courts, holds schools accountable with legal mandates and the threat of sanctions.

Legislative Mandates   Rules and regulations that stipulate the policies associated with a legislative act.

Longitudinal Data   Data collected at multiple time points.

Managing by Rules   Educational leadership method that focuses on programmatic and procedural compliance with the end goal of efficiency.

Market Accountability   Type of accountability that works through customer choice based on school performance where the ultimate consequence for schools is that they can lose their students.

Measurement   The standardized quantification of student learning outcome variables.

Measuring Gains in Achievement   With the use of longitudinal assessments, individual student progress over time can be assessed. By comparing the academic achievement of students with their own achievement in previous academic years, educators can distinguish between prior learning and the learning that occurred in the given school year.

Mediating Factors   Programmatic components that specify the essential processes of the reform initiative that must occur in order to transfer an effect.

Minimum-Competency Tests   A form of assessment developed in the 1970s that set out to establish levels of basic skills and create remediation mechanisms for low performance.

Minimum "n"   The minimum number of students needed in a subgroup in order to provide statistically reliable information about that subgroup. Additionally, the minimum number of students in a subgroup must be large enough to avoid revealing personally identifiable information about an individual student.

Minimum Targets   Annual objectives that states develop for the percent of students that must be proficient in the content areas, participation in assessments, attendance rates, graduation rates, and dropout rates in order to meet adequate yearly progress. In developing minimum targets, states are required to identify a starting point of percent proficient and establish the annual increments it will take for schools to reach 100% proficiency.

Modeling Behavior   Strategy used by educational leaders and teachers to demonstrate effective instructional practices.

Monitoring   A signaling system used within educational accountability systems to indicate the progress schools have made in meeting academic proficiency.

Moral Accountability   Type of accountability where educators improve schools based on their personal obligation or sense of duty for the school system.

Multiple Assessments   As single tests are limited in their ability to provide adequate information about student performance, multiple indicators of student performance may provide enough pieces of information to gauge student performance in regards to academic standards, as well as allow educators to make informed improvements in instructional practices.

National Assessment of Educational Progress (NAEP)   Referred to as the Nation's Report Card, the nationally representative assessment is administered by the National Center for Education Statistics (NCES) to a sample of students in grades 4, 8, and 12 in the subject areas of reading, mathematics, science, writing, U.S. history, civics, geography, and the arts.

National Percentile Rank Score Range from 1 to 99 and represent a score that tells the student what percentage of students in a representative group scored lower on the same test. For example, a student in third grade with a national percentile rank score of 81 scored higher than 81 percent of third grade students in the nation.

Needs-Assessment An ongoing process of identifying strengths and weaknesses within the school to determine where improvements should be made to improve the practices of teaching and learning.

New Professionalism A term that refers to the transformation of the teaching profession from one of isolation to teaching as a part of a communal and collaborative endeavor.

Norm-Referenced Tests Norm-referenced tests measure student performance on a broad range of academic content with test items that can differentiate between high and low achievers. The assessments are designed to provide student performance scores that can be compared and ranked with a sample of the target population, such as a national sample of the grade level tested. Academic content covered by the tests is typically taken from a selection of national textbooks rather than from content and curricula developed at the state or district level.

Normal Distribution Curve A bell-shaped curve where the outcomes, such as test scores, are distributed so that half of the students score below the average while half of the students score above the average. Additionally, most students will score around the average while fewer students score at the top or the bottom of the curve.

Objectives The goals or learning expectations intended for the content areas within particular subject areas, such as for the content areas of reading and writing within the subject area of language arts.

One-Size-Fits-All Education Programs School-reform initiatives that do not take into account the context of the school when recommending school improvement strategies. Educational accountability is a process-oriented reform initiative that encourages educational leaders to identify the needs of their school, set school improvement goals, develop learning goals, and guide teachers in tailoring instruction to individual student needs.

Ongoing Observation and Feedback Strategy used to critically examine teaching practices and student learning in order to identify strengths and weaknesses, implement evidence-based practices, and evaluate its effectiveness.

Organizational Capacity Present in schools in which human, technical, and social resources are organized into an effective collective enterprise.

Peer Coaching A school-reform strategy that utilizes the expertise of effective educators to mentor, share aspects of teaching, plan together, and pool experiences. The characteristics of effective peer coaches consist of being thoughtful reflectors, facilitative initiators and maintainers of the relationships, and capable of building relationships built on trust and respect.

Performance Levels Levels of mastery aligned with the academic standards. In general, states have developed three performance levels including basic, proficient, and advanced.

Policy Churn A term used to refer to the phenomenon by which low-performing schools are asked to implement new programs and practices in response to changing legislation and policies before it has been determined whether the old programs and policies are effective.

Policy-Practice Gap Discord between policies mandated by the federal, state, or district levels and the instructional practices that take place in classrooms. The gap emerges when policies do not match what educators believe needs to be done to improve student learning. In turn, teacher buy-in is critical to the implementation of education reform efforts.

Political Accountability Type of accountability that functions through elected representatives taking into account constituents' value preferences to improve schools.

Pressure and Support The theory of educational accountability suggests that pressure or support alone will not create the necessary motivation to bring about large-scale improvements in instructional practices. Instead, the combination of pressure and support produces the suitable mechanisms for monitoring schools while also providing low-performing schools with resources and technical assistance for making improvements.

Procedural Compliance Education practices that focus on conformity to program and policy rules to improve input efficiency. The unintended consequence of procedural compliance was that many educators were constrained by the rules and regulations, limiting innovation and experimentation to improve student learning.

Process-Oriented Reform Education reform that does not prescribe specific curriculum or instructional practices. Rather, process-oriented reform recommends strategies and processes for identifying school needs, matching instructional practices with strengths and weaknesses, and evaluating the effectiveness of reform efforts.

Professional Accountability Type of accountability where educators take responsibility and ensure professional standards of practice for teaching and learning.

Professional Culture A school environment conducive to the practices of collaboration and team building where teachers can exchange advice and reflect on teaching practices and student learning in a comfortable and collegial fashion.

Professional Development Continual, consistent, coherent, and intensive activities geared toward providing educators with the knowledge and skills to improve instructional practices and increase student learning.

Professional Learning Communities A school-reform initiative designed to promote school improvement and change through shared leadership, a common vision focused toward student learning, regular interaction among teachers and administrators, collaborative work by way of reflective dialogue, and shared learning. Professional learning communities address the intrinsic social nature of interactions within schools and the importance of individual and organizational learning for school change.

Protocols for Reflective Dialogue A set of guidelines for promoting in-depth conversations about instructional practices that all participants develop and agree upon beforehand.

Public School Choice An accountability mechanism designed by NCLB that allows students to transfer to another public school in the district if their school has been identified as low performing for two consecutive years.

Pull-Out Instruction When students are removed from their regular classroom for remedial or enrichment instruction.

Reciprocal Accountability If educators at the school level are held accountable for producing student performance results, then educators at the district, state, and federal level are accountable for providing sufficient support and resources to schools. Educators at the school level cannot be the only individuals held accountable within the education system trying to bring about large-scale improvement.

Reconstitution A corrective action process for continually low-performing schools where the state or district take over the school and replace all or most of the school staff and administration.

Relational Trust A term that refers to the presence of respect, competence, personal regard, and integrity among individuals within a school. High levels of relational trust may facilitate a school's ability to implement school-reform initiatives that require mutual support and coordinated efforts among leadership, teachers, and other community members.

Reliability Indicator of the internal consistency of tests. Reliability provides information about how well test scores remain stable from one testing instance to another. Reliability is desirable for assessments since we want test scores to be constant measures of student performance over time.

Reporting Process of providing accurate and frequent reports of results from student assessments in order to provide information for a variety of educational decisions.

Restructuring A stage of NCLB school improvement applied to low-performing schools after failing to make adequately yearly progress for five consecutive years. Restructuring may include reopening the school as a charter school, replacing school staff, contracting with a private management company, or turning the operation of the school over to the state.

Results-Driven Leadership An educational leadership theory that encourages school leaders to develop strategic thinking to focus on the best practices for student performance results. Practices include planning school improvement strategies using backward-mapping, linking teaching and learning to results, and employing high-quality professional development to address educational problems.

Re-Teaching A remediation strategy that is part of an ongoing diagnostic process of identifying students' strengths and weaknesses within the classroom.

Rubric An instructional tool that matches stated learning objectives and demonstrated performance characteristics with predetermined levels of performance.

Safe Harbor Provision Used in the determination of adequate yearly progress. The safe harbor provision states that a school will make adequate yearly progress even if one or more of its subgroups fails to meet the minimum targets for academic proficiency if each of the subgroups that failed to meet the minimum targets have decreased by 10 percent from the preceding academic year and the subgroups have made progress on additional indicators.

Sampling Variation A testing issue that arises when comparing student achievement from different samples of students. For example, when 4th grade students from the current year are compared with 4th grade students from the past year, nonrandom fluctuations in tests scores will increase the volatility of the school's average achievement score.

Sanctions A set of consequences applied to continually low-performing schools in educational accountability systems. Sanctions may include school improvement plans, school choice, supplemental educational services, restructuring, or reconstitution.

School Improvement A stage of NCLB school improvement applied to low-performing schools after failing to make adequately yearly progress for two consecutive years. Schools identified for school improvement must develop a two-year school-improvement plan and offer school choice.

School-Improvement Plans Schools identified as low-performing for two consecutive years must develop a two-year, ten-point proposal that addresses the ways in which the school will make improvements in teaching and learning. The district must review and approve the school-improvement plan (SIP).

School Report Card A tool used in educational accountability systems to present clear and pertinent information regarding the progress of students and schools in attaining proficiency on academic standards.

Schoolwide Programs A regulatory change applied to Title I programs that permits educators to use federal Title I resources on reform throughout the school, rather than targeting resources to eligible students, to bring about improvements in student performance.

Scientifically Based Research Programs Programs that have been researched with rigorous, systematic, and objective procedures to obtain reliable and valid knowledge relevant to education activities and programs.

Shared Planning Time A tool for encouraging collaboration and ongoing interaction among educators. Educational leaders may want to arrange for shared planning time for teachers in the same grade level and/or subject area.

Signaling System Refers to the mechanisms within the educational accountability system that report and monitor school performance.

Standard Scores Scores from norm-referenced tests that use the normal curve to report student performance in terms of how many standard deviations the test score is from the mean test score. Standard scores can be in the form of z-scores (mean = 0, standard deviation = 1), standard score scale (mean = 100, standard deviation = 15), or normal curve equivalents (mean = .50, standard deviation = 21.06).

Standardized Tests A form of assessment that is taken by many students under identical conditions to ensure that student achievement in a given subject is examined with the same criteria. Scores from standardized tests are statistically compared to standard norms from a nationally representative sample of students.

Standards-Based Assessments A form of assessment where the content on the test is aligned with the learning expectations of high quality academic standards.

Standards-Based Reform A reform initiative that called for creating high expectations for student performance. Standards-based reform found fault in differentiated curriculum and claimed that all students can perform well irrespective of background characteristics. Standards-based reform maintained that students learn as a consequence of what is taught; the implication being that educators must take a different approach with teaching, one defined by skill and understanding.

Stanines Scores that rank students in nine groups. Stanine scores of 1, 2, and 3 are considered below average; 4, 5, and 6 are average; and 7, 8, and 9 are above average.

Starting Points A baseline for determining academic proficiency. In selecting a starting point for NCLB, states were permitted to choose between the percent of students proficient on the state standards-based assessment in the lowest-performing subgroup and the percent of students proficient in the school at the 20th percentile in the state, whichever was higher.

Status Model A method used to measure change in student performance that examines changes in average achievement scores from one academic year to the next. The status model uses a longitudinal cross-sectional approach in which the average achievement of a cohort of students is compared to the average achievement of the same cohort composed of different students in the following year (e.g., 4th graders). The cohort of students can include all students in a school, students in a fixed grade level, or students in a subgroup, such as race/ethnicity, eligible for free- or reduced-price lunch, or English language learner.

Steady Stair-Step A strategy for determining annual improvements toward academic proficiency. The steady stair-step approach requires that the percent of students meeting proficiency will increase incrementally every two or three years to meet the 2014 deadline.

Subgroups Groups of students that must be examined separately to determine if they have met academic proficiency. Subgroups include economically disadvantaged students, students from major racial and ethnic groups, students with disabilities, and limited English proficiency (LEP) students.

Supplemental Educational Services Tutoring or other enrichment programs that are provided to students in schools identified as low performing in addition to instruction in the regular school day and composed of effective strategies designed to increase academic achievement of the students involved.

Teaching to the Test redundant While educational accountability encourages innovation, flexibility, experimentation, and the enhancement of curriculum to achieve high levels of student performance, some educators are concerned that accountability and high-stakes tests will narrow content coverage, in other words, encourage teachers to "teach to the test."

Technical Assistance Support that states and district must provide to low-performing schools in educational accountability systems. Technical assistance may be in the following forms: analyzing data from state assessments and other examples of student work to identify and address areas of need; identifying and implementing professional development, instructional strategies, and methods of instruction to improve a school's weak areas that caused the school to be identified for school improvement; or reallocating the school budget to better use resources to improve student academic achievement.

Theory of Change Explanation of the causal links and underlying assumptions that tie program components to expected program outcomes.

Tight-Loose Coupling Strategy where schools are given flexibility, authority, and autonomy to make educational improvements as long as they produce expected results.

Title I The largest federal education program for elementary and secondary schools. Title I provides additional funding to schools with high percentages of high-poverty and low-achieving students.

Transformational Leadership An educational leadership theory that focuses of the process of influencing school outcomes based on a particular school vision. In the transformational leadership model, educational leaders tackle resistance to school-improvement initiatives and work to produce commitment to the reform.

Transitory Variables One-time factors independent of the sample of test items that may attenuate reliability and impact test scores. Transitory variables are nonpersistent changes that occur as a result of factors such as the time of day the test was administered, disruptive students in the classroom, fire drills, or the weather.

Validity Indicator of the extent to which test items reflect a specified content domain. Evidence of validity demonstrates that the content covered reflects the knowledge and skills of the academic standard that the test is supposed to measure.

Walk-Throughs A nonevaluative tool used by educational leaders to collect quick snapshots about instructional practices and student learning. Information gathered from walk-throughs should be used to identify school needs and to engage educators in conversations about student learning.

Bibliography

Acker-Hocevar, M, & Touchton, D. (2002). How principals level the playing field of accountability in Florida's high-poverty/low-performing schools—Part I: The intersection of high-stakes testing and effects of poverty on teaching and learning. *International Journal of Educational Reform, 11*, pp. 106–124.

Ackland, R. (1991). A review of the peer coaching literature. *The Journal of Staff Development, 12*(1), 22–27.

Adams, J. E. & Kirst, M. W. (1999). New demands and concepts for educational accountability: Striving for results in an era of excellence. In J. Murphy & K. Seashore Louis (Eds.), *Handbook of research on educational administration: A project of the American Educational Research Association*. San Francisco: Jossey-Bass Publishers.

Ainsworth, L. (2003). *Power standards: Identifying the standards that matter the most.* Englewood, CO: Advanced Learning Press.

American Association of School Administrators (AASA). (2002). *Using data to improve schools: What's working.* Retrieved June 1, 2005, from http://www.eric.ed.gov/ERICDocs/data/ericdocs2/content_storage_01/0000000b/80/27/d3/58.pdf.

American Productivity and Quality Center. (2000). *Benchmarking best practices in accountability systems.* Houston, TX: Author.

Angus, D. L., & Mirel, J. E. (1999). *The failed promise of American high school, 1890–1995.* New York: Teachers College Press.

Anthes, K. (2002). *No Child Left Behind policy brief: School and district leadership.* Denver, CO: Education Commission of the States.

Archer, J. (2004, March 17). Weaving webs. *Education Week 23*(27), 50.

Archer, J. (2005, September 14). Theory of action. *Education Week 25*(3), S3.

Archer, J. (2005, September 15). Tackling an impossible job. *Education Week 25*(3), S3.

Armstrong, J. (2002). *What is an accountability model?* (Issue Paper). Denver, CO: Education Commission of the States.

Baker, E. L. & Linn, R. L. (2002). *Validity issues for accountability systems* (CSE 585). Los Angeles: Center for the Study of Evaluation.

Ballou, D. (2002). Sizing up test scores. *Education Next, 2*(2), 10–15.

Barfield, B. (1981). *Rethinking federalism: Block grants and federal, state, and local responsibilities.* Washington, DC: American Enterprise for Public Policy Research.

Barnes, F. D. (2004). *Inquiry and action: Making school improvement part of daily practice.* Annenberg Institute for School Reform, Brown University. Retrieved June 1, 2005, from http://www.annenberginstitute.org/tools/guide/index.php.

Barr, R., Dreeben, R., & Wiratchai, N. (1983). *How schools work.* Chicago: The University of Chicago Press.

Becker, J. M. (1996). *Peer coaching for improvement of teaching and learning.* Teachers Network. Retrieved February 6, 2004, from http://teachersnetwork.org/TNPI/research/growth/becker.htm.

Bellevue School District. (2005). *State third grade testing program.* Retrieved June 5, 2005, from http://www.bsd405.org/ITBS3.pdf.

Berry, B., Turchi, L., & Johnson, D. (2003). *The impact of high-stakes accountability on teachers' professional development: Evidence from the South.*

Chapel Hill, NC: Southeast Center for Teaching Quality, Inc.

Betts, J. (1998, March). The two-legged stool: The neglected role of educational standards in improving America's public schools. *FRBNY Economic Policy Review*, 97–116.

Bishop, J. H. (1996). The impact of curriculum-based external examinations on school priorities and student learning. *International Journal of Education Research*, *23*(8), 653–752.

Boone, W. J., & Kahle, J. B. (1997). Implementation of the standards: Lessons from a systemic initiative. *School Sciences and Mathematics*, *97*(6), 292–299.

Bond, L. A. (1996). Norm- and criterion-referenced testing. *Practical Assessment, Research & Evaluation*, *5*(2). Retrieved June 5, 2005, from http://PAREonline.net/getvn.asp?v=5&n=2.

Brown v. Board of Education, 347 U.S. 483 (1954).

Brubacher, J. W., Case, C. W., & Reagan, T. G. (1994). *Becoming a reflective educator: How to build a culture of inquiry in the schools*. Thousand Oaks, CA: Corwin Press.

Brunner, C. C. (2002). A proposition for the reconception of the superintendency: Reconsidering traditional and nontraditional discourse. *Educational Administration Quarterly*, *38*(3), 402–433.

Bryk, A., & Driscoll, M. (1988). The high school as community: Contextual influences and consequences for students and teachers. Madison: University of Wisconsin, National Center on Effective Secondary Schools.

Bryk, A., Camburn, E., & Seashore Louis, K. (1999). Professional community in Chicago elementary schools: Facilitating factors and organizational consequences. *Educational Administration Quarterly*, *35*(Suppl.), 751–781.

Bryk, A. S., & Schneider, B. (2002). *Trust in schools: A core resource for improvement*. New York: Russell Sage Foundation.

Buchanan, R. D., & Roberts, R. A. (2001). *Performance-based evaluation for certified and non-certified school personnel: Standards, criteria, indicators, models*. Lewiston, NY: The Edwin Mellen Press.

Bush, T. (2003). *Theories of educational leadership and management* (3rd ed.). Thousand Oaks, CA: SAGE Publications.

Butzin, S. M. (2004). Stop the insanity! It takes a team to leave no child behind. *Phi Delta Kappan 86*(4), 307–309.

Chatterji, M. (2002). Models and methods for examining standards-based reforms and accountability initiatives: Have the tools of inquiry answered pressing questions on improving schools? *Review of Educational Research*, *72*(3), 345–386.

Cicchelli, T., Marcus, S., & Weiner, M. (2002). Superintendents' dialogue in a professional development model. *Education and Urban Society*, *34*(4), 415–422.

Cohen, D. K., & Hill, H. C. (2000). Instructional policy and classroom performance: The mathematics reform in California. *Teachers College Record*, *102*(2), 294–343.

Coleman, J. S., & Hoffer, T. B. (1987). *Public and private high schools: The impact of communities*. New York: Basic Books.

Cook, S. D., & Yanow, D. (1993). Culture and organizational learning. In M. D. Cohen & L. Sproull (Eds.), *Organizational learning* (pp. 430–459). Thousand Oaks, CA: Sage.

Copland, M. A. (2003). Leadership of inquiry: Building and sustaining capacity for school improvement. *Educational Evaluation and Policy Analysis*, *25*(4), 375–395.

Cotton, K. (2001, March). *Principals of high-achieving schools: What the research says*. Portland, OR: Northwest Regional Educational Laboratory.

Council of Chief State School Officers (CCSSO). (1996). *Interstate school leaders licensure consortium (ISLLC): Standards for school leaders*. Washington, DC: Author. Retrieved February 1, 2005, from http://www.ccsso.org/content/pdfs/isllcstd.pdf.

Council of Chief State School Officers. (2002). *Making valid and reliable decisions in determining Adequate Yearly Progress*. Washington, DC: Author. Retrieved June 5, 2005, from http://www.ccsso.org/content/pdfs/AYPpaper.pdf.

Council of the Great City Schools. (2003). Urban school superintendents: Characteristics, tenure, and salary. *Urban Indicator*, *7*(1), 1–6.

Crocker, L., & Algina, J. (1986). *Introduction to classical and modern test theory*. Belmont, CA: Wadsworth Group/Thomson Learning.

Cross, R. W., Rebarber, T., Torres, J., & Finn, C. E., Jr. (Eds.). (2004). *Grading the systems: The guide to state standards, tests, and accountability policies*. Washington, DC: The Thomas B. Fordham Foundation.

Crow, G. M., Hausman, C. S., & Scribner, J. P. (2002). Reshaping the role of the school principal. In J. Murphy (Ed.), *The educational leadership challenge: Redefining leadership for the 21st century* (pp. 189–210). Chicago: The University of Chicago Press.

Darling-Hammond, L. (1996). What matters most: A competent teacher for every child. *Phi Delta Kappan, 78*(3), 193–200.

Darling-Hammond, L. (1997). *The right to learn: A blueprint for creating schools that work*. San Francisco: Jossey-Bass Publishers.

Darling-Hammond, L., Ancess, J., & Falk, B. (1995). *Authentic assessment in action: Studies of schools and students at work*. New York: Teachers College Press.

Datnow, A., & Stringfield, S. (2000). Working together for reliable school reform. *Journal of Education for Students Placed at Risk, 5*(1&2), 183–204.

Dayton, J. (1996). Examining the efficacy of judicial involvement in public school funding reform. *Journal of Education Finance, 22*, 1–27.

Debra P. v. Turlington, 730 F.2d 1405 (11th Cir. 1984).

DeMoss, K. (2002). Leadership styles and high-stakes testing: Principals make a difference. *Education and Urban Society, 35*(1), 111–133.

DeRoche, T. (2004, November 24). Not just a necessary evil: When teachers embrace standards and testing. *Education Week 24*(13), 37.

Desimone, L., Porter, A. C., Birman, B. F., Garet, M. S., & Yoon, K. S. (2002). How do district management and implementation strategies relate to the quality of professional development that districts provide to teachers? *Teachers College Record, 104*(7), 1265–1312.

Desimone, L., Porter, A., Garet, M., Yoon, K., & Birman, B. (2002). Effects of professional development on teachers' instruction: Results from a three-year longitudinal study. *Education Evaluation and Policy Analysis, 24*(2), 81–112.

DeVellis, R. F. (2003). *Scale development: Theory and applications*. Thousand Oaks, CA: Sage Publications.

Dorward, J., Hudson, P., Drickey, N., & Barta, J. (2001). Standards, instruction, and accountability: Teaching to test or testing to teach? *Teaching and Change, 8*(3), 247–258.

DuFour, R. (1991). *The principal as staff developer*. Bloomington, IN: National Educational Service.

DuFour, R. (2004, May). What is a "professional learning community"? *Educational Leadership, 61*(8), 6–11.

Dutro, E., Fisk, M. C., Koch, R., Roop, L. J., & Wixson, K. (2002). When state policies meet local district contexts: Standards-based professional development as a means to individual agency and collective ownership. *Teachers College Record, 104*(4), 787–812.

Education of All Handicapped Children Act, P.L. No. 94–142 (1975).

Educational Research Service. (2003). *Building on a professional learning community*. ESR On the Same Page Series.

Education Week. (2004). *Quality counts 2004: Count me in: Special education in an era of standards*. Washington, DC: Editorial Projects in Education.

Education Week. (2005). *Quality counts 2005: No small change: Targeting money toward student performance*. Washington, DC: Editorial Projects in Education.

Education Week. (2006). *Quality counts at 10: A decade of standards based education*. Washington, DC: Editorial Projects in Education.

Elementary and Secondary Education Act of 1965, P.L. No. 89–10 (1965).

Elmore, R. F. (1993). The role of local school districts in instructional improvement. In S. H. Fuhrman (Ed.), *Designing coherent education policy: Improving the system*. San Francisco: Jossey-Bass.

Elmore, R. F. (2000). *Building a new structure for school leadership*. Washington, DC: The Albert Shanker Institute.

Elmore, R. F. (2003). A plea for strong practice. *Educational Leadership, 61*(3), 6–10.

Elmore, R. F., Abelmann, C. H., Fuhrman, S. H. (1996). The new accountability in state education reform: From process to performance.

In H. F. Ladd (Ed.), *Holding schools accountable: Performance-based reform in education* (pp. 65–98). Washington, DC: Brookings Institution.

Elmore, R. F. & Fuhrman, S. H. (2001). Holding schools accountable: Is it working? *Phi Delta Kappan 83*(1), 67–72.

Enz, B. J. (1992). Guidelines for selecting mentors and creating an environment for mentoring. In T. M. Bey and C. T. Holmes (Eds.), *Mentoring: Contemporary principles and issues* (pp. 65–78). Reston, Virginia: Association of Teacher Educators.

Evertson, C., & Smithey, M. (2000). Mentoring effects on protégés' classroom practice: An experimental field study. *Journal of Educational Research, 93*(5), 294–304.

Farkas, S., Johnson, J., Duffett, A., Foleo, T., & Foley, P. (2001). *Trying to stay ahead of the game: Superintendents and principals talk about school leadership.* Public Agenda.

Fennell, H. A. (1994). Organizational linkages: Expanding the existing metaphor. *Journal of Educational Administration, 32*(1), 23–33.

Feuerstein, A., & Dietrich, J. A. (2003). State standards in the local context: A survey of school board members and superintendents. *Educational Policy, 17*(2), 237–257.

Fink, S., & Thompson, S. (2001). Standards and whole system change. *Teaching and Change, 8*(3), 237–247.

Firestone, W. (1985). The study of loose coupling: Problems, progress and prospects. *Research in Sociology of Education and Socialization, 5*, 3–30.

Foley, E. (2001). *Contradictions and control in systemic reform: The ascendancy of the central office in Philadelphia schools.* Philadelphia, PA: Consortium for Policy Research in Education.

Foriska, T. J. (1998). *Restructuring around standards: A practioner's guide to design and implementation.* Thousand Oaks, CA: Corwin Press.

Fuhrman, S. H. (1993). The politics of coherence. In S. H. Fuhrman (Ed.), *Designing coherent education policy: Improving the system.* San Francisco: Jossey-Bass.

Fuller, H. L., Campbell, C., Celio, M. B., Harvey, J., Immerwahr, J., & Winger, A. (2003, July). *An impossible job? The view from the urban superintendent's chair.* Seattle, WA: Center on Reinventing Public Education, University of Washington.

Garet, M., Porter, A., Desimone, L., Birman, B., & Yoon, K. (2001). What makes professional development effective? Analysis of a national sample of teachers. *American Education Research Journal, 38*(4), 915–945.

Gersten, R., Morvant, M., Brengelman, S. (1995). Close to the classroom is close to the bone: Coaching as a means to translate research into classroom practice. *Exceptional Children, 62*(1), 52–66.

Goertz, M. E. (2001). Redefining government roles in an era of standards-based reform. *Phi Delta Kappan, 83*(1), 62–66.

Goertz, M. & Duffy, M. (2003). Mapping the landscape of high-stakes testing and accountability programs. *Theory into Practice 42*(1), 4–11.

Goldring, E. & Greenfield, W. (2002). Building the foundation for understanding and action. In J. Murphy (Ed.), *The educational leadership challenge: Redefining leadership for the 21st century* (pp. 1–19). Chicago: The University of Chicago Press.

Goldring, E., Rowley, K., & Sims, P. (2005). *The Institute for School Leaders: A study of Tennessee's state challenge grant from the Bill and Melinda Gates Foundation.* Nashville, TN: Peabody College of Vanderbilt University.

Grant, G., & Murray, C. E. (1999). *Teaching in America: The slow revolution.* Cambridge, MA: Harvard University Press.

Green, R. L. (2001). *Practicing the art of leadership: A problem-based approach to implementing the ISLLC standards.* Upper Saddle River, NJ: Prentice-Hall.

Gregory, G. & Kuzmich, L. (2004). *Data driven differentiation in the standards-based classroom.* Thousand Oaks, CA: Corwin Press.

Griffin, B. W., & Heidorn, M. H. (1996). An examination of the relationship between minimum competency test performance and dropping out of high school. *Educational Evaluation and Policy Analysis, 18*(3), 243–252.

Grimmett, P. (1987). The role of district supervisors in the implementation of peer coaching. *Journal of Curriculum and Supervision, 3* (Fall), 3–28.

Grogran, M., & Andrews, R. (2002). Defining preparation and professional development for the future. *Educational Administration Quarterly, 38*(2), 233–259.

Guthrie, J. W., & Springer, M. G. (2004). *A nation at risk* revisited: Did "wrong" reasoning result in "right" results? At what cost? *Peabody Journal of Education, 79*(1), 7–35.

Hall, D., Weiner, R., & Carey, K. (2003). *What new "AYP" information tells us about schools, states, and public education.* Washington, DC: The Education Trust. Retrieved June 5, 2005, from http://www2.edtrust.org/NR/rdonlyres/4B9BF8DE-987A-4063-B750-6D67607E7205/0/NewAYP.pdf.

Hallinger, P., & Murphy, J. (1985a). Assessing the instructional management behavior of principals. *The Elementary School Journal, 86*(2), 217–247.

Hallinger, P., & Murphy, J. (1985b). Instructional leadership in the school context. In W. Greenfield (Ed.), *Instructional leadership: Problems, issues, and controversies* (pp. 779–203). Boston: Allyn and Bacon.

Hamilton, L. S., & Koretz, D. M. (2002). Tests and their use in test-based accountability systems. In L. S. Hamilton, B. M. Stecher, & S. P. Klein (Eds.), *Making sense of test-based accountability in education* (pp. 13–49). Santa Monica, CA: RAND.

Hanushek, E. A., & Raymond, M. E. (2002). *Improving educational quality: How best to evaluation our schools?* Paper prepared for Education in the 21st Century: Meeting the Challenges of a Changing World, Federal Reserve Bank of Boston, MA. Retrieved June 5, 2005, from http://edpro.stanford.edu/eah/papers/accountability.BostonFed.final%20publication.pdf.

Harvey, J. (2003, February). *The urban superintendent: Creating great schools while surviving on the job.* Orlando, FL: Council of the Great City Schools.

Hasse, C. (2001, August 2). Accountability is a shared responsibility. *The Seattle Post-Intelligencer,* B.7.

Hawkins-Stafford Elementary and Secondary School Improvement Amendments of 1988, P.L. No. 100–297 (1988).

Hess, F. M. (1999). *Spinning wheels: The politics of urban school reform.* Washington, DC: Brookings Institution Press.

Hightower, A. M., & McLaughlin, M. W. (2005). Building and sustaining an infrastructure for learning. In F. M. Hess (Ed.), *Urban school reform: Lessons from San Diego* (pp. 71–92). Cambridge, MA: Harvard Educational Press.

Hill, P. T. (2000). *It takes a city: Getting serious about urban school reform.* Washington, DC: Brookings Institution Press.

Hill, P. W. (2002). What principals need to know about teaching and learning. In M. S. Tucker & J. B. Codding (Eds.), *The principal challenge: Leading and managing schools in an era of accountability* (pp. 43–75). San Francisco: Jossey-Bass.

Hoban, G. F. (2002). *Teacher learning for educational change: A systems thinking approach.* Philadelphia: Open University Press.

Hord, S. M. (1997). *Professional learning communities: Communities of continuous inquiry and improvement.* Southwest Educational Development Laboratory.

Hornbeck, M. (2003). What your district's budget is telling you. *Journal of Staff Development, 24*(3), 28–32.

Hoyle, J. R., Bjork, L. G., Collier, V., & Glass, T. (2005). *The superintendent as CEO: Standards-based performance.* Thousand Oaks, CA: Corwin Press.

Huitt, W. (1996). Measurement and evaluation: Criterion- versus norm-referenced testing. *Educational Psychology Interactive.* Valdosta, GA: Valdosta State University. Retrieved June 5, 2005, from http://chiron.valdosta.edu/whuitt/col/measeval/crnmref.html.

Hurst, D., Tan, A., Meek, A., & Sellers, J. (2003). *Overview and inventory of state education reforms: 1990–2000.* NCES 2003-020. Washington, DC: National Center for Education Statistics, U.S. Department of Education.

Iannaccone, L., & Lutz, F. W. (1995). The crucible of democracy: The local arena. In J. D. Scribner & D. H. Layton (Eds.), *The study of educational politics* (pp. 39–52). Bristol, PA: The Falmer Press.

Illinois State Board of Education. (2003). *Illinois Standards Achievement Test sample social science materials*. Retrieved June 5, 2005, from http://www.isbe.net/assessment/PDF/2003SSSample.pdf.

Illinois State Board of Education. (2005). *Illinois Learning Standards*. Retrieved June 5, 2005, from http://www.isbe.state.il.us/ils/Default.htm.

Illinois State Board of Education. (2005). *Illinois state report cards*. Retrieved June 5, 2005, from http://statereportcards.cps.k12.il.us/.

Illinois State Board of Education. (2005). *Introduction to the Illinois learning standards*. Retrieved June 5, 2005, from http://www.isbe.state.il.us/ils/pdf/ils_introduction.pdf.

Improving America's Schools Act of 1994, P.L. No. 103–382 (1994).

Individuals with Disabilities Education Act, P.L. No. 108–446 (2004).

Izard, J. (2002). Using assessment strategies to inform student learning. In P. Jeffery (Compiler), *Proceedings of the annual conference of the Australian Association for Research in Education Brisbane December 2002*. Melbourne: Australian Association for Research in Education.

Jacob, B. A. (2001). Getting tough? The impact of high school graduation exams. *Educational Evaluation and Policy Analysis, 23*(2), 99–121.

Jacobs, H. H. (2004). Development of a consensus map: Wrestling with curriculum consistency and flexibility. In H. H. Jacobs (Ed.), *Getting results with curriculum mapping* (pp. 25–35). Alexandria, VA: Association for Supervision and Curriculum Development.

Johnson, L. (1965, June 4). *To fulfill these rights*. An address at Howard University.

Johnson, R. S. (2002). *Using data to close the achievement gap: How to measure equity in our schools* (2nd ed.). Thousand Oaks, CA: Corwin Press.

Kane, T. J., & Staiger, D. O. (2002). Volatility in school test scores: Implications for test-based accountability systems. In D. Ravitch (Ed.), *Brookings papers on education policy 2002* (pp. 235–283). Washington, DC: Brookings Institution Press.

Kane, T. J., Staiger, D. O., & Geppert, J. (2002). Randomly accountable: Test scores and volatility. *Education Next, 2*(1), 57–61.

Kelleher, J. (2003). A model for assessment-driven professional development. *Phi Delta Kappan, 84*(10), 751–756.

Kendall, J. S., & Marzano, R. J. (1996). *Content knowledge: A compendium of standards and benchmarks for K–12 education*. Aurora, CO: Mid-continent Regional Education Laboratory.

Kennedy, M. (1998). *Form and substance in in-service teacher education* (Research monograph no. 13). Arlington, VA: National Science Foundation.

Killeen, K. M., Monk, D. H., & Plecki, M. L. (2002). Using national data to assess local school district spending on professional development. In W. J. Fowler, Jr. (Ed.), *Developments in school finance, 1999–2000*. NCES 2002–316. Washington, DC: National Center for Education Statistics, U.S. Department of Education.

Kingsbury, G. G., Olson, A., Cronin, J., Hauser, C., & Houser, R. (2003). *The state of state standards: Research investigating proficiency levels in fourteen states*. Northwest Evaluation Association.

Kohler, F. W., Crilley, K. M., Shearer, D. D., & Good, G. (1997). Effects of peer coaching on teacher and student outcomes. *The Journal of Educational Research, 90*(4), 240–251.

Koret Task Force on K–12 Education. (2003). *Our schools and our future: Are we still at risk?* Stanford, CA: Hoover Institution Press.

Kruse, S., Seashore Louis, K., & Bryk, A. (1994). Building professional community in schools. *Issues in Restructuring Schools, 6*. Center on Organization and Restructuring of Schools.

Ladd, H. F., & Zelli, A. (2002). School-based accountability in North Carolina: The response of school principals. *Educational Administration Quarterly, 38*(4), 494–530.

Le, V., & Klein, S. (2002). Technical criteria for evaluating tests. In L. S. Hamilton, B. M. Stecher, & S. P. Klein (Eds.), *Making sense of test-based accountability in education* (pp. 51–77). Santa Monica, CA: RAND.

Learning Point Associates. (2004). *Guide to using data in school improvement efforts: A compilation of knowledge from data retreats and data use at Learning Point Associates*. Naperville, IL: Learning Point Associates.

Leithwood, K., Leonard, L., & Sharratt, L. (1998). Conditions fostering organizational learning in schools. *Educational Administration Quarterly, 34*(2), 243–276.

Leithwood, K. A., & Poplin, M. S. (1992). The move toward transformational leadership. *Educational Leadership, 49*(5), 8–12.

Lewis, A. C. (1997). Standards for new administrators. *Phi Delta Kappan, 79*(2), 99–101.

Linn, R. L. (2000). Assessments and accountability. *Educational Researcher, 29*(2), 4–16.

Linn, R. L. (2003). *Accountability: Responsibility and reasonable expectations* (CSE 601). Los Angeles, CA: Center for the Study of Evaluation.

Little, J. W., Gearhart, M., Curry, M., & Kafka, J. (2003). Looking at student work for teacher learning, teacher community, and school reform. *Phi Delta Kappan, 85*(3), 185–192.

Loehlin, J. C. (2004). *Latent variable models: An introduction to factor, path, and structural equation analysis* (4th ed.). Mahwah, NJ: Lawrence Erlbaum Associates.

Loveless, T. (2003). Charter school achievement and accountability. In P. E. Peterson & M. R. West (Eds.), *No child left behind? The politics and practice of school accountability* (pp. 177–196). Washington, DC: The Brookings Institution.

Lugg, C. A., Bulkley, K., Firestone, W. A., & Garner, C. W. (2002). Understanding the challenges of school and district leadership at the dawn of a new century. In J. Murphy (Ed.), *The educational leadership challenge: Redefining leadership for the 21st century* (pp. 20–41). Chicago, IL: The University of Chicago Press.

Lunenburg, F. C., & Ornstein, A. C. (1991). *Educational administration: Concepts and practices.* Belmont, CA: Wadsworth Publishing.

Malen, B., Croninger, R., Muncey, D., & Redmond-Jones, D. (2002). Reconstituting schools: "Testing" the "theory of action." *Educational Evaluation and Policy Analysis, 24*(2), 113–132.

Marion, S. F., & Sheinker, A. (1999). *Issues and consequences for state-level minimum competency testing programs* (Wyoming Report 1). Minneapolis, MN: University of Minnesota, National Center on Educational Outcomes. Retrieved June 5, 2005, from http://education.umn.edu/NCEO/OnlinePubs/WyReport1.html.

Marks, H. M., & Seashore Louis, K. (1999). Teacher empowerment and the capacity for organizational learning. *Educational Administration Quarterly, 35*(Supplement), 707–750.

Marks, H. M., & Printy, S. M. (2003) Principal leadership and school performance: An integration of transformational and instructional leadership. *Educational Administration Quarterly, 39*(3), 370–397.

Marsh, D. D. (2002). Educational leadership for the twenty-first century: Integrating three essential perspectives. In M. S. Tucker & J. B. Codding (Eds.), *The principal challenge: Leading and managing schools in an era of accountability* (pp. 126–145). San Francisco: Jossey-Bass.

Marshall, C., & Gerstl-Pepin, C. (2005). *Reframing educational politics for social justice.* Boston: Pearson Education.

Martin, R., & McClure, P. (1969). *Title I of ESEA: Is it helping poor children?* Washington, DC: Washington Research Project of the Southern Center for Studies in Public Policy and the NAACP Legal Defense and Education Fund.

Massachusetts Department of Education. (2000). *Massachusetts mathematics curriculum framework.* Retrieved June 5, 2005, from http://www.doe.mass.edu/frameworks/math/2000/final.pdf.

Mazzoni, T. L. (1995). State policy-making and school reform: Influences and influentials. In J. D. Scribner and D. H. Layton (Eds.), *The study of educational politics* (pp. 53–73). Bristol, PA: The Falmer Press.

McCombs, J. S., Kirby, S. N., Barney, H., Darilek, H., & Magee, S. (2004). *Achieving state and national literacy goals, a long uphill road: A report to Carnegie Corporation of New York.* Santa Monica, CA: RAND Corporation.

McMillan, J. H. (2001). *Essential assessment concepts for teachers and administrators.* Thousand Oaks, CA: Corwin Press.

McUsic, M. S. (1999). The law's role in the distribution of education: The promises and pitfalls of school finance litigation. In J. P. Heubert (Ed.), *Law and school reform: Six strategies for promoting educational equity* (pp. 88–159). New Haven, CT: Yale University Press.

Mintrop, H. & Trujillo, T. (2005). *Corrective action in low-performing schools: Lessons for NCLB implementation from state and district strategies in first-generation accountability systems.* Paper presented at the Annual Meeting of the American Educational Research Association, Montreal, Canada.

Murphy, J. (1990). Principal instructional leadership. In L. S. Lotlo & P. W. Thurston (Eds.), *Advances in educational administration: Changing perspectives on the school.* Greenwich, CT: JAI Press.

Murphy, J. (2002). Reculturing the profession of educational leadership: New blueprints. In J. Murphy (Ed.), *The educational leadership challenge: Redefining leadership for the 21st century* (pp. 65–82). Chicago: The University of Chicago Press.

Murphy, J. (2003, September). *Reculturing educational leadership: The ISLLC standards ten years out.* Paper prepared for the National Policy Board for Educational Administration.

Murphy, J. T. (1971). Title I of ESEA: The politics of implementing federal education reform. *Harvard Education Review, 41*(1), 35–63.

Murray, S. E., Evans, W. N., & Schwab, R. M. (1998). Education-finance reform and the distribution of education resources. *The American Economic Review, 88*(4), 789–812.

National Center for Education Statistics. (2003). *Digest of education statistics and figures.* U.S. Department of Education. Retrieved June 1, 2005, from http://nces.ed.gov//programs/digest/d03/tables/dt156.asp.

National Commission on Excellence in Education (NCEE). (1983). *A nation at risk: The imperative for education reform.* Washington, DC: A Report to the Nation and the Secretary of Education, U.S. Department of Education.

National Council of Teachers of English (NCTE). (1996). *Standards for the English language arts.* Urbana, IL: NCTE.

National Council of Teachers of Mathematics (NCTM). (1989). *Curriculum and evaluation standards for school mathematics.* Reston, VA: National Council of Teachers of Mathematics.

National Council of Teachers of Mathematics (NCTM). (1991). *Professional standards for teaching mathematics.* Reston, VA: National Council of Teachers of Mathematics.

National Council of Teachers of Mathematics (NCTM). (2000). *Principles and standards for school mathematics.* Reston, VA: National Council of Teachers of Mathematics.

National Research Council (NRC). (1996). *National science education standards.* Washington, DC: National Academy Press.

National School Reform Faculty. (2005). *Protocols.* Retrieved August 1, 2005, from http://www.nsrfharmony.org/protocols.html.

Neuman, M., & Pelchat, J. (2001). The challenge to leadership: Focusing on student achievement. *Phi Delta Kappan, 82*(10), 732–737.

Newmann, F. M., King, M. B., & Rigdon, M. (1997). Accountability and school performance: Implications from restructuring schools. *Harvard Educational Review, 67*(1), 41–69.

Newmann, F. M., King, M. B., & Youngs, P. (2000). Professional development that addresses school capacity: Lessons from urban elementary schools. *American Journal of Education, 108*, 259–299.

No Child Left Behind Act of 2001, P.L. No. 107–110 (2001).

Northouse, P. G. (2004). *Leadership theory and practice* (3rd ed.). Thousand Oaks, CA: SAGE Publications.

Norton, M. S. (2005). *Executive leadership for effective administration.* Boston: Pearson.

Oakes, J. (1985). *Keeping track: How schools structure inequality.* Binghamton, NY: Vail-Ballou Press.

O'Day, J. A. (2002). Complexity, accountability, and school improvement. *Harvard Educational Review, 72*(3), 293–329.

O'Day, J. A. (2005). Standards-based reform and low-performing schools: A case of reciprocal accountability. In F.M. Hess (Ed.), *Urban school reform: Lessons from San Diego* (pp. 115–138). Cambridge, MA: Harvard Educational Press.

Odell, S. J. (1990). *Mentoring teacher programs: What Research says to the teacher.* Washington, DC: National Education Association.

Ogawa, R. T., Sandholtz, J. H., Martinez-Flores, M., & Scribner, S. P. (2003). The substantive and symbolic consequences of district's standards-based curriculum. *American Educational Research Journal 40*(1), 147–176.

Olson, L. (2005a). States hoping to 'grow' into AYP success: Federal officials are considering alternatives for measuring progress. *Education Week, 24*(37), 15.

Olson, L. (2005b). Benchmark assessments offer regular checkups on student achievement. *Education Week, 25*(13), 13.

Olson, L. (2005c). States confront definition of 'proficient' as they set the bar for lots of new tests. *Education Week, 25*(15), S10.

Olson, J. F., & Goldstein, A. A. (1997). *The inclusion of students with disabilities and limited English proficient students in large-scale assessments: A summary of recent progress.* Washington, DC: National Center for Educational Statistics.

Olson, L., & Hoff, D. J. (2005). U.S. to pilot new gauge of 'growth': Ed. Dept. to permit shifts in how states track gains. *Education Week, 25*(13), 1.

Organisation for Economic Co-Operation and Development (OECD). (2005). *Formative assessment: Improving learning in secondary classrooms.* Paris: Author.

Perkins, S. J. (1998). On becoming a peer coach: Practices, identities, and beliefs of inexperienced coaches. *Journal of Curriculum and Supervision 13*(3), 235–254.

Peterson, P. E. (1981). *City limits.* Chicago: The University of Chicago Press.

Peterson, P. E., Rabe, B. G., & Wong, K. K. (1986). *When federalism works.* Washington, DC: Brookings Institution.

Peterson, P. E., Rabe, B. G., & Wong, K. K. (1988). The evolution of the compensatory education program. In D. P. Doyle & B. S. Cooper (Eds.), *Federal aid to the disadvantaged: What future for Chapter 1?* (pp. 33–60). Philadelphia: Falmer, Taylor & Francis.

Pierce, J. (2003). *Minimum size of subgroups for adequate yearly progress (AYP).* Denver: Education Commission of the States. Retrieved June 5, 2005, from http://www.ecs.org/clearinghouse/49/76/4976.htm.

Popham, J. W. (1975). *Educational evaluation.* Englewood Cliffs, New Jersey: Prentice-Hall.

Popham, J. W., Cures, K. L., Rankin, S. C., Sandifer, P. D., & Williams, P. L. (1985). Measurement-driven instruction: It's on the road. *Phi Delta Kappan, 66*(9), 628–634.

Porter, A., & Chester, M. (2002). Building a high-quality assessment and accountability program: The Philadelphia example. In D. Ravitch (Ed.), *Brookings papers on education policy 2002* (pp. 285–337). Washington, DC: Brookings Institution Press.

Porter, A., Garet, M., Desimone, L., & Birman, B. (2003). Providing effective professional development: Lessons from the Eisenhower Program. *Science Educator, 12*(1), 23–40.

Portin, B. S. & Knapp, M. S. (2001). Readiness for reflection: Two schools' response to a data-driven school improvement process. *International Journal of Educational Policy, Research and Practice, 2*(2), 103–125.

Pressman, J. L., & Wildavsky, A. B. (1984). *Implementation: How great expectations in Washington are dashed in Oakland* (3rd ed.). Los Angeles, CA: University of California Press.

Rallis, S. F., & Goldring, E. B. (2000). *Principals of dynamic schools: Taking charge of change.* Thousand Oaks, CA: Corwin Press Inc.

Raudenbush, S. W., & Bryk, A. S. (2002). *Hierarchical linear models: Applications and data analysis methods* (2nd ed.). Thousand Oaks, CA: Sage Publications.

Ravitch, D. (1995). *National standards in American education: A citizen's guide.* Washington, DC: Brookings Institution Press.

Reeves, D. B. (2002a). The six principles of effective accountability. In M. Pierce & D. L. Stapleton (Eds.), *The 21st-century principal: Current issues in leadership and policy* (pp. 18–25). Cambridge, MA: Harvard Education Press.

Reeves, D. B. (2002b). *Making standards work: How to implement standards-based assessments.* Denver, CO: Advanced Learning Press.

Reeves, D. B. (2004). *Accountability for learning: How teachers and school leaders can take charge.* Alexandria, VA: Association for Supervision and Curriculum Development.

Reid, K. S. (2004). States' roles prove tough on big scale. *Education Week 24*(7), 16.

Reitzug, U. C. (1997). Images of principal instructional leadership: From supervision to collaborative inquiry. *Journal of Curriculum Supervision, 12*, 356–366.

Rettig, M. D., McCullough, L. L., Santos, K. E., & Watson, C. R. (2004). *From rigorous standards to student achievement: A practical process.* Larchmont, NY: Eye on Education.

Reys, R., Reys, B., Lapan, R., Holliday, G., & Wasman, D. (2003). Assessing the impact of standards-based middle grades mathematics curriculum materials on student achievement. *Journal for Research in Mathematics Education, 34*(1), 74–96.

Richardson, V. (2003). The dilemmas of professional development. *Phi Delta Kappan International, 84*(5), 401–409.

Roderick, M., & Engel, M. (2001). The grasshopper and the ant: Motivational responses of low-achieving students to high-stakes testing. *Educational Evaluation and Policy Analysis, 23*(3), 197–227.

Roeber, E. D. (2002). *Appropriate inclusion of students with disabilities in state accountability systems.* Denver: Education Commission of the States. Retrieved June 5, 2005, from http://www.ecs.org/clearinghouse/40/11/4011.htm.

Ross, J. A., McDougall, D., Hogaboam-Gray, A., & LeSage, A. (2003). A survey measuring elementary teachers' implementation of standards-based mathematics teaching. *Journal for Research in Mathematics Education, 34*(4), 344–363.

Rossi, P. H., Freeman, H. E., & Lipsey, M. W. (1999). *Evaluation: A systematic approach* (6th ed.). Thousand Oaks, CA: SAGE Publications.

Rowan, B. (1990). Commitment and control: Alternative strategies for the organizational design of schools. In C. Cazden (Ed.), *Review of research in education, volume 16* (pp. 353–389). Washington, DC: American Educational Research Association.

Ryan, K. (2002). Shaping educational accountability systems. *American Journal of Evaluation 23*(4), 453–468.

Sandholtz, J. H., Ogawa, R. T., & Scribner, S. P. (2004). Standards gaps: Unintended consequences of local standards-based reform. *Teachers College Record, 106*(6), 1177–1203.

Seashore Louis, K., & Kruse, S. D. (1995). *Professionalism and community: Perspectives on reforming urban schools.* Thousand Oaks, CA: Corwin Press.

Schlechty, P. C. (2002). Leading a school system through change: Key steps for moving reform forward. In M. S. Tucker & J. B. Codding (Eds.), *The principal challenge: Leading and managing schools in an era of accountability* (pp. 182–201). San Francisco, CA: Jossey-Bass.

Schmoker, M. (2003). First things first: Demystifying data analysis. *Educational Leadership, 60*(5), 22–24.

Schnur, J., & Gerson, K. (2005). Reforming the principalship. In F. M. Hess (Ed.), *Urban school reform: Lessons from San Diego* (pp. 93–114). Cambridge, MA: Harvard Educational Press.

Schumaker, D. R. & Sommers, W. A. (2001). *Being a successful principal: Riding the wave of change without drowning.* Thousand Oaks, CA: Corwin Press.

Schwartz, A. E., Stiefel, L, & Chellman, C. (2005). Subgroup reporting and school segregation. *Education Week, 24*(28), 31.

Scribner, J. P., Hager, D. R., & Warne, T. R. (2002). The paradox of professional community: Tales from two high schools. *Educational Administration Quarterly, 38*(1), 45–76.

Sebring, P. B, & Bryk, A. (2000). School leadership and the bottom line in Chicago. *Phi Delta Kappan, 81*(6), 440–443.

Sergiovanni, T. J. (1987). *The principalship: A reflective practice perspective.* Newton, MA: Allyn and Bacon.

Shadish, W. R., Cook, T. D., & Campbell, D. T. (2002). *Experimental and quasi-experimental designs for generalized causal inference.* Boston: Houghton Mifflin.

Shields, P. M., & Knapp, M. S. (1997). The promise and limits of school-based reform: A national snapshot. *Phi Delta Kappan, 79*(4), 288–294.

Shipps, D., & Firestone, W. A. (2003, June 18). Juggling accountabilities: The leaders' turn. *Education Week 22*(41), 56.

Showers, J. & Joyce, B. (1996). The evolution of peer coaching. *Educational Leadership, 53*(6), 12–16.

Sirotnik, K. A., & Kimball, K. (1999). Standards for standards-based accountability systems. *Phi Delta Kappan, 81*(3), 209–215.

Skria, L. & Scheurich, J. J. (Eds.). (2004). *Educational equity and accountability: Paradigms, policies, and politics.* New York: RoutledgeFalmer.

Smith, T. & Desimone, L. (2003). Do changes in patterns of participation in teachers' professional development reflect the goals of standards-based reform? *Educational Horizons, 81*(3), 119–129.

Smylie, M. A., Conley, S., & Marks, H. M. (2002). Reshaping leadership in action. In J. Murphy (Ed.), *The educational leadership challenge: Redefining leadership for the 21st century* (pp. 162–188). Chicago: The University of Chicago Press.

Solomon, J., & Weissbourd, R. (2001, January 14). To improve schools, focus on teachers. *The Boston Globe*, D.7.

Spillane, J. P. (1999). State and local government relations in the era of standards-based reform: Standards, state policy instruments, and local instructional policy making. *Educational Policy, 13*(4), 546–573.

Spillane, J. P., Halverson, R., & Diamond, J. B. (2004). Towards a theory of leadership practice: A distributed perspective. *Journal of Curriculum Studies, 36*(1), 3–34.

Spillane, J. P., & Seashore Louis, K. (2002). School improvement processes and practices: Professional learning for building instructional capacity. In J. Murphy (Ed.), *The educational leadership challenge: Redefining leadership for the 21st century* (pp. 83–104). Chicago: The University of Chicago Press.

Spotsylvania County Schools. (2004). *Curriculum Map.* Retrieved June 5, 2005, from http://www. spotsylvania.k12.va.us/cmaps/pdf/science/ Science%205.pdf.

Sroufe, G. E. (1995). Politics of education at the federal level. In J. D. Scribner & D. H. Layton (Eds.), *The study of educational politics* (pp. 75–88). Bristol, PA: The Falmer Press.

Stay on reform track. (2002, January 13). *The Denver Post*, D06.

Stiggins, R. J., and Conklin, N. F. (1992). *In teachers' hands: Investigating the practices of classroom assessment.* Albany, NY: State University of New York Press.

Stout, R. T., Tallerico, M., & Scribner, K. P. (1995). Values: The 'what?' of the politics of education. In J. D. Scribner & D. H. Layton (Eds.), *The study of educational politics.* Bristol, PA: The Falmer Press.

Strahan, D. (2003). Promoting a collaborative professional community in three elementary schools that have beaten the odds. *The Elementary School Journal, 104*(2), 127–146.

Sunderman, G. L., Tracey, C. A., Kim, J., & Orfield, G. (2004). *Listening to teachers: Classroom realities and No Child Left Behind.* Cambridge, MA: The Civil Rights Project and Harvard University.

Taylor, F. W. (2001). The principles of scientific management. In J. M. Shafritz & J. S. Ott (Eds.), *Classics of organization theory* (5th ed.) (pp. 61–72). Belmont, CA: Wadsworth Group/ Thomson Learning.

Teddlie, C., & Reynolds, D. (2000). *The international handbook of school effectiveness research.* New York: Falmer.

Tennessee State Board of Education. (2001). *English/Language arts curriculum standards.* Retrieved June 5, 2005, from http://www.state. tn.us/education/ci/cistandards2001/la/ cilag8reading.htm.

Thompson, S. (2001). The authentic standards movement and its evil twin. *Phi Delta Kappan, 82*(5), 358–363.

Thum, Y. M. (2003). *No Child Left Behind: Methodological challenges and recommendations for measuring adequate yearly progress* (CSE 590). Los Angeles: Center for the Study of Evaluation.

Thum, Y. M., & Bryk, A. S. (1997). Value-added productivity indicators: The Dallas system. In J. Millman (Ed.), *Grading teachers, grading schools: Is student achievement a valid evaluation measure?* (pp. 100–109). Thousand Oaks, CA: Corwin Press.

Timar, T. (1994). Program design and assessment strategies in Chapter 1. In K. K. Wong & M. C. Wang (Eds.), *Rethinking policy for at-risk students* (pp. 65–89). Berkeley, CA: McCutchan.

Trejos, N. (2001, June 28). A challenging offer for potential principals. *The Washington Post*, T.01.

Tucker, M. S. & Codding, J. B. (2002). Preparing principals in the age of accountability. In

M. S. Tucker & J. B. Codding (Eds.), *The principal challenge: Leading and managing schools in an era of accountability* (pp. 1–40). San Francisco: Jossey-Bass.

Tyack, D., & Cuban, L. (1995). *Tinkering toward utopia: A century of public school reform.* Cambridge, MA: Harvard University Press.

U.S. Department of Education. (1991). *America 2000: An education strategy.* Washington, DC: Author.

U.S. Department of Education. (1993). *Reinventing Chapter 1.* Washington, DC: Author.

U.S. Department of Education. (2000). *Study of education resources and federal funding: Final report.* No. ED 445178. Washington, DC: Author.

U.S. Department of Education. (2003). *Education department budget history table.* Retrieved June 1, 2003, from http://www.ed. gov/offices/OUS/BudgetHistory/index.html.

U.S. Department of Education. (2005). *Approved state accountability plans.* Retrieved January 15, 2005, from http://www.ed.gov/admins/lead/account/stateplans03/index.html.

Valencia, S. W., & Wixson, K. K. (2001). Inside English/language arts standards: What's in a grade? *Reading Research Quarterly, 36*(2), 202–217.

Virginia Department of Education. (2003). *Standards of Learning.* Retrieved June 5, 2005, from http://www.pen.k12.va.us/VDOE/Superintendent/Sols/science5.pdf.

Vogler, K. E., & Kennedy, R. J., Jr. (2003). A view from the bottom: What happens when your school system ranks last? *Phi Delta Kappan, 84*(6) 446–448.

Wang, J., & Odell, S. J. (2002). Mentored learning to teach according to standards-based reform: A critical review. *Review of Educational Research, 72*(3), 481–546.

Waters, T., Marzano, R. J., & McNulty, B. (2003). *Balanced leadership: What 30 years of research tells us about the effect of leadership on student achievement.* Aurora, CO: McREL.

Weber, M. (2001). Bureaucracy. In J. M. Shafritz & J. S. Ott (Eds.), *Classics of organization theory* (5th ed.) (pp. 73–78). Belmont, CA: Wadsworth Group/Thomson Learning.

Weick, K. (1976). Educational organizations as loosely coupled systems. *Administrative Science Quarterly, 21,* 1–19.

Weiss, C. H. (1998). *Evaluation* (2nd ed.). Upper Saddle River, NJ: Prentice-Hall.

Weiss, C. H., & Cambone, J. (2002). Principals, shared decision making, and school reform. In M. S. Tucker & J. B. Codding (Eds.), *The principal challenge: Leading and managing schools in an era of accountability* (pp. 266–389). San Francisco: Jossey-Bass.

Weiss, I. R., Knapp, M. S., Hollweg, K. S., & Burrill, G. (Eds.). (2001). *Investigating the influence of standards: A framework for research in mathematics, science, and technology education.* Washington, DC: National Academy Press.

Westheimer, J. (1999). Communities and consequences: An inquiry into ideology and practice in teachers' professional work. *Educational Administration Quarterly, 35*(1), 71–105.

Wildman, T. M., Magliaro, S. G., Niles, R. A., & Niles, J. A. (1992) Teacher mentoring: An analysis of roles, activities and conditions. *Journal of Teacher Education, 43*(3), 205–213.

Winter, P. A., & Morgenthal, J. R. (2002). Principal recruitment in a reform environment: Effects of school achievement and school level on applicant attraction to the job. *Educational Administration Quarterly, 38*(3), 319–343.

Wong, K. K. (1992). The politics of urban education as a field of study: An interpretive analysis. In J. G. Cibulka, K. K. Wong, & R. J. Reed (Eds.), *The politics of urban education in the United States.* London: Falmer Press.

Wong, K. K. (1999). *Funding public schools: Politics and policies.* Lawrence, KS: University Press of Kansas.

Wong, K. K. (2003). The politics of education. In V. Gray & R. Hanson (Eds.), *Politics in the American States: A Comparative Analysis* (pp. 357–388). Washington, DC: CQ Press.

Wong, K. K., Anagnostopoulos, D. (1998). Can integrated governance reconstruct teaching? Lessons learned from two low-performing Chicago high schools. *Educational Policy, 12* (1–2), 31–47.

Wong K. K., Anagnostopoulos, D., Rutledge, S., Lynn, L., Dreeben, R. (1999). Implementation of an educational accountability agenda: Integrated governance in the Chicago public schools enters its fourth year. Chicago: University of Chicago.

Wong, K. K., & Meyer, S. J. (2001). Title I schoolwide programs as an alternative to categorical practices: An organizational analysis of surveys from the Prospects study. In G. D. Borman, S. C. Stringfield, & R. E. Slavin (Eds.), *Title I, compensatory education at the crossroads*. Mahway, NJ: L. Erlbaum Associates.

Wong, K. K., & Nicotera, A. C. (2004a). Educational quality and policy redesign: Reconsidering the *NAR* and federal Title I policy. *Peabody Journal of Education*, 79(1), 87–104.

Wong, K. K., & Nicotera, A. C. (2004b). Toward stronger accountability in Title I: Fiscal implications in the implementation of the No Child Left Behind Act. In K. DeMoss & K. K. Wong (Eds.), *Money, politics, and law: Intersections and conflicts in the provision of education opportunity*. Larchmont, NY: Eye on Education.

Wong, K. K., & Shen, F. X. (2003, October). When mayors lead urban schools: Toward developing a framework to assess the effects of mayoral takeover of urban districts. Paper prepared for School Board Politics Conference, Program on Education Policy and Governance, Harvard University.

Wong, K. K., & Sunderman, G. L. (2000). Implementing districtwide reform in schools with Title I schoolwide programs: The first 2 years of Children Achieving in Philadelphia. *Journal of Education for Students Placed at Risk*, 5(4), 355–381.

Text Credits

Pages 15–20: As first appeared in *Education Week*, September 15, 2005. Reprinted with permission from Editorial Projects in Education.

Pages 20–22: As first appeared in *Education Week*, September 14, 2005. Reprinted with permission from Editorial Projects in Education.

Pages 36–37: Shipps, D., & Firestone, W. A. June 18, 2003. Juggling accountabilities: The leaders' turn. *Education Week 22*(41), 56.

Pages 55–56: © 2001, *The Washington Post*. Reprinted with permission.

Pages 72–73: Hasse, C. August 2, 2001. Accountability is a shared responsibility. *The Seattle Post-Intelligencer*, B7.

Pages 105–107: As first appeared in *Education Week*, December 14, 2005. Reprinted with permission from Editorial Projects in Education.

Pages 128–129: *The Denver Post*, editorial, January, 13, 2002. Reprinted with permission.

Pages 157–158: Schwartz, A. E., Stiefel, L., & Chellman, C. March 23, 2005. Subgroup reporting and school segregation: An unhappy pairing in the No Child Left Behind equation. *Education Week 24*(28), 31.

Pages 170–173: As first appeared in *Education Week*, November 30, 2005. Reprinted with permission from Editorial Projects in Education.

Pages 190–191: Solomon, J. & Weissbourd, R. (2001, January, 14). To improve schools, focus on teachers. *The Boston Globe*, D7.

Index

Page numbers followed by f and t represent figures and tables respectively.

"A Challenging Offer for Potential Principals" (Trejos), 55–56

A Nation at Risk (1983), xi, 1, 3–5, 64
  recommendations, 209–215

academic performance
  goals for, 27–28
  public expectation on, 2
  tools to improve, 32–33

academic press, 28

academic standards, 76, 78–89
  design and function of, 77–78
  instructional practices and, 31
  performance standards and, 90–91
  professional development and, 179
  rating schemes for, 80, 81t
  reporting of, 133–134
  TCAP reading benchmarks in, 85, 86t–88t
  Virginia science objectives and indicators in, 92, 93t–94t
    curriculum guidelines, 94, 95t–100t

Academy for Educational Development, 184

accelerated curve, in AYP determination, 146, 147f

accountability. *see* educational accountability

"Accountability Is a Shared Responsibility" (Hasse), 71

achievement, measuring change in
  average achievement, 125–126
  gains in achievement, 126–128

achievement gain analysis, 126–128

achievement gap, 158

Ackland, R., 188

Adams, J. E., 4, 27, 46, 70

adequate yearly progress
  determining, approaches for, 143, 146, 147f
  reporting of, 136
  safe harbor provision and, 148, 149t
  school improvement and, 152, 153t–154t, 154

administrators. *see* school administrators

aggregated data, reporting of, 134–136

Ainsworth, L., 76

American Association of School Administrators, 164

Ancess, J., 122

Andrews, R., 39, 47

Annenberg Institute for School Reform, 163

Archer, J., 53
  "Tackling an Impossible Job," 15–20
  "Theory of Action," 20–22

assessments. *see also* classroom assessment
  in accountability theory, 26f, 28
  aligning standards with, 101–102, 103t–104t
  benchmark, 170–173
  large-scale external, 110
  reporting of, 133–134
  student (*see* student assessments)
  vs. traditional testing, 109

average achievement, measuring change in, 125–126

AYP. *see* adequate yearly progress

Baker, E. L., 9–10, 124, 132

Ballou, D., 127

Barr, R., 65

Barta, J., 101, 179

Bassett, Eric, 173

Bell, Terrell H., 3

"Benchmark Assessments Offer Regular Checkups on Student Achievement" (Olson), 170–173

benchmarks
  for assessment, 170–173
  learning objectives and, 79
  performance standards and, 89
  TCAP reading performance and, 85, 86t–88t

Betts, J., 76

Birman, B. F., 175

Boone, W. J., 177

Brown v. Board of Education (1954), 60

Bryk, A., 53, 127, 183, 186

Bulkley, K., 45

bureaucracy, 1–2
  managerial roles and, 41

bureaucratic accountability, 9
  professional accountability *vs.*, 37

Burrill, G., 5, 25

Bush, George H. W., 5

California Achievement Test, 111
California Standards Test, 114
Camburn, E., 186
Campbell, D., 25
Campbell, Jeremy, 56
capacity, system-wide, 13
  accountability implementation and, 69–70
  building, 46, 65–66, 69–70
Carey, K., 135
Casserly, Michael D., 21
CAT (California Achievement Test), 111
CCSSO (Council of Chief State School Officers),
  43–44, 44t, 64
Charlottesville Summit (1989), 5
Chatterji, M., 7, 28
Chellman, Colin, Amy Ellen Schwartz, and
  Leanna Steifel, "Subgroup Reporting
  and School Segregation: An Unhappy
  Pairing in the No Child Left Behind
  Equation," 157–158
classroom assessment
  aligned with academic standards, 102, 104t
  formative, elements of, 122–123
  purposes of, 122
coaching, reciprocal, 188
Coalition for Essential Schools, 163, 184
Cohen, D. K., 69
collaboration, between teachers
  peer-coaching strategies, 186–189
  professional learning communities, 183–186
collaborative inquiry
  in distributed leadership, 50
  in educational leadership, 46–47
  for effective school-improvement decisions,
    162–165
  local and state support for, 164
  in professional learning communities, 185
  professional norms for, creating, 163
  time required for, 164
confidence interval, subgroup size and, 135–136
congruence, principle of, 10
Conklin, N. F., 119–120
Conley, S., 47
consequences, in accountability system, 149–156
  corrective action, 154–155
  restructuring, 155–156
  school improvement (*see* school improvement,
    as accountability consequence)
  unintended, 34–35
    professional learning communities and, 186
content, higher-order, 174–175
continuing education, 45
Cook, T. D., 25
Cooke, Donald, 55
corrective action, as accountability consequence,
  154–155
Council of Chief State School Officers (CCSSO),
  43–44, 44t, 64

Cox, John, 55, 56
Crilley, K. M., 189
criterion-referenced tests, 113–118, 115t–116t,
  117f–121f
Cronbach's coefficient alpha, 124
Crow, G. M., 50, 165
CST (California Standards Test), 114
Cuban, L., 13, 67
Cunningham, Ronald, 55
curriculum
  aligning standards with, 91–92, 93t–94t, 94
  and instruction quality, 101
  standards and, 31
  tests aligned to, 110–111
  Virginia science guidelines, 94, 95t–100t
Curry, M., 47, 184–185

Darling-Hammond, L., 76, 122
data
  aggregated, reporting of, 134–136
  disaggregated, reporting of, 135–136
  for school-improvement decisions, 163
    data-driven strategies, 32, 167–168
decision-making strategies
  conditions for effectiveness, 162–166 (*see also*
    school improvement, effective
    decisions in)
  data-driven, 32, 167–168
  readiness dimensions and, 164–165
DeMoss, K., 54
Denver Post, "Stay on Reform Track" (editorial),
  128–129
de-privatization, of instructional practices, 183,
  185
derived score, *vs.* raw score, 111
Desimone, L., 76, 175
disabled students
  assessment requirements for, 135
  progress reports and, 134
disaggregated data, reporting of, 135–136
distributed leadership, 49–51
  real-life findings in, 53–54
diversity, respect for, 10
Dorward, J., 101, 179
Doughery, Chrys, 22
Dreeben, R., 65
Drickey, N., 101, 179
Duffy, M., 70
Dutro, E., 77

economically disadvantaged students, progress
  reports and, 134
education funding
  allocation of, 58–59, 63
  revenue sources for, 61, 61t
  Title I (*see* Title I funding)
education governance
  intergovernmental

federal level, 60–63
  nature of, 59
intergovernmental nature of
  changes in, 66–67
  at local level, 65–66 (*see also* school districts;
    schools)
  state level, 63–65
  structure of, 58–59
Education for All Handicapped Children Act, 60
education reform. *see also* school-reform strategy
  implementing, 33–34
  organization capacity and, 34
  process-oriented, 45
  standards-based, 76
education system
  efficiency of (*see* organization efficiency)
  governance structure of (*see* education
    governance)
  improvements in, motivation for, 28–29
  institutional fragmentation of, 59
  leadership roles defined by, 40–41
  nature of problems in, 24–25
  procedural compliance *vs.* measuring student
    performance in, 40, 41–42
  professional development in, 180–182
  resistance to change in, 25–29
Education Week rating scheme, 80, 81t
educational accountability
  challenges to, 33–35
  defined, 2, 29–33
  emergence of, 2, 3–8
  implementing, 67–70
    capacity, 69–70
    challenges, 70–71
    variability, 67–69
    weakly, 33–34
  operational components of, 29, 30f
  performance-based (*see* performance-based
    educational accountability)
  reciprocal (*see* reciprocal accountability)
  as school-reform strategy, 161
  standards and, 10, 26f, 27–28 (*see also* standards)
  system of, 26f, 28–29
  theory of, 25–29, 26f, 30f
  tools for, 32–33
educational leaders. *see also* school leaders
  duties of *vs.* management by, 40–41
  peer coaching and, 189
  policy reform challenging, 1–3
  professional development and, 45, 174–176, 179
  professional learning communities and, 186
  shared leadership and, 47–48
educational programs, evidence-based, 161
educational roles, changes in, 30–31
Educational Testing Service, 40
Eduventures report, 172
Elementary and Secondary Education Act (1965),
  7, 60, 61

Hawkins-Stafford Amendments (1988), 7
  testing and, 110
ELL (English language learners), federal
  legislation and, 60
Elmore, R. F., 25, 42–43, 45, 49–50, 68
English language learners, federal legislation
  and, 60
enrichment programs, 152, 154
equal yearly goals, in AYP determination, 146,
  147f
equality, Johnson's views on, 61
ESEA. *see* Elementary and Secondary Education
  Act (1965)
ETS (Educational Testing Service), 40
Evans, W. N., 64
evidence-based educational programs, 161
evidence-based instructional practices, 11–12
expectation
  education accountability and, 108–109
  new leadership, response to, 53–54
  public, 2, 10

Falk, B., 122
FCAT. *see* Florida Comprehensive Assessment
  Test
federal government
  education governance and control, 60–63
  reauthorization of legislation by, 6–8
Fink, S., 71, 180
Firestone, W., 45
  "Juggling Accountabilities: The Leaders' Turn"
    (with Dorthy Shipps), 36–37
Fisk, M. C., 77
Florida Comprehensive Assessment Test, 90, 114
formative assessments, 119–120, 173
  in the classroom, 122–123
4Sight test, 171
Fry, Betty, 18
Fuhrman, S. H., 49–50
Fullan, Michael, 22
funding. *see also* education funding; Title I funding
  for professional development, 180–182, 181t

Garet, M. S., 175
Garner, C. W., 45
Gates Foundation, 182
Gearhart, M., 47, 184–185
Geck, Carol, 56
Geppert, J., 123
Gerson, R., 12
Goertz, M. E., 70
Goldring, E., 42, 46, 47, 51
Good, G., 189
grade-equivalent scores, 112
grants, for professional development, 182
Greenfield, W., 42, 46, 51
Griffith, Kelly, 10, 15, 17
Grimmert, P., 189

Grogan, M., 39, 47
growth models
    in achievement gain analysis, 127
    adequate yearly progress and, 136, 148

Hager, D. R., 186
Hall, D., 135
Hallinger, P., 48
Hamilton, L. S., 110–111
Hammond, Jane, 20
Hanushek, E. A., 126
Harvard Project Zero, 184
Hasse, Charles, "Accountability Is a Shared
        Responsibility," 71
Hausman, C. S., 50, 165
Hawkins-Stafford Amendments (1988), 7
Hess, Frederick M., 17
higher-order content, 174–175
high-quality standards. see standards
Hightower, A. M., 181–182
Hill, H. C., 45, 69
Hogaboam-Gray, A., 101
Hollweg, K. S., 5, 25
Hord, S. M., 186
Hornbeck, M., 180
Hudson, P., 101, 179

Iannaccone, L., 65
IASA (Improving America's Schools Act of 1994),
        7–8
Idaho Standards Achievement Tests, 114
IDEA (Individuals with Disabilities Education
        Act), 60
IEP (individual education plan), 135, 140
Illinois
    academic standards, for social studies, 102, 104t
    elementary school report card of, 137,
        138t–139t
Illinois Standards Achievement Test, 102, 103t, 137
Illinois State Board of Education, standards
        development criteria, 79
improvement. see also instructional improvement;
        school improvement
    goals for, setting, 168–169
Improving America's Schools Act (1994), 2, 7–8
indicators
    in formative assessment, 120, 122
    learning objectives and, 79
    performance standards and, 89
    of school performance, 160–161
    of student performance, 109–110, 160–161
    Virginia academic standards for science, 92,
        93t–94t
    curriculum guidelines, 94, 95t–100t
individual education plan, 135, 140
individualism, 177
Individuals with Disabilities Education Act, 60

information
    management systems, 4
    on student performance (see testing)
Institute for School Leaders, 182
instruction standards, 94, 95t–100t, 101. see also
        academic standards; performance
        standards
instructional improvement
    assessment results informing, 31
    assumptions for, 26–27
    case study, 20–22
    continuous, principle of, 10
    policy talk and, gap between, 13
instructional leadership, 48–49
    characteristics of, 49
    weaknesses in, 49
instructional practices, 11–12
    academic and performance standards guiding, 31
    adapting, 162–163, 169
    aligning standards with, 94, 95t–100t, 101
    changes in, 149
        questions concerning, 45
        resources and support for, 67
    implementation of standards and, 76–77
    outcomes and, link between, 108–109
    sharing (de-privatization), 183, 185
intergovernmental roles
    implementing educational accountability, 67–70
        capacity, 69–70
        challenges, 70–71
        variability, 67–69
    school governance (see education governance,
        intergovernmental)
Interstate Leaders Licensure Consortium,
        standards, 43–44, 44t, 222–228
Iowa Test of Basic Skills (ITBS), 111
ISAT (Idaho Standards Achievement Tests), 114
ISAT (Illinois Standards Achievement Test), 102,
        103t, 137
ISBE (Illinois State Board of Education),
        standards development criteria, 79
ISL (Institute for School Leaders), 182
ISLLC (Interstate Leaders Licensure
        Consortium), standards, 222–228

Jacobs, H. H., 92
Johnson, Carol R., 20
Johnson, Lyndon, 60–61
Joyce, B., 186
judicial rulings, on education funding, 64
"Juggling Accountabilities: The Leaders' Turn"
        (Shipps and Firestone), 36–37

Kafka, J., 47, 184–185
Kahl, Stuart R., 172
Kahle, J. B., 177
Kane, T. J., 123

Kelleher, J., 177
Kennedy, Carole, 19
Kim, J., 183
Kimball, K., 109
King, Don, 56
King, M. B., 26–27, 34, 46
Kingsbury, G. G., 68–69
Kirst, M. W., 4, 46, 70
Klein, Joel I., 36–37
Klein, S., 123
Knapp, M. S., 5, 25, 164
Koch, R., 77
Kohler, F. W., 189
Koret Task Force on K–12 Education, 4
Koretz, D. M., 110–111

Ladd, H. F., 28
large-scale testing, 110
Larsen, Marissa A., 172
latent variable modeling, 124
Le, V., 123
leadership. *see also* "leading by results"
    distributed (*see* distributed leadership)
    instructional (*see* instructional leadership)
    results-driven, 52
    shared, 47–48, 184
        professional development and, 179
    theories for educational accountability, 48–52
    theories of, 48–52
    transformational, 51–52
"leading by results," 41–42
    building capacity for, 46
    collaborative inquiry in (*see* collaborative inquiry)
    knowledge and skills for, 42–45
    reflective process in (*see* reflective practice)
    sharing leadership in, 47–48
learning. *see* student learning
learning objectives, 78–79
    Virginia academic standards for science, 92, 93t–94t
        curriculum guidelines, 94, 95t–100t
Learning Point Associates, 164
legal accountability, 9
Leithwood, Kenneth, 16
LEP (limited English proficiency) students, 134
LeSage, A., 101
licensure
    ISLLC standards, 222–228
    school leaders' assessment modules, 219–221
limited English proficiency students, 134
Linn, R. L., 6, 9–10, 89, 105, 109, 124, 132
Lissitz, Robert W., 106, 107
Little, J. W., 47, 184–185
Locke, Gary, 73
low-performing schools, 65–66, 130–131
    applying consequences to, 149–150
    corrective action in, 155
Lugg, C. A., 45

Lunenburg, F. C., 41, 49
Lutz, F. W., 65

Magliaro, S. G., 187
management/managing
    information systems for, 4
    by objectives, 4
    by rules, *vs.* measuring student performance, 41–42
    Weber's theory of, 1–2, 41
managerial roles, in education system, 41
Marion, Scott, 106
market accountability, 9
    vs. moral accountability, 37
Marks, H. M., 47
Marsh, D. D., 40, 52
Marzano, R. J., 43
Massachusetts Department of Education, mathematics
        performance standards, 80, 82t–83t, 84
mathematics
    NAEP long-term trends by race/ethnicity, 115, 118f
    NAEP performance levels
        for mathematics, 115–117, 120f
        for reading, 115–117, 119f
    performance standards, 80, 82t–83t, 84
Mazzoni, T. L., 64
MBO (management by objectives), 4
McCullough, L. L., 102
McDougall, D., 101
McLaughlin, M. W., 181–182
McMillan, J. H., 122
McNulty, B., 43
McUsic, M. S., 63–64
Menino, Thomas M., 190
Meyer, S. J., 62
minimum-competency tests, 110
Mintrop, H., 71, 131, 152, 155
MIS (management information systems), 4
monitoring mechanisms, in accountability system, 31–32, 130–132, 141–149
moral accountability, 9
    market accountability *vs.*, 37
Morgenthal, J. R., 48
Murphy, J., 48–49, 61
Murphy, Joseph F., 16, 41
Murray, S. E., 64

NAEP (National Assessment of Educational Progress), 110, 114
    achievement-level definitions, 114, 115t
    long-term trends by race/ethnicity
        mathematics, 115, 118f
        reading, 115, 117f
    performance levels
        for mathematics, 115–117, 120f
        for reading, 115–117, 119f
            and cut scores, 114–115, 116t

National Commission on Excellence in
Education. *see A Nation At Risk* (1983)
National Council of Teachers of Mathematics, 5, 84
National Council on Educational Standards and
Testing, 5
National Education Goals Panel, 5
National Educational Association, federal
mandates and, 60
lawsuit against, 229–230
National Governors Association, 64
National School Reform Faculty protocols,
163–164
National Science Foundation, 53
Nation's Report Card. *see* NAEP (National
Assessment of Educational Progress)
NCEE (National Commission on Excellence in
Education). *see A Nation At Risk* (1983)
NCEST (National Council on Educational
Standards and Testing), 5
NCLB. *see* No Child Left behind Act (2001)
NCTM (National Council of Teachers of
Mathematics), 5, 84
NEA. *see* National Educational Association
needs assessment, 168
networking organizations, state-level, 64
Neuman, M., 42
Newmann, F. M., 26–27, 34, 46
NGA (National Governors Association), 64
Niles, J. A., 187
Niles, R. A., 187
No Child Left Behind Act (2001), xi, 1
Colorado legislation concerning, 216–218
consequences of, 132
evaluation mechanisms in, 31–32
federal legislation before, 131
federal role in, 60, 76
legislative intent of, 8
local educational agency programs and,
192–208
monitoring school improvement under, 150,
151f
state responses to, 64–65
student performance and, 2
subgroup reporting provisions under, 157–158
unfunded mandates, NEA lawsuit against,
229–230
normally distributed curves, 111, 112f
norm-referenced tests, 111–113, 112f, 113t
norms and values, of professional learning
communities, 185–186
Northouse, P. G., 51
Northwest Evaluation Association, 114
Norton, M. S., 51
NWEA (Northwest Evaluation Association), 114

Oakes, J., 4

objectives learning (*see* learning objectives)
management by, 4
O'Day, J. A., 29, 35, 66
Odell, S. J., 188, 189
OECD (Organization for Economic Co-Operation
and Development), 122–123
Ogawa, R. T., 69, 76
Olchefiske, Joseph, 10–11, 22
Olson, Lynn
"Benchmark Assessments Offer Regular
Checkups on Student Achievement,"
170–173
"States Confront Definition of 'Proficient' as
They Set the Bar for Lots of New
Tests," 105–107
Orfield, G., 183
organization efficiency, 40–41, 46. *see also*
capacity, system-wide
Organization for Economic Co-Operation and
Development, 122–123
organizational inertia, 2
Ornstein, A. C., 41, 49
Ouchi, William G., 19
outcomes
instructional practices and, link between,
108–109
unintended, 34–35
professional learning communities and,
186

peer coaching, 186–189
limitations, 189
roles in, 188
strategies for, 187, 187t
Pelchat, J., 42
percentile rank scores, 111–112, 113t
performance indicators, school improvement,
160–161
data collection and, 167–168
in decision-making process, 166, 166f
school leaders and, 161, 167–168
performance standards, 76, 89–91
accountability tools and, 32–33
design and function of, 77–78
goals for, 27–28
instructional practices and, 31
Massachusetts Department of Education, 80,
82t–83t, 84
professional development and, 179
reporting of, 133–134
TCAP reading benchmarks, 85, 86t–88t
performance-based educational accountability
analytic perspectives in, 8–10
conditions for, 9–10
effect of, 5
logic of, 8–10

Perkins, S. J., 188
"policy churn," 33
policy-practice gap, 13, 175, 183
policy-theory gap, 25
political accountability, 9, 36–37
political effects, on education system, 60–61
Porter, A. C., 175
Portin, B. S., 164
PPBS (programming, planning, and budgeting systems), 4
pressure mechanisms, 28
    as motivation for change, 131
    in system of accountability, 28
    in transformational leadership, 51
Preston, Mary Bea, 55
principals
    as educational leaders, 2
    responsibilities of
        case study, 15–20
        examples, 55–56
    successful, common characteristics of, 53
    tenure and, 12
principalship, core beliefs in, 12
process-oriented reform, 45
professional accountability, 9, 174–176
    vs. bureaucratic accountability, 37
professional development, 32
    criteria for, 175
    design and implementation of, 175
    for educational leaders, 45, 174–176
    effective strategies in, 176–182
        research on, 177–179
    elements of, 178
    spending on, 180–182, 181t
    system-wide, 180–182, 181t
    traditional activities, problems with, 176–177
professional learning communities, 183–186, 185
    characteristics of, 186
    common elements of, 184
    guiding principles of, 185
    impact on student performance, 186
    norms and values of, 185–186
proficiency. see also assessments; student assessments
    baselines for monitoring, 142–143, 142t, 144t–146t
    performance levels for, 117
    proficient achievement, focus on, 10
    school report cards on, 137, 140–141
        Illinois elementary schools, 138t–139t

"race gap," in student performance, 158
race/ethnicity
    NAEP long-term trends by
        mathematics, 115, 118f
        reading, 115, 117f
    progress reports and, 134

Rallis, S. F., 47
RAND Corporation, performance level study by, 117, 121f
rating schemes, academic standards, 80, 81t
raw score, vs. derived score, 111
Raymond, M. E., 126
readiness dimensions, 164–165
reading
    ISBE standards development criteria, 79
    NAEP long-term trends by race/ethnicity, 115, 117f
    NAEP performance levels and cut scores, 114–115, 116t
    RAND study performance level results, 117, 121f
    TCAP performance benchmarks, 85, 86t–88t
    Tennessee Language Arts Curriculum standards for, 231–236
Reagan, Ronald, 1, 3, 6–7
reciprocal accountability, 26f, 27
    federal governance and, 66
reciprocal coaching, 188
Reeves, D. B., 78, 114, 162, 171
reflective dialogue, 47
    in professional learning communities, 184
    school-improvement decisions and, 163
reflective practice
    in distributed leadership, 50
    in educational leadership, 47
    for effective school-improvement decisions, 162–165
    local and state support for, 164
    in professional learning communities, 184
    professional norms for, creating, 163
    time required for, 164
    traditional supervision vs., 47
Reid, K. S., 67
relevance, principle of, 10
reliability, of testing, 123–124
reporting mechanisms, in accountability system, 31–32, 131, 132–141
restructuring, as accountability consequence, 155–156
results-driven accountability
    assumptions of, 26–27
    leading by results and, 41–42
results-driven leadership, 52
Rettig, M. D., 54, 102
revenue sources, for schools, 61, 61t
Richardson, V., 177
Rigdon, M., 26–27, 34, 46
Roeber, Ed, 107
Roop, L. J., 77
Ross, J. A., 101
rules, managing by, vs. measuring student performance, 41–42
Ryan, K., 161

safe harbor provision, AYP and, 148, 149t
sanctions, in accountability system, 31–32
  unintended consequences of, 34–35
Sandholtz, J. H., 69, 76
Santos, K., 102
Santos, Oscar, 18
SAT (Stanford Achievement Test), 111
Schlechty, P. C., 27, 42, 161, 176
Schneider, B., 183, 186
Schnur, J., 12
school administrators
  building capacity, 46
  role of, 2, 41
  school-improvement decisions and, 164, 166
school districts
  accountability implementation in, variability of, 69–70
  administrative roles in, 2, 41
  changing roles in, 30
  leadership roles in, 2, 12 (*see also* school leaders)
  professional development and, 179
    spending on, 180–182, 181t
  supplemental services provision and, 154
school governance
  changes in, 30–31
  restructuring, 156
school improvement
  as accountability consequence, 150–154
    schools identified for, 153t–154t
    stages of, 150, 151f
  Annenberg Institute for School Reform guidelines, 163
  data-driven process in, 163, 167–168
  decision-making process for, 166–170, 166f
    adapting instructional practices, 169
    data collection, 167–168
    impact evaluation, 169–170
    improvement goals, 168–169
    needs assessment, 168
  effective decisions in, 162–166
    collaborative inquiry and reflective practice for, 162–165
    data for, 163, 164
    data-driven, 165–166, 167–168
    readiness dimensions and, 164–165
  performance indicators of, 160–161
  social interactions and organizational learning for, 183–184
school leaders. *see also* educational leaders
  accountability and, 30, 36–37
  challenges facing, 10–13
  expectations of, 39–40
  licensure assessment modules, 219–221
  professional learning communities and, 186
  skills and knowledge requirements, 12

student- and school-performance indicators and, 161
school readiness dimensions, 164–165
school report cards, 137, 140–141
  for Illinois, 137, 138t–139t
  state-level, 133–134
school-improvement plan, 150, 152
school-reform strategy
  accountability and, 29
  educational accountability as, 161
  initiatives, types of, 43
  professional learning communities and, 183–186
schools
  accountability evaluation mechanisms in, 31–32
  administrative roles in, 41
  improvement (*see* instructional improvement)
  level, principles of educational accountability, 10
  low-performing (*see* low-performing schools)
  performance indicators for, 160–161
  principles of accountability in, 10
  professional development and, 179
  revenue sources for, 61, 61t
Schwab, R. M., 64
Schwartz, Amy Ellen, Leanna Stiefel, and Colin Chellman, "Subgroup Reporting and School Segregation: An Unhappy Pairing in the No Child Left Behind Equation," 157–158
science, Virginia academic standards for, 92, 93t–94t
  curriculum guidelines, 94, 95t–100t
scores
  cut, NAEP performance levels and, 114–115, 116t
  grade-equivalent, 112
  individual, criterion-referenced tests and, 115
  intra-individual variation, 127
  percentile rank, 111–112, 113t
  raw *vs.* derived, 111
  standard, 112
  stanine, 112
  student gain, 127
Scribner, J. P., 50, 69, 76, 165, 186
Seashore Louis, K., 50, 178, 183, 186
Sebring, P. B., 53
Second International Mathematics Study, 3
Sergiovanni, T. J., 47
Shadish, W. R., 25
Shearer, D. D., 189
Shepard, Lorrie A., 171
Shipps, Dorothy, and William A. Firestone, "Juggling Accountabilities: The Leaders' Turn," 36–37
Showers, J., 186
Simmons, Warren, 21

SIMS (Second International Mathematics
    Study), 3
SIP (school-improvement plan), 150, 152
Sirotnik, K. A., 109
Slavin, Robert E., 171, 173
Smith, T., 76, 175
Smylie, M. A., 47
social science, ISAT results for, 103t
social studies, assessments aligned with Illinois
    academic standards, 102, 104t
society, equality in, 61
Solomon, Jesse, and Richard Weissbourd, "To
    Improve Schools, Focus on Teachers,"
    190–191
specificity, principle of, 10
Spillane, J. P., 5, 35, 50, 69, 178, 183
Staiger, D. O., 123
standard scores, 112
standardized achievement tests, large-scale, 110
standards
    alignment of
        with assessment, 101–102, 103t–104t
        with curriculum, 91–92, 93t–94t, 94
        with instruction, 94, 95t–100t, 101
    design of
        and function, 77–78
        and implementation, 75–76
    in educational accountability, 10, 26f, 27–28
    ISBE development criteria, 79
    ISLLC, 43–44, 44t, 222–228
    professional development and, 179
    reform movement and, 5–6
    Tennessee Language Arts Curriculum,
        231–236
    tests aligned to, 110–111
standards-based reform movement, 5–6
Stanford Achievement Test, 111
stanine scores, 112
state governance, 63–65
    school practices and, variability of, 68–69
states. see also individually named states
    established starting points for, 143, 144t–145t
    intermediate goals for, 143, 144t–145t
    reports by, 133–134
"States Confront Definition of 'Proficient' as
    They Set the Bar for Lots of New Tests"
    (Olson), 105–107
status models
    achievement gain analysis vs., 127–128
    in average achievement analysis, 125–126
"Stay on Reform Track" (Denver Post editorial),
    128–129
steady stair-step, in AYP determination, 146,
    147f
Steifel, Leanna, Amy Ellen Schwartz, and Colin
    Chellman, "Subgroup Reporting and
    School Segregation: An Unhappy

Pairing in the No Child Left Behind
    Equation," 157–158
Stiggins, R. J., 119–120
student assessments, 24, 28, 109–123. see also
    subgroup reporting
    criterion-referenced, 113–118, 115t–116t,
        117f–121f
    formative, 119–120, 122–123
    for minimum competency, 110
    norm-referenced, 111–113, 112f, 113t
    standardized large-scale, 110–111
student gain scores, 127
student learning
    collective focus on, 185
    focus on, 11
    indicators of, 160–161
    teacher practices and, 11–12
student performance
    changes in, measuring, 124–128
        average achievement, 125–126
        gains in achievement, 126–128
    expectations and, 10
    impact of professional learning communities
        on, 186
    indicators of, 160–161
    Linn on, 6
    measuring, 2, 108–109 (see also student
        assessments)
        procedural compliance vs., 40
    "race gap" in, 158
    rewards and consequences for, 109
students
    accountability and, 31
    schoolwide decisions impacting, 165
subgroup reporting, 134–136
    minimum group size for, 135–136
    NCLB provisions, 157–158
"Subgroup Reporting and School Segregation: An
    Unhappy Pairing in the No Child Left
    Behind Equation" (Schwartz, Stiefel, and
    Chellman), 157–158
Sunderman, G. L., 59, 183
supervision, traditional, vs. process of reflection,
    47
supervisory roles, in education system, 41
support mechanisms
    in accountability system, 28, 31–32
    changes in instructional practice and, 67
    for collaborative inquiry and reflective practice,
        164
    for professional learning communities, 185
    in transformational leadership, 51

"Tackling an Impossible Job" (Archer), 15–20
TCAP (Tennessee Comprehensive Assessment
    Program), reading performance
    benchmarks, 85, 86t–88t

teacher collaboration, 183
  through peer coaching, 186–189
  through professional learning communities,
    183–186
teacher practices, and student learning, 11–12
teachers
  accountability and, 30–31
  adapting instructional practices, 162–163
  effectiveness of, 190–191
  professional development for, 174–176
  schoolwide decisions impacting, 165
  time for meetings between, 164
technical assistance, 67
  professional learning communities and,
    184–185
Tennessee Comprehensive Assessment Program,
    reading performance benchmarks, 85,
    86t–88t
Tennessee Department of Education, 182
Tennessee Language Arts Curriculum
  standards for reading (eighth-grade), 231–236
  TCAP reading performance benchmarks, 85,
    86t–88t
TerraNova, 111
testing
  academic and performance standards guiding, 31
  criterion-referenced, 113–118, 115t–116t,
    117f–121f
  effects of, 76
  large-scale, 110
  for minimum-competency, 110
  norm-referenced, 111–113, 112f, 113t
  reliability of, 123–124
  standardized, 110
  student performance, 24, 28
  traditional, assessments vs., 109
  validity of, 124
test-retest reliability, 124
"Theory of Action" (Archer), 20–22
thinking skills, 174–175
Thomas B. Fordham Foundation rating scheme,
    80, 81t
Thompson, S., 71, 77, 90, 94, 180
Thum, Y. M., 127
Timar, T., 4
Title I funding, 62–63
  appropriations, 62f
  evaluations mandated for, 110
  proficiency reports and, 141
  supplemental services provision and, 154

"To Improve Schools, Focus on Teachers"
    (Solomon and Weissbourd), 190–191
Tracey, C. A., 183
training programs, 45
transformational leadership, 51–52
Trejos, Nancy, "A Challenging Offer for
    Potential Principals," 55–56
Trujillo, T., 71, 131, 152, 155
Tucker, Marc S., 16, 18
tutoring, 152, 154
20th percentile method, for proficiency
    monitoring, 142–143, 142t
Tyack, D., 13, 67

uniform accounting systems program
    evaluation, 4

Valencia, S. W., 77, 80, 91
validity, of testing, 124
Vallas, Paul, 9
Van Sickle, Ann, 19
Vander Ark, Tom, 21
Virginia, academic standards for science, 92,
    93t–94t
  curriculum guidelines, 94, 95t–100t

Wang, J., 188, 189
Warne, T. R., 186
Waters, T., 43
Watson, C. R., 102
Weber, Max, 1–2, 41
Weiss, C. H., 5, 25
Weissbourd, Richard, and Jesse Solomon, "To
    Improve Schools, Focus on Teachers,"
    190–191
What Works Clearinghouse, 161, 167–168
Wiener, R., 135
Wildman, T. M., 187
Wiliam, Dylan, 173
Winter, P. A., 48
Wiratchai, N., 65
Wixson, K., 77, 80, 91
Wong, K. K., 59, 60, 61, 62
WWC (What Works Clearinghouse), 161,
    167–168

Yoon, K. S., 175

Zelli, A., 28
zero-based budgeting, 4